M, J, Hands is an avid historian regarding the era of British history before, during and after the Norman invasion of 1066, with a particular interest in Wild
 Edric, who was an English landholder dwelling in what was then
 part of the old Kingdom of Mercia.(Now the county of Shropshire)
 The author has had a varied career.
 He has been a Gamekeeper and Farmer, before he joined an Insurance company, graduating into the world of banking, and retiring in 1998 in the east end of London.
 He now lives in Shropshire with his wife

The Cover for this book is part of a single plate, copied from the detail of the 11th century Bayeux Tapestry. With special permission from The City of Bayeux

The right of M, J, Hands is identified as the author, and sole owner of the copyright of this work, in accordance with section77 and78 of the Copyright, Designs and Patents act of 1988.
 All rights reserved.
 No part of this publication may be reproduced, stored in a retrieval system, or transmitted in any form, or by any means, electronic, mechanical, Photocopying, recording, or otherwise, without prior permission of the Author.
 Any person who commits any unauthorized act in relation to this publication may be liable to criminal prosecution and civil claims for damages.

Novels by same author = The Shieldwall.
The Broken Shield.

A small English village of some twenty or so cottages is suddenly invaded by thirty armed men, who slay the few men who dare to resist them, beat the remainder into submission and enslave the population.
This is England in the 11th century, following the Norman Conquest.
The Norman invaders occupied every village, town and city, evicting the English noblemen, and replacing them with their own people.
These new Lords consolidated their occupation, by forcing the population to construct a Motte and Bailey, (Fortress) in every town and village, in order to control their rebellious subjects.
Despite their iron rule, their occupation was contested with rebellions, which erupt like a rash, in almost every part of England
English warriors either died in their attempt to rid England of the Normans, or were forced to seek their fortunes abroad.

Although many of the characters and places in this novel are based on real people and places which existed in the 11th century, all other characters are fictitious and purely the product of the Authors imagination.

In order to portray country dialects and an occasional Anglo/Saxon phrase, I have inserted the following;=
   Frae.   = Friend.
   Hwaet aert thu= How are you.
   Oi b.'   = I am.
   A Nithing.   =A nothing. A person of no worth.

AELNOTH.

Simon Le-Mare urged his men onwards, as they marched along muddy tracks and over heathland that seemed to be never ending.

He had led them through miles of squelching marshlands and through dense forests.

There were loud sighs of relief when they eventually reached the end of the moorland, and were able to look down into the final valley, where they could see the outline of the village, a mere mile ahead, perched on the top of a wooded hill.

The climb down the hillside had been treacherous, but when they reached the foot of the hill, their elation turned into groans, as they found their way blocked by yet another peat bog.

'We will have to make our way along the side of the hill until we reach dry ground,' said Wilfred the Englishman, who had been bribed with two pieces of silver to betray his own people, and to lead Simon Le-Mare and his men to the village of Wentnor.

'How far now'? Growled Sir Simon.

'About another two miles my lord.' Was the mumbled reply.

'Lead the way,' snapped Sir Simon, who was beginning to lose his temper at yet another unforeseen delay.

Simon Le-Mare of Trouville was the fourth son of a minor Lord, who owned a small estate on the island of Le-Tamaris, in the gulf of Morbihan, overlooking the azure Mediterranean Sea.

The thirty men who had sworn allegiance to him, and who now followed him on this gruelling trek through this damp and cold land, had named him 'Simon the sword,' due to the heroic deeds he had performed whilst protecting his liege lord. 'Duke William of Normandy,' during the long and bloody 'Battle of Hastings.'

Theoretically speaking, Simon Le-Mare was the leader of this small section of the mighty Norman army, although not one of his men knew that it was his wife Mari was the real leader, and it was Marianne who made all the decisions.'

Marianne was one year his senior and it had been due to her persuasive manner that her husband had accepted the Lordship of this remote village.

She had trudged alongside her husband since dawn, scorning any offer of help, and had adamantly refused to ride the one and only horse that they possessed, ordering the animal to be laden with additional food, spears and arrows.

Whilst a number of the men had stumbled and cursed during the march, Marianne had merely stared at them with a scornful look, shaming them to cease their grumbling and to keep up with herself and her husband.

Prior to her marriage, she had been the unwanted daughter of a minor lord, who dwelt with his two sons and one other daughter, in a small villa, some three miles from Trouville, and she had been the best match that Le-Mare's father could obtain for Simon.

Marianne was not a raving beauty, but she was tall and strong, with wide hips and the stature and strength that was the envy of many a man.

She had dressed for the journey in a common leather jerkin, and wore thick leather breeches, which she had tucked inside her new deerskin boots.

For most of the past day she had marched bareheaded and proud alongside her husband through the wind and the rain, allowing her usually immaculate dark hair to become drenched and wind-swept.

Although she would never admit it, her legs ached more than she could imagine possible, and she knew that the boot on her left foot was saturated with blood, from one of the numerous thorns she had stepped on, but rather than show any signs of weakness in front of the men, she suffered in silence, and steeled her mind to dream of the wealth, which she and her husband would soon inherit, in order to drive the pain out of her mind.

Nothing! Nothing could mar her utter delight at her new title of 'LADY Marianne' of Wentnor,' despite the fact that she fully expected the place to be a slum and nothing like her own sunny home overlooking the Mediterranean.

It was a title that some of her husband's warriors had already called her, and despite her painful foot and the atrocious weather, the mere word 'LADY' had caused her whole being to glow with pride, each time she was addressed as such.

'I'll show my cow of a sister, when I return home with my rich clothes, golden arm rings and silver buckles on my fancy shoes.' She muttered under her breath.

Her husband had also been overjoyed to learn that he had been given the ownership of a village and its surrounding lands, but his elation had been speedily dashed, when, after asking one of the Kings scribes about its location, he had been curtly informed that the village of 'Wentnor' was not in the balmy south of England, as he had hoped, but was in the extreme west of the country, bordering the tribal lands of the Welsh, and in an area where Norman rule had yet been consolidated.

The scribe had also informed him that the village had once belonged to a famous English warrior called 'Edric Sylvaticus,' or 'Wild Edric,' but the man had not been seen for many years, and it was rumoured that he had disappeared and died somewhere in the vast forests, which covered that part of the country.

Le Mare was delighted that he now held the title of 'The Lord of Wentnor,' and as such, he too, fully expected to glean great wealth from his new holding.

Like his wife, he was more than a little apprehensive about this particular adventure, for he anticipated that the inhabitants of his new Hall would probably not welcome him and his men as the liberators that they purported to be, and as such, he would probably have to fight for his new Hall, and may be forced to kill a few of them, in order to impress his will upon them.

'Not too many,' he muttered to himself. 'For a lord cannot extract taxes, beef, mutton or wool from dead peasants.'

Despite the years of weapon practice with his brothers on the practice field, his three elder and more robust brothers had habitually beaten him.

Simon had never considered himself to be a warrior, and had been slightly amazed by his own courage, during the one and only real battle in which he had fought, where he had slain two of the enemy.

However, he had been shocked and appalled when he had witnessed the bravery and savage slaughter that the English, warriors and peasants alike, had wrought amongst his fellow warriors, with their razor sharp Saex's and long handled battle-axes.

Simon had always been a man who planned ahead, and had decided that on this particular occasion, he must take the initiative and pre-empt any resistance, by taking his new domain by force.

'I'll be damned if I am going to knock politely on the gates, and beg to enter my own Hall,' he had muttered to his wife.

He gazed up at the darkened sky and felt the cold rain on his face, cursing his good luck, as well as his misfortune at being here at this particular moment in time.

He wished that he had been the eldest son of his fathers' brood, and not the fourth in line.

Had he been the eldest, he would have eventually inherited his Fathers beautiful estate, which overlooked the sunny gulf of Morbihan, and it would have been his three brothers who would have been evicted, and forced to seek THEIR fortunes, by joining the host of landless sons of noblemen, who roamed the countryside in search for a lord to serve, and ply their skills as Knights, or even men-at-arms.

'Then it would be one of them who would be standing here in the rain, gazing up at this bleak hill fortress,' he mused to himself, as he looked up towards the small fortress, which he could see protruding through the trees up ahead of him, 'and I would be basking in the sunshine at the Mediterranean.'

He halted his men an hour after midnight, and allowed them to rest in a small hollow besides a clear babbling brook.

He hardly slept, and roused his men as soon as he saw the eastern sky begin to show its first signs of the dawn.

'Up, up my brave fellows,' he said quietly, for he was aware that sound carried far in the cold morning air.

'Come now; prepare yourselves, for we have work to do.' He said as he chivvied one of the older veterans, who groaned as he stretched his back, after a night of attempting to snatch a little sleep on the sodden earth.

He began to lead the way up the slippery, tree studded incline towards the fortress.

A chill breeze stirred the new leaves of the woodland, as the thirty men crept warily towards the verge of the dense undergrowth, which bordered the fortress.

A sudden gust of wind blew one of the lower branches of a beech tree, making it swirl about the heads of the men, causing one man to curse softly, as a wet branch flapped across his face.

A much larger branch crashed against another man's shield with an audible thump.

'Quiet. All of you,' he hissed. 'Or you will wake up the villagers, and if you do rouse the fortress, then you will have a fight on your hands, and you dozy idiots who were with me at Hastings, will do well to remember that these are the same people who caused such injury amongst us with their damned axes.'

'We must surprise them and catch them asleep.' He added quietly.

Those men who had been at the Battle of Hastings looked towards one another with apprehension, as they were reminded of the carnage that the English axes had caused at Hastings, when their new King William had lost no less than three stallions slain from under him, and had come to within a hairsbreadth of losing his life by men wielding the dreaded long handled axes, which made the Danish and English warriors amongst the most feared warriors in Europe.

Nonetheless, most of these Normans were experienced veterans, who had been with their Lord, Le-mare of Trouville for over a year, and had come through a number of skirmishes unscathed.

'I lost my only brother at Hastings,' snarled a gnarled veteran, in a very low voice, 'and I'll make the sods pay for his death before this day is out.'

Another younger man nodded his head in agreement, and glanced towards Le-mare, as his wet hand grasped the hilt of his sword, in his eagerness to cease this infernal waiting.

The scout, who had been sent ahead in order to reconnoitre the small fortress, crept back and reported to Le-mare.

'My Lord,' he whispered.

'There are two sentries on the gate, both half asleep, and it looks like they have been on duty for most of the night.'

Le-mare nodded, and said to the four crossbowmen, who had been assigned to the task of silencing any sentries.

'Off you go,' and the four men sidled their way past Le-mare, and silently disappeared into the thick undergrowth.

The two sentries, who stood on the walkway above the gate, were huddled up against the savage wind, which seemed to cut through them like a knife.

They stamped their feet and slapped their own bodies, in a futile attempt to keep warm.

They did not see or hear the iron headed bolts, which thudded into their bodies and flung them backwards onto the sodden earth, on the inside of the fortress.

The four crossbowmen scrambled up the wooden walls with the ropes that they had carried wrapped around their shoulders, and dropped silently onto the ground, inside the fortress, discarding the ropes and running to the inside of the gate.

It took the four of them several precious seconds to lift the huge oak locking beam, and carry it to one side, lowering it as quietly as possible onto the ground.

They ran back to the gates, and swung them open, in order to allow the waiting warriors to enter.

The majority of the Villagers were asleep, or perhaps there were a few who were in the process of rising from their beds, in order to face the new day.

Aelnoth Edricson, who was the second son of 'Wild Edric,' had risen before dawn, and had almost finished eating a hasty breakfast.

He was a young man of seventeen summers, of average height, with a sturdy torso, which belied the hidden strength that lay beneath his loose deerskin jacket.

As is the habit of young men, he had gobbled down his cold porridge and snatched up a chunk of cold bread, which had been left over from yesterdays evening's meal.

He had swiftly bridled and saddled his horse whilst gulping down the last of the bread.

He was about to mount his father's ancient warhorse. 'Chieftain,' in order to set off on a hunt, with the hope of bagging a big fat stag, before the small herd of deer, which oftimes grazed in the meadows below, made their way out of the meadows, to return to the depths of the woodland, where they knew they would be much safer from hunters, such as he.

The wind ruffled his fair hair, but as he rose into the saddle, a slight movement caught his eye, causing him to freeze and stare at the spot.

Suddenly, the form of a man materialised out of the shadows from behind a cottage.

Another man appeared from behind the first man, and then another and another, until a long line of men appeared, and commenced to creep silently into the sleeping village.

The men were dressed in Iron helmets and war gear of leather and chain mail, and were fully armed with swords, spears and shields.

Their large kite shaped shields immediately identified them to be Normans, and not the usual Welsh marauders, who tended to cross Offa's Dyke from time to time, in search for cattle slaves and booty.

'Normans.' Uttered the shocked youth to himself. He quickly gathered his wits and shouted at the top of his voice, 'Normans. Normans,' as he wrenched his horse around, digging his spurs into the flanks of his stallion, and galloped as fast as he could down the main street of the small village.

'Normans, Normans,' he bellowed as he sped through the village, in an attempt to rouse his people.

'To Arms. To Arms.' He shouted at the top of his voice. 'We are attacked.'

When he reached the far end of the muddy street, he reined in his stallion and wrenched the reins around so that he could retrace his steps.

Shutters and doors were being flung open as men emerged in various states of dress and undress.

Aelnoth was pleased to see that most of them carried weapons.

He charged back through the village to his starting point, but was dismayed to see that the large band of Normans had already passed through the gates, and were in the process of slaughtering any man who dared to confront them.

He spurred the stallion towards his home, and snatched the old shield, which his father had always left on a stake outside the front door, in order to tell the inhabitants of the village that their lord was in residence.

When Aelnoth and his brother had inherited the fortress, they had continued the tradition, and had left their fathers shield in its usual place.

Clutching the shield in his left hand and his Saex in his right hand, Aelnoth guided Chieftain with his knees, and spurred the horse for a second time, causing the old stallion to leap forward towards the raiders, so that it seemed to Aelnoth that the stallion had remembered some of the aggression, of which Aelnoth's father had often spoken about, for on many occasions, his father had stated with pride, that Chieftain was the most aggressive war horse he had ever known, having been trained to kill and maim anything that came within reach of his three inch long teeth and steel clad hooves, be that intruder mankind, or even members of his own equine tribe.

Chieftain took his rider into the very centre of the fray, where four of the raiders were in the process of attacking one of the village youths, who were manfully fending off his four foes with his Saex.

In the few short heartbeats that it took Aelnoth to reach the youth, the four Normans had slain the boy, and were in the process of turning to seek other prey, when they were suddenly struck by a big black whirlwind called Chieftain, and a young man who sat astride the savage beast.

Chieftain struck two of the men like an avalanche, sending them flying into the air, and crashing to the ground in a jumble of arms, legs, shields and swords.

Aelnoth brought his Saex down upon the helmet of one of the man, causing the Norman to drop to the ground like a stone, where he lay, either dead or unconscious.

The fourth man was now behind Chieftain, and was about to thrust his spear into the rear of the stallion, when Chieftain gave an aggressive snort, and kicked with both of his hind legs, catching the man in the chest and propelling him some ten feet through the air, until his lifeless body fell against a discarded wheelbarrow, where it lay twitching.

Aelnoth glanced around to see his father's old friend. The fierce old warrior, named 'Garth Blood-axe,' who was standing over two dead Normans, whilst a further five men circled him, standing just out of reach of the Englishman's famous axe.

Aelnoth watched in horror, as he saw the old warrior pierced by a shower of crossbow bolts, causing the white haired warrior to drop his axe, and sink slowly to his knees, where he hovered for a brief moment before he fell, face forward onto the ground.

Aelnoth spun Chieftain around, in order to face yet another foe, but was shocked when he saw that during the few short minutes, which had elapsed since he had charged into his four opponents, the remainder of the Normans had formed themselves into a solid shield wall, and were advancing along the single track of the village, driving everyone before them and leaving dead, wounded and stunned men women and children in their wake.

As he turned Chieftain towards the fighting, he saw his brother Godwin emerge from a the small knot of warriors, and charge into the Normans, plunging his long handled axe into the nearest Norman, and wrench it out of the man's body as he fell to the ground.

He was in the act of attacking a second man, when he suddenly froze, with his axe raised in the air, as a spear plunged into his back.

He staggered forward a few paces, and then slowly collapsed onto the ground.

Many of the villagers screamed in alarm, as they saw the eldest son of 'Wild Edric' die, for he was a famous warrior, and much loved by his people.

Aelnoth was even more shocked, when he saw a woman stand over the prone body of his brother, and place one foot on his body, and wrenched the spear out of his back.

Aelnoth could not believe what he had witnessed, and shook with anger and shock at the death of his beloved brother.

'Godwin,' he screamed at the top of his voice, as he stared at the prone figure of his only brother.

Over the past few years Godwin had been the most stabilizing force in young Aelnoth's life, and had been a young man whose strength and prowess had been little short of legendary.

Aelnoth's mind refused to register that this prone body lying in the mud was his beloved brother.

He screamed unintelligible words of shock and anger, which echoed down the silent, bloody street.

The woman held her gory spear above her head, and screamed something which he could not understand, causing her fellow warriors to join her, as they added their own shouts of victory to that of the still screaming, triumphant woman.

Aelnoth bellowed with rage, and yet the noise of the beast that had been awakened within him, did not seem to emit from his own mouth, but appeared to him to have been uttered by a savage animal, which dwelt somewhere within his chest.

At the very moment that he was about to charge into his enemies, he was horrified to see the few remaining men of fighting age, cease their struggle against such overwhelming odds, and throw their weapons onto the ground in surrender.

Another loud cheer rose from the Normans.

It was a cheer that was speedily silenced by their leader, whose eyes fell upon Aelnoth and his savage war-horse, who stood defiant amongst the lifeless looking bodies of four of his men.

'Get that Bastard,' screamed Simon Le-mare, pointing his bloodied sword towards Aelnoth, causing at least ten of his men to run towards the now stationary figures of Chieftain and Aelnoth.

Realising that he had little chance of success against the crowd of armed Normans who approached him, Aelnoth steadied his steed and raised his fist into the air and yelled at the top of his voice.

'You murdering bastards.' He screamed

'I will be back.'

Three of the men launched their spears towards him, and Aelnoth watched with horror and fascination, as the three projectiles arched high into the air, in their seemingly gentle way towards him, causing his eyes to follow their course, as is the way with many young men who are new to battle.

Realizing, much too late the lethal purpose of the spears, he wrenched his reins around in an attempt to avoid them, only to see one thud into the ground about three feet to his right, whilst a second spear fell short, but the third spear cut a six inch gash into the rump of Chieftain.

Being the battle tested stallion that he was, he had sustained numerous injuries much more severe than this small cut, and was speedily brought under control, but just as he had begun to move, a bolt from a crossbow thudded into his rump, causing him to rear onto his hind legs, and once his front legs returned to the ground, the wounded horse ran straight and true, through the village and the open gate, over the newly planted field of oats, and into the woodland, forcing Aelnoth to hang on for dear life, as Chieftain crashed through the woodland, before he eventually allowed himself to be brought under control.

Chieftain shuddered to a halt, and stood panting with his four legs splayed out in utter exhaustion.

Aelnoth dismounted, and after a short examination of the stallions wounds, he pulled the crossbow bolt out, with a sudden tug, causing Chieftain to rear and snort loudly, before he calmed down again, and nuzzled into his masters shoulder, as if he was explaining to Aelnoth that he knew that the bolt had to be extracted, and he forgave Aelnoth for causing him pain.

Aelnoth was pleased to note that the bolt had no barb, and had penetrated a few short inches away from the spear wound.

He was also relieved to see that the spear had done nothing other than to slice through the skin, causing a long clean wound, which should heal within a few days.

He coaxed Chieftain a few paces towards a nearby stream, and watched as the stallion quenched his thirst, before he knelt down and scooped up a couple of handfuls of the clear refreshing liquid for himself.

As Chieftain began to recover, Aelnoth contemplated riding back to Wentnor, but then dismissed the idea, as he knew that it would probably take at least an hour before his horse would be fit enough to be ridden again, and if he did return to Wentnor, he realised that an inexperienced youth such as himself, stood little chance of success against twenty or so experienced oath sworn warriors, and would certainly achieve little, other than to get himself either killed or captured.

He knew that he was strong for his age, and had been schooled in the art of war by both his father and Garth Blood axe, who had both assured him that he had the strength and skill, superior to many experienced warriors.

'And yet here I am,' he said aloud, 'a youth of seventeen summers, alone, friendless, and penniless, with nothing other than an ancient, wounded warhorse and the meagre weapons of a huntsman.'

With a mood like thunder, he moved further into the depths of the woodlands, where he lit a fire, and although he did have a chunk of dried meat in his saddlebag, he was too miserable to bother to cook or eat it.

As he sat on his blanket, his fire did seem to offer him a little solace as he racked his muddled brain, attempting to decide what to do and where to go.

'I will return.' He muttered to himself, and then he rose to his feet and threw his arms above his head, as he stared up at the cloudy sky.

He shouted at the top of his voice.

'I will return.'

'I will return.' He screamed into the emptiness.

'I will avenge my brother and take back my land.' He shouted, and fell onto his knees, as if in exhaustion.

He sat down on his sheepskin horse-blanket, and delved into the depths of his still angry and muddled mind; in order to devise some way which he could recover his home and his inheritance.

'Wealth and warriors.' he eventually muttered to himself.

'If I can become rich, then my riches will attract warriors to me.'

'I will recruit warriors and mercenaries. Men who have survived our defeat at the Battle of Hastings.'

'Thieves, vagabonds, deserters and malcontents.'

'Anyone who can wield a weapon and kill a bloody Norman.'

But almost before he had finished mumbling the words to himself, he knew that he would not use such men, for his father had often remarked that such men were not to be trusted, and would invariably revert back into their old ways.

'Once a traitor, always a traitor,' his father had said on more than one occasion.

Over the past few years Aelnoth and his friends had been eager to reach an age when they would be old enough to take up arms, and fight the Normans, who were still making their way northwards, taking over each and every town and village which came within their reach.

'I will seek out some of my friends, and we will wage war against them.' He silently vowed.

'I will find friends and money, and I will furnish an army to fight the Normans.'

'I will perfect the skills which my father has taught me until no man can beat me.'

'I will gather riches and warriors to help me to re-gain my lands.' He mumbled to himself, as he gazed into the flickering fire.

As dusk fell, he rose and walked over to Chieftain, who had pretty well recovered from his wounds, and pushed his soft nose into Aelnoth's chest.

'There there old man.' He said soothingly as he examined the wounds. 'Everything will be all right.'

'We will both be fine in the morning.' He lied.

He tethered Chieftain to a sturdy sapling, giving him ample space to roam over a small area, where tussocks of new grass grew, and returned to the fire, where he rolled himself into his blanked and settled down for the night.

He rose after a damp and unpleasant night to a grey dawn, and strode over to his horse.

After examining Chieftains wounds yet again, he was pleased to see that they had ceased bleeding, and were already beginning to heal.

This pleased him immensely; as it seemed to him that this gnarled old war-horse was the only friend that he had in the world, especially so after the disappearance of both his mother and his father some years ago.

The steady and systematic encroachment of the Norman occupiers of England continued to depress him, for they had, yet again, broken their sacred oath, by taking over all of the Halls, which had once belonged to his father, despite the assurances that his father had been given by King William himself, as a reward for his father's courage at the battle of Alnwick.

First Kenley had been taken. Then the township of Clunn, which had been his fathers pride and joy, and after Clunn, all of his father's other Halls had been usurped, until the Manor of Wentnor had been the only one that had remained.

And now, that also had been lost.

He decided that he would ride to Pitchford to find Edward, who was the elder of the two sons of the Lord of Pitchford, and was one of his closest friends.

Two or three years ago, Edward and Aelnoth had sworn that when were old enough; they would join together and fight the Normans.

He was aware that the Lord of Pitchford has also been robbed of his Hall, but he hoped that his friend still lived in or near the village, and if he could meet up with Edward, than perhaps things could be sorted out, and if not sorted out, then at the very least, he would have a friend and an ally.

He reached Pitchford late in the evening, and sat astride Chieftain on a hill above the village, peering down at the peaceful village, which now contained a small wooden Motte and Bailey.

Once darkness had descended, he tethered Chieftain to a small tree and crept slowly towards one of the outlying cottages, which was situated about one hundred yards south of the main village.

He had almost reached the cottage when two dogs began to bark, causing him to freeze.

A moment later the cottage door was flung open, and the large figure of a man emerged, casting a long shadow across the front of the yard.

'Who's there?' demanded a gruff voice.

Aelnoth thought that he recognised the man, so he stepped out of the shadows, to stand in the light, which shone through the doorway of the cottage.

'I am called Aelnoth,' he said in the bravest voice that he could muster. 'And I am looking for Edward, who was the son of the Lord of this place, some two or three years ago.'

'Aelnoth,' Aelnoth.' Answered the man.

'I know of no Aelnoth. Where might you be from?' he demanded.

'I am from Wentnor, and I am the son of Edric, who was the lord of that village, until he disappeared some years ago.'

'Ha,' exclaimed the man.

'Now him I have heard of and you claim to be his son do you?'

'I do'

'Oh well, I see no reason to doubt you, and if that be the case, then you had better come in.'

Aelnoth followed the man into his cottage, and was quite surprised to see a corpulent middle aged woman stirring a metal pot over a fire, whilst no less than five fair haired children of varying ages sat at a rough table, waiting, or so Aelnoth thought, to consume whatever was in the pot, which steamed and hissed over a fire.

'I am called Leofric. Leofric of Pitchford and I was a freeman on his lordships estate until the Normans came,' he said glumly.

'And now we are just serfs, like the rest of the villagers,' muttered the woman.

'This is my wife Elfreida, and these are our children.' He added.

Aelnoth sat on a stool near the table, and glanced casually at the children, noting that there were four girls and one boy, who all looked to be in need of a good meal, whilst the eldest girl seemed to be the thinnest of the brood.

'This young man is called Aelnoth.' Said Leofric in a loud voice, 'and he has come seeking young Edward who used to live at the hall.'

'Oh dear,' replied Elfreida.' He doesn't know then?' She said in a sad voice.

'Don't look like it, do it?' said Leofric.

'Know what?' asked Aelnoth in a quiet, apprehensive voice.

'Shall I tell him, or will you?' Said his wife.

'I will,' said the man in a low voice, and continued in the same tone.

'I'm sad to tell you that both young Edward and his brother were slain, when they tried to defend their father, when the Normans came and took over the village.' He sighed in a soft voice.

'He was a lovely lad too.' Said his wife in a sympathetic tone.

'We had high hopes that he would wed our eldest there, as he nodded to one of his daughters.

'The girl has hardly uttered a word since it happened, and that was over nine months ago. Aint that right Ingrid?' But the eldest girl, who looked to be around the age of fourteen or fifteen, kept her head lowered over the table, with her long fair hair almost touching her empty wooden bowl.

The girl merely nodded just once without saying a word.

Aelnoth noticed that the girl's shoulders shuddered a little, and he suspected that she was silently crying.

Unnoticed by anyone, Ingrid had raised her head slightly to gaze at the young man who sat opposite her across the table, and the vision, which she saw through the veil of her blond hair, caused her eyes to open wide.

The boy, for he was no more than a boy, appeared to be bathed in an eerie glow, which encompassed his entire body, dazzling her so much that she was forced to close her eyes and shake her head, in an attempt to make herself believe what she was actually seeing, but when she opened her eyes again, the light still encompassed the boy, as if his whole being was being illuminated by a hundred candles.

She shook her head again and a convulsive sob pulsated through her body, but when she looked again, the lights had subsided and the boy was just a boy again.

Elfrieda broke the silence, as she heaved the heavy iron pot off an iron rod, and hauled it onto the table, where it still simmered and steamed, causing the entire family including the dumb struck girl and Aelnoth to look up and gaze at their intended meal.

'Smells good,' said Leofric, as he sniffed loudly.

Aelnoth nodded in agreement, for he had not eaten in more than twenty-four hours, and was ravenous.

Despite his rumbling belly, he could not help himself thinking of Edward, and was still stunned at the death of his childhood friend, as well as the slaughter of his own brother and his old mentor, Garth Bloodaxe.

'What a day.' He muttered quietly to himself, and shook his head in order to chase the ugly thoughts away.

Elfrieda scooped several spoonfuls of the soup onto everyone's bowl, giving one additional scoop to both her husband and their guest.

Whilst the aroma of the soup was wonderful, and it did taste good, Aelnoth did note that it consisted mostly of wild garlic, nettles and other vegetables, plus an odd scrap of undetermined meat here and there.

Before Elfrieda sat at the table, she brought out a large jug, and began to fill his cup with warm beer.

'There thee be young sire that should help to fill yer belly.' She said before she moved on to fill her husband's cup, and the cups of each of her children.

Aelnoth thanked her, but did not partake of the small beer until his wooden bowl was so empty that one of the waiting hounds, which sat obediently under the table, would have found it futile to lick it any cleaner.

After they had eaten, the daughters helped their mother clean away and take the bowls and cups outside to wash in a nearby stream.

Leofric moved his stool so that he was close to Aelnoth, and asked quietly. 'What will e' do now that young Edward is dead?'

'Not really sure.' Answered Aelnoth. 'I think I will probably go to one of my fathers other halls, and see if any other of my friends have survived this Norman onslaught.'

The family gave Aelnoth an old sheepskin to sleep on, and he joined the rest of the family as they all settled down for the night on the floor of their small cottage.

Despite his low spirits, the meal and the small beer seemed to have worked wonders, and he had a surprisingly good nights sleep, waking with the dawn, refreshed and determined to make his way to the village of Shifnal, which was several miles to the south.

After a welcome breakfast of freshly baked bread and cheese, washed down with a cup of small beer, he thanked his hosts profusely, and bade them goodbye as he mounted Chieftain, and set out towards the south.

*   *   *

'What in God's name do you think you are doing?' shouted Leofric, as he saw Ingrid carrying a small sack, and walking purposefully towards their one and only horse.

'I'm going with him.' She said, as she reached the horse and threw the small sack over the saddle horn.

'With who?'

'Aelnoth of course.'

'Why?'

'He is the one.'

'The one what?'

'He is the one who I will marry, and the man who will avenge the death of poor Edward and his family.'

'He is not a man. He is just a boy, who the Normans will squash like an ant and go on to find a man-sized meal.'

'He will grow.' She said adamantly, as she stuck her chin out as she placed her foot in the stirrup, and mounted the horse.

Her father held the reins saying. 'He has been long gone, and you will never catch him up on this old nag.'

'Besides.' He added. 'He won't want a slip of a girl like you with him.

'He was near penniless and starving when he came here, and I am sure that even if you do find him, he will send you home with a flea in your ear.'

'Nevertheless father. I shall find him and he WILL NOT send me home.' She said forcefully.

'Gods blood child; you always were a strange one. Stubborn to a fault.'

'Just like your mother.'

'You have not thought this thing through my darling,' said Leofric, as a kind smile crossed his weathered face.

'Your mother and I would grieve for you, and you would be sorely missed, for you are still little more than a child.'

'Nay, dearest father.' She said as she smiled down at him. 'I am almost full grown, and have long known that my Knight in shining armour would come one day, and if I were to let him go, without at least trying to follow him, then I would regret it for the rest of my life.'

'My dearest Ingrid,' said her father, as a tear oozed out of his eye. 'Wait a moment, for I have something to give you before you go.' And he turned and trotted ungainly off towards the cottage, reappearing a few moments later carrying a small package.

He stood alongside her and unwrapped the cloth to reveal an ornate slender dagger.

'Here,' he said, as he reached up and handed the dagger to her.

'I took this off a dead Norman at Hastings. I think it is called a 'Poniard.'

'May it help to keep you safe on your travels?'

'God speed my lovely daughter.' And he slapped the horse on its rump sending it off at a gallop along the rutted cartway.

* * *

Aelnoth by-passed most of the towns and villages by keeping to the woodlands, noting with foreboding that almost all of them were either in the process of having a Mott built, or already contained a defensive mound, which was topped, either by a wooden or a stone tower, thus dominating the villages and their immediate countryside.

On several occasions he approached close enough to see that the people who were actually working on these defensive buildings were local villagers, who were being urged, and in some cases whipped as if they were slaves, and not the free born Englishmen who, a few short years ago had farmed their own strips of the fertile soil of England.

Many of the farms and holdings, which he encountered, were either run down or derelict, but he had half expected that to be the case, for it was a well known fact that the Norman's had robbed and slaughtered their way across southern and central England in the few short years, since their victory at Hastings.

Most of the population seemed to consist of old men, women and children, and the few men of fighting age that he did encounter, were despondent, miserable, and beaten men.

Those men of fighting age, who still retained their aggressive nature, had already been slain, driven overseas, or pressed into the service of their new masters as serfs, workmen or foot-soldiers.

After a restless night, when Aelnoth had been forced to sleep under the stars, he had wakened with his cape soaking- wet, to a dark and dismal morning, causing him to rise, stiff, cold and miserable.

His still confused mind went over the events, which had taken place in the last few years of his life.

He wished he knew the real reason about the disappearance of both his Mother and his Father.

His black mood deepened to such an extent, that when he reached the next village, his mind was still in turmoil and a state of delayed shock that his Fathers old black stallion took him down the main track, which led directly into the centre of a village.

Chieftain halted before a small crowd of English serfs, who were toiling under the lash of a Norman overseer, who sat regally on a bay gelding, and was in the process of urging his mount around the workers, striking at any man who came within reach of his long leather whip, but to the man's surprise, his own mount halted a few paces away from Aelnoth, but more importantly, a few paces away from Chieftain, who, being the savage war-horse that he was, immediately flew at the Normans horse, biting the horse on its neck, whilst chieftains iron shod hoofs rained down on the startled horse, throwing its rider to the ground.

The Norman overseer lay stunned for a moment.

He quickly recovered his wits, and as he jumped to his feet, he drew his sword and slashed at the stallion and its rider, catching Chieftain and leaving a half-inch long cut down the stallions left shoulder, causing chieftain to rear, throwing Aelnoth, whose turn it was, to land in the mud.

The enraged Norman boldly strode the few long strides towards Aelnoth, who had risen to his feet, shaking his head in order to clear it, as he retreated a couple of paces whilst he drew his own Saex to face his attacker.

Aelnoth judged his attackers first lounge and allowed the mans sword to hiss past his left shoulder, whilst he countered with his much shorter weapon, grazing the Normans left cheek, causing the man to retreat whilst his left hand flew involuntary towards his damaged face.

He stared in amazement at his bloodied hand, and glared savagely at this young man who had dared to challenge his authority.

With a shout of rage, he launched into a flurry of swipes as he advanced towards Aelnoth, who calmly retreated through the small crowd of onlookers and out of range of the man's sword.

As he retreated, he caught sight of another horseman savagely spurring his horse towards him, which made him realise that if did not bring this particular duel to an early close, he would find himself fighting one man on foot, as well as another man on a horse, so using one of the tactics that his father had drilled into him whilst he was still a youngster, he stepped forward and kicked the man in the groin, sending him to the ground in pain, and quickly brought the handle of his Saex down on the back of his head, sending him into an unconscious heap in the mud.

The horseman charged towards Aelnoth and attempted to run his steed into and over him, but Aelnoth sidestepped and grabbed the mans leg, wrenching his attacker out of the saddle as the horse galloped on, causing the man to land virtually at Aelnoth's feet in a heap, where he remained moaning and groaning, clutching his back in agony.

Yet another horseman spurred his steed towards Aelnoth, and in a flurry of mud and sods of turf, slithering to a halt some eight or ten feet away from Aelnoth, and almost casually alighted from his horse.

Aelnoth could see that by the very nature of this man, that he was not one of the guards, for his stallion was at least two hands taller than the other horses, and was groomed so well that his coat glistened in the weak morning sun, which had now begun to peer through the grey clouds.

The man was dressed in an expensive green cloak with a collar of ermine, and he carried one of the modern and much smaller kite shaped shields, which was now the fashion for horsemen.

The pommel of the man's sword appeared to be gold, with a hilt that was girt in silver.

All that De-Bracy could see was a stripling of a boy, who had just bested two of his finest warriors, and had caused the vital work on his new keep to be abandoned, at least for a few short minutes, before he put the stupid English peasant in his place, (which would be his new graveyard on the edge of the village of Broseley), but then he noticed Chieftain, who despite the small wound he had just suffered, had returned to Aelnoth, and now stood slightly to one side of his master.

'Where did you get that stallion?' he snarled.

'It is a Norman horse.' He spluttered.

'So you are a thief as well a wolfshead, who has been lucky enough to best two of my men.'

'I am neither a thief nor a wolfshead.' Answered Aelnoth, 'nor was it luck that I bested these two oafs.' Nodding disdainfully towards the two fallen warriors.

'Nonetheless,' he added. 'I shall bother you no further and will be on my way.'

He turned towards Chieftain, grasping the stallion's bridle, and was about to mount, when he felt the touch of cold steel prodding his neck.

In the blink of an eye Aelnoth spun around, deftly knocking the offending sword away from his neck, whilst in his right hand he held his own razor sharp Saex under the un-bearded chin of the Norman.

Aelnoth noticed that the man not only had a sword in his right hand, he noted that the man's left hand contained a slim Norman poniard.

'It would be wise of you to allow me to leave in peace.' He stated quietly.

'For I have been known to kill men for less offence than you have already given me.' He lied.

'So Have I.' was the reply, as the man thrust his sword towards Aelnoth's chest.

'That was a mistake,' snarled Aelnoth as he moved his body slightly to allow the sword thrust to pass by his right side, and countered, not with the blade of his Saex, but with the hilt of the weapon, which caught the startled Norman on his chin, sending him backwards to the ground where he lay in a heap, as his left hand flew to his chin.

The man shook his head in order to dispose of the stars, which were flying around, inside his brain.

'Kill the bastard,' came a voice from the crowd, as a man stepped out from the huddle of labourers, who had watched this young Englishman defeat two of their most brutal guards, from amongst more than twenty other Normans who were dotted about the area, as well as get the better of the new lord of Broseley, who they all knew as De-Bracy the Bastard.

Aelnoth turned towards the man who had spoken, and saw a ragged man of perhaps thirty years of age, although it seemed to Aelnoth that beneath his rags and his grubby unkempt beard, that he could be aged anywhere between twenty to forty.

The things that appeared to set him apart from his fellow serfs, was the man's stature, and his refined voice.

He also noticed that the man was only of average height, whilst his shoulders were unusually broad, which seemed to give the man the bearing of a warrior.

The man strode the few paces out of the crowd towards De-Bracy, who was now in the act of standing up.

The man scooped up De-Bracy's fallen sword, and held it aloft in order to bring it down upon the Normans head, but the sword was halted in mid-flight by Aelnoth who caught the sword on its downward journey with his Saex.

'Nay my good fellow.' Said Aelnoth. 'He has been beaten. Leave it at that.'

'I suggest that you go your own way whilst you still have a chance, and I too must be away from this place before this Normans henchmen are upon us.' He added.

'Aye,' snarled De-Bracy. 'I too suggest that you run, or else my men will skin you alive when they catch you. Which with any luck will be within a few short minutes time, for I see that they are on their way?' His eyes glanced over Aelnoth's shoulder' towards a group of men who were in the process of mounting their horses.

'Quick.' Said Aelnoth. 'Grab that horse and follow me,' as he grasped the bridle of his own stallion and leapt into the saddle.

Chieftain needed no urging and raced off at a gallop, leaving the startled man still attempting to mount De-Bracy's horse.

It was a task that took longer than he had hoped, and by the time that he had mounted the nervous steed, no less than eight Norman horsemen were a mere 50 yards away.

Luckily the man was a good horseman, and De-Bracy's stallion was known to be one of the strongest and fastest horse's in the district, so as the stallion got into its stride, the gap between the pursuers and the pursued widened.

After a couple of miles, the Norman pursuers horses began to flag, until all but one gave up the chase, and stood with their legs splayed and their heads down, as their frustrated riders dismounted and stood alongside their exhausted animals.

Aelnoth turned in the saddle and slowed chieftain a little, in order to allow the man to catch up with him.

He also noted that a lone Norman horseman was not only still in the chase, but had actually closed the gap between him and his prey to about one hundred yards.

As the ragged stranger came alongside Aelnoth they spurred their mounts onwards and the man stretched out his hand towards Aelnoth.

Aelnoth took the hand and as he shook the man's hand he said, 'I am called Aelnoth.'

'Magnus.' Said the man.

'Well met Magnus,' said Aelnoth as he returned the handshake.

He smiled and then looked back towards the lone rider.

Aelnoth noted the look of alarm on the face of his new found ally, and glanced to the rear, where he too could see that the Norman was a little less than 50 yards behind them, and was in the process of untying his hunting bow from his saddle.

'I know this sod.' Shouted Magnus.

'He is Roland. De-Bracy's son, and is said to be the finest archer in the Shire, and if we don't do something rather quickly, that bastard will soon be skewering us with those bloody arrows of his.'

'Head for those trees over yonder.' Shouted Aelnoth, as he wrenched the rein to the shield side, and headed across a meadow towards a small copse.

Magnus followed, but was slightly behind Aelnoth as the first arrow zipped past his shoulder.

Roland steered his horse with his legs, as he fitted another arrow to his bow, and he mused to himself just how easy a shot this would normally be, as the broad backs of these two English peasants loomed ever nearer, but the movement of his horse and the uneven contours of the ground made it quite difficult not only to fit the arrow, but once it had been fitted, he knew it would still be a reasonably difficult shot.

It was a shot that he could almost make with his eyes closed when he was on foot, and at this range he would usually score at least eight bulls out of ten.

Roland was just about ready to shoot, when the nearest of the two wolf-head's horse's had suddenly been reigned in and brought to an abrupt halt, in a shower of mud and stones.

As both of his hands were occupied with his weapons, he was unable to rein in his own horse, as it continued its gallop, and it was something of a shock when he found himself suddenly alongside his intended target, who he recognised as being one of the serfs from Broseley.

Suddenly Magnus swung the sword which he had stolen from his Lord and master, using it as a backward slice, which sent the razor sharp sword through the ash hunting bow itself, before it ended its journey half way through the body of Roland, sending him backwards over the rear of his horse onto the ground.

In the meantime Aelnoth had reined chieftain in, and had returned to the side of Magnus, who sat on his horse looking down at the body of Roland.

Aelnoth dismounted and said. 'Give me a hand to get his body over his horse and we can lead the horse into yonder copse, and bury him.

Magnus jumped down and eagerly removed his sword, wiping the blade clean before he helped Aelnoth to heave the body over the saddle.

Aelnoth led the two horses ahead of Magnus, who followed with the third Norman horse, as he struggled to balance Roland's body, which seemed unwilling to remain slung over the horses back.

Before burying the body, Magnus wrenched Roland's boots off, in order to replace the rags, which he had on his own feet, and exchanged his own ragged shirt and jerkin for the much newer clothes of the dead Norman youth.

As they rode slowly through the woodland, Aelnoth remarked. 'That was a canny blow that you made when you slew that archer.'

'Where did you learn to handle a sword like that?

'I take it that you have not always been a serf?' He asked.

'Nay, I was not always an underling.' Was the answer.

'I fought with King Harold at Stamford Bridge, but was wounded and was unable to journey with him to Hastings.'

'Lucky for you.'

'Aye, perhaps so, although sometimes I wish I had been there, for Harold was my own uncle and my other uncle and my brother died with him.' He said sadly as he shook his head, as if to dispel the memories of his brother and King Harold.

'You mean to tell me that you are King Harold Godwinson's nephew? Asked the astonished Aelnoth.

'Indeed I am, although I too find it hard to believe, after spending a year and a half as a serf of the Normans.'

They dismounted and took the saddles off their mounts, allowing the horses to drink from a small river, which flowed lazily though the forest.

Aelnoth took his flint from his satchel, and after he had gathered a few dry sticks and a clump of dry leaves, he struck the flint and coaxed a small fire into life.

He unsaddled Chieftain and settled down to chew on a chunk of dried venison.

'Have a bite of this.' He said as he offered a lump of meat to his companion.

'My thanks to you, for my so called masters have nearly starved me to death.'

As he chewed the tough dry meat, he said. 'I would hazard a guess that you too are no peasant, by the way that you handled those two guards.'

'Well, No, not really. I am called Aelnoth Edricson. My father was known as 'Wild Edric,' as well as 'Edric the Savage,' along the Welsh borderlands and my Mother was named 'Godda.' She was a Queen of the Fairy folk, although some people did gainsay that, and considered her to be nought but a Welsh Princess.'

'Gods blood,' said the shocked Magnus. 'I have heard my father speak of 'Wild Edric.' Didn't he slay some Welsh chieftain, and bring peace to the borderlands?'

'And if I remember correctly.' He added, without waiting for an answer. 'Was he not one of King Harold's men, who fought at the battle of Hastings?

'Aye, He did. And he was at Stamford Bridge.'

'Now that was a bloody day.'

'I got this at Stamford Bridge' said Magnus as he eased his shirt down over his left shoulder, to reveal a scar, which ran down from his shoulder to his left nipple.

'Ug, that looks nasty. Sword or Axe?' asked Aelnoth.

'Axe.'

'The Danes are masters of the Axe.' Said Aelnoth.

'Tell me something I don't know?' Was Magnus's reply, as he rubbed the scar and grimaced?

'I have yet to see a real battle' said Aelnoth with a wry smile.

'My sire taught me the ways of war, but he ordered me stay at home and guard our holding, when he rode off to fight the Vikings and the Normans.'

'You have not yet slain a man?' asked Magnus, as he looked at the younger man who he reckoned could be no more than sixteen or seventeen years of age.

'No,' came the mumbled reply. 'At least I don't think that I have, although I did not see one of those Normans back there get up, after I had bested him.'

'That man I slew today.' Said Magnus.

'What about him?'

'Well he wasn't just another Norman.' Answered Magnus.' He was the only son of De-Bracy, and when

De-Bracy learns that we have slain his boy, he will move heaven and earth to wreak his revenge upon us.'

'It seems we have made yet another enemy amongst these damned Normans.' Said Aelnoth, as he rubbed the few sparse hairs, which covered the lower half of his face.

'It does indeed.'

CHAPTER 2

'What was that?' said Aelnoth quietly.

'What?'

'I thought I heard something.'

'What Like?'

'I don't know what like.' Answered Aelnoth angrily.

'If I knew what it was, I wouldn't bloody well ask you what it was, would I?'

Magnus had never liked being spoken to like that, and was on the point of rising to his feet with his hand on the hilt of his sword when Aelnoth said. 'There it is again. Didn't you hear that?'

'I did. At least I think I did.' Said Magnus who was immediately convinced that one of De-Bracy's men had found them.

'Hello in the camp.' Called a child like voice.'

'I am a friend.' It said.

Both Aelnoth and Magnus drew their swords and retreated out of the light from their small fire.

'Come on in.' Called Aelnoth in the gruffest voice that he could muster.

A diminutive figure appeared out of the shadows, holding its right hand in the air to show that it held no weapon, whilst it lead a horse that limped so badly that it appeared ready to be turned into horse steaks.

The small figure halted in front of the fire, where it dropped the reins of the horse and couched before the fire, warming its hands over the flickering flames.

'Who are you and what do you want with us?' asked Aelnoth as he and his new found friend sheathed their swords, and walked towards the fire.

The figure did not answer, but merely raised its head and took off the grubby cap, allowing a cascade of blond hair to fall around its shoulders, revealing the childlike face of Ingrid.

'By the saints, it's the girl from Pitchford. Ingora.' Said Aelnoth in amazement.

'Ingrid.' She said with a huff, for she was livid that she had travelled so far, and had already undergone so many near disasters and dangers, only to find that this boy, with whom she had decided to spend the rest of her life with, couldn't even remember her name.

'Of course. Ingrid. How could I forget?' he lied, for although he did remember seeing the eldest of the girls around the table in Pitchford, he could not remember that he had ever actually seen the face of the eldest girl of Leofric's brood.

'What on earth are you doing here dressed in boys clothing?' asked the still shocked Aelnoth, as he walked the few paces towards her.

'I have come to join you.'

'Join us?' Queried Aelnoth.

'Well you have indeed joined us, but the question is, now that you have joined us, what shall we do with you?'

'Take me along with you of course.' She said snootily, as she tossed her head from side to side, in order to emphasise the point, sending her long blond hair cascading from one side of her head to the other.

'But we don't know where we are going.'

'That doesn't matter. Wherever you go, then I shall go with you.'

'Why would you want to do that?'

'It will probably be dangerous.'

'It matters not.' She said as she shook her head in defiance again.

'If it is dangerous, then I shall share the danger with you.' She added.

'You could get hurt.'

'So could you.'

'And if you do get hurt, then I shall be with you to protect you, or to heal you. I am good at healing.' She said haughtily.

'We should send her back.' Intervened Magnus.

'If you do, then I will follow you.'

Aelnoth took the arm of his friend and led him a few paces away, so that Ingrid could not hear him.

'It seems that we have no choice other than to take her with us.'

'Over my dead body.' Said Magnus.

'She will hold us up, and will be a hindrance to us rather than a help, especially if we get into another fight.' He added in a gruff and surly voice.

'She could cook for us, and if we do get into a fight, then she may be able to care for our wounds.' Countered Aelnoth.

'Besides,' he added. 'I cannot help but admire the girl, for it is several days since I left her in the care of her parents, and yet she has managed to follow our trail, and has found us, which in itself is quite a feat, and I must admit that there is certainly something in my being, which is telling me that she has been appointed to join me, and that her fate is somehow entwined with my own.

'But she is a mere child.' Argued Magnus.

'She is but a few short years younger than me.' Countered Aelnoth.

'And,' he added, 'both she and myself will not always be youngsters.'

Magnus could see that he was fighting a losing battle, and in order to save face he shouted to Ingrid. 'Girl, can you cook?'

'Probably a lot better than you can.' Was the answer from the smiling maiden?

'I will show you if you will give me something to roast over this excuse that you call a fire.'

'But I must warn you.' She added with a beguiling smile that a girl of 15 or 16 should not have possessed. 'I will do my fair share of the cooking and the washing of clothes, but I have not joined you to be your slave.'

'I have joined you so that I can help you with your quest.'

'What quest is that?' asked Aelnoth.

'Your quest of vengeance for the death of your brother and the loss of your Hall.'

Aelnoth was totally shocked that this child should know that he was set upon revenge, for he was certain that he had not mentioned it when he had spent the one and only night with the girl and her family

'And are you prepared to share the dangers that I know we will face?'

'I am.' She answered as she looked up and smiled at him.

*   *   *

De-Bracy was white with anger as he saw Robert join the chase after his runaway slave, and the youngster who had aided his escape.

He fully realised that his hot-headed son would probably try to perform some stupid heroic deed, and get himself killed, unless he could catch up with him in time to prevent such a disaster from happening.

And when the other men urged their tired horses back into the paddock without his son, his rage knew no bounds.

'Why did you leave him to chase those two wolfheads alone?' He fumed.

'Why didn't you stay with him? You know he's is no match for two men.'

'I should have you hung up by your balls, and leave you for the crows.'

'We had no choice my lord.' Answered the bravest of them.

'Our horses were blown and the slave took your own stallion, and young Lord Robert had the only other horse in the valley that could keep up with your lordships own steed.'

'Excuses. Excuses. That's all I hear from you cowards. And my only son is out there chasing two English savages, with nought but a hunting bow and a stupid smile on his silly young face.'

'It's all a game to him.' He bellowed as he strode towards the stables.

'Gather as many men as you can and get yourself a fresh mount. We must get to the boy before he does something foolish.'

'Make haste.' He roared as he flung the stable doors open and ran towards the small paddock, which was situated at the other end of the stable block, where he kept his small stock of riding horses.

Within a few minutes, no less than fourteen fully armed Normans rode out of the paddock, and spurred their mounts in the direction the runaway slave and his son had taken.

They urged their horses across the meadow, scattering the small flock of sheep, which the new lord of Broseley had recently stolen from one of his new tenant farmers.

They splashed through the brook and up the steep bank into the woods, which were now the sole hunting grounds of De-Bracy and his family.

His villagers had been banned from hunting in his woodlands, and could not collect so much as a stick of firewood without his permission, and lo and behold any villager caught in the forest, for he had decreed that any man woman or child caught in his forest would suffer severe pain.

By nightfall they had lost the tracks, and De-Bracy cursed himself for being in such a rush, and he had neglected to bring his hunting dogs.

'I should have known better.' He said aloud.

'Sorry My Lord?' questioned one of his liegemen, who had failed to hear what his Lord had said. 'What did you say'? He added.

'Nothing.' He snarled at the man. 'Mind your own damned business.'

'Make camp here.' He shouted.

'We can't pick up their trail until it gets light in the morning.'

They unsaddled their mounts and tended to their needs, spreading their saddle blankets on the damp earth, where they spent a damp and restless night.

As dawn broke De-Bracy woke and kicked some of his men awake, and without eating a morsel of food, they mounted and retraced their steps to the spot where they had last seen any sign of the fugitives.

'Here My Lord.' Called one of his men.

'They made camp here My Lord.

'Only two men slept here, and another one here.' Said Osborn, who was noted to be a man who could read the signs of the forest.

'Was one of them my son?' Screamed De-Bracy.

'No. My Lord.'

'Why not?' roared De-Bracy.

'The other one appears to have turned up after darkness, and joined the two who we are after.'

'Where is my son then?' He demanded.

'Perhaps he returned home.' Suggested one of the men.

'Mmmm. Lets hope so. Mount up. We will return to Broseley.' He said, hoping that the man was correct, and that his headstrong son had indeed returned home.

They had followed the trail for about half a mile when Osborn suddenly reined his mount in, and gazed fixedly to the ground on his shield side.

'My Lord.' He said, as he held his hand up and pointed towards a clump of bushes that nestled along the side of the woodland.

'They seem to have turned off here.'

The small cavalcade veered off to the left, as they followed Osborn along an almost invisible trail that led into the small copse.

'Someone has made a good attempt to cover his tracks.' He said admiringly.

'Can't fool me though.' He added smugly as they entered the bushes.

He suddenly yanked his horse to a halt.

'Oh my God.' He exclaimed.

'What?' shouted De-Bracy, who was directly behind Osborn?

'What is it?' He snarled.

'A grave, my Lord.'

'Someone's dug a grave.'

'Where?'

'I can't see a bloody grave.'

'It's there my Lord, covered by those dead leaves.'

'Damn and Blast.' Swore De-Bracy, fearing the worst.

'Shall I dig it up? My Lord. Asked Osborn hesitantly.

'Yes! Yes! Spluttered the distraught De-Bracy.

'Of course you should dig the bloody thing up. Get on with it.' He spat.

'You and you.' He snarled as he pointing to two of his other men.

'Give him a hand.'

The three men used their swords to dig, and within a few short minutes they had uncovered the body of Robert, who had been placed on his back with his hands crossed over his chest, with a small piece of cloth covering half of his face.

De-Bracy dropped onto his knees, and muffled sobs emitted from deep in his chest, as the tears oozed out of his eyes, and cascaded down his beardless face.

'Those English bastards even took his boots.' He screamed with rage and flung his leather gauntlets onto the ground.

'They were new boots, which I had especially made for him only two weeks ago.' He raged.

He unclasped his own cloak and handed it to Osborn. 'Wrap him in this and hand him up to me.' He ordered, as he mounted his horse.

'I shall carry him home.' He uttered amid another flurry of sobs.

On their return to Broseley manor, there was much tears and wailing, for the Lords young son was loved by many, especially the serving maidens with whom he had spent many a happy hour, dallying in the hay lofts.

His burial was a sad affair, being attended not only by De-Bracy and his wife, but also by every Norman who belonged to the old English Hundred of the area, for the English system of 'Hundreds' was much admired, and had been adopted by the new Norman overlords,

As the grieving father threw the first handful of earth onto the hand carved coffin, he said, as his sobs welled up in his chest and welled up from his open mouth.

He placed his right hand on his aching chest, and uttered. 'I swear upon my dead son's coffin that I shall not rest until I have the heads of these two English murderers in my own two hands.' And he held his hands up towards the sky as his stony gaze stared into the heavens.

For the next two and a half months his mood became blacker and blacker, causing his shrewish wife and his household servants to avoid his company whenever possible.

His English subjects fared even worse, and felt the full fury of his venom for the slightest of misdemeanours.

He had two men flogged by his brutish overseer, and hung a young man who had been found poaching in his new (off limits) woodland, leaving the youngster's corpse hanging on the newly erected gallows for all to see, as a gruesome warning, should any other serf be foolish enough to upset the new lord of Broseley.

Within two days of his son's death he had dispatched an envoy to Normandy, and had provided the man with two of his finest mounts, in order that he could reach the city of Le-Mans in the shortest time possible.

Le-Mans was a pleasant city, which stood on a high point above the river Sarthe in southern Normandy.

He had given the man a heavy purse of silver, with orders that he must return with all speed, accompanied by the famous assassin, John de Moren.

John de Moren was known to the many Lords who employed him as 'John the Slayer,' for he was the most famous assassin in the Kingdoms of Frankia, Normandy and Aquitaine.

He was also a man who had never failed to carry out an assignment.

John was the ninth son of a tanner, and despite being the runt of the litter, he was the most aggressive and ambitious of all of his siblings, for whilst they were content to spend their lives in their fathers' tannery, squelching around in huge butts full of other men's piss.

John's aggressive and sly nature, as well as his undeniable courage, had eventually made him dominant over all of his male and female siblings, who, over the course of time, had learned that the jibes and insults, which they had heaped upon him whilst he was still a toddler, were returned ten-fold, with at least half of them carrying scars and broken bones by the time John reached the age of thirteen.

He left home at the age of fourteen, never to return.

In adulthood John of Le-Mans, (as he was also known) gave people the impression that he was the most mild and un-assuming man imaginable, shocking many of the noblemen who had hired him for the trade in which he specialised, for he was a small, almost timid looking man, and not at all like the cold hearted butcher, which they had expected.

He had lost his hair at an early age.

He had a clean-shaven baby face, making him look at least ten years younger than he actually was, but despite his innocent looks, John was an accomplished assassin, who had learned his trade from a noted killer, and by the age of twenty, he had been employed by nearly half of the great lords of Europe.

He was a master of disguise, and had the skill to alter his appearance so swiftly and so thoroughly, that on one occasion he had been able to fool his own wife and children into believing that a total stranger had just entered their modest house, and had shared a meal with them.

He was a master of the garrotte.

He could throw a knife thirty feet with unerring accuracy, and could place an arrow from his small, but powerful crossbow into the centre of an acorn at thirty feet.

John and his faithful servant, the sadistic Pierre, had found the journey to be long and tiresome, as they rode slowly across a large part of Normandy in order to reach the port of Honfleur, where they were delayed for a further ten days before they had been able purchase a passage to Dover.

The crossing of the narrow seas had been an experience that had caused him, for the first time in his life, to pray to God. Beseeching the almighty that the huge waves that appeared to toss the small trading vessel about like a toy, would not send him to a watery grave, for although in most situations he was totally fearless, water was, in his opinion, only fit to be drank on the rare occasion when he could not obtain passable wine or beer. Indeed he rarely washed and was unable to swim, so he avoided water like the plague.

At Dover, John had purchased a sturdy stallion that was approaching it's old age, as well as an old pack horse for his servant and their belongings, and rode slowly through southern England, pausing for only two days in the smelly English capital city of London, before they began to make their way through the north gate towards the midlands, arriving at the village of Broseley late on a dull Sunday evening, at the precise time when the villagers were emerging through the open door of the village church.

Six men at arms preceded De-Bracy, who was the last man to leave the church, and it was not until De-Bracy had spoken at length to the priest, that he noticed a ragged old man sitting astride a very old stallion, with a second man on an equally bedraggled horse, which was in the process of nibbling at a tuft of grass that had sprung up through the cobbled pathway.

'Get you gone from here.' He shouted at the two grubby men. 'Tis the Sabbath and I will not tolerate tramps and vagabonds harassing my people on the lords' day.'

'Be gone before I set my men upon you.' He roared, causing the villagers to look at him in alarm and hasten on their way.

'The grubby old man merely looked towards the angry Norman, and then, as if in distain, he turned his head away, to gaze nonchantly at the sparrows, which fluttered and chirped in a nearby Holly (holy) tree.

De-Bracy went red with anger. 'Reynauld,' he screamed.

'Kill the insolent pigs and confiscate their wares.'

'My Lord,' said the priest as he held his hands up in horror.

'It is the lord's day. A day of forgiveness.'

De-Bracy ignored him and nodded towards Reynauld, who strode over to the man and placed his gauntleted hand on the old man's leg, with the intention of yanking him off his horse.

In the blink of an eye, the ragged man leapt off the other side of his horse, kicking Reynauld under his chin as he did so, landing on the ground like a cat, only to reappear from under the belly of his horse in front of the startled Reynauld, who was still shaking his head, in order to clear the stars, which whirled about the inside his skull, only to be confronted by this grubby old man, who clouted him under his chin and sent him to the ground unconscious.

De-Bracy was beside himself with rage, and he drew his own dagger as strode up to the man, but as he reached him, the stranger said quietly in a rather refined voice.

'I am John of Moren.'

At this totally unexpected announcement, De-Bracy halted as if he had walked into a stonewall, for he was completely nonplussed that this grubby old man should turn out to be the most famous assassin in Western Europe.

'I, Err. Herrum.' He found himself to be speechless, and cleared his throat as he willed himself to calm down, and it was only after a very long silence that he found that he could speak.

'Welcome. John of Moren. 'I trust you had a good journey.' He muttered.

'Bloody awful.' Was the reply.

'I am weary and hungry and would murder my own grandmother for a glass of good burgundy.'

'John. John,' repeated De-bracy, as he shook the man's hand. 'I should have known it; the minute I saw you put down that clod Reynauld, although I must admit that I had expected you to be a much younger man.'

'Oh, I am much younger than I look.' Exclaimed John, as he removed his ragged hood, and as the hood came off, so did the white hair, followed by the white beard, to reveal a man who was aged somewhere in his mid twenties.

'Come my good fellow.' Muttered the shocked Lord of the manor.

'Come with me to my Hall and I shall wine and dine you with the finest food and wine that my humble Hall can provide.'

As he escorted the assassin through the door, he asked 'I have been told that you are the most reliable assassin in Western Europe. Is that so?

'We shall see.' Answered John.

'If I get your man. Perhaps I will be. If not. Then, perhaps not.'

'Have you ever failed?'

'No.'

'I have been told that you can track a mouse through a meadow.' Is that true?'

'Don't know. I usually track more savage game than mice.' Was the reply from the killer, who was already getting annoyed at this stupid little man, and his stupid little questions?

'Pray tell.' He asked amiably. 'Who is your companion?'

'Ah. This is Pierre. My servant.'

'Oh. I see. Well the stables are good enough for him.' He said haughtily as he escorted John into the house.

*   *   *

The sound of a fish jumping after an insect echoed from the river, at almost the same time that a blue flash of a kingfisher zipped along the far bank.

'My Father Edric used to tell me of a tale of your Grandmother, the lady Gytha,' said Aelnoth quietly.

'And of the day after the Battle of Hastings, when she pleaded with Duke William for King Harold's body.'

'And how she offered to give William an amount of gold, which weighed the same as her son's body, and yet he refused her.'

'Do you think there is any truth in the story?' he asked.

'Indeed. It was so.' Answered Magnus thoughtfully.

'That is a lot of gold.' Said Ingrid, who had been listening avidly to their conversation.

'Was he a heavy man?' she asked in her childlike voice.

Aelnoth looked down towards Ingrid, but he merely smiled at her and continued to speak with Magnus.

'And yet it is rumoured that Lady Gytha's gold was never found.'

'No. At least, not as far as I know.' Muttered Magnus, as he sadly shook his head.

'That gold would draw a lot of warriors to our cause.' Said Aelnoth.

'What cause is that?'

'Well, if we could gather enough men, we could rid our country of this plague of Norman swine.' Said Aelnoth thoughtfully.

'And just where would we get enough men to do that? 'Asked Magnus.

'They are building a Mott and Bailey in every village in England.'

Aelnoth ignored the last remark and continued.

'From what I have been led to believe, not all of King Harold's brothers were slain at Hastings.'

'It is rumoured that your own father fled to Ireland, did he not?

'So'?

'Well, if we were to recover the Lady Gytha's gold, and persuade your father to lead us, we could recruit enough men from Ireland to cross the Irish Sea, and help us to lead a rebellion, and rid our land of these damned Normans.'

'I've never been to Ireland.' Said Ingrid. 'Is it far?'

This time it was the turn of Magnus to look down at this thin girl who, by her silly questions was beginning to annoy him, and although he felt that he had cause to give her a slap for her impudence, something within him stopped him, and he scowled and looked away, to continue to speak with Aelnoth.

'Mmmm' answered Magnus, as he stroked his short fair beard, and brought his mind back to the task in hand. 'Might work.' He muttered.

'But first we would need to get the treasure, and I for one, have no idea where my grandmother hid it.' My family owned half of the Kentish lands and it could be just about anywhere in the county.'

'Or even in the lands of the West Saxons.' He added.

'You really have no idea?' Said Aelnoth with a shake of his head.

'No.' answered Magnus. 'No idea at all.'

'But surely you must know some of the places where she favoured, and could have hidden the treasure? You must know the countryside well, having spent your childhood there.'

'Oh I know both Wessex and our Kentish lands like the back of my hand, but I really have no idea where she buried the gold.' He said, as he turned his back to the fire and rolled into his sheepskin, in order to fend off the evening chill.

They settled down in their sheepskin saddle blankets near the fire in order to sleep, but sleep eluded Aelnoth, as his mind flitted from one thing to another, as he thought of how he and his two new friends could get hold of the Godwinson hoard, and when they had it in their keeping, just what would be the best way to use such a large treasure?

Aelnoth was wakened by an unfamiliar noise, and as he quickly rose to his feet he could see that Ingrid was already up and attempting to rekindle the few glowing embers that remained from yesterday evenings fire.

'Ah, there you are,' said Magnus in a cheerful manner as he too wakened. 'I'll go and catch a few trout for breakfast.'

'As a boy I was an expert at tickling trout,' as he knelt beside Ingrid and threw a few dry leaves and sticks onto the small flame. He watched them catch alight, before he rose to his feet and strode off merrily towards the stream.

Ingrid looked up at him and scowled as he turned his back on her.

'Be back soon.' He said, as he walked away, delighted to be alive and free from the Norman yoke, which he had been made to endure over the last year and a half.

'Make sure you build up the fire so that we can cook the fish over it as soon as I get back.'

Aelnoth was a little abashed, as he was not used to taking orders, and thought that building the fire up to cook the fish was just a little premature, as his new friend had not even reached the stream, let alone caught any fish for breakfast.

'Cocky sod.' He mumbled quietly to Ingrid, as they watched Magnus stroll slowly and almost nonchalantly towards the riverbank.

They both walked amongst the tangled woodland gathering dry sticks, and soon had arms full of wood; chatting as they walked the few yards back towards their campsite.

As he neared the fire Aelnoth was quite surprised to see Magnus on his way back from the stream, with no less than three good-sized trout dangling from his hands.

God's blood! You were quick.' Exclaimed the startled Aelnoth.'

'Just you wait until you taste them.' Was the reply as Magnus knelt down to clean and gut the fish.

'You see,' said Magnus to Ingrid. 'I too can cook.'

The fish were filleted, filled with wild garlic, spitted onto a stick, and were soon sizzling over the fire.

The three youngsters enjoyed their meal as the morning sun crept higher into a cloudless sky.

After four days of travel, they halted at an isolated farmstead, where they enjoyed a delicious meal of roast pork flavoured by wild garlic, and washed down with several jugs of small beer, which the farmer and his wife willingly provided, once they realised that the travellers were English fugitives.

After the meal, the old farmer said. 'The village of Brownhills is a mile up the track, and you might find some young men there who would be willing to join you.'

'Ask for 'Oscar.' He is the son of Lord Wilfred, who was slain at Hastings.'

'He is the sort of man you are looking for. Mind you. He is a bit strange.'

'Strange. How? Asked Aelnoth.

'Well. I can't rightly say, but he don't talk much, but, but.' The old man hesitated and appeared unwilling to continue, but he tapped his nose a couple of times with his index finger? 'But when you do see him, you will see what I mean.'

'Despite his looks, he is still a good man.' He added.

'We have grown up with him, so it makes no difference to us, but he might look a bit odd to you. You being strangers an' all.'

The man would say no more, but as the two men mounted their horses, he solemnly waved them farewell and shouted. 'Make sure you find Oscar now.'

An eerie howling sent shivers down their spines long before they reached the township of Brownhills, and it was not until they were almost within sight of the village that they discovered the origins of the noise.

Two hounds periodically howled, as they sat beneath two sturdy trunks of birch trees, which formed the shape of a large cross, and on the cross was a naked man who was spread-eagled, with his hands and his legs firmly tied with thick leather straps.

To say that the man was naked was not quite correct, for the man's head was covered with a leather hood, on which the word 'Traitor' had been written in large white limestone letters.

Ingrid was shocked to the core at the poor mans predicament, and averted her eyes away from the scene.

The dogs snarled and barred their teeth as the riders halted their horses, forcing Aelnoth to draw his Saex and wave it in their faces.

'Shift.' he snarled back at the dogs as he approached the cross.

The hounds retreated a few feet, and watched him as he hacked through the ropes, which held the man's legs.

A low feral growl emitted from the man as the weight of his body sagged.

'Take some of his weight while I cut his hands free.' Said Aelnoth and Magnus rushed forward to help his friend cut the man down.

As the final rope was cut, the man literally fell into the arms of Magnus, causing both the rescued and the rescuer to end up in a heap at the bottom of the cross.

The hounds immediately leapt forward and whined aloud as they licked the masked face and body of the man.

Aelnoth cursed under his breath as he fumbled with the double knot, which had been tied in order to prevent the hood from slipping off, and stepped backwards, crying aloud in alarm as he removed the hood, for he was confronted with a chalky white face with shiny white hair, and eyes, which were so pink that he wondered for a brief moment whether the man who they had just saved was a human, and not one of the changelings or trolls, which his mother had told him about, when he had been a child.

'God.' Cursed Aelnoth.

He was aghast at the strange startling white man who sat before him.

'No,' replied the man with a wry smile.

'Oscar.' The next best thing. 'He added, with a grimace.

Ingrid, who had been kneeling beside the man, recoiled in horror and turned her head away from the poor man, who, she felt, must have been cursed by God himself to have been afflicted so.

Aelnoth felt a hand on his shoulder and turned to find Magnus standing over him with a smile on his face.

'Fear not my young friend.' He said. 'He is an Albino, and what's more important, his name is Oscar, so he must be the very man who the old farmer advised us to contact.'

The man struggled to his feet and tottered unsteadily for several moments until he eventually stood upright.

He slowly stretched to a height that astounded Aelnoth, for the Albino had looked to be just a normal man, when he had been stretched taut on the cross, but now Aelnoth was forced to look upwards towards the mans face, which appeared to be at least four or five inches above his own.

The man rubbed his wrists where the ropes had cut into him, and let out a low moan as he squinted down at both of his rescuers. 'I thank you for my life, for Herbert of Lisieux was due to return before nightfall to finish me off.'

'Knife?' mumbled Oscar' as he nodded towards the hunting knife, which nestled in its sheath in Aelnoth's belt.

Aelnoth took the knife out of its sheath and handed it to Oscar without saying a word, but he was more than a little apprehensive, as he really did not know what this newcomer intended to do with it.

Oscar stooped and retrieved the hood, which had covered his head a few minutes ago, and made two long cuts in the hood, and as his bemused companions watched, he placed his legs through the slits, and struggled to pull the hood up over his waist as far as the lower end of his hips, stretching the leather towards breaking point as he proudly looked down at his new, very brief breeches.

'There.' He uttered. 'That's a bit better.'

'I don't think that I am dressed elegantly enough to attend a dance, but at least we'll not get too many maidens swooning at the sight of such a beautiful, naked man.'

Ingrid had not turned to look at the man, and had walked a few paces away in order to avoid embarrassing herself, and stood gazing into the woodland, as if she was a hunter studying the countryside.

Before the two younger men could reply, Oscar continued. 'Do either of you possess such a thing as a strip of cloth that I could use to cover my eyes?'

'The brightness from the sun is hurting my eyes.'

Both of the young men fumbled in their pouches and pockets until they both shook their heads.

'I could cut the bottoms off your breeches and cut two slits in for your eyes,' said Ingrid, 'and you could wrap that around his eyes.'

Whilst Aelnoth was a little reluctant to lose a couple of inches off his breeches, and searched around for another solution, he eventually nodded his head rather reluctantly in agreement, and allowed the young girl to cut two inches off the bottom of one of his trouser legs.

'That looks bloody silly.' He said scornfully as he looked down at her handiwork.

'I think you will have to cut a chunk off the other leg to even things up a bit.'

Ingrid grinned, and without a word she knelt down again and commenced cutting the other trouser leg, which she held aloft and said. 'Is this of any use to you?'

No one actually answered, so she tossed it away.

After a little fumbling, Oscar tied the cloth around his head, leaving two slits for his eyes, and sighed with relief, saying 'Ah that's much better.'

'I can see better now.'

'I am not too good in the daylight, but in the darkness. Now that is a different stripe on the badger.'

Aelnoth and Magnus looked briefly at each other, both not quite understanding what he meant by the remark but, erring on the side of caution, he made no comment.

Oscar called the dogs over to him and stroked their heads lovingly, but then with a gruff voice, he said, 'Go Home.' The dogs did not move but looked up at him with a look that almost spelt out their disbelief, that they were to be sent home, but when he repeated 'Go Home,' in an even gruffer voice, they both reluctantly slunk off in the direction of the village, but halted after they had covered some twenty feet, and sat on their tails, refusing to go any further.

Despite shouts and snarls from Oscar, they refused to budge.

To the three young men's astonishment, Ingrid casually strolled up to the dogs and knelt by them, fondling them and speaking to them in a low and soothing voice for a few minutes, before she rose to her feet again and pointed towards the distant village.

'Go,' she said in a low voice, and the dogs obediently rose and trotted away towards the village.

The three young men exchanged looks, but said nothing, until Magnus broke the silence.

'I think it's time we moved on,' he said as he urged the horse that had belonged to Robert De-Bracy, a few short hours ago.

'Can you ride?' he asked, and with a smirk across his chalky white face, Oscar took hold of the reigns, and with one leap, he landed daintily in the saddle and looked down to Aelnoth with the smile still on his face and said. 'Probably better than you young man, for I was practically born in the saddle.'

They urged their horses southwards across the meadows and into the woods, not easing their pace until they were some five or six miles away from the cross that had meant to be Oscar's death marker.

It was not until they had made their camp that evening, that they began to learn from Oscar, exactly why he had been sentenced to death, and after hearing his brief account, Aelnoth thought that the new Norman Lord of that Manor had cause to seek revenge on their new companion, for Oscar had not only slain one man. He had wounded two other Normans who had been assigned the task of supervising and building the new Lords Keep.

'He is just the sort of man we need.' He thought to himself, and smiled.

As they were gathering wood for the fire, Magnus said quietly to Aelnoth. 'I reckon that he is only telling us half of the truth.'

'It seems to me that our new friend has been a thorn in this side of this Norman Herbert of Lisieux for quite a while, still,' He added quietly. 'He is a dangerous looking character and seems to have endured his ordeal with little or no effect, so I think it might be prudent for us not to dig too deeply into his past, and let sleeping dogs lie.'

Oscar returned with an armful of sticks for the fire, and as he sat down, he started to throw on an odd stick onto the fire, and began to study his two companions, noting that the one called Aelnoth was obviously the younger of the three, and yet it appeared to him that it was Aelnoth who gave the orders to Magnus, and that alone seemed to be odd, for Magnus was obviously the elder and more experienced of the two, and it was he who carried a number of white scars on his arms, as well as a huge scar across his chest, indicating to Oscar that Magnus had stood in a shield wall on at least one occasion.

Oscar had not been deemed experienced enough by his father, to fight either at Stamford Bridge or at Hastings, and it had been a decision for which he had never really forgiven his father, for one of Oscar's dearest wishes had been to fight alongside King Harold.

Oscar mused to himself, that as he had slain a number of men, and as he was obviously the eldest of this trio of Noblemen's sons, he really ought to proclaim himself to be the leader.

However, for the sake of acquiescence, he simply decided to leave things as they were, for he had already realised that despite Aelnoth being the youngest and less experienced of the three men, he recognised the fact that the youngster was a natural leader, and seemed to possess a certain something that was lacking in both Magnus and himself.

He poked at the fire as he decided that he would leave the hierarchy as it was, and wait a while to see how things worked out. 'Nothing is forever,' he whispered to himself.

CHAPTER 3

An owl hooted from a nearby oak tree, and somewhere in the distance, the night's silence was broken by the eerie yowl of a mating vixen.

Aelnoth broke the silence that had descended on the four young people, as he more or less echoed the thoughts that had crossed the mind of Oscar a few moments before.

'Well, here we are.' He said thoughtfully.

'Three fugitives and a girl.'

'We are three sons of Lords who have been dispossessed of our birthright.'

'Our Fathers have either been slain or exiled.'

'You are a believer in the old gods of Thor and Woden, he said, as he nodded towards Magnus.

'And I am a Christian.' He added.

'Are you a Christian?' he asked Ingrid.

'I am.' She said proudly.

He gazed towards Oscar. 'And you are a seer who believes in the mystic powers of all things,' he said.

Oscar nodded solemnly.

'The three of us are men who have narrowly escaped death, and we are now hiding like frightened deer in the depths of the woodlands, almost afraid to show our faces amongst our own people, let alone face up to these Norman bastards who have stolen our lands, and the Halls of our Fathers.'

Aelnoth paused for a moment, and just as Magnus was about to say something, he continued in a low voice.

'Well, I am sick of running, and sick of hiding in these wet woodlands.'

He turned towards Oscar and said. 'Before we met you, Magnus and myself were talking about going down into the lands of the Kentish men, and into Wessex, where we thought that might try to find the riches, which the Godwinson's held before the invasion.'

At this stage Magnus took up the story.

'That's right.' He said with savage enthusiasm.

'We thought that if we could find the treasure which my grandmother held, then we could take it to my Father, who is in Ireland and use it to raise an army of Irishmen and Norsemen, or even a few of the English exiles who now dwell in Ireland with my Father.'

'We might be able to win back our country from these Norman pigs.'

Before he could say more, Aelnoth intervened, saying, 'What think you of that?'

'Are you with us?'

Almost before Aelnoth had asked the question, Oscar gasped 'Aye.' I am with you.'

'Let us make it so.'

'Me too.' Shouted Ingrid. 'I will help.'

Aelnoth patted her gently on her shoulder but failed to look down into her face.

Had he done so, then he would not have seen the face of a child, but he would have seen the face of a maiden in the throes of her blooming. He would also have seen a maiden who was head over heels in love with him.

The three young men clasped hands and slapped one another on the back with genuine joy, as they talked excitedly about the adventure and the pitfalls, which lay ahead of them.

Ingrid remained a step or two away from the trio, smiling, and yet rather annoyed that she had not been included in the embrace.

As Aelnoth's two companions spoke to one another, he gazed at his friends, noting that Magnus was the only one with any real experience of warfare, and that perhaps Magnus, and not he should be the leader of the trio, but he shook his head violently in order to push that particular thought out of his mind.

Whilst Magnus was of average height, his shoulders and arms testified that he had spent many years training with sword, axe and shield.

Aelnoth turned his attention to the strange Albino, guessing that he was perhaps twenty two or twenty three years of age, who claimed that he had also slain men, albeit in something that must have resembled a brawl, and perhaps may not have been a real battle.

Oscar was the tallest of the three at a little over six feet, but he was rather thin and wiry, and his pure white hair, (which he kept hidden for most of the time) gave him the aura of a female, and yet his strange eyes reminded Aelnoth of a painting, which he had seen many years ago in Shrewsbury Cathedral.

The painting had been that of an angel who had brandished a short sword, and had hovered over the mother of Jesus, as she held the baby Jesus to her breast.

This strange man, who they had rescued from a cross, also appeared to possess the same sort of aura that Aelnoth had seen in the painting.

Was he a freak or a holy man? Or merely a man, like other men? He asked himself.

And then, he tried to assess himself.

'Here I am, a mere boy of seventeen summers,' he mused, 'who has never wielded a weapon in a real battle, despite the constant training, which my father and my old mentor, Garth blood-axe had insisted that I carried out every afternoon, since I have been old enough to hold a sword or an axe. And yet these two new friends seem to have elected me to be their leader.'

Why? He asked himself, but it was a question, which puzzled him, and he was unable to answer.

They were still talking loudly when Oscar suddenly froze, and held his finger up to his mouth. 'Shh.' He said quietly. 'Cease your chatter.' and without saying another word, he rose and walked over to where Aelnoth had placed his ash hunting bow and bag of arrows.

'May I borrow these for a moment?' He whispered, and before Aelnoth could answer, he stooped, picked up the bow, and a single arrow, and disappeared silently into the dark woodland.

'That was strange.' Whispered Aelnoth, as his hand touched the hilt of his sword.

'I didn't hear anything. Did you?'

Magnus and Ingrid both shook their heads, and joined him as the three of them stared silently into the blackness of the woodlands.

Suddenly, there was the sound of something falling; followed by complete silence.

The local owls and other night creatures appeared to have suddenly lost their voices, as an eerie silence encompassed the darkness.

The bushes on the edge of the clearing suddenly shook violently, causing the two young men to leap to their feet with their weapons at the ready, only to see the grinning white face of Oscar step nimbly into the clearing, carrying a young Buck over his broad shoulders.

'Now we have some food, as well as a fine new cloak to cover my nakedness,' said the smiling Albino, as he threw the carcass onto the ground.

He knelt beside it and made a long slit along the belly of the Buck, and with a quick movement, he allowed the guts to spill out onto the grass.

He peered long and hard at the stringy, steaming intestines, as his three companions gazed at one another in awe, realising that their strange new friend was studying the Buck's innards, as if he was a soothsayer, or a sage.

'Can you really see the future in the guts of a dead deer?' asked a bemused Magnus as he turned and winked at Aelnoth.

Although his face was turned away from Oscar, the Albino did not look up from his study and said in a low and cynical voice.

'Sometimes I can and sometimes I cannot.'

'What do you see today?' asked Magnus.

'Blood and guts.' Answered Oscar

'Is that all?' Scoffed Magnus.

'Well, no. Not really.' Mumbled Oscar, as he sliced through the heart and liver with his knife and peered into the bloody mess.

'The heart is strong and without blemish, as is the liver and the lungs, and that tells me that the four of us are now strong together, and have become an army who will be able to beat any enemy, three times our numbers.'

'Some army! Three landless men.' Growled Magnus.

'And a maiden.' Said Ingrid.

'Scoff all you like my sceptical friends.' Answered Oscar.

'But we shall see. Shall we not?'

His strange eyes appeared to glaze over, as he peered more intently at the tangle of guts, which lay steaming on the ground before him, causing his two companions to glance at one another.

'He's gone into a bloody trance.' Growled Magnus quietly, and was about to add to his remark when Oscar said clearly, not in his own voice but in the voice of a child.

'I see the three Nones.'

'They are at a loom, and are weaving the destinies of the four of us.'

'They stare at me, but they have no faces.'

'They are speaking to me, but they have no voices.'

'We shall cross four seas, but only three of us will return to England.'

'I see an army of many thousands.'

'Four men stand on a hill.'

'Thousands of warriors are swept away.'

'I see swathes of slain warriors.'

'There are Crows, and the eaters of carrion, and beasts that I do not recognise.'

'I see a slain man in a tree. And the face of a wolf.'

'No. It is the face of a girl. A beautiful girl and she is smiling at me.' He shuddered.

'IT IS a wolf. No, it is a girl, and she has a human hand in her mouth.'

He slumped forward and his face was only just prevented from falling into the steaming guts by the hand of Aelnoth, who lurched forward and caught him.

'He didn't mention me.' Said Ingrid.

'What about me?' She huffed.

'What is going to happen to me?'

'Oh, I will look after you. You will be safe with me.' Said Aelnoth with the conviction that he did not feel.

Magnus steadied the still shaky Oscar, and as he did so, he glanced towards Aelnoth and said in a voice that was full of bravado.

'Well my young friend. What do you think of that?'

'Four men on a hill and yet we are now four, if we count Ingrid.'

'Four seas, but only three of us will return.

Which one of us will not return?

'Will that man be slain or will he be left stranded in some foreign land?

'Or She?' intervened Ingrid.

'Mayhap I will be the one who will not return.'

'Ask him.' Aelnoth said as he nodded towards the now recovered Oscar who had obviously heard their remarks, and was looking wistfully towards his three companions.

'Only the Gods know the answer to that one.'

Answered the Albino, and gazed wistfully away into the darkened forest.

They skinned the deer and staked a number of large slices of venison over the fire.

Magnus asked 'How is it that you can hunt a deer in the forest at night time?'

'I can barely see a foot beyond the fire.'

'Ah well.' Came the answer. 'You see. Although my eyes are weak, and do not like bright lights. I am totally at home in the dark, and have better eyesight than any owl you've ever met.'

'I've never met an owl,' said Magnus jovially.

'Mind you, I have eaten one or two of them when times got tough.'

'I'll wager that the owl's meat was damned tough.' Said Aelnoth with a smile.

As the four hungry youngsters watched the meat sizzle on their relevant skewers, Oscar added. 'They called me Oscar after a baby owl, which I reared when I was a boy.'

'My real name is Alfred. Alfred. Son of Beorn. Lord of Brownhills.'

'Or at least he was, until the Normans killed him.'

'The villagers named me Oscar when I was a boy, and we spent many a summer night playing in the woodlands that surrounded Brownhills, and if I hid from them, no one could ever find me.'

'I could not only hear them blundering around in the forest.'

'I could also see them as they crashed around with torches to light their way.'

'What would you like us to call you?' asked Magnus. 'Oscar or Alfred?'

'Oscar will do'.

'Oscar it is,' echoed the two men.

'I think that we should set out for Wessex first thing in the morning, said Aelnoth.

'Agreed?'

The other two young men and Ingrid nodded in agreement.

A little while later, they ate their roasted venison with relish, and settled down for the night, wrapped in their sheepskin horse blankets, with their bellies full to bursting for the first time in many days.

On the advice of Aelnoth, they rested for most of the day and did not set out on their journey to Wessex until late the following evening, passing through the towns of Tamworth and Nuneaton in the dark, and reaching the outskirts of Atherstone by dawn the following morning, where they made their camp in a small patch of woodland.

After two more days of travelling in the dark, Oscar's companions fully accepted his boast about his eyesight being as good as an owl, for each night he guided them unerringly past darkened towns and villages, through woodland and heath lands, crossing streams and rivers by small bridges or stepping stones, which would have taken an eagle-eyed youngster to spot, even in broad daylight.

They purposely by-passed London, but as they were in the act of crossing the Isis at a ford near to the village of Richmond, they met their first real problem.

The suns had barely risen in the east as they climbed the riverbank; they were met by a troop of Normans who were topping the rise, with the intention of crossing the Isis on the very same ford that the four youngsters had just crossed.

Aelnoth had inherited his fathers annoying habit of counting things, like herds of deer, ducks in flight, and similar things, including groups of people, and had almost automatically noted that this band of horsemen consisted of no less than ten men.

The three Englishmen were not only outnumbered, but were disadvantaged, with the Normans being on the higher point of the riverbank.

However the Normans were riding three abreast, with the leader some two horses' lengths in front of the leading row of three men.

The gods of good-fortune were with the youngsters, or perhaps it was due to the rising sun, which was now shining directly into the sergeant's face, for his startled horse misjudged the lip of the embankment, causing both horse and its rider to stumble, and then tumble sideways down the bank.

The three leading riders pulled their horses to a halt, and watched with horror as their sergeant's horse rolled onto the man and tumbled into the water, leaving the prostrate sergeant on the ground.

The few brief moments of the accident gave the three Englishmen time to assess the situation, and with a scream of anger, Magnus, followed by Oscar and Aelnoth spurred their steeds up the incline and into the still hesitant Norman horsemen, cutting down two men before they realised what was happening.

Magnus slashed his sword at the man on his right, who was in the act of trying to swing his shield from off of his back, in order to protect his front, but the shield seemed reluctant to be moved, thus allowing the Englishman's sword to slash across the mans chest, sending him reeling to the ground.

Two men who were in the second rank attacked Magnus, who valiantly tried to ward off their sword thrusts, until Aelnoth urged his horse up the embankment and into the fray, attacking the burly Norman who was on the right hand side of Magnus.

Using the tactics that his father had drilled into his brain whilst he had still been a boy, Aelnoth thrust and swayed as his opponents sword swished past his face, then thrust again as the man was in the act of bringing his sword upwards, plunging his sword into the mans unprotected neck.

The man dropped his sword and brought his hand up to the gash in his neck, presenting Aelnoth with a brief moment that enabled Aelnoth slash again at his neck, sending him toppling to the ground.

He looked around with trepidation towards his two companions, and to his amazement he saw Oscar standing by his mount, in the act of taking a shield off one of the two dead Normans who lay at his feet, whilst Magnus was still battling with two very much alive Normans, who were in the act of attacking him from both sides.

Aelnoth immediately urged his stallion forward to attack one of the men in order to ease the pressure from Magnus.

The Norman saw Aelnoth coming, and turned his horse to meet him, thrusting his sword to the fore, hiding most of his body behind his shield.

As they met, the Normans sword descended in a series of savage blows, which sent waves of pain down the sword-arm of the English youth, as the more powerful and experienced Norman warrior slashed down again and again, causing Aelnoth's sword to be forced lower and lower, almost reaching the unprotected head of his horse.

Aelnoth managed to guide his horse a little way away from his adversary, thus allowing him a moment to snatch his Saex from his belt, and with his knees, he urged his stallion around to face the Norman, who was in the act of bringing his sword down again onto the unprotected legs of the Englishman.

Aelnoth managed to ward off the blow with his sword, whilst at the same time he lunged forward with his left arm, and plunged his Saex into the unprotected midriff of his opponent.

He twisted the Saex and wrenched it out of the startled mans belly.

Aelnoth quickly turned in his saddle, fully expecting the rest of the Norman troop to be upon him, but was surprised to see that the remaining Normans had turned tail, and were in the act of disappearing in the distance.

The sound of a loud groan caused him to turn his face towards the river again, where he saw the sergeant, who had regained his feet, and who was in the act of bringing down his raised sword to plunge it down onto the unprotected back of Oscar, but the man slowly sank to his knees and fell forward onto his face with Ingrid's poniard protruding out of the back of his neck.

'God's blood.' Swore Oscar. 'That was close.'

'Saved by a fourteen year old girl.' Said Magnus contemptuously.

'Fifteen.' Hissed the white faced, trembling girl, who turned and retched into the fast flowing river, shocked and appalled by her own bravery.

Oscar and Magnus had already dismounted and gazed towards Aelnoth with broad grins across their sweaty faces.

'By Odin's balls,' shouted Magnus. 'That was well done.' He stooped to search through the clothing of a dead Norman.

'T'was so,' added Aelnoth as he grinned towards his friends. But then he added in a more serious note. 'But I think it is time to glean whatever we can from these dead buggers and get the hell out of here, or else their friends may get it into their thick heads to pay us another visit.'

Still white faced and shaken, Ingrid watched as the three young men speedily rifle through the dead men's belongings, where, to their delight they collected four purses of silver coins of varying amounts, plus two gold rings and a jewelled poniard, which, a few brief moments ago, had belonged to the sergeant who now lay dead on the side of the river bank, with his left arm dangling in the fast flowing river.

Aelnoth helped Ingrid take the saddle off her old horse and place it the most docile looking of the Norman horses, and helped her up into the saddle. 'There,' he said.

'You will be able to keep up with us now, and gave the horse a friendly pat on its neck before he returned to his friends.

With the looted Normans shields slung over their backs and fully armed with the captured weapons, they cantered their horses for a mile before they slowed them down into a slow walk.

Aelnoth rode alongside Magnus and said quietly. 'Do you realise that there were ten Norman's in that troop we just tangled with?'

Magnus shook his head and looked towards Aelnoth, and said. 'So?'

'Well did not Oscar say that we three could hold our own against three times our number?'

'Mmmm, so he did.' Was the bemused answer, as the elder of the trio rubbed his chin in thought?

'Four threes are twelve.' Hissed Ingrid.

They rode on in silence.

As they sat around their morning camp near the village of Sutton, chewing on chunks of venison. Magnus turned to Aelnoth and said with a wry smile.

'Well, my boy. You killed your first man today.'

'Two' chirped in Oscar.

'What about Ingrid.' Said Aelnoth in an attempt to take the attention off himself, and give credit to young Ingrid.

'She is only fifteen, and she saved your life by killing that bloody sergeant.'

'She is the one who we should be praising.'

'Indeed.' Said Oscar, and he raised his horn tankard, and despite the fact that it was only filled with water, he said. 'To Ingrid,' and, followed by his two companions, they echoed in unison. 'Ingrid,' and drank to the health of the young maiden.

CHAPTER 4

At dawn on the following morning, Oscar led them around the city of Basingstoke, and they camped in a secluded hollow in woodland, near to the village of Alton, which was a pretty little village, perched on the edge of the downs, adjacent to the lands that had once been owned by Earl Magnus Godwinson.

The Following day they entered the lands of the late King Harold Godwinson and his family.

'My Grandmother, the lady Gytha died over a year ago.' Said Magnus.

'I will take you to her Hall and we shall find there what we will.'

His two companions merely nodded and urged their horses after him.

Magnus brought his mount to a halt on the edge of a small coppice.

He pointed to a building, which stood on a small mound.

'That is the boyhood home of my father and his mother, the Lady Gytha.' He stated glumly, adding.

'My Grandmother took King Harold's body there before she had him buried in the Abbey at Waltham.'

All three of his companions knew the story, and grunted in agreement.

Aelnoth turned and walked back to his waiting horse. 'We will camp here and as soon as we have eaten the last of the venison, Oscar can have a look around and see if it is safe for us to approach the Manor.'

Without another word, they commenced to unsaddle their horses, made a small hidden fire and roasted the remaining strips of venison, which they ate with relish as darkness fell upon the woodland.

Oscar smeared some mud over his white hair and his face, and stood, stretching his arms high over his head.

'Time to go.' He said as he rose from the fire, and without another word, he disappeared into the darkness.

Oscar made his way silently through meadows, and small fields of oats and barley, seeing the landscape, the village and the great hall, as clearly as a normal man could see them in the daylight.

Nothing stirred. No dogs barked, and there did not appear to be any livestock in the fields.

Two owls hooted as if they were conversing across the meadows and informing each other of this strange white human, who glided silently across their dark domain?

The only light that he could see, glowed out of an open window in the great Hall, which stood on a slight rise, surrounded by a dry moat.

He approached the Hall cautiously, carefully picking his way down into the moat, making sure that he evaded the sharpened spikes, which had been embedded into its base and sides.

He reached the wall beneath the room from which the light shone, and peered in, almost gasping as the bright light sent pangs of pain shooting through his sensitive eyes and into his head.

Inside, he saw a man and a woman, who he assumed must be the new Norman Lord and his lady, who were sitting at a large carved table, which was laden with food and drink.

An elderly man and woman were attending the table.

Oscar hastily ducked his head as the old man passed the window, and retreated silently down into the dry moat, and up onto the level ground, pausing behind a small clump of bushes, which grew alongside the main uneven road that led to the Hall.

After what seemed to be many hours, but was in truth little more than one hour, the heavy oak doors of the

Hall swung open to allow two people to pass through, and clanged shut again, as soon as they were out.

As the couple walked slowly towards him, he realised that the two people were non other than the old man and woman, who he had seen serving at the table of the new lords of the Manor.

Oscar allowed the couple to amble slowly passed his hiding place, before he silently rose and stepped into the road a few yards behind them.

He glided silently past them and as he a halted a couple of feet in front of them, his hands shot out and covered the startled couple's mouths. 'Fear not.' He hissed in the friendliest of way that he could muster, without throwing the old couple into a panic, which could have caused the women either to faint, or to scream at the top of her voice.

'I am a friend and will not harm you.'

They were both dumb with shock at this strange being who had simply appeared out of the darkness in front of them.

'Hwaet eart thu?' (Who are you?) The old man managed to squeak in a voice that was on the verge of panic.

Oscar slowly took his hands away from their mouths.

'I am a friend and will not harm you.' He repeated.

'I am an Englishman, and merely wish to take you over yonder to meet a friend who used to live here.'

'Who be he?' said the old man in a more confident voice.

'His name is Magnus. He is the son of Earl Magnus Godwinson.'

'He is the Nephew of our late King. Harold Godwinson.'

The old man staggered backwards, but was caught from falling by his wife, who knew of his ways, and had prevented him from falling on more than one occasion in the past.

'It cannot be so.' He mumbled as he steadied himself. 'Young Magnus was slain at Stamford Bridge some years ago.'

'Not so my friend.' Said Oscar. 'He was only wounded and was captured by the Normans, and has been their slave for many a long year.'

'Gods blood.' Swore the old man. 'It cannot be.'

'It is indeed so. Come and see for yourself, for at this very moment he is no more than two hundred yards away from this very spot.'

The man looked at his wife, who seemed to more trusting than her husband, who smiled and nodded her consent to him.

The old man reluctantly grunted his own consent, and followed Oscar, who led the way unerringly through the darkened landscape towards the place where his companions were waiting.

'I am Alfred,' said Oscar. 'Son of Beorn, who was the Lord of Brownhills, but my friends call me Oscar. How are you named?'

'I am Sabert.' Answered the man. 'And this is my wife Edith.'

Edith nodded and gave a half smile towards Oscar, but added in a braver voice than her husband. 'And I hope that you are telling us the truth young man, and not leading us into the woodland to rob us, for the good Lord knows, we have little or nothing worth so much as a copper penny.'

'Believe me dear lady. You are quite safe with me, and I do assure you that Magnus is but a few steps yonder.'

Complete silence ensued, other than a series of grunts and gasps, as the old couple struggled through the woodland in their attempt to follow their strange abductor, who strode forward as if it was broad daylight.

The old couple felt that they were blundering though woodlands, which were as black as pitch, as they stumbled and tripped over each and every stick and bush, which seemed to block their passage.

It was with a loud sigh of relief from both of the old people, when they suddenly found themselves out of the tangled woodland, as they stepped into a small clearing, which consisted of a small fire, where two men and a young girl were lying on sheepskin blankets, as they watched a chunk of venison roasting over the fire.

The two men and the girl rose from their blankets, and the younger of the two men walked casually over towards Oscar and his two companions, as if he had been expecting them.

'Welcome. Welcome.' He said jovially. 'We were wondering what had taken Oscar so long.'

'I am Aelnoth,' said the young man. 'And these are my friends Magnus and Ingrid,' as he pointed towards his two friends who were still some paces away.

'This is Sabert and his wife Edith.' Said Oscar, as he stooped down to examine the roasting venison, which he prodded with his knife, in order to ascertain if it was ready to eat.

'They work for the new Norman Lord at the Hall.' He added.

Old Sabert stepped towards Magnus and gasped. 'Tis true. Look you Edith. It is the young Lord Magnus. Alive and well.'

'I cannot believe my own eyes.'

Edith hobbled up to Magnus, and as she placed her hands on his cheeks and looked up into his eyes.
'Thanks be to God.' Thanks be to God.' She repeated. 'You be the same young rascal that I used to bounce on my knee for your mother. God rest her soul.'

'Edith, dear Edith,' said Magnus as he gently touched her shoulder. 'I remember you from what seems to be another lifetime ago. Before the disaster at Hastings.' He added with a sigh and a faraway look, which neither of the old people could see in the flickering light of the small fire.

Aelnoth interrupted her by saying. 'Come Edith. You too Sabert.

Sit with us and have a slice of venison.'

Aelnoth had been trying to repair his father's old shield, and although he had glued a fresh piece of boiled deerskin on top of the old leather, it still needed more work in order to make it sturdy enough to turn a spear thrust, or a well-aimed arrow.

68

As the venison was taken off the spit, he placed the half repaired shield on the floor and set to cutting the still sizzling meat into six more or less equal portions, which he then shared out amongst the six people.

Sabert chewed the stringy venison with his few remaining teeth, for he was now completely at ease with the situation in which he had his wife had found themselves.

'My Lord,' he said, as he struggled with mouthful of half chewed venison. 'What do you want of me that is so important to have abducted me in the middle of the night?'

Aelnoth swallowed the chunk of venison and cleared his throat before he answered the rather blunt question, unused as he was to answer such a straightforward question from a mere peasant.

'Well, as you work for the new Norman lord, presumably you were on the estate before the Normans came?'

'Aye my Lord,' Was the reply. 'I have lived here man and boy. Long before young Lord Magnus here was born.' He said with a wide grin, which displayed his two remaining front teeth.

'What sort of a relationship did you have with the lady Gytha?'

'A fine lady she was my Lord. Right fond of my wife Edith she was. Edith was one of her handmaidens in her younger days.'

'She was quite a beauty when she was young, was my Edith.'

'Have you seen the Lady Gytha lately?'

'Nay, I have not. But I did hear that she had fortified the town of Exeter in the shire of Devon, and fought off the Normans there.'

'You are correct, my good Sabert, but alas, she finally lost the town to the Normans, and has since died.'

'Oh.' Said Sabert. 'Now that is a shame. She was a good un.'

'Heart of a lion she had.'

'So you have not seen her since? He asked. She has not been back here?' Asked Magnus.

No my lord.' Answered Sabert glumly, as he was shocked and crestfallen at the news that he had just received.

'Was she killed at Exeter?' he asked.

'Don't really know.' Was the quiet reply? 'I have been a slave of the Normans and have heard sparse news from the world outside the shackles of my slavery.'

'But, my Lord, I do recall seeing your own Father. Lord Magnus.' Added Sabert as he turned his face towards Magnus.

'Oh.' Said the startled Magnus, for this was a revelation that he had not expected.

'When was that?' He asked in an excited voice, for he had heard that his father had been killed, at either Stamford Bridge or Hastings.

'Oh, about six months since,' came the answer as the old man continued to chew on his venison.

'Wh.' Magnus started to ask but was interrupted by Sabert who said.

'His Lordship was looking for the Godwinson treasure. Or so I heard.'

He swallowed the last morsel of meat.

'Did. Did he find it?' asked the now very alert Aelnoth.

'Aye. Indeed he did.' He muttered. 'Dug it from the graveyard by the castle of Lok.' 'Or so I heard. Never did see it myself.'

'Would 'ave loved to have seen it though.'

'Would've loved to 'ave seen a piece of gold afore I go to meet me maker.'

'And if I had a piece of gold on me I would willingly give it to you for what you have told us, but alas, I too have no gold.' Said Magnus sadly.

'Just one more thing Sabert, before I ask my friend Oscar to escort you and Edith to your home.' Said Magnus in a friendly way.

'Do you know what my Father did with the gold?'

'No! Not really my lord, but my Cousin Edgar helped 'im dig it up, and he said that he thought his Lordship was taking it back to Ireland.'

'Ireland. Are you sure?'

'Well Not really sure my Lord, but that's what my cousin said, and he's not a one to tell lies. Honest as the day is long, is our young Edgar.'

'Young Eadbald the hunter was with 'im.'

'You could ask him.'

'He helped Edgar, and he only lives over yonder.' He added as he pointed towards a cottage that was a few hundred yards away.

'Let's do just that.' Said Aelnoth.

'Ireland is too far to travel on a wild goose chase.'

'Aye,' added Oscar. 'Better to be safe than sorry.'

The small party walked over to the cottage.

Magnus banged on the door.

'Is anyone in? He said in a loud voice.

'Who wants to know? Was the reply.

'It's me Sabert, and I've got young Lord Magnus with me.'

The door opened, and a young man who was in his mid twenties stood and blinked into the darkness.

'Young Lord Magnus was killed at Stamford Bridge,' he muttered, but then as his eyes focused on Magnus, and he gasped with surprise and said. 'Praise the heavens. It really is you Lord Magnus.'

'I cannot believe it. What service can I do for you?'

'Come in. Come in.' repeated the smiling young man.

Magnus entered the room and said. 'Sabert here tells me that you helped his cousin Edgar dig up the Godwinson treasure from the castle of Lok.

He paused for a moment before he asked. 'Is that so?'

'Indeed it is, my Lord.'

'Do you know where they took the treasure?'

'I do my Lord. They said they would take it to Ireland and raise an army.'

'Did they? And where exactly in Ireland were they going?'

'I don't know exactly where, cos I have never been to Ireland. Never been out of this Shire.'

'But I did hear the name of King Diarmait and Leinster mentioned.'

'Of course.' exclaimed Magnus excitedly. 'I should have guessed. For where else would they go to raise an army, but to the King of Leinster?'

'He is the high King of Ireland, and has holdings here in England, as well as in Wales and the Isle of Man, and if the rumours that I have recently heard are true, he also holds some lands in the Hebrides. Or, at least he did, before Hastings,' he added.

'I've never heard of him.' Said Aelnoth.

'Me neither,' echoed Oscar.

'Never heard of 'Diarmait mac Mail na-m Bo?' 'The High King of Ireland?' Gasped the shocked Magnus, who found it hard to believe that his two companions did not know of the most famous Overlord of Ireland.

But then he realised that from what young Aelnoth had told him, the village of Wentnor, where he had spent most of his life was, in Aelnoth's own words. (The back of beyond.) So he surmised that he really shouldn't have been so surprised at Aelnoth's lack of knowledge regarding Diarmait Mac Mail na-m Bo.

'Well, lets say that apart from these Norman thieves, Diarmait is probably one of the most wealthy men in these isles of Britain, and apart from being wealthy, he is also one of the most ambitious men that I have ever heard of, and the ideal man to help us on our venture.'

Magnus felt a timid tap on his shoulder and turned to find Eadbald standing behind him. 'What?' said Magnus who was rather annoyed to be interrupted from what he was about to say?

'S'sorry my Lord,' stammered Eadbald, 'But there is one thing.'

'Oh, and what is that?' snapped Magnus.

'Well my Lord,' whispered Eadbald, as if he did not want any of the others to hear him. 'They didn't take all of the treasure my Lord.'

'There was too much silver.'

'They left some at Lok.'
'Left some you say? How much did they leave?'
'Where? Do you know where it is?
'Aye my Lord.'
'How much?'
'Quite a lot.'
'I helped them hide it my Lord.'
'Find this man a horse.' Ordered Magnus.
'There aren't any my lord. The Norman lord has all the horses.' answered Sabert
'Then we must steal one.' Snapped Magnus.
'There are only three horses in the district my lord, and the new Lord keeps them in the stables, and the stables are inside the walls.'
'If we attempt to steal them, then it might get us into a fight, and that would certainly alert the new Lord of our presence, as well as endanger the villagers who we would be leaving behind to face his wrath.' Said Aelnoth soberly.
'How far is Lok?' he asked.
'Eight or ten miles, or even twenty.' Answered Eadbald.
'He can ride behind me.' Said Ingrid. 'You three are heavier than me, so it would be no trouble for my new Norman horse to carry the two of us.
'Let's go.' Said Oscar, as he kicked his horse into motion.
'It's nearly dark, perhaps we should wait till morning,' said Aelnoth as he momentarily forgot Oscar's ability to see in the dark.
'So much the better.' Answered the Albino.
'We had best be on our way.'
Magnus and Aelnoth mounted their horses and Eadbald clambered up behind Ingrid, and they urged their mounts to follow Oscar into the woodland.
'Thank you for your help,' called Aelnoth, as they left the three villagers who stood and gazed at the three young English Lords and Eadbald, who held on to little Ingrid as if his very life depended upon it.

By midnight they had reached the forest, which lay to the west of the castle of Lok.

'Over there.' Said Eadbald quietly into Ingrid's ear, as he pointed towards the darkened centre of the woodland.

'Aelnoth repeated the direction to his two friends and Oscar veered off towards the centre of the woods.

'How far now?' he asked.

'Not far my Lord.' Adding. 'Thank the Good Lord that the moon has come out or I could never find my way around here in the dark.'

'Never mind that,' said the tense voice of Aelnoth.

'Just keep on following Oscar.'

'Tell him where to go.'

'He can see well in the dark.'

'Follow that track over there to the left.' he said almost inaudibly for he was totally overawed by the way that the strange chalky white man could find his way over fields, meadows, through brooks and across rivers in the blackness of the night.

After a while he tapped Ingrid on his shoulder again and said.

'There. That oak tree.'

'The big one with the broken branch.'

'That's where we hid the silver.'

Aelnoth shouted to Oscar, for he was pretty certain that no one was likely to be abroad in the middle of a forest at this hour.

'Eadbald says it's over there. By yonder oak.'

They guided their horses towards the tree where they all alighted, and tied their horse's reins to a part of the broken branch, and looked towards Sabert.

'Well, said Magnus. 'Where did you bury it?'

'There my Lord,' answered Sabert. 'Where that broken limb touches the ground.' As he pointed to the spot where part of the massive branch touched the ground.

The three young Lords knelt by the spot and began to dig, Magnus and Oscar with their knives and Aelnoth with his much sturdier Saex.

'No. Not there my Lords. Just a little to the left.'

'That's right. That's where we buried it.'

Magnus looked up in disgust and pointed his knife to the left. 'Here?' he queried.

'Aye, my Lord. Right there.'

The three men moved a foot to their left and started to scoop out the earth, finding nothing until they had reached a depth of two feet, when Aelnoth's Saex made the noise of metal striking metal.

'I've found something.' He said excitedly.

They renewed their efforts, enlarging the hole, and were rewarded by unearthing no less than twelve iron chests, which had been placed in a row.

It took two men to heave the heavy chests out of the hole and place them one by one onto the ground alongside the hole.

They scraped below and around the area of the last chest in order to satisfy themselves that they had retrieved the complete hoard before they turned their attention to the twelve chests.

'The bloody things are locked.' Said Oscar as he cleaned the clay from around the front of one of them.

'Of course they are locked.' Said Magnus almost scornfully.

'What do you expect'?

'Well I haven't seen many earthworms who would want to get into iron chests.' Have you?' answered the slightly annoyed Albino, who considered that the remark that Magnus had just made, had been totally uncalled for.

Fortunately, after such a long time in the damp earth, the chests were beginning to rust, so it did not take Aelnoth long to prise one open with his sturdy Saex, revealing a gleaming Kings Ransom in silver coins.

'By Thor's sacred balls.' Exclaimed Magnus.

'Jesus Christ.' Said Aelnoth.

Ingrid gasped aloud as her hands flew up to her mouth as she stared at the silver hoard.

'What is? Will be.' Stated Oscar, almost nonchantly.

They opened the other chests, which revealed similar hoards of silver, causing Magnus to stammer. 'These things would take a few sturdy carts to carry.'

'Little wonder they took all the gold and left the silver here.' He added.

'I can't imagine how much it weighs.'

'Which leaves us with something of a problem? Does it not?' Said Aelnoth.

'It does indeed,' said Oscar. 'Just how are we going to transport this lot to Ireland?'

'Three carts. That's what we need.' Said Magnus.

'And three horses.' Added Aelnoth.

'We've got three horses,' retorted Magnus.

'We can't use three Norman warhorses to pull carts.' Said Oscar.

'Why not? Asked Aelnoth.

'We could, providing we only moved at night.'

'True. True.' Said Oscar reluctantly.

'Well, we have got enough silver to purchase three sturdy carts.' Said Oscar light-heartedly.

'Enough to buy three hundred and thirty three carts, and then some.' Said Aelnoth jokingly.

'Where is the nearest town?' asked Oscar.

'That'll be Fareham.' Answered Magnus. 'I've spent many a happy day at Fareham when I was a boy.' He added.

'Is there a carter there? Asked Magnus.

'No I don't think there is, but there is one at Wickham and a bloody good one too.'

'My Father used to deal with him.'

'How far is that?'

'Not far. Maybe six or eight miles.'

Before he was asked, Magnus said. 'I'll go to Wickham and bring back three carts.'

'One of those silver pennies should do the trick.'

'You will need another one to buy three mules or horses to pull the damn things.'

'Ah' True. True, but what shall we do with the mules when we get here? Asked Magnus.

'Let us cross that bridge when we come to it,' said Aelnoth.

'You can't drive three carts by yourself.' Tutted Oscar. 'Magnus and I can take Eadbald, and you can stay here and guard the silver.'

'I will stay with Aelnoth,' offered Ingrid as she dramatically drew her Poniard from its calfskin sheath and flourished it in front of her scrawny figure.

Aelnoth and Magnus glanced towards one another and smiled.

Oscar glanced towards Magnus, and it was a look that Aelnoth noticed, and he said with a tone or irony in his voice. 'Oh. Don't worry, we won't run off with the treasure.'

'We are as keen as you are to rid our land of these Normans, and if I did run off with it, I am sure that you would chase me to the ends of the earth to get it back.'

'Too bloody right,' said Oscar as a grim smile crossed his chalky white face.

Magnus returned late in the afternoon, driving one cart with his own steed tethered behind the cart, whilst the other two carts were driven by and Eadbald and Oscar.

'My word that was quick,' said Aelnoth as he stepped forward to greet them, but added in a quieter tone. 'Did you have any trouble?'

'None at all.'

'But it looks like you spent some of the silver on those six coffins.' as he pointed to the six wooden coffins that were on the three carts.

'Indeed I did.'

'Well, there are only four of us, and I suppose you expect our murderers to cut each of us into little bits and bury us in six coffins.' He said in jest, as a wide grin spread across his face; although he had guessed that the coffins had been purchased to carry the silver.

'Two chests in each coffin.' answered Magnus haughtily.

'Good idea.' Said his friend as he slapped Magnus on the shoulder in a friendly way.

'What about the mules? Asked Aelnoth.

'I am afraid that they were only on loan and must be returned to their owner before nightfall,' was the answer.

'That's not a problem,' said Aelnoth. 'These Norman horses can pull those puny wagons just as well as any old mules.'

Oscar turned towards Eadbald and took two silver coins from one of the chests, which he handed to him. 'Can you make your own way home now?' he asked.

'I can indeed my Lord.' Answered the startled man, for he had never seen, let alone owned a silver coin in his life, and stood dumbfounded as he stared down at the shining coins which seemed to be burning a hole in his hand.

'Safe journey.' They called in unison as the man sat astride the leading mule and pulled the two spare mules behind him as he urged them out of the clearing.

Two iron chests were placed inside each of the coffins, which were in turn loaded onto the carts, and covered with branches before they commenced their journey westwards.

They purchased a small haystack from the first farm they came to, in order to cover the coffins with the hay, so that it looked like the carts contained nothing but hay.

They placed their Norman weapons, clothing and shields close to the sides of the carts, in case they were needed in haste, covering them with a thin layer of hay before they commenced their journey, trying to look like normal English peasants who were on their way to market in order to sell their loads of hay.

They slowly made their way along the roadway until they reached a convenient wood, where they stopped for the day.

*   *   *

Aelnoth and his friends were not the only travellers who neared the river Isis that moonlit night, for John the Slayer and his servant were heading south, having gleaned snippets of information about his prey that other men would have missed.

His journey had taken him from Broseley to Bridgenorth, where the trail had become cold, and only after ranging far and wide, did he sniff out news that the men who they were hunting had passed through the town of Brownhills, leaving behind them a furious Norman Lord bent on vengeance.

He had learned all he could about the Albino runaway who had joined the duo, and discovered that he had been the only son of the previous lord of that Manor.

The Norman Lord, Herbert of Lisieux had told him all he knew about 'Alfred the Albino.' Explaining to him in vivid detail of how the young Alfred had slain three of his men in the space of a few short seconds in a dispute over a village maiden. 'A maiden,' (he said, with a smirk, which fled across his swarthy face like a swallow across a darkened lake.) 'A maiden,' he repeated. 'Who I gave to my men, and after the men had finished with her. I had them strip her naked, and forced her to watch as they had whipped Alfred, and hung him high on a cross, to suffer and await his execution.

'Alas.' He snarled. 'Two wolfheads who happened to be passing released the pig.'

'Do you know what they looked like?' asked John, trying, without much success to hide his keenness to know if these two wolfheads could be the same men who he was hunting.

'Afraid not old chap.' Said the man, 'but I asked one of my serfs who claimed to have seen them, to describe them to me. To no avail.' He added. 'Most of these ignorant English serfs wouldn't know the difference between a pigeon and a woodcock.'

'Would you mind terribly if I questioned the man?' asked John in a polite way.

'Good lord no my dear fellow.' Was the reply as Herbert raised his glass.

'I will have him brought to you as soon as we have broken our morning fast.'

After a pleasant night, sleeping on a duck down mattress, John enjoyed a breakfast of bacon, sausage and eggs with freshly baked bread, which he washed down with two tankards of passable wine.

As he was about to thank his host, and had began to rise to his feet, but was prevented from speaking, as Herbert said. 'Wait a moment my friend.'

'I have that English serf in the next room.'

'Perhaps you would like to speak to him now?'

John nodded cordially and followed his host through a large oak door into the next room, which, to his surprise, had none of the plush furnishings that had been rife in the dining room, but consisted of a small room, which contained one small table and two chairs.

He noted with satisfaction that one of those chairs was firmly nailed to the floor, and on the chair sat an old peasant of perhaps fifty years of age, who had his hands firmly tied to the arm rests, whilst his legs were tied to the sturdy legs of the chair.

The peasant was obviously terrified, and as he stared in horror at John, he tried unsuccessfully to retreat, but the only thing that he was able to move was his neck, which he stretched backwards as far as it would go, before the man realised that all he was doing was presenting his 'would be torturers' with a very tempting target.

'He's all yours.' said Herbert pleasantly as he turned and exited through the doorway, closing the door quietly behind him.

Silence prevailed, as John stood and gazed at the man.

The silence was broken by a loud sob, which seemed to emit from deep in the man's chest.

'What.' What are you going to do? Groaned the man in a terrified voice.

John did not answer, but walked slowly towards the table and stared down at an array of knives, saws and other instruments that lay on the table, studying each one carefully in turn.

'Tell me of the two men who took Alfred.' He said quietly.

'I've already told the lord all I know.' Sobbed the man.

'Perhaps there is something that you have forgotten?' he asked as he cleaned his thumbnail with a slender Poniard that had been honed down throughout the years by constant sharpening, and was now little more than a thick needle.

'No. My Lord. Nothing! I have told him everything.'

John leaned forward and pointed the Poniard under the man's chin.

The man cowered away. Sweating profusely and causing the perspiration to cascade down his forehead and merge with the saliva that dribbled out of the sides of his mouth.

John moved the dagger slowly across the mans throat, leaving a line of blood, as the knife reached his ear, which John slashed with vigour, causing the man to scream loudly, reducing him to a quivering wreck.

'No. My Lord. No, screamed the man.

'I have told you the truth. I know nothing.'

'Tell me again.' Snarled John, 'or I shall start to really hurt you.'

'First I will cut off your ears, and then your nose.'

'And then your fingers one by one.'

'And then your ball's '

'But I am a kind man, so I shall start with your fingers, and with a sudden leaped towards his prisoner. He landed nimbly to one side of the fettered man.

He lunged down with the razor sharp Poniard and with a satisfying grunt, slashed off the mans little finger so quickly that it was several moments before the man realised what had happened, and screamed loudly as the blood spurted out from the stump of his finger.

'There.' Said John with a sly smirk crossing his face. 'That wasn't so bad, was it?' and then he returned to his chair and sat down, proudly admiring the man's little finger, which he held up in front of him.

'Now tell me again.'

'What did these two men look like?'

'I've already told his lordship.' Sobbed the man.

'Describe them to me.' Snarled John. 'Were they young? Old? Fat? Thin? What colour hair did they have? What were they wearing? What colour were their horses?'

'Were they stallions? Mares? Geldings?

'Tell me or do I need to take another finger?' he said as he wrenched the man's other hand towards the arm of the chair.

'They were both young men your lordship.' Sobbed the man. One was perhaps twenty five or thirty years of age whilst the other was naught but a boy.'

'How old was the boy? Ten? Fifteen? Eighteen?' he snarled.

'Sixteen or seventeen I think.' Stuttered the captive.

'I think they were riding Norman horses. Stallions I think, although one of them could have been a grey gelding, but I'm not sure.' He added.

'How close were you to them?'

'Oh, I was a good fifty feet from them and they flashed past me in an instant my lord.'

'Honest. I didn't really get a good look at them.' He sobbed.

John studied the man for a full minute without saying a word, and when he rose, it was with such speed that it caused the man to jerk backwards, fearing that he was about to lose another finger or even an ear or an eye.

John walked to the rear of the quivering man and stooped.

The man whimpered loudly fully expecting to feel the Poniard plunged into his back, but to his surprise he felt the bonds cut, allowing his arms to flop loosely down.

John cut his legs free.

'There. You see. I was telling the truth when I told you that I am a kindly man, especially so, when there is no profit in it for me to slay a man.'

'You are free to go. And thank you for your help,' he added, as if he had merely asked the man for directions, and was about to leave such a helpful individual and continue on his travels.

During the morning he questioned all of the servants, as well as the field hands, in order to learn all he could about the fugitives.

He was delighted when one of the serfs revealed that the elder of the two was none other than a family member of the Godwinson's, who John knew were related to the late King Harold, who had held wide lands and many manors in the Shires of Wessex and Kent.

With a wave and a shout of thanks, John and his servant left their host.

John was in a much happier mood, for he was sure that he was again on the right trail, and that his intended victims were somewhere ahead of him, heading he thought into the lands of the West Saxons, or even to the lands of the Kentishmen.

John and his servant questioned people at every farmstead, village and town that they passed through. They frequented the markets and taverns, in order to glean news of the three men who they were hunting.

It felt as if God was helping him, when John asked an innkeeper in Wickham if he had heard of three strangers riding Norman horses. Two stallions and a grey gelding?

'Indeed I do,' was the answer to the surprised hunter. 'But there was a youngster with them, who may have been a boy or a girl, and they were here less than three days ago. Stayed in my best room.'

'Well it is my only room.'

'Paid me in silver.' He added with a wry smile.

'Where were they going?' queried John, trying not to show his excitement.

'Wouldn't really remember where they were heading.' Said the Innkeeper as he purposely looked down at his own open palm, which he had placed on the table.

'Ah,' said John, who had been dealing with men like this Innkeeper for many a long year.

He ferreted around in the leather purse, which hung around the front of his belt, and eventually pulled out two coins. One of copper and one of Silver, which he held in his open palm as he looked into the man's eyes with a gaze that was as sharp as steel.

He chose the small silver one and held it towards the man.

'Can you remember now?' he said grimly.

'Well I just might.' Answered the Innkeeper, as he attempted to snatch the coin from John's outstretched hand, only to find that the coin had suddenly vanished, and John had not only grabbed his hand with a grip of iron, but in Johns other hand was a thin dagger, the like of which he had never seen before, and that dagger pricked his neck just a hairsbreadth away from his jugular vein.

'I. I did hear talk yer Lordship.' Stammered the man.

'What talk?' snapped John.

'I overheard them talking my lord. Of how they were going to get to Ireland.'

'Ireland?' snarled John. Furious that his preys had doubled back, and were now on their way to the Island of Ireland, which was, in his opinion, just about as far as a man could go before he fell off the edge of the world.

'Why Ireland?' he snarled, as his own mind battled just how a man from Kent would get from Kent to Ireland.

'Don,' don't know my Lord.' Choked the man, who could feel a trickle of blood running down his neck.

'Honest, I don't know, but I did hear the word Wales whispered a couple of times.'

'Wales.' Bloody Wales, Bloody Ireland.' Swore the assassin. 'Why in the name of Hell don't they head for bloody Jerusalem and be done with it,' as he released the Innkeeper, and handed him the copper coin, whilst he returned his poniard to its hiding place, and replaced the silver coin to its rightful place in his purse.

The Innkeeper flopped back into a chair with relief, and when he eventually managed to stand up, he staggered through a door into the back room, where he took a long swig from a special bottle of very strong wine, that in normal circumstances he kept under the counter for himself, and perhaps one or two very special customers.

He heard a loud voice roar 'Pierre' and a door slam, as the servant of the man who had nearly killed him entered the room.

'Ha, there you are Pierre.' Shouted John who was totally indifferent that his voice carried across the hushed room. 'Saddle the horses. Quickly now! We have little enough daylight left, and we must be on our way.'

'Which way do we ride' asked the startled servant.

'Back the same bloody way we came. And now there are bloody four of them. They have a child of some sort with them.' Snarled the still angry Assassin.

'That should make them easier to find.' Whispered the astute Pierre.

CHAPTER 5

Despite being pulled by three strong warhorses, the slow pace of the carts annoyed all three of the young men, who tried their best not to swear in the presence of Ingrid, as they tried in vain to urge their horses into a faster pace.

'I think we should exchange our horses for three less conspicuous ones,' said Aelnoth in a reluctant voice.

'God's blood why?' asked Magnus.

'Well, I am rather reluctant to say it, but I think it was a mistake to send those mules back with old Sabert. It would have made more sense if we had kept them and sent these bloody war-horses back with him.'

'As Aelnoth said.' Intervened Oscar.

'They stick out like a sore thumb, and normal farm nags or oxen would fit in with the fact that we are lugging carts full of hay.'

Adding after a short pause. 'Farm horses would be better suited to pulling carts, and we may even be able to travel faster.'

'Why don't we just swap them for three ordinary farm horses, and we can come back for our own horses in perhaps six months or so.' suggested Aelnoth, who was very reluctant to part with his father's old steed, Chieftain.

'All right.' Said Magnus. 'If we can find three suitable nags, we'll do a swap.'

His companions nodded and grunted approval as they urged their horses forward.

After two further nights of travel, Oscar led them into small wood overlooking a small village north of Warwick, where they could hide during the daylight hours.

After they had eaten, Aelnoth strolled towards the edge of the wood to survey the countryside below.

He noted that the village contained a newly built Mott and Bailey, which stood on a small rise that was surrounded by cottages and fields, and to his surprise and delight, one of the fields contained no less than five farm horses, which were lingering around the gateway, where they would probably receive their morning bucket of oatmeal, before the farm workers would lead them off for the days work.

Magnus was usually wide-awake by mid day, and whilst he had been taking his turn to guard the camp and watch for intruders, he had got into the habit of sitting on one of the carts, where he had began to carve the names of his family members on the coffins.

The carvings were the names of his family members who had been slain in the battles of either 'Stamford Bridge' or 'Hastings.'

In the eyes of his friends, these carvings, which contained a horse's head, as well as the crest of arms of his family, were little short of masterpieces.

'Too good to bury and to be left in the ground to rot.' Remarked Oscar as he admired the final coffin, which Magnus was working on.

Aelnoth strolled back to the camp at dawn, just as his two companions were about to snatch a few hours sleep.

'Come and have a look at this.' He said.

'I think I have spotted the horses that we have been looking for.'

His three friends rose and followed him to the edge of the wood.

'There.' He said as he pointed to the horses below who were now nuzzling into their wooden feed buckets, which were being held by the farm workmen, who would soon be leading them away to begin their day's work.

'Indeed you have found the horses.' Said Magnus. 'But how are going to persuade yon fellows to exchange their work horses for three Norman war-horses?'

'That is a good question.' Remarked Oscar sarcastically.

'I don't suppose that those nags belong to those men.' said Aelnoth.

'They probably belong to the Lord who lives in yonder keep.'

'He is the man we should talk to then' said Aelnoth.

'Let's get some shut eye.' Said Oscar.

'We have been up all night and I am dead tired.

'We can pay his lordship down there a visit this evening, when he has eaten his evening meal and is likely to be friendlier towards us.' He added.

'I'll give the bugger friendly.' Snarled Oscar, as he tapped the hilt of his sword a couple of times.

'I don't think that is such a good idea,' said Aelnoth. 'We must not let these Normans know that we are in the area, because once they do, they will have no trouble tracking three carts laden with silver, and it is vital that this silver reaches Ireland, or else our cause is lost.'

*   *   *

It was a bemused Sir Godfrey de la Sable who was called away from his morning meal by one of his underlings. 'Sire. Sire,' said the Norman overseer as he stepped as quietly as he could into the room.

'The peasants are revolting.' He gasped.

'They are standing around and are refusing to do their work.'

'Oh. We shall see about that.' Snapped Sir Godfrey as he gulped down the mouthful of sausage and snatching up his sword belt, he followed his man through the doorway and into the courtyard, strapping on his sword belt as he strode manfully towards his horse, which had been saddled and was waiting for him.

He mounted and galloped through the gateway, followed by four of his men, screeching to a halt in a shower of mud and stones, which peppered the small group of his serfs who were standing idly at the entrance of the paddock, where his farm horses were normally kept.

'What's all this?' he demanded in a loud voice.

'Why aren't you working in the fields?' he hissed.

The young man, who had been promoted to be the spokesman, stepped out of the crowd.

'My Lord. We cannot work with them.' He said hesitantly.

'With who you idiot?' snapped Godfrey.

'With them, My Lord.' Said the man, who then pointed to the horses that were grazing peacefully in the paddock.

'And why in the name of heaven not?' he shouted angrily, but then he looked at the horses again, and for the first time he noticed that four of the horses were not the normal run of the mill farm horses, which he had seen on countless occasions, but had miraculously been turned into sturdy Norman war horses.

'What' What the Devil. How?' he gasped but then he turned to his sergeant who was also staring at the warhorses, who were happily munching their way through the swards of rich green grass.

'Who in the world would exchange my useless farm nags for valuable steeds like these?' he said to himself.

His sergeant, who was standing beside him, assumed that his lord was asking him the question, and answered in a low and servile manner, as was his duty when addressing his lordship? 'No idea my Lord, for surely your lordship could buy a dozen farm horses for the price of just one of those warhorses.'

'True. True,' answered Godfrey, for although he had been given this manor by King William for the courage that he had shown at the Battle of Hastings, he was not the brightest of men, and in truth, he possessed perhaps half of the wit of some of his own men, especially his sergeant, William de-La-feate who was standing alongside him.

William's comment cheered Godfrey, for his true love was not the beautiful English woman he had married over a year ago, neither was it his sturdy fair haired son, which she had produced a mere three months since.

His first love was the glint of silver and gold, and the amounts of these commodities were growing ever greater in the chest, which he kept in his locked bedroom.

His love for gold and silver was followed closely by his love of fine horseflesh.

His eyes glinted with greed as he studied his three new horses.

'One of them is a gelding.' He said.

'And one of the others looks to be past his prime, so I think you could let some of our neighbours know that I have a fine Norman steed for sale, and you can get rid of the old Stallion, and purchase three or four new nags to pull the plough.'

'Mind you. No funny business and I shall want to see the letters of sale and purchase, so that I can keep my books in order.'

'And fill your chest with more silver.' Thought William, as the wryest of smiles crossed his weathered face.

*   *   *

The fresh horses hauled the three carts at twice the speed of the Norman war-horses, having spent their entire adult lives pulling loads, which had been three and four times the weight of these small carts, which contained nought but a few chests, that lay under the small loads of hay.

Aelnoth and his companions were delighted when they realised that the distance that they covered with the new horses during the past three nights, had brought their quest to reach Wales, and of course, the Welsh coast much closer.

Aelnoth's two companions were becoming concerned at the annoying habit which Aelnoth appeared to be developing, by halting his cart, which was the last cart of the three, and peering behind him for long periods of time.

As the sun began to make its watery appearance through the low cloud on one particular morning, Magnus finally voiced his concerns.

'Aelnoth.' He said in a pleasant voice. 'What ails you? Are we being followed?

'Have you seen someone?'

Aelnoth did not immediately answer the question; he gazed wistfully along the path that they had just covered. 'I don't really know.' He said.

'But I do have the feeling that we are being followed.'

'I haven't actually seen anyone,' he added, 'but I seem to have inherited an uncanny knack from my parents, to experience strange things like this.

'Both my Sire and my Mother had the gift of foreseeing things, and I have had prickles on the back of my neck a number of times during the past couple of days, and I really do have the strange feeling that we are being followed.'

'Well I haven't seen anyone,' said Oscar, 'and I can see better than you, especially in the darkness.'

'In that case.' Said Magnus. 'Whilst it is still not full daylight. I will leave the camp as if I am collecting sticks for the fire, and then I'll double back the way we came, and see if I can see anything suspicious.'

After they had made camp that morning, Magnus left the campsite, returning twice with sticks for the fire, but on the third occasion that he left the camp, he made his way deeper into the woodland, in a wide circle around the camp, creeping quietly through the woodland, close to the pathway which they had used when they had entered the wood.

He followed the pathway for more than half a mile, and was on the verge of returning to the camp when his sensitive nose caught a whiff of wood smoke.

He froze as he tried to locate the location of the fire, but there was so little breeze in the thick woodland, that he failed to catch another scent of the smoke.

He crouched down and slowly inserted his index finger into his mouth and after withdrawing his wet finger from his mouth; he held it cautiously above his head.

The almost miniscule breeze caught his wet finger, telling him that the wind was reaching him from a westerly direction, so he slowly made his way westwards through the woodland, making sure that he kept himself under cover whenever he could, carefully avoiding stepping on any bracken or dry branches.

His caution was finally rewarded when he spotted a small glade, where an individual was in the process of crouching over a tiny, hidden fire.

Two horses were tethered nearby.

He automatically noted that one was a sleek war-horse, whilst the other was an animal of a much lower pedigree.

Magnus circled the fire, and approached silently from the rear of the man, who at the very last moment must have heard the slight rustle of the leather jerkin, which Magnus wore, and sprung to his feet, holding a foot long dagger in his left hand.

'Damn,' cursed Magnus silently, as he realised that the man was a left-hander, and as such, he would be a more difficult opponent to overcome than a normal right-handed man.

He drew his Saex and faced the man.

The grubby old man was slight of build with a mottled grey beard, and wore rags that a beggar would have refused to wear, giving Magnus an immediate feeling of superiority.

It was a feeling that was dashed to smithereens as the first movement which the man made was to step back, which was obviously a move that invited Magnus forward, only to be countered by a stab from the mans left arm, which was swifter than a striking snake, leaving a neat, bloody hole in the shoulder of the surprised Englishman, who stepped back in alarm, as a shriek of pain shot through his shoulder and up into his brain.

Although Magnus had been wounded before during the battle of Stamford Bridge, he knew that if he allowed the pain of this wound to hinder him, it would be the end of him, so he forced his mind to ignore the throbbing pain, and flexed his fingers in order to revive the full use of his arm.

Pierre smiled slyly to himself, thinking how easy it had been to wound this stupid clod of an English peasant

'I shall play with the fool before I end his miserable life,' he thought to himself, for, like his master, one of the greatest pleasures in his life was inflicting as much pain as possible for the longest period of time upon his many victims.

He nimbly switched his poniard from his left hand to his right, and slashed at the peasants face, missing the man's neck by a hairsbreadth, as the startled man stepped backwards, almost falling over the small pile of sticks, which had been collected for the fire.

'Christ alive,' swore Magnus aloud, as he felt the wind from the man's knife pass his face.

His brain cried out to him, telling him that this grubby looking peasant had been well schooled in the gory business of the cut and thrust of battle, as well as being an expert in the art of single combat.'

The grinning man circled him with his knife held towards the Englishman.

Magnus continued to face the man.

The ragged man sliced again and again, but was met by the Englishman's solid Saex.

The grinning man became more and more confident as he jeered at his opponent.

'I shall slice you into little bits, you English peeg.' He sneered in a strange accent.

'And then I will roast you bit by bit over the fire,' as he glanced at the fire which lay between them.

It was that small momentary glance that was the man's undoing, for as his eyes left his opponent for a split second, Magnus stepped forward, and as he did so, he sank his razor sharp Saex in the man's left shoulder and grabbed his right hand with his own left hand in a grip that numbed the mans hand, and, at almost the same instant, he brought his left knee up into the mans groin, causing the man to double up in agony.

Magnus vigorously shook the man's wrist several times before the man's numbed hand reluctantly dropped the poniard, causing him to look up into the icy blue eyes of the much younger and stronger Englishman.

He could see no mercy.

Magnus forced the groaning man's hands behind his back and wrenched at the leather belt that the man wore around his waist.

He ripped the belt from around the man, and used it to tie the man's hands securely behind his back, before he stepped back and looked at his prisoner.

His own shoulder throbbed with pain, causing him to search through the scattered belongings that lay on the ground, where he eventually found a cleanish piece of rag, which he stuffed inside his jerkin, in an attempt to stem the flow of his blood that oozed out of the wound.

'Why are you following us?' he demanded.

The man stared at him with bored eyes, and then he looked away with distain.

'There are two horses, and this camp looks big enough for two.' He said out aloud.

'Where is your companion?' he snarled.

Pierre was not merely the servant of John the slayer, but in his youth he had been a warrior of some repute, and had slain more men than he could count.

Although he was adept with a sword and axe, his real skill had always been with knives, and he never left his bed with less than three knives secreted about his body.

This stupid English peasant had not even bothered to search him, and if he had searched him, he might, just might, have found the small knife that he carried hidden in a special sheath that had been sewn into the inside of his breeches, but Pierre was confident that the stupid man would not have discovered the small and very sharp poniard, which he carried strapped around the inside of his ankle of his left leg.

With a loud groan he flopped to the floor. Not from exhaustion, or from the shoulder wound, which throbbed so much that he feared that if it were not treated soon, he would be in danger of losing the use of his arm, or even his life, for he could feel his life's blood dripping down his chest.

The real reason that he had dropped to the floor was to be able to manoeuvre his hands into a position that would enable him to reach the knife that was strapped to his left leg, cut the bonds and slay this arrogant English pig before his master returned.

As he watched his captor search through the baggage, he eased the leather breeches up his left leg and smiled as his hands touched the knife, which he eased out of its scabbard and held the razor sharp knife in one hand, whilst he cut his leather bonds.

Within the space of a heartbeat, he had jumped to his feet and leapt at his captor whose back presented a very tempting target.

Magnus felt, rather than saw the movement, and spun around as the man launched himself onto the startled Englishman, who luckily still held his Saex in his right hand.

Years of training, and with the experience of battle behind him, Magnus brought the Saex up a split second before the man's knife reached him, and felt it enter the man's chest and plunge into his heart.

The man stopped as if he had run into an oak tree, and his mouth opened in shock, as if he was trying to say something, but the only sound that emitted from his open mouth was a low groan, as he sank to the ground, where his eyes stared up towards his slayer before they glazed over, as his soul left him.

There appeared to be little of value amongst the man's belongings except the two poniards, which he thrust into his belt, before he grabbed the reins of the two horses and led them through the woodland towards his companions.

CHAPTER 6

John the slayer had been crouching in the undergrowth watching the two men and the girl, who lay on their saddle blankets around the fire, but he was reluctant to shoot with his crossbow, as he knew that although he could definitely hit one of them.

The other two would be more difficult targets, and the missing Englishman could well be upon him before he could reload another bolt to his bow, so he lowered his bow.

'No,' he mused silently to himself. 'Three men and a girl are too many to tackle in such a haphazard way, especially a time like this, when there are too many unknowns.'

I have seen men kill their attackers despite having two or even three bolts inside them.' He mused.

'Now is not the time. There are too many risks, and I am a professional, and act only when the risks are either non-existent, or at least negligible.'

'I have not lived this long by taking stupid risks.' He mused.

This was turning out to be one of the strangest assignments that he had ever been on, he thought to himself. 'Here I am, in the depths of a forest in a foreign country.'

'I am following three warriors who are the sons of Lords. All three are young landless men who have exchanged their valuable war-horses for farm horses?'

'They only travel at night and hide up during the daylight hours.'

'Why?' he asked himself.

'And why travel the length and breadth of the country with carts full of hay.

'Ah! I am an idiot.' He exclaimed out loud.' And then he realised that he had spoken aloud in the silence of the forest, and cursed himself for a fool.

But then his mind flew back to the three young warriors and their three carts.

'Of course.' He felt angry with himself and with his servant Pierre.

'Why didn't I think of it before?' he asked himself.

'There is obviously something valuable hidden under the hay in those bloody carts.'

'Silver or even gold,' he mused, and his eyes shone with greed at the thought of the gold, which he had just convinced himself lay under the hay in those old farm carts.

He crept through the forest at a slightly faster pace in his haste to reach Pierre in order to plan his next move.

'I will need Pierre with me, in order to watch my back at a time of my own choosing, and then I shall see if there is gold under those loads of hay.'

As he approached his camp, his senses told him something was amiss.

He halted and dropped into a crouching position whilst his eyes darted hither and thither, as he searched the quiet woodland for the slightest sign of danger.

Nothing stirred. No sounds of alarm sounded.

He rose and commenced to circle around the site of his camp, creeping ever nearer until he reached the very edge of the glade, where he had left Pierre and their two horses.

'Damn and blast' he exclaimed aloud as he recognised the body of his servant, which lay amongst his belongings that were strewn around the clearing.

'The bloody horses have gone.' He swore. More concerned that he had lost his horses than he was about Pierre, who had been not only his servant, but also his constant and only companion for more than ten years?

He gazed at the body, and his clinical mind noted that nothing appeared to have been stolen other than the two horses, and two of the three poniards that Pierre habitually carried with him.

He searched through his servants body for the silver that he suspected his servant always had about his person, but found nothing, but he did untie the thin

Poniard, which Pierre always carried strapped to a leather thong that hung around his neck, and looped it over his own head.

'That is too valuable to leave here to rust.' He mumbled to himself.

He walked quietly around the glade, searching for clues, but picking up nothing with the exception of one of his blankets and a fur-lined cape, muttering to himself. 'I'd better take this or I shall freeze to death in this damp hell hole of a country.'

He silently followed the tracks that the stolen horses had left in the damp earth.

'It is the third man.' He muttered to himself.

'He will be the thief who killed Pierre and took my horses.'

'He must be pretty good, for Pierre was the devil incarnate with those knives of his.'

'I know exactly where they will be.' He said quietly to himself, as he made his way quietly through the woodland.

The camp was deserted, and all that remained were the embers of a small fire that emitted a thin, almost invisible wisp of smoke.

He cursed aloud, and threw the Poniard into the trunk of a nearby oak in his frustration, leaving the poniard quivering in the tree, whilst he raged and fumed

'Bloody horses stolen. Bloody servant killed. No food and no bloody Wine. And now these three swine have high tailed it to God knows where.'

'Damn and Blast. Horse shit and Cow dung.' He shouted at the top of his voice.

He tossed his cape onto the ground and sat with his head in his hands for a while, willing himself to calm down.

'Think. Think.' He repeated.

'All is not lost.' He said to himself. 'I still have my crossbow, and my sword, plus half a dozen knives, AND my garrotte. I will soon get food and a horse.'

'I'll find them.'

'I will find you.' He yelled at the top of his voice.

'I will find you.' He yelled again and held his face up towards the heavens as his words echoed through the silent forest.

*   *   *

The arrival of the wounded Magnus leading two horses drove his two companions into a flurry of activity, as well as a barrage of questions, and it was only after his wound had been cared for, and the questions answered, that they made the decision to make a speedy exit from their hidden camp.

They broke their golden rule of not to travel during the daylight.

It was a move that turned out to be ill advised.

They did not run away from trouble, but in fact ran directly into it, for they had travelled no more than three miles along the rutted roadway, when they urged their carts around a sharp corner, only to find themselves face to face with a patrol of no less than five Normans, who were lolling at the side of the road, huddled around a fire, on which they were in the process of roasting a large chunk of beef.

'Ah. What have we here?' Shouted one of the men, who Oscar immediately recognised by his attire to be a Norman sergeant, and as such, he would be the man who was in charge of this small band of his enemies.

'A fine gaggle of farm boys on their way to market, I'll wager,' said the sergeant in a loud voice.

'And a girl.' He added in a jeering voice.

He walked up to the now stationary carts and held the bridle of the leading horse.

'Where are you heading lads? He asked in a jovial way.

'To market my lord.' Answered Oscar in a country accent and with a forced smile.

'To sell our masters hay and these two spare horses.'

'Oh.' Said the sergeant, who was about to lose interest in three farm boys and a girl who were off to market, when his eyes fell on the Norman boots, which Oscar had failed to conceal.

'And where did you get those nice boots?' asked the sergeant in sinister voice.

'Steal them off some dead Norman I'll wager.' He added with a snarl, as his hand flew to his sword.

'No, My Lord,' stammered Oscar with feigned terror. 'They belonged to my master who discarded them and gave them to me.'

'A likely story.' Snapped the Norman as he drew his sword from its scabbard.

'Up. Up you lazy lot.' He shouted to his four friends. 'And bring your bloody weapons with you. We shall see what these peasants have in these carts of theirs.'

All three of the Englishmen realised that their silver was about to be discovered and if these Normans found the silver, then they would have a fight on their hands.

It was Oscar who was the first to react, as his right arm shot to his rear and grasped his own sword, which he had hidden under the hay directly behind his seat.

His hand rose from the hay clutching the sword, which immediately descended as fast as a falcon, slicing through the leather cap that covered the sergeant's head before it halted near the man's chin, sending the already dead Norman to the ground.

With a heave, he withdrew the sword and jumped off the cart and stood facing the four Normans who were now advancing towards him.

Despite his wound, Magnus grabbed his own sword and shield, and joined Oscar and Aelnoth as they faced the four Normans, who were slightly shocked at the simple and sudden death of their leader.

However, the Normans were experienced warriors, and had seen battle and death in many forms, so they gripped their weapons and strode forward.

The slight hesitation caused by their sergeant's death proved to be their undoing, as the three Englishmen, as if ordered by some hidden sign, launched themselves simultaneously at their foes.

Magnus was the most experienced warrior of the three, and feinted with his sword, and as the Norman raised his spear and shield in order to ward off the expected blow,

Magnus dropped to his knees and sliced across the ankles of his enemy, cutting completely through the mans one leg and crippling the other, sending the man to the ground with an ear splitting scream.

Magnus cut his scream off with a slice across the Norman's neck, and strode around the mans still quivering body towards his next opponent.

Aelnoth and Oscar were battling with the three remaining Norman's as Magnus entered the fray, thus easing the pressure off his two friends as he slashed and parried at his new opponent.

Without warning one of the men suddenly stepped backwards, turned and ran for his horses.

He leapt up onto the back of his own horse and disappeared in a flurry of clods of earth and pebbles.

The two remaining Normans glanced at one another in alarm, as they realised that these three English peasants had already slain two of their number, and their friend Alaine had just turned tail and deserted them, leaving the two of them to defend themselves against three men, who they now realised were not mere farm boys, but seasoned warriors who seemed to know their way around a battlefield.

They both stepped back and looked at one another, uncertain to fight, run, or surrender.

The decision was made for them by Aelnoth, who immediately took advantage of their hesitation and slashed down with his sword, cutting half of his opponents sword hand off, causing both the sword and half of the mans hand to drop to the ground in a small cascade of blood.

The man screamed and clutched his right hand with his left hand, and dropped to his knees, sobbing in agony and frustration.

'I yield. I yield.' He cried.

His companion immediately allowed his own weapons to fall to the ground and dropped to his knees.

'Mercy. Mercy. In the name of the one true God I beg for mercy.' He said in a hoarse voice.

'Do you mean Thor or Woden,' asked Magnus with a sly grin, for he was a believer in the old Gods

He turned to Aelnoth. 'That was well done my young friend.' He said

'Indeed it was,' said Oscar. 'Made these two pigs make up their minds in double quick time.'

'Right. Let's kill them and be on our way.' snarled Magnus.

'No.' said Aelnoth. 'I think there has been enough killing.'

And then he added. 'It is almost as if you enjoy killing.' He accused.

'I do not.' Answered Magnus adamantly. 'It is merely the fact that these men are my enemies, and I am just a warrior doing my task in the best and most efficiently way possible.'

Before Aelnoth could reply, Magnus continued. 'I think it is simply stupid to allow these men to go free, only to meet them again on some future battlefield.'

'Just you remember who they are.' Snarled Magnus. 'These are the swine who have killed and exiled our Kinfolk, and have stolen our lands.' He said hotly, as he snarled and waved his sword over the heads of the two kneeling men.

'No more killing I say.' Said Aelnoth menacingly.

'Strip them and gather up all their clothes, and all of these weapons, and stuff them under the hay in the carts, and then we can be on our way.'

'Not before I sink my teeth into that chunk of beef that's roasting over yon fire.' Said Oscar as he walked purposefully over towards the fire.

'Good idea.' Echoed Aelnoth as he left Magnus who was still hovering menacingly over the two Norman captives.

'Take your clothes off.' Snarled Magnus as he slapped one of the men across the side of his face with the flat of his sword, causing the men to rise to their feet.

'Strip. Get 'em off.' Growled Magnus who was even more annoyed now that he could see his two companions standing around the fire, chewing on portions of the meat, which they had cut off the roasting joint.

The two captives stripped down to their underpants.

'Them too.' Snarled Magnus. 'And the boots. Come on now. Get the bloody things off.'

'Here.' Shouted Aelnoth. 'Have a slice of this beef,' as he walked towards Magnus with a large slice of beef held out on his outstretched knife.

Magnus grunted his thanks as he sank his teeth into the beef.

He kicked the Norman who was the only one without a wound, sending the man into a heap of nakedness alongside his wounded companion.

To the young men's surprise, Ingrid suddenly appeared by the wounded man, whose arm was still dripping with blood, and despite the fact that he was naked, she stood before him and held his arm, wrapping a large piece of cloth around the wound in an attempt to stop the man from bleeding to death.

'Hold it tight.' She said haughtily to the man.

'Until you can get it attended to properly.'

'Unless he bleeds to death first.' Growled Magnus, whose hatred for the Normans was becoming more savage with each passing day.

The three young English warriors hid the captured clothes and weapons under the hay, and pocketed the few coins that they had found in the Norman's clothing.

They commenced their journey, but before they left, Aelnoth unhitched the two spare horses, which they had previously tied to the carts, and untied the four Norman horses.

He then turned their heads in the direction of the way that they had travelled and urged them on their way with a shout and a slap on the rump of the horse that was nearest to him.

'Why in the name of the Gods did you do that?' Snapped Oscar who was annoyed to see such valuable horseflesh disappearing in the distance.

'It is just too risky to keep them for they would invite every Norman to eat at our table.' Answered Aelnoth.

He slashed at the rump of his carthorse with a stick to urge him on his way, leaving the two naked, shivering Normans standing over the bodies of their sergeant and their friend Barnard, who had both been their constant companions since they had left their home town of Parthenay over three years ago.

* * *

A mere two miles down the road, the small herd of horses that he found grazing along the lush green grass of the overgrown road were a godsend to the weary John, who had been up for most of the night, and had been trudging along this damp overgrown road for most of the morning, for he was a man who was not used to walking and was thus becoming very footsore.

'There. There my Beauties.' He cooed, as he limped up to the grazing animals.

'Where did you come from? All alone with no one to care for you.' He said in a soothing voice, for the only real loves in his life were money, and the small herd of Palomino's, which he kept in a secluded valley near his home.

'Come my beauty.' He cooed, as he gently held the bridle of a large brown stallion.

'I shall look after you from now on. I know we shall be the best of friends,' as he breathed into the stallions nostrils and held his own face at the side of the stallions muzzle for a minute or two.

From an early age, he had always had a way with horses, and this stallion soon fell under John's spell, allowing this stranger to mount, and with a slight nudge from the man's knees, he trotted happily away from the rest of the herd.

John reined his new steed to a halt within the space of a few hundred yards, for as he rounded a bend in the overgrown roadway, nearly riding directly into two naked men, who were standing dejectedly in the middle of the road, surrounded by what must have been a small battle, for not only was one of the naked men nursing a bloody arm that appeared to have his hand, or perhaps half of his bloody hand missing.

John could see the bodies of two men strewn on the ground, close to the two stark naked men.

The two men retreated a couple of steps, looking up in horror at this stranger who rode the wounded mans own horse.

Were they to be attacked again by another madman, like the three who had decimated their own small war-band less than an hour ago?

John could see by their savage hairstyle that the men were Normans.

'What happened here?' he demanded in a commanding voice.

'We were attacked.' Spluttered the man who was not wounded.

'By whom?'

'Three ruffians who were posing as peasants.' Answered the man who was almost in tears with the humiliation of standing here naked, and in broad daylight before this ugly bald man, who sat astride his friend's stallion as if he owned the bloody thing.

'Describe them.' Demanded John.

'Well there were young.' Whispered the man.

'One was a beardless boy.'

'Speak up man. I can hardly hear you.' Shouted John who had not bothered to dismount from his stallion.

'Sorry my Lord,' said the man as he bowed his head.

'Like I said,' he continued in a louder voice. 'There were three of them.'

'All youngish and they were driving three carts full of hay.'

'And they had a young girl with them.' He added almost as an afterthought.

John did not wait to hear more. He dug his heels into the side of his horse and galloped away, but as he rode he shouted over his shoulder. 'Go back down the road a way, and you will be able to get your horses back.' And he disappeared around a bend in the road.

He shouted out aloud again. 'I will find you.' Blessing the very same Gods who he had been cursing a short time ago.

'Thank you.' He bellowed into the morning air.

'You, who allowed that English swine to slay my servant and steal my horses.' He muttered to himself.

'You have truly redeemed yourself to me.'

'You have provided me with a fresh mount and given me a trail that is so hot that it is burning my fingers.'

'I shall play no more with these pigs.' He swore to himself.

'I shall take them one by one or all at the same time. It matters not.' He said aloud in a jovial manner, as a savage grin passed fleetingly under his cold blue eyes.'

CHAPTER 7

They drove their horses with sticks cut from an ancient willow tree, urging the tired horses to haul the three carts as speedy as they were able, until some time around mid-morning; they halted in a small overgrown wood where they remained for the rest of the day.

Fortunately, Magnus's stab wound had ceased to bleed and already contained a soft scab that covered the neat hole, where the slim poniard had entered.

Ingrid dabbed the wound with some herbs she had found, and although the wound remained sore, after flexing his arm a little, Magnus was delighted to find that it seemed to be working as normal.

They decided to take it in turns to stand guard whilst the other two young men caught up on some sleep, thus allowing Magnus to rest until his two friends had finished the first and second watch.

It was an hour before dusk when Oscar shook Magnus gently. 'Time for your watch.' He said, and the still sleepy Magnus rose, groaning quietly at the spasms of pain that shot through his arm and up into his brain.

'All seems quiet enough,' said Oscar.

'Although I have been watching a couple of peasants working down there in that small wood over yonder.' He pointed to his left, where Magnus could see a small wood, and he caught an occasional glance of a movement deep in the woodland.

'I think they are collecting wood to build something.' Muttered Oscar, 'so there is nothing to worry about there.'

Magnus nodded and slowly walked over to the edge of the wood where he sat with his back to a tree and watched the panorama below him.

It was close to mid-day when Magnus had merely turned his head at the sound of a hen sparrow hawk, which had just alighted onto its nest and had begun to feed its nestlings, when a bolt suddenly thudded into the tree exactly where his head had been a second before.

Totally shocked by this unexpected attack, he scrambled quickly around the tree so that he would be protected from the hidden crossbowman.

'Where the devil did that come?' he muttered angrily as he peered cautiously out, and scanned the empty scene that looked exactly as it had for the last four hours.

He could see several places where a crossbowman could hide, and he knew full well that a man using such a weapon needed far less space than an archer using an English longbow.

He shaded his eyes and stared at the hedge that at least two hundred yards away, knew that the distant hedge would be the normal limit of the range of a crossbow, but could see no sign of the archer.

He scanned the reeds where he could see the outline of a patch of yellow irises.

A second bolt screamed past his face, causing him to curse, as he jerked his head violently away, shocked and annoyed that he was the target of a hidden assassin.

'Aelnoth. Oscar. Ingrid.' He shouted.

'Take care. I am being shot at by some hidden bowman.'

Although he could not see them, he heard his friends making their way cautiously towards him through the undergrowth.

'Take care.' He shouted. 'Keep yourselves hidden behind a tree.' Adding in an even louder voice. 'This sod is good. He has nearly hit me twice.'

'Can't be that bloody good then can he?' Came the almost jovial retort from Oscar.

'Stop there.' Shouted Magnus. 'I'll come to you as he turned and begun to make his way back towards his friends.'

'No,' called Oscar who was the nearest to him.

'You stay where you are behind that oak and wait 'till it gets dark. Then I'll sort him out.'

Magnus settled back behind the tree, only peering quickly out from time to time in order to make sure that the sniper didn't get any closer to him.

Hour after hour passed before the sun sank in the west, and dusk began to settle over the landscape, but it seemed to be at least a day and a half to Magnus, as he crouched behind his protective tree, fearing to feel the stab of a crossbow bolt at each and every moment.

Oscar did not move until the twilight turned into the inky blackness of night.

He then removed the cover from his sensitive eyes and sat for at least three hundred heartbeats whilst his eyes became accustomed to the darkness.

With his senses on full alert and his night vision honed to perfection, it seemed to him that daylight had returned, as he crept in a wide circle around the spot where his friend was still cowering behind the oak tree.

He silently reached the spot where the hedge met the edge of the wood, and waited for twenty heartbeats before he crept silently along the side of the hedge.

At the end of the hedge he slowly lowered himself into a damp ditch, which had been dug into the peaty soil in order to drain the field, and crawled along it on his hands and knees, fully expecting to find the hidden bowman at any moment.

He found an indentation in the grass where the man had crouched on the low embankment, and he could clearly see the tree where Magnus still lay hidden, but the man himself was nowhere to be seen.

Erring on the side of caution, Oscar continued to follow the ditch and hedge until it reached the overgrown roadway, where he could see patches of trampled grass where the man had left the ditch, and had walked over to where he had tethered his horse, before the tracks of both horse and its rider disappeared along the old road.

Confident that the bowman had gone, he walked openly across the field to where Magnus lay. 'He's gone.' He shouted to his friends as he reached their camp.'

'Nonetheless I think it wise that we alter our journey a little, and I do recall a farm track that is heading northwards at the edge of this forest.'

'Good idea.' Said Oscar. 'If we head off along an alternative track, then we are less likely to be ambushed by whoever it was trying to skewer us with his crossbow bolts.'

By midnight they had hacked their way through the undergrowth to reach the end of the small forest, and after Oscar had located the farm track, they urged their horses along it.

They passed through a small farm yard, where the only beings that appeared to be awake were three farm dogs, whose incessant barking woke up the farmer and his family, who eventually appeared in the doorway of their cottage, just in time to see the last of the three carts disappear into the darkness.

The track led them to a more substantial road, which headed northwards, and after passing through the silent township of Leamington, they halted for the day in a tiny copse near to the town of Warwick, where they covered their carts with fern, fed and watered their horses and settled down for the day.

The following night they passed through the sleeping town of Redditch, making their camp a mile or so from Bromsgrove.

Two days later they rested their tired horses on a mound overlooking the township of Wellington, where Aelnoth and Magnus roused themselves from their blankets late in the afternoon.

Leaving Oscar in charge of the three carts they made their way down the hill and across the river, labouring up the long street before they entered into the township, where the market stallholders were in the process of taking down their stalls and packing up the wares that they had not sold during the day, with the intention of leaving for their respective homes.

'Good,' said Aelnoth. 'Things should be cheaper now. They will not want to take their unsold goods home with them.' As he and his friend approached a stall holder who was packing up several wicker baskets with a dozen or so loaves of bread.

A few minutes later, loaded with a sack full of bread, they moved on to another stall where they bought four live hens, which were tied in twos, and Magnus soon had four squawking chickens hanging over his shoulders.

They ate well for the next few days.

One morning, as shafts of light stabbed through the dark clouds, threatening them that daylight was virtually upon them, they urged their horses as fast as they could, in order to pass over the large stretch of heathland that lay ahead of them, not wanting to find themselves in this type of open heathland in the broad daylight.

'Let us get off these moorlands.' Shouted Oscar, who was in the leading cart, 'and find somewhere to rest up for the day.'

'We should be safe from ambush in this open countryside.' He added as he lashed his horse with his willow wand.

As the final word left his mouth, an iron-tipped bolt with leather feathers slammed into his left shoulder, throwing him backwards onto the hay and bringing his horse to an immediate halt.

'What the hell was that?' Shouted Magnus who was directly behind Oscar's cart.

He had heard Oscar's shout of pain, but had only just caught a glimpse of his friends head as he had been thrown backwards.

Magnus leapt off his own cart and ran forward to the front of Oscar's cart, where he found the wounded Oscar clutching at the bolt that had been driven pretty well through his left shoulder.

Magnus jumped up onto the cart and was about to stoop down in order to help his friend, when a second bolt thudded into his back, throwing him into a heap on top of Oscar.

Aelnoth and Ingrid were in the third cart, and brought their cart to a halt.

Aelnoth jumped down from the cart and was in the process of walking, rather casually forward in order to see what was holding up their small procession, when a ragged man rose from the heather some fifty feet from the roadway, and strode arrogantly towards him as he fitted an iron studded bolt to his crossbow.

Aelnoth froze, and took a quick glance towards his own cart where his father's old shield was hidden under the hay in his cart. He immediately realised that it was too far away for him to reach, before this evil looking man skewered him.

The man stepped onto the roadway and approached Oscar's cart, where he casually stroked the nuzzle of the horse, before he stepped a couple of paces forward to gaze at the two men who were lying on the hay, groaning, as they were both attempting, without success to withdraw the bolts, which protruded out of their bodies.

John of Moren stared for a moment at the youth, who stood and gazed open mouthed at him, noting that the lad had no weapon except what looked like an old, out-dated Saex.

'A mere boy with bum fluff for a beard.' He muttered to himself as he casually dropped his crossbow to the ground and drew his sword.

'You are not the one who stole my horses and slew my servant.' He said.

'Therefore it must be one of these pigs,' he spat as his gaze returned to the two wounded men.

'I chose not to kill them outright.' He said smugly.

'You see. I want to see them suffer.' He explained as a cynical smile crossed his face.

He wagged his index finger and shook his head as he added. 'You have led me such a merry dance.'

'Still, I had better sort you out before I skin these two pigs alive.' He added as he drew his sword and advanced towards Aelnoth.

'And the girl. Ah, the girl. I shall have such fun with her before I put her out of her misery. Such fun.' He repeated.

'I will give you a purse full of silver if you will leave us in peace.' Said Aelnoth.

'Young man, I cannot accept your silver,' snarled the man, as a cruel smile briefly flitted across his face.

'I have sworn an oath to kill the slayer of De-Bracy of Broseley's son, and I am a man who has a reputation to protect, and I never renege on a contract.'

'Reputation is everything in my line of work, you know.' He added.

'Which one of you three swine killed Robert of Broseley?' he snarled.

As Aelnoth drew his own short sword he noticed that a slim dagger had suddenly appeared in the man's left hand.

He swallowed hard and retreated a step in apprehension, or was it fear?

John feinted with his sword, and as he stepped forward, he stabbed with his poniard, but the boy merely stepped back out of range.

Anxious to eliminate this boy quickly, so that he could enjoy the pleasure of skinning the other two wounded

Englishmen alive, and learn which one of them he had been paid to kill, before they died.

He raised his sword above his head with the intention of slaying the boy with his poniard, but as the poniard sped forward with its usual lightning speed, it was met with equal speed by a solid Saex, which numbed his hand.

His sword swooped down again, only to be met with the boy's Saex, jolting his arm yet again.

These responses were not the usual counters that John had met on his many, many previous assignments, nor were they the type of responses that he should have encountered from an inexperienced farm boy.

He stepped backwards two paces, allowing the numbness to ease from both of his arms.

Aelnoth used the brief pause by spinning around on his heels, and racing back to his own cart, where he fumbled beneath the hay and grasped one of the Norman swords, which he had hidden.

By the time he turned to face this cold faced killer, the man was barely three feet from him, and in the process of slashing down with his sword towards Aelnoth's unprotected head.

Aelnoth jumped backwards to avoid the blow, and retreated a further three steps, giving himself the few seconds needed to switch the sword to his right hand whilst in his left hand he grasped his sturdy Saex.

He stepped forward slashing right and left with his weapons. Thrusting and parrying in attack and counter attack.

 He took the fight to his opponent, causing the man to retreat past Aelnoth's cart, and then past the middle cart, until they battled furiously before the leading horse, where, it seemed to him, that the man had sworn to retreat no further, and stood as he slashed and parried as if his back was against a stone wall.

The face of Aelnoth's opponent had ceased to smile, and was now set in a grim and determined manner.

Aelnoth used all the tactics and skill that his father had drilled into him, whilst he had been a boy.

They were skills, which he had perfected by constant practice to such a point, that there were few men in the midland shires who would have been able to match him.

It was fortunate that he had been born ambidextrous, and could use both of his hands with equal skill, and it was this talent that was probably helping him today, for from the start of this particular contest, he had realised that this killer could also use both of his hands with a skill that matched, or even surpassed his own.

Whilst this killer was obviously more experienced, Aelnoth realised that he had youth on his side, and as a result of his youth, he should also have stamina, and perhaps the agility, which may help him to outlive his opponent, but that particular thought was thrust out of his mind as the man attacked again and again, forcing him to retreat as the man parried and danced about like a year old foal, showing no sign of fatigue.

Aelnoth attacked from his shield side and from his sword side.

He slashed high at the man's head, and then crouched as he slashed at the man's legs.

To no avail, as the man parried and skipped daintily out of the way.

The killer, who was still showing no signs of tiring, was, nonetheless being frustrated by this boy, who annoyingly countered his every move, and parried all of his attacks with apparent ease.

He snarled aloud and grunted with every thrust and slash that he made.

For Aelnoth, the world seemed to slow down, and an eerie silence descended into his head, allowing him to anticipate his opponent's every move, thus allowing him to counter the move.

He knew not only where his opponent would be, but also what kind of move the man was about to make, and although he could see the marks where his weapons had touched the man, he seemed unable to land the fatal blow.

Aelnoth noticed that at the side of the roadway there was a tree, which had been snapped off some two feet from the ground, probably during one of the gales that the countryside had endured during the previous winter.

Several savage splinters of wood protruded like spears towards the roadway.

After several attempts Aelnoth managed to manoeuvre his opponent into a position where he faced Aelnoth, with his back towards the broken tree.

Aelnoth slashed to his right and to his left, forcing the killer backwards and leaving the man's chest unguarded for a split second, and in that split second, Aelnoth jumped forward, and with both of his feet, he kicked the man in his chest, propelling the man with such force that his opponent fell backwards onto the wooden splinters, which entered his unprotected back and protruded out of his chest and abdomen.

The killers eyes opened wide and his mouth opened as if he was in the process of speaking, but the only thing that came out of his mouth was a thick trickle of blood, which cascaded down his chin and onto his chest, to mingle with the blood that was seeping out of his shattered chest and abdomen.

Aelnoth fell to his knees before the man as if he was giving thanks to god, but the only thing that he could think of, was the fact that he had just slain a man who was, without a doubt, the finest swordsman that he had ever met.

A thin cheer of approval caused him to turn his head and remember his two wounded friends, who, despite their own predicaments, had watched the contest between their friend and this strange man, with awe and admiration.

'Well done my boy.'

'By Odin's balls, that bugger was faster than a fart, ' shouted Magnus, but then he fell back onto his bed of hay in agony from the iron bolt that still protruded out of his chest.

'Aye, well done two swords.' said Oscar who was sitting with his back propped up by a bundle of hay.

'What are these two swords?' grumbled Magnus.

'What do you mean? What's this two swords?' he questioned.

'You saw the lad with two swords. Didn't you?'

'He was bloody good. Don't you agree?'

Oscar didn't answer. He merely nodded his head as a spasm of pain shot through his body.

Suddenly another attacker assailed Aelnoth, as Ingrid raced over to him and flung her arms around him, kissing him repeatedly on his sweating face and neck.

'Oh Aelnoth,' she sobbed, 'that was wonderful. Thank God you are unhurt.' And then she released her hold on him; she took a step backwards and stood embarrassed with her head on her chest in order to prevent the three young men from seeing her reddened face.

'From now on we will call the lad 'Two swords.' Said Magnus loudly.

'Enough of this nonsense.' Snapped Aelnoth. 'Let's get these carts into yonder wood, and see to your wounds,' as he pointed to a small wood that loomed on the distant horizon.

'We need to hide the carts and get those bolts out of you two, and get them out quickly, or these carts, and more importantly, the silver, will get no farther than this bit of god-forsaken moorland.'

'You two sit here on this cart.' He ordered, and I will drive the carts one by one into the woodland.'

'Oh, just wait a moment,' said Aelnoth as he walked over to the limp body of the slain man.

He searched the man's clothing but found nothing, until he removed the mans belt, where, to his delight he found no less than six golden coins stitched into the wide leather belt.

'Look at this.' He shouted as he held up the coins.

'This is the start of the fortune, which will help me regain my inheritance.'

He helped Ingrid to make his two wounded friends as comfortable as possible, before he drove the first cart across the moorland, where he deposited his friends on sheepskin rugs on the ground.

He unhitched the horse and rode it back to the second cart and repeated the procedure.

Again he rode back for the remaining cart, but before he left, he heaved the body of the dead assassin off the broken tree trunk and rolled it into a ditch.

As he drove the third cart into the woodland, he noted that Ingrid had collected a small pile of dry timber and was trying, unsuccessfully, to strike her flint in order to light a fire.

Oscar was attempting to rise to his feet in order to help her.

'Sit down.' Ordered Aelnoth, 'or that wound will turn bad. 'I will light the fire.'

He knelt by Ingrid and struck his own flint, lighting a tiny handful of moss, which he placed on the ground before he added a few dry twigs, and soon had a small fire crackling away.

'Now, I will try to get this dart out of you,' he said as he helped Oscar to the ground.

'Now let me have a look at the damned thing.' He said.

Oscar untied the thongs of his shirt and groaned quietly as he eased his one arm out of his shirt, and groaned a little louder as Aelnoth cut a long slit in the other side of his shirt, before he edged the shirt over the offending bolt.

'Thank god these things don't usually have barbs.' He said as he studied the iron bolt.

'Get on with it. Just pull the damned thing out.' Groaned Oscar.

'If you insist.' Answered Aelnoth. 'Remember, this is going to hurt you a lot more than it is going to hurt me. Here. Bite on this.' He added as he thrust a small chunk of wood into the wounded man's mouth.

Aelnoth grasped the few inches of the iron bolt that was visible as firmly as he could and with his left hand on the right hand shoulder of Oscar.

He gave the bolt a savage half turn and with a hard tug, he wrenched the bloody bolt out of his friends shoulder.

Oscar groaned aloud as he spat the chunk of wood out of his mouth, and then spat a bloody goblet of saliva onto the ground.

'My thanks to you my friend.' He groaned. 'Now piss on it.'

'What?' In front of Ingrid?' Questioned Aelnoth?

'I said piss on it. Its one of the best things to do to clean a wound.'

'Go on, two swords. Piss on it.'

He turned to Ingrid and ordered her to turn her back, and as soon as she had done so, he commenced to untie the belt that held up his breeches.

'Both sides. Back and front.' Added Oscar, as he lay back on the ground.

Aelnoth allowed his breeches to drop around his ankles and obliged his friend, sending his steaming urine over, and into the wounds on the front and on the back of Oscar's bleeding and swollen shoulder.

Aelnoth covered his friend with his own sheepskin saddle blanket and told him to lie still until he felt better.

'Now for you.' He said as he turned towards Magnus who was sitting on his own blanket and had watched the previous operation with growing apprehension.

'Mine's worst than his.' He said glumly.

'I think it's gone right through.'

'I am not sure that it's wise to just yank this bloody thing out. It may have gone through my lungs.'

Aelnoth nodded in agreement and said, 'I agree that it may have gone through your lungs, and although I'm no healer. I think that if it had hit either your lungs or your heart, then by now you would be either dead or coughing up a lot of blood, and as you seem to be doing neither, I think that the bolt must have missed your organs, and with a bit of luck should come out without too much trouble.' He added with the confidence that he did not feel.

He knelt down alongside Magnus and after a lot of cutting; he managed to get his shirt off, and looked at the bolt, which had indeed gone right through the centre of his body.

'Come here.' He said to Ingrid, who still had her back to them.

'Help me to hold him whilst I try to get this damned thing out.'

The leather flight feathers were all that he could see protruding from below his friend's shoulder blade.

However, perhaps two thirds of the bolt stuck out from his chest.

'I'm going to cut these leather flights off and pull it through from the front.' He said.

'It's going to be painful.' He added.

'Oh, I bloody know that. Just get it on with it. I can hardly stand, and I can't bloody well lie down with this damned thing sticking out of me.'

'Suck on this.' Said Aelnoth as he handed the same stick that Oscar had chewed on.

'I'm not sucking on that thing.' He said indignantly.

'Find me a clean one.'

'Aelnoth slowly walked around the campsite until he found a suitable chunk of wood and handed it to Magnus.

'This has got mould on it.' He moaned, as he attempted to scrape the mould off before he put it into his mouth and sank his teeth into it.

'What are you trying to do? Poison me?'

Aelnoth could not suppress a grim smile at his friend's fussy nature, although both of them were well aware that if the bolt could not be removed, and removed soon, then there would be no doubt whatsoever that Magnus would die.

Aelnoth gently cut the leather flight feathers off the bolt, and scraped the bolt as clean as he could with his knife, before he returned to the front of Magnus, and sat in front of him, and grasped the offending shaft with both of his hands, and using the same technique that he had used on Oscar, he twisted the bolt and withdrew the bolt as firmly and as gently as possible.

As the bolt left Magnus's chest, it made an audible sigh as if it was reluctant to leave its nice new warm home.

Magnus fell back onto his blanket, completely unconscious.

Aelnoth called to Oscar. 'I used all my piss on you.'

'It's now your turn to initiate our friend to the joys of warm piss.'

Oscar groaned as he rose and walked over to the prostate body of Magnus, undid his breeches and covered the front and back of his friend with steaming urine.

During the following two weeks Aelnoth and Ingrid did nothing except tend their wounded friends.

They had already eaten the chickens and food, which they had bought at Wellington, forcing both Aelnoth and Ingrid to forage far and wide, across woodland, stream and meadow, in order to find sufficient food in order to sustain the four of them.

Whilst they were out hunting, they did manage to catch a number of birds, rats and moles as well as a varied collection of herbs, roots and bulbs, which they hoped, would help to heal their friend's wounds.

Oscar was up and about after a few days, but Magnus suffered from a fever, which was so stubborn that both all of his friends feared for his life, and were obliged to force feed him with thin soup made from scraps of meat, mixed with crushed willow bark and feverfew.

Ingrid's talents came to the fore during this worrying period, and despite her tender age; she seemed to know all of the herbs of the heath and woodlands, which she threw into the pot, making the thin, palatable and healing gruel.

Aelnoth eventually managed to shoot a half grown boar and had just heaved it off his shoulders onto the ground near the campfire, when a voice said. 'It's about time you returned. I've been waiting for a good meal since dawn.'

Aelnoth looked towards the familiar cutting voice, and saw Magnus smiling up at him from under the sheepskin blanket, which had been his home for more than two weeks.

'So the old bugger has returned to us.' Came the quip from Oscar who was in the process of returning from watering the horses.

They ate well for the next four days as they waited for Magnus to recover his strength.

'I'm anxious to continue our journey.' Said Oscar.

They left their camp the following evening, travelling along cart tracks and by-roads, reaching the town of Bridgenorth two days later.

The following night they headed westward along a lush green valley as they followed a track alongside the river Corve, which meandered lazily through woodlands and meadows.

To their left were woods, which rose up and over the tops of the hills; whilst ahead of them their views were obscured by even more woodlands and mountains.

There was cover and game aplenty as they travelled through the last English hamlets and villages and across the Welsh border, where villages and farmsteads were few, which was probably the result of the border raids, that had been carried out by both the Welsh and English people over the past three or four hundred years.

As they travelled even further north western, the land became wilder and wilder.

The hills became higher and the valleys more overgrown, causing their progress to dwindle to a few miles for each laborious day's travel.

*   *   *

'Anwen the fair' was a Princess and a beauty amongst her people, who were part of the once powerful Cornovi tribe, and although her people had been decimated by the Roman legions, which had passed through their lands many years ago, they were still a proud people.

They were proud of their heritage.

Proud of their cold savage lands and proud of the courage that was still the very essence of their warrior society.

'Anwen the fair' did not show her beauty today, as she sat huddled over a small fire, grilling the small trout, which that she had just tickled out of the nearby stream that gurgled over the rocks and boulders alongside her.

She was weary and unwashed, having travelled alone to the very edge of her people's territory, following a wounded hind, which her brother had shot, and had been too vain to follow.

She had come to realise that the hind had not been mortally wounded after all, for it had ran for at least fifteen miles since her brother had placed an arrow into it's side.

Being of a very stubborn nature, she would have carried on and trailed the beast for at least another couple of miles, but she had been so engrossed in following the tiny droplet's of blood, which the hind had left in its wake, that she had failed to notice, rather a little late in the day, that she had already entered the territory of her neighbours, 'the Ordovice.'

Her own people and the Ordovice were not officially at war, and lived in an undeclared truce, which had hovered precariously between war and peace between the two tribes for more than ten years.

There always had been, and still was, a lot of animosity between the two tribes, with each tribe continually trespassing into the other's territory whilst hunting, as well as the old British custom's of cattle rustling, sheep stealing and of course, 'Bride snatching.'

Anwen was in the process of taking the trout off its wooden spit, when she heard a slight rustle behind her.

She turned and was shocked to see a middle aged man standing a few yards behind her.

She rose and spun around to face him, clutching the still sizzling trout in one hand and her razor sharp hunting knife in her other.

She backed away from the man, who grinned as he slowly approached her.

'Come any closer and I'll open you up with this.' She said as she made a gesture with her knife.

'That'd be interesting.' Said the man in a pleasant enough way, as his eyes looked to his left and then to his right.

Her head spun quickly to her left, where she saw a second man walking towards her with his hunting bow in one hand, noting that he was in the process of notching an arrow into the bowstring.

She turned to her right hand side in order to make a run for it, but was dismayed to see yet another man approaching her from that direction.

She turned on her heel only to see that a fourth man had stepped out from behind a high gorse bush, barring her escape.

'I am Cornovi,' she spat. 'And my brother is the Prince of our people.'

'If you harm me, he will hunt you down and hang your heads in his hall.' She said with venom.

'How will he ever know?' asked the eldest man, who appeared to be the leader.

'Oh, He will know.' She spat as she jabbed her knife towards the man.

'I won't tell him. Will you Emrys?' he said with a chuckle.

'No, I won't tell him. Said the man called Emrys, with a sly smile.

'I don't see him here.' Said one of the other men.

She heard another of the men chuckle, and as she turned to see exactly where the chuckle had come from, the fourth men jumped nimbly in and grabbed her wrist, which he shook until her knife fell from her numbed hand.

'Now our little wild cat has lost her claws.' Said the man as he held her in a grip of steel.

'Hold her still.' Said the leader. I shall have her first.'

'He threw her to the ground and immediately leapt on top of her, sitting on her belly as he ripped her shirt off and began to pull her breeches down, whilst at the same time he grunted with frustration as he tried to untie his own breeches.

His friends hooted and shouted, egging him on.

'My turn next,' bawled Emrys.

His friends did not readily agree, and a slight fracas ensued between the three men, as the leader finally grunted with satisfaction as he wrenched his own breeches down.

The arrow that thudded into his chest threw him off Anwen, where he lay on his face, with his bare buttocks shining like snow amongst the greenery of the moss that he was dying upon.

Had Emrys reacted with more speed, as was expected from a warrior of his category, he would not have received the second arrow, which threw him over his leader's prone form, and left him writhing in his death throes with an arrow in his heart.

His two comrades stooped to snatch up the weapons that they had cast upon the ground, in their expectation of a lively romp with this half naked girl, who still lay upon the ground

Anwen could scarcely believe her eyes as she stared at the man who, a mere heartbeat or so ago, had been about to rape her, and who now lay dead a mere two feet away from her face, staring directly into her face with unseeing eyes.

She sat up and gazed stupidly in the direction that her two remaining abductors were looking at a boy. Yes. A boy, who almost casually tossed his ash hunting bow to the ground and strolled slowly towards the two men.

She watched with fascination and horror as the boy advanced.

He drew his sword, and then brought out a second and much smaller sword, which he held in his left hand.

She was not the only one who was surprised by this boy, who was strutting up to these two experienced warriors, for Arella, who was the elder of the two, and had no less than six tattoos on his forehead, depicting that he had slain no less than six warriors in battle.

He glanced at his cousin, Alouarn, who stood beside him.

Alouarn was also a proud warrior, and had been so named due to the fact that as a child he had possessed such black brows that his parents had named him 'Alouarn' (Iron Brow.)

Throughout his youth and into his manhood he had lived up to his austere name, thrashing, or even slaying men who gave him the slightest cause.

Alouarn had nine tattoos, and was something of a legend in the lands of the Ordovice.

'Stupid English pig,' growled Alouarn, for he was quite happy now that this stupid youth, who by his appearance was obviously English, had thrown down his bow.

'Let us slay this stupid boy quickly, and then we two can enjoy this damned Cornovi bitch.' He sneered, as he strode around the fire and advanced towards Aelnoth.

They spread out and attacked him from both sides, raining blows upon his head and his body, but the blows failed to reach the boy, for they were either blocked by one of the youngsters' swords, or the youth simply ducked or danced out of harms way.

None of their slashes and thrusts reached their target. Not only did they not reach their intended victim, but the two men found themselves counter-attacked by this youngster, as the boy danced about them, as if he was enjoying a summer equinox dance with a couple of maidens, raining blows, which cascaded upon them with the speed of a shower of hailstones.

Both of the Ordovice warriors were forced backwards as the youth's arms seemed to whirl like a waterwheel.

In their many battles with other tribes, and on the two occasions that they had raided into England, they had never encountered a situation such as this, and had slain and maimed their enemies with impunity, and yet they both knew that this particular fight was being wrested away from them.

As they were forced backwards, they almost tripped over the bodies of their two slain comrades.

'Come.' Roared Alouarn as he puffed his chest out with bravado.

'He is only a boy. Kill the bastard,' and stepped forward again, thrusting his sword at the boy's body only to find his sword knocked away as if it was a toy.

Grateful for the small respite, Aelnoth stepped back towards the girl, and stood over her like an avenging Demon.

Arella approached the dead body of one his friends, making a mistake by glancing down so that he would not step on the corpse, and thus prevent its soul on its journey to Heaven.

It was a glance that took a mere blink of an eye, and yet it was enough to allow Aelnoth to slash across his opponents neck causing the man to drop to his knees as his life blood gushed out from his half severed neck.

With a savage roar Alouarn charged forward slashing to his right and to his left, only to find that his weapon caught nothing but the empty, sweet smelling mountain air.

The boy counter attacked, raining blows upon his opponent until fear took hold of the warrior, forcing him to retreat yet again until he could take no more, but the youth pursued him and seemed reluctant to let him go.

'This was not how battles are fought,' his muddled brain told him.

'If a man has had enough, then he has always been allowed to quit, and leave the field, and yet this mad youth will not allow me to quit.'

Alouarn was a proud warrior. Bred from warrior stock.

Was he not a member of his tribe's foremost society? The ferocious society of wolves.

He had been trained to perfection and betrothed to battle, and thus he was also betrothed to death.

'But not today.' He snarled.

He tried again and again to retreat, hoping beyond hope that his cousin would step in and defend him.

His beloved cousin was nowhere to be seen, for he had been wise enough to take to his heels, once he had seen that this fight was doomed, realising that he would probably be the only survivor to reach home, where he could spin a tale about his own courage, tall and elaborate enough to be believed.

'Perhaps I shall come out of this as a hero,' he mused to himself as he spurred his horse, and disappeared around the end of the valley.

The end came suddenly as Alouran's sword was forced down by a flurry of blows, which suddenly ceased, as the sword that was in his opponent's left hand stabbed forward into his chest with the speed that was so fast that his brain refused to believe it.

His body froze for a moment as his own sword dropped from his lifeless hand, and he stared down in horror at the short sword, which protruded from the centre of his chest.

Aelnoth wrenched his poniard out of the man's body and allowed the man to fall to the ground.

He turned and walked towards the woman, who still sat on the ground where she had watched the fight in awe, as this young Englishman had slain four warriors of the dreaded Ordovice clan.

'Anwen the Fair' became tense, as this baby-faced killer, who was covered in the blood of his victims, strode confidently up to her.

He smiled down at her and held his bloodstained hand down towards her.

'Come Lady.' He said. 'You have naught to fear from me.'

Still in a state of shock, she took his outstretched hand, and with his help, she rose.

As she stood, the grubby cowl, which had covered her head, fell off.

It was now the turn of Aelnoth to be shocked, for, as the cowl fell, it revealed, not the middle aged hag that he had expected, but a stunningly beautiful young maiden.

Certainly. He noted. Her Auburn hair was greasy and unkempt, and her face was covered with grime, through which small rivers of tears had made their way down her cheeks, in her anger, shame, and frustration at the ordeal, which she had undergone, but her beauty shone through this grease and grime, like a pure white swan swimming in the middle of a muddy lake.

'I am called Aelnoth.' Stammered Aelnoth, as he stared at this vision of the gods.

'My friends and I.' He pointed oafishly towards the end of the valley, which was no more than a hundred yards away, where for the first time Anwen could see three carthorses, which were being held by Aelnoth's companions, 'are travelling through these lands, so that we can sail to Ireland and bury our sacred dead.'

Anwen dumbly nodded, for although she did not speak the language of the English, she knew just enough to understand what this handsome young killer had said.

'Come.' She said.

'This is the territory of my enemies.'

'We should leave.'

Fortunately, as Aelnoth had been born and bred in the lands bordering the Welsh Kingdoms, he was in pretty well the same situation as the girl, for although he did not speak the Welsh language. He also understood just enough of it to get by.

He walked quickly back to his two wounded friends.

'God's blood.' Exclaimed Magnus whose arm was still in a sling.

'I think we named you well.'

'I have never seen a man wield two swords with such skill.'

'Remind me to never get on the wrong side of you.' He added with a grin as he slapped Aelnoth on his shoulder.

Oscar merely nodded, and with a smile he turned and walked towards his cart.

'Come.' Said Aelnoth. 'The girl says that we are in the territory of her enemies and says we should make ourselves scarce.'

Aelnoth was, once again assaulted, but this time it was not by wild Welshmen wielding weapons, but by a thin girl child who, only a few short days ago had celebrated her sixteenth birthday.

Aelnoth smiled as he forcibly unwound Ingrid's arms from around his neck and walked up towards his own cart.

As Aelnoth's reached his cart, he noticed that Anwen had hesitated for a moment, before she took his outstretched hand and climbed onto the cart, where she sat quietly beside him.

After a little while she looked back towards the following cart and noticed that what little hay remained on Aelnoth's cart was failing to cover what looked like coffins.

'What's in the coffins?' she asked.

'Oh, we are taking the remains of Magnus's family to Ireland for burial.'

'How did they die?'

'They were slain at Hastings. Well most of them were.'

'What about the one's that weren't?'

'We dug them up so that they could all be together in Ireland.' He lied.

Aelnoth, not wanting to be questioned any further about the coffins, tactfully tried to change the subject.

'How far is your home?' he asked.

'Not too far.' Was the reply.

'We should be there before dark.'

'Good.' He said. 'These nags won't last much later without a day or so of rest.'

Anwen guided them through a maze of valleys and soggy meadows, through passes and woodland, until they reached a wide valley, which was dotted with cottages, meadows and fields of oats.

She pointed to the far end of the valley, where Aelnoth could see a high stonewall, which surrounded a township, which was itself overshadowed by a stone castle.

'There.' She pointed.

'Not far now.'

'Stop.' Said a voice from the rear.

Aelnoth brought his cart to a stop and looked behind him to see Oscar hobbling towards him.

'Stop.' He shouted again.

'Why?' Aelnoth demanded, as he could see no threat.

The meadows and plough-land seemed to be deserted, except for the odd labourer here and there.

'Danger.' Blurted Oscar, as he stopped and looked up towards Aelnoth.

'Where?' asked the bemused Aelnoth, for he could see no armed men approaching them, nor could he see any place nearby, which could conceal hidden bowmen.

'There.' He said emphatically, as he pointed towards the township.

CHAPTER 8

Anwen looked at Oscar, and then to the township, but could detect no sign of danger, either on the approach to the fortress, or on the walls.

She could see the usual sentries walking their beat along the palisade, but even they seemed not to have noticed the three carts that were at least half a mile from the town.

'There is no danger.' She said. 'It is completely safe.'

'They are my people and once they see me, everything will be fine.'

'Danger,' said the frustrated Oscar again.

Anwen turned to Aelnoth and said in a low voice. 'I can see no danger.'

And then she added in an even quieter voice.

'Is he mad?' for in truth, since she had been in the company of the three men, she immediately took a liking to both Magnus and Aelnoth, but at the first sight of this strange startling white man, who possessed the weirdest eyes she had ever seen, she had avoided him as if he had the plague.

Indeed he frightened the living daylights out of her.

His white face and his white hair were the nightmares of her dreams.

However, her feelings towards Ingrid hovered between love and hatred, for some of the time Ingrid was child like and amusing, whilst at other times she seemed full of hatred and venom towards Anwen, especially when the Welsh girl seemed to be near to Aelnoth.

Aelnoth answered her questioning about Oscar in an equally quiet voice as he looked down towards his Albino friend. 'No, he is not mad,' he said, 'but he sees things.'

'Sees things?' she questioned aloud.

'Yes, he sees things. You know. Things that happen in the times to come.'

'Oh. I see. You mean he is a Seer?'

'Yes. Well something like that.' Answered Aelnoth.

He looked down at Oscar.

'We have no choice my friend.' He said.

'We must go on.'

'On your head be it.' Answered Oscar, who shook his head as if in disgust.

By the time they had reached the township, crowds had gathered along the walls and around the double gates, shouting, cheering and clapping their hands.

'What's all the fuss?' asked Aelnoth.

'Haven't they seen three carts and a few coffins before?'

'They are pleased to see me. Answered the young woman.

'Why? Are you famous or something? He queried with a tired smile.

'Something like that.' She answered with a smile.

She directed him through the gates and along the main track, which appeared to lead to the centre of the township, but their progress was painfully slow, as the roadway was choked with people of all ages, small flocks of sheep, and milking cows that seemed to be free to wander aimlessly hither and thither.

She indicated to Aelnoth to pull up in front of a large building, and as he halted his cart, a young man strode jauntily out of the buildings large double doors.

He was as dark as she was fair, and was dressed in striped woollen leggings and a knitted sleeveless jerkin that was edged in ermine.

Around his slender waist was a belt made of silver links, which had been intricately woven to resemble a rope, which was buckled at the front by the largest silver buckle that Aelnoth had ever seen.

'Sister.' The man shouted at the top of his voice as he held his arms aloft and rushed down the three stone steps to embrace her.

Anwen leapt off the cart and jumped into his arms, throwing her arms around the young mans neck and showering him with kisses.

After she had unwound herself from him, she turned towards the three waiting Englishmen and the young girl, who had dismounted from their carts, and were standing in a small group as they surveyed the two young people who had been absorbed in a long embrace.

Anwen turned to the trio and said in a demure and an almost revered voice.

'This is my brother Arnallt.'

The three young men nodded their heads towards Arnallt.

'He is soon to be made King.' Said Anwen in a rather stern voice.

'And as such, should be shown more respect.'

'What do you want us to do?' asked Magnus.

'Get on our knees before him?' he added in a very sarcastic tone.

'Careful.' Said Aelnoth.

'It is unwise to insult a Prince inside his own Keep.'

'Sod him.' Growled the ever-defiant Magnus.

'I am a nephew of King Harold Godwinson. I kneel to no man.'

'My sister did not ask you to kneel.' Said Arnallt in perfect English.

'A good handshake would suffice.'

Aelnoth stepped forward and shook his hand, followed by his two companions as all three were introduced to the brother of Anwen.

'You saved my sister from being raped, which would have resulted in either death or a life of slavery, which has put me in your debt for ever.' He said as a wide smile creased his handsome young face.

'Had she been taken by those savages, we would now be at war with them and the good lord himself knows how many of my warriors would have died fighting the Ordovice.'

'They are formidable warriors you know.' He added.

'Come! Come my friends, and allow me to break bread and drink wine with you.'

The four young travellers followed Arnallt through the doorway.

'Aelnoth shouted politely to his host. 'Will the coffins be safe there?

Arnallt spun around and glared at Aelnoth. 'Of course they will be safe.'

'None of my people would dare to touch the things, no matter how smelly they are.'

But then his stern face broke into a half smile as he added. 'If you would feel more comfortable I shall have them moved into the stable over there, where your horses can be tended and the coffins can rest in the shade.'

The three men nodded in agreement, causing Arnallt to commence his walk into the hall.

Once their eyes were accustomed to the darkness of the room, they could see that the hall contained nothing other than a long trestle table with benches all around it, and a large carved chair at the far end of the table.

The table was laden with food and drink.

More and more warriors followed the three Englishmen into the hall, which was soon buzzing with so much noise that they could hardly make themselves heard.

As if by some hidden signal, the noise suddenly ceased and all eyes turned to the door.

Nothing happened for the space of a hundred heartbeats, until the eerie silence was broken with the sound of, thud, shuffle, thud, shuffle, thud, as slowly, an old man appeared in the light of the doorway and continued to advance into the room. Thud, shuffle, thud, shuffle, thud, broke the silence, as he limped slowly with the aid of a stout, ornately carved, ash walking pole, and the help of a handsome young man who assisted him, as he shuffled forward.

Thud, shuffle, thud, he slowly made his way passed the silent warriors until he reached the head of the table, where he sat down on the chair, uttering a loud sigh of relief.

After a long silence, the old man looked up.

'Son.' He said, and Arnallt rose from the eating table and walked over to his father, where he dropped to one knee and bowed his head before him.

'Sit by me.' He ordered, and Arnallt sat on the bench by his father, causing the warriors to shuffle up the benches in order to make room for him.

'I see that you have brought Englishmen to my table.' He said wearily with a grimace, which cracked his heavily tattooed and wrinkled face, so that his face took on the look of a ploughed field that had seen six months of drought, and was covered with black crows.

'Why is that?' he said in an even quieter and more sinister voice.

The silence of the room seemed to echo with the sound of his whisper.

'They are friend's father.' Answered Arnallt.

'They are English.' He hissed.

'I know father,' answered the son.

'They saved Anwen from the Ordovices.' he added quietly.

'This young warrior prevented her from being raped and taken into captivity.'

'He slew four of them.'

The King was silent for a moment before he hissed 'four? And then he looked up and said.

'Where are their heads?' He asked in a voice that was full of suspicion.

'The English do not take the heads of their enemies.' My Lord.

'Why ever not? How can they say they have killed a man, if they do not take the head?

'Any man can gainsay their courage.' He added as he stared, bemused at his son.

'Even the Irish take heads.' He hissed, as his old eyes narrowed in suspicion.

'I. I am not sure Father.' Answered his son.

'They are a strange people to be sure.'

The old man looked at the four young travellers, and turned again to his son, saying rather reluctantly.' I suppose you had better present them to me.'

Arnallt stood and bade the three Englishmen stand. 'Come forward.' He said.

The three Englishmen joined Arnallt in front of his father.

Ingrid stood behind Aelnoth as if she feared this fetid old Welsh King.

'My friends.' He said.

'This is my Father, King Llewellyn. King of the Cornovi.'

'Father. May I present Magnus, who is the nephew of the late King Harold Godwinson, and this is Oscar, who is the son of an English nobleman, and this young man is Aelnoth Edricson, and he is the son of the famous Edric Sylvaticus, who slew the Welsh Chieftain, 'Madoc the lucky.'

'The girl is called Ingrid.'

The old King ignored Ingrid.

'Mmm,' mumbled the King. 'I have heard of Wild Edric.'

'He was no friend to our people.' he said sourly.

'Did he not marry Godda? The Queen of the Light Elves?'

'I believe so father.'

'She was rumoured to be a Welsh princess.'

'So I have heard, father.'

'Did Edric not slay Madoc the Lucky?' he questioned.

'I do not know,' answered Arnallt.

'I do,' snapped the old King.

'He was a Welsh king. He added.

And added with a snarl. 'A bad one.'

He sniffed loudly as if he was attempting to expel some snot from his nose, before he turned his gaze towards Magnus.

'So you are the nephew of Harold who was slain at Hastings?'

'I am my Lord.'

'Mmm,' he said snootily.

'He also was not a friend of my people, and lay waste many parts of Wales, slaying many Welshmen.'

'But he did not venture this far into our sacred mountains, and he slew many warriors who were also not our friends, so I suppose we must abide by the old saying that my enemies' enemy is my friend.'

He then turned his bleary eyes towards Oscar.

'Why does the tall one wear a hood in my Hall?' Snapped the King.

'Father. I am told that he is a soothsayer and has sensitive eyes and skin, and he suffers much pain from bright lights such as the sun, and burning torches.'

'I would see his face.' Demanded the King in a stern voice that belied his frailty.

'He is not the one who saved Anwen.' Said Arnallt as he tried to avert what he thought would be a disaster if Oscar's cowl were to be removed, for he had seen his features just the once, and in his opinion, that one time had been one time too many.

'I am aware of that you fool.' He spat at his one and only son.

'I will see his face.'

'Take the hood off.' He snarled at Oscar, and although Oscar did not understand what the King had said, he knew by the tone of the King's voice that something was amiss.

'I must ask you to take your hood off.' Said Arnallt in an apologetic voice.

Oscar reached up with both of his hands and dragged the hood over his chin and up over his head, revealing his startling white face and his pink eyes, which were framed by the type of white hair, that a man might expect to see on the head of a very ancient man.

The silent hall was broken by cries of alarm, as the warriors forgot their vow of silence whilst in their King's presence.

Many of them stumbled back in terror and reached for their eating knives, which was the only weapon that they were allowed to bring into the Kings Hall.

'Kill him. Kill him.' Shouted the warriors.

'Slay the freak.' 'Kill the monster.' Roared other men whilst one huge warrior to rush forward and bowl over one of the Kings personal bodyguards with a shoulder butt, and as the guard fell, the warrior nimbly scooped up the man's spear and rushed at Oscar, who was standing slightly dazzled by the torches that burned in the hall.

'Die,' screamed the warrior as he thrust the spear at Oscar's chest.

Arial was one of the most famous warriors of the Cornovi people, and a man whose courage and fame was known, not only in the valleys of Mid Wales but also in the south and the North of the Welsh hinterland.

Arial had not been born with that name, and had carried a Christian name until he was nine years of age, but as he was enjoying a honey cake, which his mother had baked especially for him on his 9th birthday, his village had been raided by a war band of his enemies from the Demitae tribe, and two Demitae warriors had burst into his home whilst he was licking the last of the honey off his sticky fingers.

He failed to lick all the honey off as his hand froze a few inches from his lips, as one of the raiders hacked his father down before his father had been able to reach his own sword, which hung over the fireplace.

The second raider grabbed his mother by her hair and flung her to the floor, where he straddled her and savagely ripped her loose bodice to shreds.

Whilst he was abusing his mother, the man glanced at the nine-year-old boy and snarled, 'you'll be next,' and then returned to the task in hand.

As the first raider was occupied rummaging through Arial's fathers clothing, the boy leapt to his feet and dashed over to the fireplace where his father's sword hung.

He stretched to reach the sword, and the heavy sword fell onto the dirt floor with a thud.

It took all of the strength of both of his puny arms to raise the heavy sword above his head, which he then brought down onto the head of the raider who was in the act of leaving the body of his father, slicing through his skull and sending him dying onto the body of his father.

The warrior on top of his mother heard his friend fall and attempted to rise, but his breeches were around his knees and Arial's mother, who had witnessed what her child had done, held onto the man and thus prevented him for a brief second from reaching his feet.

The few seconds were all that Arial needed, and he wrenched his father's sword out of the dying man's skull and stabbed it forward with all of his strength into the stooping man's chest, sending him sprawling off his mother as he clutched at the offending object, which was deeply embedded in his chest.

When the survivors of the raid entered his house, they found Arial standing in front of his mother with the sword ready to fight any other raiders who may dare to enter his home.

Hence they had re-named him 'Arial.' 'The courageous one.'

But now Arial. 'The courageous one,' was not merely courageous, he was simply fighting mad, despite the fact that his intended victim was quite obviously wounded and unarmed.

He did not see a wounded MAN standing before him. He saw a Demon.

An Inhuman being, which he believed to be the Devil incarnate.

And it was a Devil, who he would now eliminate.

Despite the fact that Oscar's right shoulder still pained him, he was able to use it, albeit in a somewhat limited way, and as he saw the spear speed towards his chest, he stepped to one side and allowed the weapon to zip a mere hairsbreadth from his chest, and as the spear came to a sudden halt, he grabbed it with both of his hands and with a twist and a sudden jerk, he wrenched the spear from his attackers hand, and neatly slapped the haft of the spear across the side of the man's head, sending him sprawling to the ground.

As the warrior shook his head in a vain attempt to dispel the stars, which circled vividly in his brain, he suddenly froze as he felt the metal of the spearhead pricking his neck.

The roars and bellowing that the throng of warriors had been making had suddenly hushed into a deathly silence, as this eerie white Englishman held their defeated champions life in balance.

'Hold.' Shouted Arnallt, who then turned to his father, who had watched the brief fight with his old eyes bright with excitement, as he had fully expected Arial to skewer the strange Englishman as soon as he had seen Arial jump to his feet.

'He has betrayed our code of honour by attacking a guest whilst he is under our roof,' Arnallt said loudly, as he pointed to the prone figure of Arial, who in turn was still scowling up at this eerie being who had un-armed him in a split second, and who could end his life with a mere flick of his wrist.

'Aye, my son,' answered the King.

'He has. But it happened too speedily for my old eyes to take it all in, and stop it.' Lied the King.

'Arial has always been a bit headstrong.' He added. 'Still, no harm done, and it has stirred my old blood to see a bit of a fight in my old age.'

'In my youth, there would have been a different outcome if I had taken a spear to another man.'

'Nonetheless. My son. You are the watchdog of my wrath, and you are correct when you say that Arial has broken our code of honour.'

He turned his face towards the three Englishmen.

'You are my honoured guests, who came to my Hall not as enemies, but of your own free will, having saved my daughter from a fate worst than death, and I have abused my own hospitality, and have shrank from my duty to give you the thanks, which I should have extended to you, the moment you entered my domain.'

'Please accept my sincere apologies.' He bowed his head reverently.

'I beg you to allow my man there to live.' He said in a pleasant voice.

'He saved my life in The Battle of the Mynd, and I would be sad to see him slaughtered like a lamb.'

'Besides,' he added. 'He is one of my best warriors and I may well need him in these troubled times.'

'What with you English lapping at my eastern borders, and the Demetae and Silures threatening my borders from the west and from the south.'

Oscar rather reluctantly took the spear point away from the man's throat, and handed the spear to the bodyguard, who looked shamefaced as he retrieved it from his hand.

The King was about to say something further when the double doors at the end of the room were suddenly flung open with a loud crash, and through it walked the King's daughter 'Anwen the Fair.'

Anwen was dressed in a white, tight fitting gown that went down to her ankles.

Around her waist was a wide silver belt with a large ornate buckle.

Her Auburn hair had been washed and brushed until it shone like burnished gold, and a large, single white daisy had been inserted inside a small ringlet of her hair on the crown of her head.

She strode silently and regally passed the silent throng, accompanied by four handmaidens who were beauties in their own right, but were totally outclassed by the their mistress.

'Surely this cannot be the grubby girl who I rescued from those four beasts, and who sat alongside me for God knows how many miles,' mumbled Aelnoth, and yet he knew it was.

But today he saw her in a totally new light. Like the Princess that she actually was.

She halted before the King, making a slight bow.

'Father, I see that you have met my saviours.' She said loudly.

'What honours did you bestow upon them for saving my life?'

'Ah!' spluttered the King. 'I was just about to do that.' He lied.

'What would you suggest my dearest?' he asked.

'Perhaps you would give my hand in marriage to one of them,' she said.

'But they are English.' He spluttered, and almost choked.

'So?'

'Well the eldest seems to be a bit of an oaf, and the white one. Well .Ug. I could not abide a grandchild of mine looking like him, and the third one is nought but a beardless youth.'

'Father. Dear Father. You could not be more wrong, for the eldest is a nephew of King Harold Godwinson who was defeated at Hastings, and the White one, as you call him, is the only son of a great Lord.'

She paused and turned towards Aelnoth, who she was beginning to believe that she was in love with.

'The boy, as you call him, is the one who slew the four warriors who would have raped me.' She said, as she felt a tear well up into her eyes.

'He is called Aelnoth Edricson, and is the son of a man who owned many manors in the old Kingdom of Mercia, and is already a famous warrior called 'Aelnoth two swords.''

'Oh! I know all that. Nonetheless.' Said the King, as he cleared his throat yet again.

'I would like you to marry one of our own, so you can forget that idea.'

He knew only too well many of the ways of women, who oftimes planted ideas into the heads of their menfolk, in order to allow those ideas to ferment for a couple of weeks, or even a couple of months, before the poor, unsuspecting man came up with the idea, which he claimed to be his own.

If four wives and three daughters had taught him one thing and nought else, it was that the average female of the species was even more cunning, and manipulative than the most cunning man who ever lived.

He was a man who hated to be lectured to by anyone, especially a woman, and even more so, when he was being confronted in the presence of his own warriors, so he did what he usually did when he found himself at such an impasse.

He blustered and said the first thing that came into his head.

'After my ancestor Griffith-ap-Llewellyn the first, returned from his exile in Ireland,' he reminisced. 'He fought more battles than I care to remember, mainly against our enemies the Romans, but he also battled against those cowardly tribes who made peace with them, and had allowed themselves to become their puppets.'

'Many were the nights when he slept wet and cold in the mountains, with a mere handful of trusted warriors, emerging through the teeth of a snowstorm or out of the mists, to wage war in the valleys and in the mountains, trapping both the Romans and their minions, slaying them in their hundreds, before he vanished like the ghost that he was.'

'He united the tribes, and we were strong.' He said loudly.

He paused to raise his golden drinking horn to his mouth and whilst he took a long drink he gazed over the rim of his horn and was pleased to see that his ruse was working.

'Alas.' He sighed aloud. 'We have all taken the wrong path from time to time, and although we are not the best of friends, at this moment in time we are not at war with any of our neighbouring tribes.'

'Have I not made peace with the Cornovi and the Demetae? Despite the fact that the Cornovi slew my only brother, who I loved more than life itself.'

'He was blood of my blood.'

'Flesh of my flesh.'

'We lived and fought together, loved together, and wenched together'

'We were ticks in the ear of the same dog.'

'I am the sixth King to take the name Llewellyn, and I lead my people in freedom and prosperity.'

He began to lose his way and the words dried up in the crowded, yet silent Hall, but then he recalled the one and only thing that his old father had drilled into his young brain, and recited it in an almost singing voice, to his silent audience.

'Ten thousand thousand we have slain.'

'Romans, Saxons, Celts and Dane.'

'All have come and all been beaten.'

'We filled the valleys with their slain.'

'Ten thousand drinks we have drunk.'

'Beer and Wine and Sacred Mead.'

'Our foes are many. Our friends are few.'

'We are Cornovi, Brave and true.'

There was a long silence after he had finished, for each and every man present had heard the saga sung again and again since they were babes on their mother's tits.

Prince Arnallt broke the silence by stamping his one foot on the floor, and banging the hilt of his eating knife on the table before him.

Others joined him until the room vibrated with noise, as they all stamped their feet and banged the hilts of their eating knives on the tables in unison.

'Ten thousand thousand we have slain.' They roared.

'Romans, Saxons, Celts and Dane.'

'All have come and all were beaten.'

'We filled the valleys with their slain.'

'Ten thousand drinks we have drunk.'

'Beer and Wine and Sacred Mead.'

'Our foes are many. Our friends are few.'

'We are Cornovi, Brave and true.'

'The Cornovi,' roared Arnallt at the top of his voice as he rose to his feet and held his drinking horn aloft.

'The Cornovi.' Bellowed his warriors, who followed his example and held their own drinking horns aloft, and as the shouting subsided, they brought their drinking horns to their mouths and emptied the warm beer down their throats.

As it was expected of her. Anwen joined in with the singing, well aware of her father's wily mind, and of his canny ability to change any subject that he was, perhaps uncomfortable with, and of course it had, yet again been successful, for the bulk of his warriors had forgotten the question of Anwen marrying one of these three strange Englishmen, as the warriors emptied their drinking horns, and sang the old saga again and again until their throats became dry, causing them to hail the serving maidens for refills.

However, she was of his blood, was she not? And had not only her father's blood running through her veins? But she had also inherited his determination and his wily, active brain, so she rose and stood before him.

The assembled warriors slowly quietened down and the room lulled again into silence.

'Father,' she said in a voice that she hoped would be loud enough to carry to the far corners of the hall.

'Father.' She repeated a little louder. 'You have yet to tell your people of the reward that you are going to bestow upon these three English warriors who rescued me.'

The King's face reddened at the sheer audacity of his daughter, knowing that she alone, or perhaps with the exception of Arnallt, had not been fooled by his attempt to avert the subject of her suggestion of marriage to one of these damned Englishmen, or by his evasion of a reward.

Marriage was out of the question, mused the King, for he had already approached the king of the Silures with a proposal of a marriage of Anwen, to the eldest of the Princes of the Silures, and even at this precise moment, he was awaiting a favourable answer, which would cement an alliance between his own Tribe and the people of the Silures.

Matching her agile mind with his own, which, despite his age and his frailty, was still as sharp as a good knife?

He said. 'You were the one who was rescued, so other than your silly suggestion of marriage, what reward would you bestow upon them?'

'A Village or a Princedom?

'Or perhaps your own weight in silver?'

'From your own coffers of course.' He added with a sly grin, causing an odd snigger from one or two of his warriors.

'Since the question of marriage is not on the agenda,' she said. 'I feel that there is nought that we have here that they need, but when they accompanied me here, they spoke of a guide to lead them to the coast, so that they can take their relics across the sea to Ireland.'

'I suggest,' she continued. 'That as two of them are wounded, you offer them a strong escort through the lands of the Silures, with enough silver to enable them to purchase their passage to Ireland.'

The King was delighted that her suggestion would let him off so lightly, and beamed with pleasure at his daughter, for such a journey, his canny mind told him, would allow him to send a gift to the King of the Silures, and thus prod their doddery old fool into make a favourable decision about his marriage proposal.

Although Aelnoth was able to follow most of the conversation, his two companions had no idea what had taken place.

Seeing that both the King and his daughter were smiling and nodding in their direction, Oscar asked Aelnoth, 'What's going on?'

'Well it looks like Anwen wanted to marry me, but the King said no. I think he has agreed to provide us with an escort to the coast, and give us enough silver to get to Ireland.'

'That's good news then,' said Magnus enthuastically, 'but they could forget the silver.'

'We've got enough bloody silver to sink a good sized ship.'

'Quiet you dolt,' snapped Aelnoth, 'lest they hear. And if we can collect more silver, then I would be able to put it into my own coffers, to help me to reclaim my inheritance when I return home to Wentnor.'

Magnus snapped his mouth shut, realising that he had already said too much, and looked furtively around to see if any of the tribesmen were close enough to have overheard his remark.

'I don't think anyone heard.' He mumbled quietly.

'Thank the good lord for that.' Said Aelnoth.

'They probably don't speak English anyway.' He added with a wry smile.

'Let's drink up and celebrate.' Said Oscar as he lifted his half empty drinking horn to his mouth.

The King rose to leave, and leaning on his stout staff, and assisted by his young attendant, he hobbled past the long table.

Thud, the staff hit the ground, followed by a slow shuffle. Thud. Shuffle. Thud. Shuffle. Thud. Shuffle, came the noise as he slowly retreated through the hall and out of the doorway.

The rest of the evening went well with a goodly supply of both food and drink, and it was long after midnight before they were shown to their beds.

They were awakened at dawn by a slave boy, who brought each of them a wooden tankards of warm ale, two chunks of freshly baked bread and a couple of chunks of cheese, which they devoured with relish before leaving the room.

They made their way to the stables, where their three horses and three carts had spent the night.

Much to their relief, the horses had been fed, watered and groomed, but more importantly, the three carts and the coffins had not been tampered with.

They were in the process of hitching the horses up to the carts when they heard the clatter of horses and the shouting of men coming from the cobbled courtyard.

'A few minutes later Arnallt jauntily entered the building.

'Ah,' he said merrily. 'I see you are nearly ready. Good.'

'I will see you outside when you are ready,' and left them to finish harnessing their horses.

They were met by an escort of twenty-five riders, accompanied by half as many pack animals, carrying a number of packages, which had been covered with cowhide and firmly tied with leather straps.

Oscar, as usual, wore his cowl in order to shade his eyes from the bright morning sunlight.

He was not too delighted to see Arial scowling down at him from the back of a large grey gelding.

The King was nowhere to be seen, but amongst the large crowd of townsfolk, Aelnoth did see the sad face of Anwen, who stood on the steps of her father's hall.

She stared directly at him, and he was sure that she pouted her lips into the shape of a kiss, before she turned around and disappeared through the darkened doorway into the Hall.

Arnallt led the way out of the township and down a well-used roadway, which meandered through lush meadows and newly planted fields, down the valley, alongside a wide fast flowing river.

They left the cultivated lands, and entered into a maze of valleys, which were thickly forested with all manner of trees, included oak trees, which seemed to Aelnoth to be nothing like the giant oaks that choked the dense forests in the English shires, for almost all of these Welsh oaks were small, windblown and stunted.

Deer and boar teemed, but speedily vanished into the dense forests as soon as the noisy cavalcade came within a dozen bowshots of them.

Arnallt approached the cart that was being driven by Aelnoth just as they had halted on the second day for their mid day rest.

'We entered the lands of the Silures about a mile back, so keep your eyes skinned. Said Arnallt, as his eyes warily scanned the thickly forested hillsides.

'I know that we are supposed to be at peace with them, but you can never really trust the pigs.' He added.

'Many of them still hate us because of the whipping that we gave them over fifty years ago.'

'Aye,' answered Aelnoth. 'There is always the odd one here and there who finds it difficult to forgive and forget.'

His gaze fell on Arial who squatted near one of the fires, who was glaring at the chalky white young man who had humiliated him in front of his fellow warriors.

Aelnoth stared into the woodland, which encroached their camping site, and asked.

'How far do you think we are from the coast?'

'Oh, not too far. We should be there in a couple of days.'

'With a little luck,' he added with a smile.

Far from hiding their presence from the Silures, it seemed to the Englishmen that the warriors went out of their way to announce to the world that they were in the territory of another tribe, for they lit three large fires over which they roasted year old lambs, and whilst they were eating their meal, they sang loud and merry songs, and roared with laughter at one of the men, who appeared to be the clown of the group.

When Arnallt made his way around the sentries in the morning, he was shocked to find that no less than three of his five sentries lay dead.

Each of the three was headless.

The slain guards lay naked and spread-eagled on the ground, amidst dark congealed pools of their lifeblood.

After a flurry of activity with warriors dashing about in utter chaos, as they grabbed their shields and weapons, they eventually formed a circle around the carts and horses,

Arnallt called to a man who was called Elwyn the F'F'F'Fox, and although they all acknowledged his skill at following a trail, it did not deter the warriors from poking fun at him, on account of the nervous stutter, which he had possessed since childhood.

Elwyn was so named because he was the finest tracker in the Cornovi, and it was his boast that he could track a ghost through a fogbank.

Aelnoth was standing by Arnallt as he spoke to the tracker, and he was not at all impressed with what he saw, for all he could see was a ragged middle aged man, who was as thin as a bean pole. He had stick thin legs, which did not look strong enough to support his meagre weight.

'Elwyn.' Said Arnallt, 'I want you to scout around the camp, and see if we are still in danger, or if it was just one or two warriors out for a head.'

Elwyn merely nodded and loped off into the surrounding woodland.

It was a long time before Elwyn returned, and it appeared to Arnallt that, unusually for the man who he had been known for most of his life as a famous tracker, the man seemed to be perspiring badly, and was gasping for breath.

'Well?' growled Arnallt.

'I f, f, found them my L,L, Lord.' He panted.

'I fol, fol, followed them for at least five miles, but they w, w, went into a small river and I l.l.lost their spoor.' He said almost apologetically as if it was a crime, or perhaps he was just a little ashamed that a man of his ability could lose a trail.

'But I tr, tr, tracked them along the stream bed, you know.' He said as his puny chest puckered out a little.

'An, an, upturned stone here a, a, and there.'

'A f, f, faint footprint on a m,m, mossy stone.'

'The usual Th, Th, thing.' As if it was an every day occurrence.

'Followed them t, ter, to their camp.' He stuttered.

'Saw ser, sev, seventeen of 'em.'

'M, m, might be more.'

'I r,ran all the way back to give you the n,n,news.' He added

'Good man.' Said Arnallt as he slapped him on his shoulder.

'At least we are safe from them for the time being.'

'Collect some wood.' He shouted to his warriors, 'and we can send the spirits of our men to heaven before we move on.'

A funeral pyre was quickly built and the bodies of the three slain men were reverently placed on top.

Arnallt said the few words of Latin that he knew before he lit the fire, which sent the souls of the dead, cloaked in dark clouds of smoke, up into the clear morning sky.

'That'll tell every man and his dog that we are here.' Mumbled Aelnoth to his friends as they followed the warriors to the horses and carts, in order to resume their journey.

'We cannot let these savages get away with killing three of our men.' said Arnallt in a loud voice.

'That would tell all our neighbours that the Cornovi are cowards and nithings.'

'You two.' He pointed towards Oscar and Magnus. 'You are still wounded and unfit to fight, but you, Aelnoth can ride with me and some of my men and you will see how the Cornovi avenge their slain comrades.'

Arnallt had assembled ten of his warriors to accompany Elwyn, and were about to leave, when their small glade was suddenly invaded by a dozen horsemen, who reined in their mounts in front of Arnallt, in a flurry of sods and flying pebbles.

'Ah, well if it isn't my old friend Arnallt.' Shouted the leader who was still in the act of bringing his pure-white stallion under control.

'What brings the prince of the Cornovi into the land of the Silures?'

Arnallt reached across from his own mare and took the outstretched hand of Owen, who he had not seen for at least five years, and who had, over those five years, developed from a pimply faced youth, into the broad shouldered, robust young man, who now sat on one of the finest white stallion's he had ever seen.

'Hail Owen,' said Arnallt in the friendliest tone that he could muster.

'Prince of the Silures.'

'It is good to see you, but alas, I was on the point of leaving to pursue some bandits who raided us in the night and slew three of my sentries.'

'Were they Silures?' asked Owen.

'I don't know who they were,' answered Arnallt honestly, 'but when we catch up with them they will be dead. Silures, Cornovi, Ordovice or whatever.'

'I will ride with you,' said the Prince of the Silures, as a wide grin spread across his young face, and he wrenched the reins of his stallion around, in order to ride alongside Arnallt.

'I expect that you are bringing gifts to my father, so that I may condescend to marry your sister?' he asked with a wide grin, which spread even wider across his boyish face.

Before Arnallt could answer, Owen continued.

'Is she fair? Or is she the usual sort of spinster that is usually left on the shelf at her age?'

'She is the most beautiful maiden in the whole of Wales.' Came the indignant answer from Arnallt.

'Oh you would say that, being her brother.'

'Believe me,' snorted the now angry Arnallt. 'She is the most beautiful woman alive, and far too good for an untried youth such as you.'

Owens face reddened and although he let the insult pass, both of the Princes knew that he was seething with rage.

Owen knew that his father had already agreed to the match, so his calculating mind told him that beauty or not, his destiny was to marry the girl in order to secure an alliance with the Silures, so he rode in silence alongside the man who had just insulted him.

'How come the Cornovi ride with Englishmen?' he asked in a low but ominous voice.

Arnallt cleared his throat in order to allow himself a little time before he answered a question that he rather resented. He was. Was he not the Prince of the Cornovi? And although the question had come from a man of equal rank, it still rankled him.

'They saved my sister from being raped, and they escorted her safely home.' He said.

'Oh.' Mumbled the Silures Prince, as he turned in his saddle to study the three Englishmen.

'Two are wounded?' he questioned.

'Was that in the fight to save your sister?'

'No. They were wounded before that.'

'That only leaves the boy then?'

'Aye.'

'He must be good.'

'I believe he is, for he slew four Ordovice warriors.

'Mmm.' He muttered as he turned again in the saddle to survey the boy, and stroking his sparse beard he said, 'Is he as good as me?'

'How good are you?'

'The best there is,' or so my father tells me.'

'Have you slain four Ordovices?

'Well no. Not yet.'

'Well, when you have, you might, just might be good enough to best that boy, for according to my sister who witnessed the fight, he was like one of God's avenging angels.'

'Mmm' said Prince Owen of the Silures as he again stroked the few sparse hairs, which had sprouted on his boyish chin, as he eased his horse back a little to rejoin his own men who were riding a short distance behind.

CHAPTER 9

The cavalcade followed Emrys the fox down the valleys and through the woodlands, until they reached the river that he had told them about.

Emrys did not enter the water, but rode along the riverbank, and placed his index finger over his lips.

'Quiet.' Said Arnallt. 'We must be nearing their lair.' Causing the riders to cease the friendly banter that had been taking place between the warriors of the Silures and the Cornovi.

Half a mile further Emrys urged his mount into a small copse of stunted oak and dismounted.

The warriors followed him, dismounted and tied their horse's reins to the branches of the low-lying trees.

'U, u.up the, there,' stammered Emrys, as he pointed to an almost hidden pathway, which followed the small river.

Arnallt called one of the warriors over to him and said, 'I want you to stay here and look after the horses. I will take the men forward and see what sort of men think that they can take Cornovi heads with impunity,'

Arnallt led the way up the path, which followed the small river up the hill, but was brought to a halt by a tap on the shoulder.

Angry at being stopped by one of his own warriors, he turned and glowered at the man, but was slightly startled when he saw that the man was no other than Aelnoth the Englishman.

'What?'

'I smell wood smoke.'

'So?'

'I suggest that we leave the river and filter through the trees on the right until we can see what we are blundering into.' He whispered into the leaders' ear.

'Blundering. Blundering.' He almost choked.

'I am not blundering anywhere.' He snarled.

'They don't know we are coming.'

'They have probably lived here for years, and will not be expecting to be attacked in such a remote place like this.' He snarled in a whisper.

'But they are bound to have a sentry or a lookout somewhere.' Said Aelnoth.

'Better to be safe than sorry.' He added.

Arnallt fumed that this English puppy should tell him what to do, and what not to do, in the mountains of HIS homeland, but then he recalled the warning that his father had given him before he set out on this venture.

'Remember,' he had said.

'You are a Prince of this realm, and the whole kingdom depends on you. For you and you alone will inherit my Kingdom when I am gone.'

'Do not. I repeat. Do not get into any fights.'

'I don't want you to return slung over the hindquarters of a pack animal.'

He recalled his father's fierce eyes, and the way that he had prodded him in his chest with his gnarled and arthritic finger. Winching as he had done so.

His hands grasped the sacred sword, which his father had given him as a gift on his sixteenth birthday, and allowed his anger to slowly subside.

'I will do as you suggest.' He said quietly to Aelnoth, as he waved his arm in the direction of the nearby woodland.

'Follow me.' He said in a quiet voice and he led the way, off the path and into the dense woodland.

After perhaps two hundred yards, Emrys the fox held up his hand, and turned as he crouched down, and faced the men who had been silently following him.

'Th,' The', There,' he stammered quietly, and pointed towards the end of the woodland, some twenty or so feet in front of them.

Aelnoth and Arnallt crawled forward and passed Emrys to the very edge of the wood, where they could see a small village that was bustling with life, for there were women, who were in the process of doing womanly chores, children shouting and playing, and men lolling around, doing manly things that men usually do in the heat of the mid-morning, such as attending to their weapons, dicing or generally doing little more than chatting with their neighbours.

The two men carefully retreated to rejoin the bulk of their men who were resting and preparing themselves for the fight, which they knew must come.

'They are not of the Cornovi,' whispered Arnallt.

'Are they Silures?' he asked Owen.

'Don't know. I'll go and have a look.' answer the baby-faced prince of the Silures, who without further ado, crept carefully towards the edge of the wood.

When he returned he said, 'Well, I did see a couple of Ordovices, but the rest could be from the moon. They are probably the same renegades who have been raiding the outlying farms of my people for the last couple of years.'

'Could never find 'em.' He snarled quietly.

'Well we have found them now and I don't care which tribe they come from.'

'If these are the same slimy bastards who killed my three guards, then revenge is mine.' Said Arnallt quietly.

'What about the women and children?' asked Prince Owen?

'Can't kill them, can we?' he added quietly.

'Take 'em prisoner,' said Arnallt. 'I could do with a new slave woman, and we can sell the youngsters on the slave block, and this journey might turn out to be profitable after all.

We will split 'em between the three of us.' Said Owen with a smile.

'I don't want any,' said Aelnoth.

'All I want is to get these bloody coffins to Ireland.' He added.

'Great!' Exclaimed Owen gleefully.

'That leaves just me and you.' He said, as he turned to face Arnallt.

His fellow Prince nodded in agreement and the two leaders commenced to organise their men into two bands in order to surround the village.

Aelnoth seemed to have been forgotten in the discussion, and was left to decide which band he should join in the coming fight.

A horn sounded three times as the sun reached its zenith, and the two bodies of men stormed out of the woodland in a semi-circle of gleaming weapons, which drove the screaming women and children before them in the direction of the river.

The men were isolated and disorganised by the sudden attack, and although many snatched up their weapons and fought, they were soon either hacked down, or forced to throw down their weapons and surrender, causing the skirmish to be over in a matter of minutes.

Aelnoth counted twenty-three women, eighteen children of varying ages and six surviving men.

Arnallt strode in front of the survivors brandishing his bloody sword in one hand and waving a head of one of his slain warriors in the other.

'I found this head in that hut over there.'

He pointed to a hut close to the centre of the village.

'Whose hut is it?' he demanded.

There was no reply.

'Search the other huts for the other two heads.' He said to four of his warriors who were standing behind him, and they sped off to do their Prince's bidding.

He continued to pace up and down in front of the cowering villagers, and whilst he realised that his very presence was menacing.

The fact that he waved his bloody sword in their faces, as strode arrogantly in front of them, caused most of the crowd to cower and look at the ground, refusing to meet his savage stare.

It was a ploy that he had learned from his father the King, and although this was the first time that he had put this particular ploy into practice, he was pleased to see that it was actually working, for no less than two of the captured warriors stared at him, with faces of stone, whilst sweat dripped down their beards and onto their shirts, as if they were not standing in the sun on a beautiful day such as this, but were standing in a heavy downpour of rain.

Three of his men returned carrying the two remaining heads of his slain sentries.

'Sorry it took so long.' Gasped one of his men. 'There was a lot to choose from, and some had been mutilated so badly that their own mothers would be hard put to recognise them.'

The last of the four warriors returned but he carried no heads.

He returned dragging a filthy half clothed woman behind him, who was still chained to the post, which he carried on his shoulder.

'What on earth have you got there?' said Arnallt.

'I found her on the edge of the wood,' answered the warrior.

'I wouldn't have noticed her, except that I followed one of the men who must have hidden and tried to escape.'

'I followed him into the wood and although I lost him. I did find her.'

'She was chained to this post.'

'I couldn't get the chain off her so I pulled up the post.' He said as he puffed out his chest, as if he was proud that he had managed to pull up the post, which had been buried at least three feet deep in the dark peaty soil.

'Now we have two dilemmas',' Said Aelnoth.

'One. We still haven't identified the men who killed your sentries, and two.'

'Why was the woman chained to a post, and not kept as a slave or claimed by one of the men?'

'Bring those two men forward.' Ordered Arnallt as he pointed out the two men who he suspected might be the slayers of his men.

The two suspects were immediately pulled out from the crowd, and forced to kneel before him.

'Did you take the heads of my men?' he snarled as one of his men held the three heads up before the kneeling men.

'No my Lord.' Stammered the eldest of the two. 'You have just slain the men who took them.' He said more boldly as he stared up into the iron hard eyes of Arnallt.

Arnallt looked at the second man, who was little more than a youth, and was still kneeling. His eyes stared down at the earth, and Arnallt could see the youth's body shaking with fear, as he fully expected that his life was about to be brought to an abrupt end.

He pointed to the younger man and said to two of his men who stood alongside him. 'Bring him.' He snarled.

The two men, who carried three heads between them, placed the heads reverently onto the ground, before they grabbed the youngster and half dragged and half carried him, as they followed their leader into a hut.

'Untie him.' He ordered, and one of the men cut through the boy's bonds.

The second man stood in the doorway, holding a bloodied axe in his right hand.

'Tell me.' Said Arnallt. 'Were you one of the men who attacked my camp and returned with the heads of three of my men?'

'No. No. Really my Lord. It was not me.'

'Who were they then?'

'You have already killed three of them.' He said hurriedly.

'Was that man out there one of them?' he snarled at the cowering youth.

'He. He. I'm not sure my Lord.'

'Tell me the truth now.' Snarled Arnallt, 'or I shall get my man here to slice off your hands, and then your feet with that nice big axe of his.' As he nodded towards the blood stained war-axe that was now resting on the ground, a few feet away from the youngsters face.

'Your friend over there can't hurt you now, so you can tell me, and save yourself.' Said Arnallt with the most reassuring a smile that he could bring his face to make.

The captive was still unwilling to name the man as one of the killers, looked down at the earth, convinced that he was about to die, whether or not he condemned the man.

'Is he one of your kin?' asked Arnallt.

The youth shook his head.

'Are you bound to him by oath?'

Again the youth shook his head.

'Come now. Tell me if he is one of the men, and I swear by all that is holy that I will not harm you, and you can join my people as a free man.'

The youth slowly stopped shaking and raised his head to look up into Arnallt's face.

'Was he one of them?'

The youth slowly made a nod that was almost imperceptible.

'Are you sure?'

This time the nod was more distinct.

'Aye. My Lord. He was one of them.' He said with more conviction.

'You are free to go' said Arnallt as he turned to exit the hut, but then he halted in the doorway and turned again towards the youth.

'How are you known?' He asked.

'Awell, My Lord.' in a voice that had begun to tremble again for the still could not quite believe that after all the slaughter that he had seen in the last hour, he was being allowed not only to live, but also to go free.

'The girl. The girl in chains.'

'Tell me of her?'

Awell gave an audible sigh of relief, for he had feared that this Chieftain had changed his mind and was about to order his death.

'She is a captive my Lord. Taken about a week since on a raid near the coast.'

'She is a warrior woman from Ireland, and slew two of our men.'

'They were going to burn her alive at the next full moon.'

Awell silently cursed himself for having been so stupid to mention the word 'OUR,' but he knew that a word once spoken, cannot be unspoken, and wished he had paid more attention to the teachings of his old grandmother, who had done her best to drill her vast knowledge into his young head.

'Ireland you say?'

The youth nodded, and silently thanked God that this killer of men had not taken offence at his use of the word, 'OUR'.

'Remain here until we have gone.' Ordered Arnallt.

Many of the people noticed that when Arnallt strode out of the hut with the two warriors who had accompanied him in, and who now followed him out, there was no sign of the youth who they all knew of as 'Awell.'

The captive who was known to all as 'Andras the cruel' especially noted Anwell's absence.

Arnallt stood before the assembly and said in a loud voice so that all could hear him.

'Cut the chains off the woman,' he ordered, and one of his men stepped forward and sliced through the chains with one blow of his axe.

She shook her body and the chains dropped to the floor like a cascade of water.

The Woman stepped towards Arnallt and knelt at his feet, uttering words that he could not understand, although he assumed, correctly, that she was thanking him for her release, and seemed to be pledging her allegiance to him.

He touched her on her head and half lifted her to her feet, indicating to her that she should stand alongside him.

She meekly obeyed his indications, and stood erect at his side.

He took a pace forward and addressed the assembled people.

'You people who have preyed upon helpless farm folk, and have slain travellers, will now pay for your sins.'

He waited a moment for the mumblings to cease.

'My warriors will be allowed to take any children and women as slaves or as bondswomen, and if those women chosen have children, then they will be allowed to accompany their mothers.'

'The rest of you will be taken to the coast to be sold as slaves.'

There were groans and cries of alarm, which were drowned by the cheering of his warriors, who scramble forward to choose the most comely of the womenfolk as their own.

After even more shouting and cries of joy, mingled with screams of alarm, the hubbub eventually died down, allowing order to be restored.

The few captives, who had not been chosen by the warriors, were tied and tethered to each other, and made ready to accompany their captors out of the encampment.

Arnallt called his personal bodyguard over to him.

'Kill him.' He ordered as he turned to 'Andras the Cruel.'

One of his men kicked the captive behind his knees forcing him to stagger to the ground with a loud grunt, but the captive raised his head and glared angrily up as one of the men raised his axe and took his head off with one blow of the razor sharp weapon.

'This.' Shouted Arnallt, as he held the dripping head up towards the watching crowd of captives and captors.

'This is what happens to men who wage war against my people.'

'This head will grace my Hall for many years to come.' He shouted as he thrust the grisly head into one of the many ready-made sacks, which all the warriors of Wales took with them when they went to war.

'Slay the rest of the male prisoners.'

'Burn the place.' He ordered and his men immediately carried out his orders.

CHAPTER 10

The captive women and children caused the pace of the warriors to slow down to such an extent that Aelnoth began to think that he would never reach Oscar, Magnus and Ingrid, but despite the delays, they did eventually reach his friends and the few guard's who he had been assigned to look after the carts, as darkness descended.

Both Magnus and Oscar were much recovered, although one of the wounds, which Magnus had received, was still inflamed, and stubbornly refused to heal.

The enlarged party commenced their journey through the valleys, passing tiny hamlets, sleepy villages and isolated farmsteads, until they reached the river Dovey.

They followed the river to the sea.

The village of Aberdovey did not have a proper port, but did possess a rocky outcrop, which appeared to have been hacked out of the living rock many years ago.

The tide was out when they reached the village, with no less than four merchant vessels resting on their sides in the mud.

Aelnoth and his two companions drove their carts onto the beach, high above the line of smelly fly covered seaweed and flotsam, which marked the line of the high tide.

Aelnoth thanked Arnallt and his warriors for escorting them to the coast, and waved them farewell, as Arnallt and his men herded their prisoners before them, and began their homeward journey.

Suddenly there was a commotion from the midst of Arnallt's warriors, who suddenly parted, as the form of a girl broke free, and raced towards the three Englishmen.

At first Aelnoth did not recognize the girl, but as she reached him, he realised that it was the girl who had been chained to the post in the bandits camp.

Yet, to him she did not look like the same girl, for when he had last seen her, she had been dressed in rags, covered in mud and filthy.

Now, the girl who stood gasping for breath a few feet before him, had somehow acquired a garment that passed for a dress.

Her hair had been washed and combed, and gleamed like burnished bronze.

Her face shone and her eyes sparkled in the sunlight.

The thing that totally captivated him as she stood and looked up at him, were her vividly blue eyes, which stood out like twin beacons from her sunburned face.

'I go with you.' She said in broken English as she patted her ample bosom with her right hand and pointed towards the ocean.

He looked into the distance and saw the tail end of Arnallt's warriors and the line of slaves, as they began to disappear in the distance, and decided that even if Arnallt and his men knew that the girl had escaped, they did not seem to be concerned about her departure, as they had not bothered to chase after her, so he had little option other than to nod in agreement to the girl, and allow her to remain with him.

As Aelnoth could speak a little of the Welsh tongue, he was elected to search out the owners or captains of the four ships, whilst Oscar and Magnus stayed with the carts in order to protect their contents.

The strange auburn haired girl savagely plonked herself down in front of the leading cart and glowered, as she watched Aelnoth make his way across the shingle towards the cluster of houses that called itself the township of Aberdovey.

There were no people visible in the single street, which curved around the estuary, but Aelnoth was only too aware that each of the cottages he passed contained eyes which literally bored into the back of his head.

He was relieved as he approached the largest house, when he saw the sign containing two crudely painted mackerels, denoting, he hoped, that that the place was a tavern, and should be a place where he would find the captains, or at least some sea farers, who would be able to help him and his companions to sail to Ireland.

He entered a room that was completely empty, with the exception of a long, roughly hewn table and a number of stools.

He sat on a stool and thumped the table with the hilt of his eating knife.

Despite the echo of the noise he made, there was no sound of movement in the house.

He knew that the occupants of the house were at home, because he had not only seen the curtains move, but he had also seen a slight movement as he had passed the one and only window, which overlooked the estuary.

He banged again, louder.

Nothing.

He rose and walked over to the door that led into the interior of the house, and banged on it.

'I have come a long way.' He said loudly in the best Welsh that he could muster, 'and my mouth is as dry as a black bears armpit.'

He heard a slight noise, and a few moments later the latch clattered.

The door opened, to reveal a small, round old woman, who was dressed in black and carried a wooden drinking cup in one hand and a leather jug brimming with ale in the other.

Without looking at her guest, she shuffled past him towards the table, where she plonked both of her charges onto the table, spilling a large quantity of beer before she turned with her hands on her hips, and gazed at her one and only customer.

Aelnoth followed her and sat down.

He reached into his purse and flipped a small silver coin towards her, which she deftly caught, and immediately placed the coin between her teeth.

Her face slowly cracked into a sly smile as she looked at this English idiot who, for the purchase of one jug of ale, had just given her enough silver to clear every last drop of beer out of her cellar.

'Silver.' She said in English.

'You speak English,' exclaimed the astonished man.

'Oh we get all sorts here,' she said.

'English. Irish. Norsemen. Celts from Scotia. Even the odd Moor.' And as the word 'Moor' left her lips, she spat generously onto her own floor.

'The silver was for the ale, some food, and a little information.' Said Aelnoth with a false smile, for in truth he had taken an instant dislike to the woman.

'So. This English pig is not as stupid as he looks.' She mused to herself.

'What sort of information?'

'Oh, nothing too severe. I just need to hire either a captain or a ship to take my friends and myself over to Ireland.' He said in a casual tone.

'Just you and how many friends?'

'Three men and two girls'

'Nothing else?' Just the five of you?'

'Yes. Well we do have six coffins as well.'

'Christ alive.' She exclaimed as she made the sign of the cross across her ample chest, but then her acute mind thought about the six coffins, for they would be yet another reason for her to raise the price of any deal that was to be made.

'What's in the coffins?'

'What do you damned well think is in the coffins?' was the curt reply.

'Why do you want to take them to Ireland?'

'What's wrong with good honest Welsh soil?' she asked as a sly smile crossed her fat, greasy face.

'They are not Welsh bodies,' said Aelnoth as calmly as he could, for he was beginning to get annoyed at this grubby old landlady, who had already asked more questions than she should, so he changed the line of the conversation in order to prevent her from asking any more difficult questions.

'Well.' He said rather harshly.

'Do you know who the ships belong to or not?'

She stroked her bristly chin and squinted a little as she looked up into his eyes.

'Indeed I do my friend.' She said.

'The largest and the finest of those ships belong to my goodself and my husband.'

'But the question is. Do you have enough silver to hire him?'

Before he could answer, she stepped a few paces towards the door, which she flung open to reveal an old bearded man, who had obviously been listening to their conversation through the half opened door.

'I knew you'd be there,' she said in a sarcastic voice.

'This is my husband Idris, who is the finest seaman in these parts, and knows these waters like the back of his hand.'

Aelnoth shook the man's dirty outstretched hand, and found the shake of the man's leathery hand to be firm and friendly.

'Enough of the niceties.' Snapped the wife.

'Let's talk money.'

She turned to Idris and said to him, (just in case he had not overheard the entire conversation).

'This Englishman wants you to take him and his friends, as well as six coffins over to Ireland.'

'How much will you charge?' she asked as she walked away, only to retrace her steps a few moments later with two leather bottles brimming with ale, as well as two additional wooden cups.

The cups were filled and refilled many times, and the stale cheese and dry bread consumed, before the bargain was sealed, and although it did cost Aelnoth a few silver pennies more than he would have liked, they did agree that Idris and his wife would provide enough food and small beer, to fulfil the needs of the crew and passengers for the journey.

The ship sailed down the estuary and out to sea on the high tide at noon the following day, complete with the three Englishmen and their coffins as well as Ingrid and the Irish girl, plus Idris and two of his sons.

The day was fine, and by mid-day the sun had burned away the sea mist, which had persisted for most of the morning.

A good breeze blew from the east, filling the single sail and sending the thirty-foot ship skimming over the millpond that was called the Irish Sea.

By dusk, the breeze had grown into a stiff wind, and the millpond had become a choppy sea with heavy swells, which seemed to the passengers to be so enormous, that they feared that the huge waves would swamp the ship.

The ship that had appeared to be so big, when it had been moored on the mud flats, now seemed to be so small and vulnerable, that the passengers doubted that they would ever see land again.

However, Idris and his two sons' seemed to be unconcerned, for they chatted merrily away as they sat and steered the ship, adjusting a line now and again in order to catch the correct amount of wind, which sent the vessel speeding gracefully up and down the enormous troughs.

Much to the obvious glee of the three seamen, the faces of the three Englishmen and the two girls had long since turned to a pallid colour of whitish green, as they continued to puke up the contents of their stomachs, until all that they could retch up was a slimy bile, which dribbled down their faces and onto their clothes.

One of the seamen steered the ship through the night whilst the other two slept, but sleep eluded the passengers, who spent a wet and very uncomfortable night clinging to their benches, as the ship, which seemed to have a mind of its own, and continued to lurch upwards, downwards, and then to one side or the other, or, as it seemed to the five seasick passengers, all of the aforementioned at the same time.

Dawn broke slowly to reveal a clear sky and a somewhat calmer sea, which stretched to the horizon in every direction.

Aelnoth was feeling slightly better and shouted across to Idris, who had again taken the tiller. 'How far now?'

'Half a day. Maybe more.' Answered Idris.

'Which way is Ireland?'

Idris nodded in the direction of the prow of the ship.

'How do you know?'

'Been there before.' Answered Idris in a voice that showed annoyance that this silly English whelp could have the nerve to ask such a stupid question, and question his seamanship.

'I know.' Said Aelnoth. 'But how can you know which way to go in the dark and with no land in sight.'

'By the stars, and now the sun.' Snuffled the angry Welsh Captain.

They could see land long before darkness fell, but by the time it was pitch black, Idris had ordered the sail be brought down, and he helped his son's to heave the large anchor stone overboard, thus bringing the vessel to a halt.

'We will wait here for the morning.' He announced as he pulled his shabby leather hat down over his eyes and settled down for a sleep.

'Why?' asked the naïve Aelnoth.

'Rocks,' was the reply from under the hat.

All five passengers slept a little before being wakened by the two younger seamen who grunting loudly as they heaved the anchor stone up from the seabed.

Idris, who was allowing his two strapping sons to haul up the anchor, pointed to the mountains on his left.

'Those are the Wicklow Mountains,' he said, 'and the mouth of that bay over there will lead us up the estuary of the river Liffey to the town of Dublin.'

'Do you know what the name 'Dublin' means? Asked Captain Idris.

'No,' answered Aelnoth. For he cared little what the name meant.

The only thing that was on his mind at that precise moment in time was to reach land, and stand again on something that was not in perpetual motion.

'It means 'Blackpool,' shouted Idris to make his voice heard over the wind that had begun to get up again.

'Probably the peat.' he added, although he said it in such a quiet voice that no one probably heard him.

Once the anchor stone had been placed as gently as possible into its niche on the deck, the two sons hauled up the sail and the ship began to make headway towards the mouth of the Liffey.

*   *   *

The port of Dublin was crowded with all manner of vessels, ranging from round coracles, through the various stages of large and small trading ships, to sleek, Viking Dragon ships, causing Idris to lower the sail, and order his sons to man the oars, in order to row the ship towards a space along the shingle beach.

They were met by a band of ten armed men.

'Vikings.' Muttered Idris.

'You lot keep quiet and let me do the talking.'

'Not likely,' said Magnus in a firm voice, as he shouldered his way past Idris and stood on the prow of the ship.

'Who are you, who enter our port without permission?' demanded the leader of the Danes.

'That space was taken.' He snarled.

'Who are you, to meet us with arms?' answered Magnus.

'Is Dublin not an open city? Ruled by my kinsman Dairmat, King of Leinster?' he lied.

'If you are kinsman to the King, then we will escort you to him?' said the leader whose weather-beaten face cracked with a savage grin.

'Before you do that.' Answered Magnus.

'I will have to hire men or carts to carry these sacred bones to my father, who is the Earl Magnus Godwinson.' He turned and nodded towards the coffins.

'And then I will accompany you to Dairmat.'

'Oh we shall see about that.' Snarled the Dane as his hand flew to the hilt of his sword.

'There is no need for that.' Said Aelnoth, who now stood to the left of Magnus with a notched arrow in his hunting bow that was pointing directly at the heart of the Dane.

'Perhaps your men would like to assist us to take these coffins to my father.' Said Magnus.

'I take it you know where he is?' he questioned.

'I do.' Said the man with a snarl. 'He is out hunting.'

'He is ALWAYS out hunting.'

He stared at the drawn bow and then turned his gaze to the steely hard eyes of Aelnoth, and saw in them, the eyes of a killer.

'There is a farm cart there.' He said to his men.

'Load those coffins onto it and we can be done with this business.'

Aelnoth relaxed his hold on the bow and slowly lowered it.

Several of the Danes scrambled aboard, and with more than a little effort, four of the men managed to manoeuvre each coffin off the ship, up the embankment and onto the cart, whilst the owner of the cart stood by helpless, and then followed, as his ox and his cart were driven up the slope and into the township.

Dublin was a small place, and it did not take long before the cart was brought to a halt before a house, which was the largest building that they had seen in the town.

Two tough looking guards stood by the doorway, holding round English shields and large English or Danish axes, for indeed it would take a good man to tell a Danish axe from an English one.

Magnus strode up to the entrance only to find that his way was barred as two shields, as they clashed together in front of his face.

'Hold Varlet.' Snapped one of the sentries.

'Where do you think you are going'?

The men reeked strongly of damp leather, sweat and stale beer.

'To see my Sire, Earl Magnus Godwinson.' Snarled Magnus as he brought his knee up into the groin of the man on his left, and then slapped the second man across his ears with the hilt of the Saex, which had miraculously appeared in his right hand.

Both men fell to the ground, and as they did so Magnus calmly stooped down and disarmed them.

He threw their weapons to one side and helped the two shocked sentries to their feet.

'I am Magnus. Son of Magnus. Who is, I believe your Liege Lord.'

'Now if you would be kind enough to escort myself and my friends and our belongings into the building, we will make ourselves comfortable and await the arrival of my father.'

The Danes and the two sentries carried the coffins into the building, and after laying them down in the Main hall; they left the travellers alone in the empty house.

It was not long after dusk, when the clatter of hooves and the racket made by shouting men announced the return of Earl Magnus, who swept into the room like a whirlwind, only to be brought to an abrupt halt when he saw that there were strangers standing in HIS hall, warming themselves before HIS fire, and more importantly, they seemed to be guzzling HIS ale.

'Who in the name of God are you?' he roared at the top of his voice.

'Who the name of hell do you think it is,' shouted his son as loudly as he could.

'Don't you recognize your own son?

You must be getting old.' He added as he stepped forward.

'God's blood.' Exclaimed the Earl as he finally glared into the face of his son.

'I thought you were dead.' He bellowed as he stepped forward and threw his huge arms around his son.

'Obviously not.' Answered Magnus the Younger.

'I was only wounded.' Adding, 'although I think it was touch and go for a while.'

'Thanks be to God.' He said loudly as he crossed himself.

'And who are these ruffians?'

Magnus the Younger introduced Oscar and Aelnoth but ignored the girls.

The formidable father of Magnus, shook hands with Oscar and Aelnoth and bade them welcome.

'How dare you wear a hood in my presence?' Snapped the Earl at Oscar.

'Are you an assassin or a thief?'

'Neither my Lord,' answered Oscar in the most pleasant manner that he could speak, for he was quite used to people's questions, as well as their shock, when on the few occasions, he had been made to take the hood off to reveal his unusual appearance.

'I'm afraid that I am an Albino, and I do have trouble with my eyes in bright lights.' He answered, 'but if your lordship insists I will take the mask and hood off.' He offered.

'Nay, Nay my boy.' Said the Earl in a jovial way.

'I have seen an Albino once and that was quite enough.'

Aelnoth could not help to notice how father and son resembled one another, for whilst Earl Magnus had streaks of white in his carefully combed beard and hair, and indeed, he was wider in the girth than his son. He still retained the same colouring and profile as his son, as well as the wide shoulders and the bearing of a warrior.

His son was exactly the same height as his father. He had the same straw-coloured hair, and his much younger face had the same strikingly blue eyes, which carried the same stark warning, that was enough to tell any potential adversary to stay clear, but they were both the faces of men who seemed to make many maidens go weak at their knees.

'Who are the girls?' asked the Father

'The thin girl is Aelnoth's sister,' he lied, for he was only too aware of his fathers liking for young girls.'

'The other one is just some girl we rescued from a band of cutthroats, and we brought her with us.'

'I think she is Irish.'

'Irish. Irish you say?'

'I have adopted one of these Heathens who speak passable English.' He said jovially.

'Paidric.' He roared at the top of his voice, and a few moments later the clump of feet announced the arrival of a dark haired youth with shifty brown eyes, and the beginnings of a youthful beard, which had begun to sprout out of his spotty chin.

'Paidric. 'Ask the girl her name and where she is from,' he commanded.

Paidric walked over to the girl, who was soon talking in a language that seemed to Aelnoth to be nearer to the ranting of a drunken Welshman, than any other tongue that he had ever heard spoken.

Paidric turned to the Earl and said.

'Her name is Teresa, and she says that she is the daughter of Mide, Conchobar Ua Maelsechalinn, who is a great lord in Navan.'

'Navan,' exclaimed the Earl.

'I know Navan. I have hunted near the town of Navan many times.'

'So! She is the daughter of a lord? We shall have to think on that,' as his agile mind immediately flew to the word, 'Ransom,' but then, for the first time since he had entered the room, he noticed the six coffins, which were stacked in the shadows along one of the walls.

'Coffins. Coffins.' He bellowed even louder, in a voice that echoed around the room and into every other room in the house.

'Who the hell brought coffins into my Hall?'

'Don't they know that to bring a coffin into a man's Hall is bad luck?'

'I brought them in father.' Said Magnus the Younger in a quiet voice, which brought an instant silence to the room.

'And I don't think that these coffins will bring you bad luck,' and added in an even quieter voice.

'In fact, quite the opposite.'

'Oh. And why is that?' Said his father in a suspicious voice, as he became a little calmer, and his red face slowly began to resume its normal colour.

'Come and see,' said his son, as he walked over to the coffins.

He took his sturdy Saex out of its sheath and commenced to prise the lid off the topmost coffin, and after a little exertion, he lifted the lid and threw it onto the floor where it landed with a loud thud and a cloud of dust.

'God's blood,' exclaimed the Earl. 'Where did this come from?' as he plunged one of his hands into the coffin and held up a handful of silver, which he allowed to dribble slowly back into the metal chest.

But before his son could answer.

'Are they all filled with silver?' He asked.

And then he realised that he had seen the chests before, and knew where they had come from.

'These are the chests that I buried back in England.' He said loudly as he placed his arm clumsily across the shoulders of his son.

'They are indeed.' Answered his son.

'I have brought them here so that they can pay for an army of Norse and Irish mercenary's to take back that which we have lost to those Norman barbarians.'

'I take it that you still have the gold? He asked warily.

'Herrum,' said his father as he cleared his throat.

'Well, yes, of course I have. Well, most of it anyhow.'

'Me and my men cannot live here free of charge,' he continued.

'The King of does not give us free board and lodgings you know.'

'King Diarmait?' queried his son.

'The same.' Said his father with a grimace.

'I get on well with him. Most of the time.'

'Although he is a canny wee fellow, who will squeeze every last penny out of you, whether you are a peasant or a Prince.' He added.

'I hope that there is enough of your gold left, to add to my silver and raise an army?' questioned the son, with a hint of menace in his voice, for he knew only too well of his fathers long established vices.

Feeling brave, for probably the first time in his life before his formidable father, he spoke his true feelings, and said with a smile as he escorted his father back towards the table.

'I do hope that you have not spent all of the gold on wine, women and song?'

His father chuckled and answered.

'Well, I have spent most of it on wine women and song, and I wasted the rest.'

'Nay, my boy. I jest. There is a goodly sum left.'

'Certainly enough to fund a good sized army, as long as we can add yon silver to it.'

'Wine.' Bellowed the Earl, as he quickly changed the subject

'Bring wine and let us celebrate the return of my son with this treasure, which will help us to win back our homeland.'

Not only did the servants bring wine, but they also brought huge flagons of beer to the Hall, and much to the astonishment of Aelnoth, two men who clutched yellow pig-skin bladders with reeds inserted into them, appeared at the two doorways of the Hall and commenced to blow on the pipes as they squeezed the pig-skins, to produce what he could only think of a sound that seemed more akin to a cat, or perhaps a live pig that was being skinned alive.

He noticed that the din did not appear to be offending either the Irish or the exiled Englishmen, who shouted over the noise in order to make themselves heard, as they carried on drinking copious amounts of ale and wine.

A number of the Earls and English Lords joined them. Men who had followed the Earl into exile, joined them in the Hall, and the wine flowed until many of them either left for their beds or ended up snoring on the rushes of the hall.

As this was such a special occasion, Oscar, Magnus and Aelnoth drank more than they would normally drink, and although they were light-headed by the end of the evening, they did not join their fellow drinkers by collapsing onto the floor, but staggered to their rooms, where they flopped down onto the duck down mattresses, which had been laid out for them.

Aelnoth was surprised in the morning when he wakened, to find the rather beautiful face of Teresa facing him on the pillow, a mere six inches away from his own face, and when he turned over, he found himself staring into the young face of Ingrid, who lay sleeping as peacefully as a child, as she snuggled up close to him.

He gazed at her as if he was seeing her for the first time, noting the wide generous lips, her beautiful eyebrows, and her tiny pointed nose.

Her beauty entranced him and he felt a stirring in his loins.

'How could I not have noticed her beauty before?' he mused to himself, as he watched her breathing through her half open generous lips.

He could not recall her drinking more than one tiny goblet of wine the previous evening, but suddenly he did remember that she had been virtually by his elbow for most, if not all of the time.

Suddenly, with a slight movement, her eyes opened and without moving her head away from him, she gazed lovingly at him with the largest and bluest eyes that he had ever seen.

With an embarrassed grunt, he eased himself over her prone body and left both of the maidens in the bed, dressing so hurriedly that he put his shirt on back to front.

CHAPTER 11

Both of the maidens followed him into the Hall, where the servants had laid the table with freshly baked bread. Bacon, Ham, Venison, eggs and cheese. All placed on wooden platters.

Large leather bottles filled with small beer had been placed at intervals along the length of the table.

The only thing that slightly disturbed Aelnoth was the fact that there were at least a dozen men still lying on the rushes, fast asleep, or so he hoped, for he did recall that there had been at least two knife fights during last nights celebrations.

Oscar and Magnus entered the Hall, followed by Earl Magnus who breezed in a few moments later, full of the joys of spring, and not in the least affected by the amount of ale and wine that he had consumed the following evening.

Earl Magnus was escorted by four of his personal bodyguards, who did not appear to share his appetite for the morning meal, as they sat sullenly alongside him, and watched him, as he guzzled down a full tankard of ale, followed by mouthfuls of Ham, bread and cheese, which Aelnoth, who was watching him from the opposite side of the table, felt sure that he would choke on, if he stuffed a single extra morsel of food into his already overfilled mouth.

Aelnoth looked as casually as he could at the two girls who sat on opposite sides of the table, glaring at one another as they nibbled and played with their food.

Earl Magnus, almost as if he was aware of the thoughts that were going through Aelnoth's mind, suddenly looked up and stared directly at him.

'How now young Aelnoth?' He said, scattering morsels of food and saliva in all directions.

'What thought you of our celebrations last night?'

'Did you enjoy yourself?' he asked as he scattered another mouthful of residue in the direction of Aelnoth.

'I did indeed my Lord,' answered Aelnoth, for despite his dislike of the man, he was aware that as Earl Magnus was the brother of King Harold Godwinson, as such, his status demanded respect.

'I noticed that the dark haired Irish temptress never left your side.' He smirked.

'Neither did that doe eyed little English wench.' He added.

'Get in there my boy.' He said with a friendly wink.

'I would if I were you.'

'In fact I have. Not with her of course, but there will be a goodly clutch of fair haired babes born hereabouts in the next few months.'

He chuckled, and clutched his ample belly as his roars of laughter resounded around the Hall.

'Right,' roared the Earl as he swallowed yet another mouthful of ham.

'Time for the hunt.'

He turned to his son and the other two travellers.

'I take it that you will be joining us?'

It was more of an order than a question, and within the hour, all three had been provided with half wild Irish ponies and Boar spears, and followed the Earl, who was accompanied by twenty other mounted men, as they galloped through the town and out into the nearby forest.

No matter how heavy the rain, the following three weeks were spent in identical ways, as the Earl and his retinue scoured the forests and moorlands in their quest to slay wild boar, deer and a variety of fowl.

The evenings also followed an identical pattern, with the Earl and most of his men consuming copious amounts of food and drink, as they endured the infernal wailing of yet more Irish pipers.

After the twenty-fourth day of hunting the ever-elusive wild boar, Aelnoth purposely sat next to the Earl, and before the Earl had finished his second tankard of beer, he turned sideways and said to the Earl.

'My Lord, whilst I have always enjoyed the hunt. Wild boar and Stags were not the reason that my friends and myself journeyed to Ireland with twelve chests of silver.'

'Do you not think it time that we started gathering an army about us, so that we can return to England and kick the Normans out of our beloved country?'

'I like it here.' Stated the Earl bluntly, for he was not used to being questioned or doubted by his underlings.

'Why my Lord?' said Aelnoth. 'It is not home.'

'Do you not miss England?' he asked.

The Earl was, yet again put on his back foot by this impudent young stripling.

'Ireland is the cleanest country in the world.' He blustered, as he quoted a saying, which he had heard countless times since he landed in Ireland.

'For the good lord God washes this country with copious amounts of rain, each and every day.'

'It rains in Kent as well.' Said Aelnoth, who was determined to pursue his case, and equally determined not to be put off by this man, who he was beginning to think of as a drunkard and a wastrel.

The Earl sullenly looked into his half empty jug of beer but made no further comment.

'My Lord,' said Aelnoth boldly.

'May your son, Oscar and myself, have your leave to send messengers out to the outlying townships and villages to recruit warriors for our cause?'

'God's blood. NO!' he stormed as he lifted his tankard and thumped it back onto the table, spilling half of its contents as he did so.

He fumed and his face reddened for a while as he struggled to control his rage, which was being caused by this pimply-faced youngster, who had forced him into a corner, which he was reluctant to be in.

'Tis not my city, nor is it my land.' He said in an angry and trembling voice.

'I am merely a guest here.'

'The city is controlled by Bjorn, and he is here under the sufferance of King Diarmait.'

'Who then, should I seek for permission to recruit?' Asked Aelnoth.

'Either or both would suffice.' Was the gruff reply as the Earl emptied his tankard in one large, noisy gulp.

'Bjorn would be the nearest? Queried Aelnoth.

'Arrg.' Consented the Earl with a nod, as he held his empty tankard aloft for it to be refilled.

'Would you be so kind as to introduce your son and myself to him on the morrow?'

'I'm hunting on the morrow.'

'We could go early, and you could still get a good days hunting in.'

'Heerum.' He cleared his throat.

'I will consent to that, but you had better be up at the crack of dawn.'

'We will be.'

Oscar roused Aelnoth Oscar and Magnus before dawn on the following morning.

They broke their fast and made their way towards the room where the Earl usually slept.

They were halted by the two bleary eyed guards, who lolled by the doorway to his room.

'What do you want at this unearthly hour?' Growled one of the men.

'We agreed to meet the Earl before first light this morning.' said Aelnoth pleasantly.

'He's still abed and will not be up for some time.' Said the man.

'We will wait.'

'You can't wait here.'

'Why not?'

'Because I bloody well said you can't.' snarled the guard as his hand grasped the hilt of his sword.

'Then we will wait in the great Hall.' Said Aelnoth as he turned and he, followed by his two friends made their way back to the Hall.

The Earl eventually arrived to break his fast; he was followed by two guards, who were apparently the men who had relieved the two guards who had stood at the doorway of his room for most, if not all of the night.

As he sat at the table, he immediately bellowed for ale, and glanced knowingly at the three youngsters, who he knew were waiting for him.

Not a word was spoken whilst he consumed three slices of freshly baked bread, four sausages, and numerous slices of ham and the breast of a quail, washed down by three jugs of ale.

'Ah! He exclaimed as he stretched his arms above his head.

'I expect you want me to introduce you to Bjorn, before you will allow me to go hunting.'

'Well. If I must.' He added

'What I would like you to remember when you meet him is that he is not the man he looks to be.'

'What do you mean?' Asked his son.

'All I will say is that he is from the far north of Norway. He's from a place called Lofoton, which is a place that is inhabited by Madmen and Trolls, and he is not a Troll.'

'Remember what I have told you. For he is not like other Norsemen.'

'All I am going to do is to introduce you to him, and then I shall be off.'

'The rest is up to you. Follow me.' He growled in a most unpleasant way as he rose and walked quickly through the doorway.

The three young men followed the Earl and his escort through the narrow streets, which were mostly devoid of people at this time of day, being inhabited by dogs, cats and a few beggars and homeless people who lay in doorways, clothed in rags.

'Watch the windows,' shouted the Earl as he pointed casually up at a window that had just been flung open.

Aelnoth, who had been born and bred in the country, did not understand what the Earl meant, and gazed upwards to the window, but was almost immediately forced to jump to one side, as a potful of piss and night soil came flying out of a window to land alongside him with a mighty splosh, covering his trousers with stale piss and shit.

'Damn and blast.' He swore as his hand automatically went down to wipe the mess off his trousers, but after a single wipe, he realised that if he attempted to wipe the stuff off, all he would achieve would be to smear it in even further, and get his hand covered with another mans waste, so he resisted the urge to wipe it off, and hurried onwards, in order to catch up with his companions, who had not stopped and were already beginning to disappear around the corner.

As he rushed around the corner he came to an abrupt halt, as he almost bumped into them, for they had already halted, and were standing on the banks of the River Liffey speaking with a hulk of a man who guarded the doorway of a large building.

This giant of a man stood over six feet in height, and was carrying a huge axe and an equally large round shield.

They were allowed to enter the building, and were ushered through the door, and into a room that consisted of several travelling chests, which had been placed along the walls, as well as a single scrubbed table, and half a dozen benches.

Several men sat at the benches, and were in the process of cleaning up the remains of their breakfast, but Aelnoth could not see any sign of a man who could be a leader of this particular band of gnarled, fair haired warriors.

The Earl strode past most of the men, halting half way along the table before a small man with a baldhead.

'Ah Bjorn, there you are. I couldn't see you for a moment amongst this crowd of ruffians.' Said the Earl in a jovial manner.

Bjorn stood, and Aelnoth was rather shocked to see that the Earl was a man of slight stature; for he was a full twelve inches shorter than the Earl, and although he did seem to possess something of an aura, Aelnoth could not quite decide what it actually was.

'This is my son,' said the Earl, 'and this is Aelnoth Edricson and his friend Oscar.'

'You will have to excuse the hood and cowl that Oscar wears. He is an Albino.'

Bjorn held his hand out to shake the hands of the three young men, but before he could speak, Earl Magnus said. 'They want to speak to you about raising an army to invade England and take it back from the Normans.'

Bjorn did not look at the Earl but stared at Oscar.

'I have never seen an Albino man.' He said quietly.

'I have seen an Albino deer and an Albino sow, but never an Albino man.'

'Is he sane? Can he fight?' he asked, but before he could be answered, he continued.

'From what I have heard about them, Albino's cannot see well. Can he see?'

'I can see and I fight, and I am sane. Well as sane as the next man, and I can see like an owl in the darkness, but I do need to shade my eyes from bright lights,' came the surly voice from behind the mask.

'However, the thing that annoys me most of all, is people who talk about me as if I am either an idiot or not here at all.'

'My apologies to you,' said the Lord of Dublin.

'I did not mean to offend you.'

Whilst this conversation was taking place, Aelnoth had almost got over the shock of meeting this man. This famous Viking who was the Lord of Dublin, as well as being the overlord of all of the Northmen, be them Danes, Finns or Norwegians, in the complete island of Ireland, for he was not the man who Aelnoth had envisaged him to be.

Certainly the Giant at the doorway of his Hall looked to be a true Viking, for he was tall, blond, bearded and savage looking, but Bjorn was none of those things.

He was small, with a dark beard mottled with grey; dark eyes and had not a single hair on his head. He also wore the type of clothing that Aelnoth could only describe as the clothing of a Fop or a Dandy.

He was shaken out of his thoughts when the Lord of Dublin said to Magnus.

'Your father says you want to raise an army to invade England?'

'What do you want of me?'

'I hold no sway in England.'

'I. We seek your leave to recruit Irishmen or even Northmen to join us in our quest to oust the Normans from our country,' said Magnus.

'Mmmm,' growled Bjorn, and after a long pause, he said. 'Irishmen you can have and be welcome to them.'

'Indeed, you do have my permission to recruit as many of them as you can take out of Dublin, and indeed out of the surrounding villages and those parts of the countryside, which come within my jurisdiction.'

'I will be pleased to have them out of my hair, for they are an unruly and wild bunch, and I shall be well rid of them.'

'You will find that they can fight like the furies in Hell, but they are as undisciplined as a herd of swine, and if you can find a way to control them, then you are a better man than I am.'

Again he paused and ran his rather womanly fingers through his motley beard.

'However,' he added.

'The Norsemen are mine, and I need them here with me, or in the Orkneys, where I shall set sail to this very afternoon, so there is no way that you can recruit them.'

'We have silver,' said Aelnoth, 'and England is one of the wealthiest countries in Europe, so the pickings would be rich for you and your men.'

Bjorn's eyes lit up, but he was adamant. 'Nonetheless, young man I am off to the Orkneys today.'

'It is a journey that has been long planned, and cannot be delayed.'

'My father the Earl, who will be the new King of England, if our venture is successful, has authorised me to offer you the counties of Devon and Cornwall in return for your help.'

'Under his overlordship of course.' He added.

Bjorn looked up and stared into the blue eyes of Magnus, and then without saying a word, he turned as if to walk away, thus closing the conversation.

Magnus was about to take his leave from the Lord of Dublin, rather pleased with himself at having obtained the concession to recruit from Dublin and the Irish provinces, when Bjorn halted in the doorway and said in his quiet voice. 'Mayhap, when I have consolidated my claim to the Isles of Orkney, I may call on my homeland, where I believe there is a surplus of young landless men who may be interested in joining our cause.'

A little later, when the three had bade farewell to Bjorn and his companions, Aelnoth said to Magnus. 'That went well did it not?'

'It did indeed.'

'Did you notice that he said the words? (OUR cause) not

'Your cause?'

'In truth I did not.'

'But if he really did refer to it as 'OUR,' then it must mean that he has approved of our venture, and WILL be joining us. Does it not?'

'It does. At least I think it does.'

CHAPTER 12

Recruiting in Dublin was all too easy for the three young Englishmen, for the city was full of young landless men, many of whom had migrated into the town in an attempt to escape the drudgery, low pay and poverty of the countryside, only to find that the things that they had sought to escape, had followed them into the city, which was full to overflowing with Irishmen, as well as exiled Englishmen and Norsemen whose ships were either in port for repair, or else the ships captains had been ordered to remain in the port by their Viking overlord, until such times as he returned from his voyage to the Orkneys and Norway.

However, whilst the quantity of men willing to accept a silver penny to join the growing army were many, the quality was poor, for the great majority of potential recruits were beggars and near-do-wells, who were more used to sleeping in doorways than using a weapon, other than a knife, and that was usually used to slit another man's throat in order to obtain a crust of bread.

'Sparrows come in flocks, but eagles fly alone.' Muttered Aelnoth, as he eyed a man who stood out from the crowd like a white stallion amongst a herd of donkeys.

'Now that one looks as if he can handle himself,' he said quietly to Oscar.

'Maybe so, but he could also be a man who could be equally as lethal to us as to any of our enemies.' Muttered Oscar, as he stared at the man.

Ignoring Oscar's misapprehension, Aelnoth strode over towards the man, who saw that he had the attention of the Englishmen, and nudged his way out of the crowd.

'I am Padraid of the Brown shields,' announced the man in a loud voice.

'I am Aelnoth and this is my friend Oscar,' said Aelnoth, as he looked at the man who towered over him by at least six inches.

The man's skin was weather beaten into a dark tan. Brown, intelligent eyes gazed down to Aelnoth, for the man was not only tall, he was broad in the shoulder and carried a brown shield, as well as a sturdy spear, a sword, and at least two knives in his belt.

Aelnoth noticed that there were many white scars, which shone from the dark skin of his muscular arms, indicating that he had experienced the cut and thrust of battle.

But the thing that also caught his attention was the ornately carved ivory hilt of a two-handed battle-sword, which protruded from its silver embossed scabbard that was slung over his back.

'What are the Brown Shields? Asked Oscar.

'You have never heard of the Brown shields?' growled the indignant Padraid.

'No.'

'You jest?'

'No.'

The man called Padraid turned his intensive gaze towards Oscar who was almost as tall as the Irishman.

'We are the foremost warriors in Ireland.'
'And you would join us to fight in England?'
'I would.'
'Why?'
'My brothers and I think that if we can kill Englishmen in England, then there will be less of them to come here to make a nuisance of themselves.

'They are Normans who we fight in England. NOT Englishmen.'

'Oh they are a damned sight worst. And far more dangerous.' He replied in a gruff voice.

'Mmmm, grumbled Aelnoth, as he ran his hand over the few hairs on his still boyish chin.

'How many are your Brown shields?'
'Perhaps a hundred.'
'Are you the leader?'
'I am, although some men may gainsay me''
'Would you be loyal to our cause?'
'We would. As long as we are in England.'
'Or Wales? Or Scotland, if we have need to go there?' questioned Aelnoth.
'We would.'
'But not here in Ireland.' He said adamantly.

Aelnoth and Oscar retreated a few feet away from the Irish warrior to confer, and returned to him a few moments later.

'We would welcome you and your fellow warriors to our cause.' Said Aelnoth as he held out his right hand towards the man.

Padraid transferred his spear to his shield arm and shook the hand of Aelnoth with such vigour that Aelnoth felt that the man was attempting to wrench his arm out of its socket.

'I shall return within the month with my men.' said Padraid as he turned and shouldered his way through the crowd of potential recruits.

The two Englishmen watched him disappear into the crowd, before they turned their attention to the waiting crowd, where they selected more and more, choosing only men who seemed to be young, fit and eager enough to join, and who possessed some sort of a weapon, which appeared to indicate that they might have had some experience in warfare.

*   *   *

The Englishmen still had plenty of silver with which they could purchase food and drink, but the area around Dublin was speedily running out of cattle, sheep, pigs and grain, as it struggled to cater for the growing army, as well as the citizens of the town.

It had been three weeks since the disappearance of Teresa, who had once been a constant companion of Aelnoth.

One evening, she had been there, all sweetness and light, and in the morning there was no sign of her.

No horse had been stolen.

No guard had seen her pass through the gate.

The reason that none of the guards had seen her pass through the gate was that she did not go through the gate, but had clambered over the ramparts at an hour past mid-night with the help of a rope, and had disappeared into the night.

Three days later, after she had found her way to the hill of Tara, from where she had seen the friendly river Boyne.

She had followed the river along its banks until she had reached Navan, footsore and weary, where she had immediately been ushered by two burly guards into the Hall of her father, Lord Mide.

'May the saints be praised?' Exclaimed her astonished father, for he had long thought that his daughter had been lost forever, since her capture by brigands over a year ago.

He flung his arms around her and hugged her to his chest.

After she had washed and changed her clothes, she met with her father who had already eaten his mid-day meal.

A serving maiden placed a steaming hot bowl of stew in front of her, which she immediately attacked with gusto, for she had not eaten for two whole days, since she had finished the half loaf of bread, which she had stolen from the kitchens, before she had left Dublin.

When she had finished and emptied her mouth of the last of the freshly baked bread, she turned towards her father, who had been waiting patiently by the side of the table.

'Father. I am to be married.' She announced boldly.

'Married.' He flew into a temper, for both he and his daughter knew that she had been betrothed to the eldest son of the King of Cork since she was the age of five.

'You cannot marry. You are betrothed.' He fumed.

'Who is the man?' he demanded, as he kicked the chair away from him and rose to his feet.

'Did he deflower you?'

'No. Of course he didn't.'

'Hrrmmm,' spluttered the king.

'Who is it? Tell me.' He roared.

'An Englishman!' she said in a determined voice.

'An Englishman.' He bellowed at the top of his voice, as his face turned from its normal colour to the colour of a red rose in full bloom.

'You cannot marry a bloody Englishman.'

'They are not even Christians.'

'This one is.' She said adamantly, as she watched the face of her father turn from a pink to a brilliant red, fearing that he would burst a blood vessel, or have a seizure, unless he calmed down a little.

'Is he wealthy?' he almost shouted in her ear.

'I don't really know.' She answered quietly as she looked up into his still ruddy face.

'But he is a warrior.'

'They call him 'Aelnoth two swords' and his father was a famous lord in the midland shires of England.'

'Christ's blood.' Fumed her still furious father.

'If your saintly mother was alive today, she would turn in her grave.' He said in all seriousness, not really realising what he had said.

'Of course, he doesn't know it yet.' She said in a stern voice, in her attempt to calm down the rage that still consumed her red-faced father.

'What!!' he bellowed. 'A bloody Englishman and he doesn't know he's going to marry you?'

'You mean to tell me that you are going to marry a penniless, damned English pauper, and he doesn't even know it yet?'

'Are you mad?'

'No Father,' she answered.

'But I will marry him. With or without your consent.'

The King of Navan shrugged his shoulders and stormed towards the door, as if he was about to leave the room, but he knew only too well that once his daughter had set her mind to do a thing, then there was no man on this earth who could persuade her otherwise.

As he reached the door, he kicked it shut with his right foot, as his mind tried to comprehend what his daughter had said.

'He is the son of a lord. You said?'

'So he is high born?'

'Yes Father.'

'I wonder just what sort of a lord.' He mused.

'Is he a powerful lord?' he asked.

'His father was.'

'He owned half of Mercia? She said as she stretched the truth just a little.

'What do you mean? He owned half of Mercia?'

'Does he not own it now?'

'No. The Normans have dispossessed him, but if he and his friends win, then they will take back that which has been taken from them, and they will all be wealthy landowners again.'

'Just you wait a minute. You said if he and his friends win.

'Win what?'

'Win the battle of course.'

'Daughter. You are talking in riddles.'

'What bloody battle?'

'Oh! I forgot to tell you darling Daddy.'

'He is going to invade England and take it back from the Normans.'

'Oh my good Lord.' Screamed her father at the top of his voice.

'How in Hell's name is he going to get to England, AND defeat the bloody Normans? Who you may or may not know, are the foremost battle hardened bloody warriors in the whole of bloody Europe?'

'He is a famous warrior father dear, and they call him 'Aelnoth two swords,' she said again, just in case her father had not heard her the first time.

'Hrrr. Never heard of him, and what sort of a bloody name is bloody Aelnoth,' shouted the King at the top of his voice, who was beginning to think that his daughter had gone insane during her captivity.

'He will have the help of King Harold Godwinson's brother, Earl Bjorn and his Vikings, AND he has twelve huge chests full of silver.'

At the mention of twelve huge chests of silver, her father seemed to calm down a little, and after he had paced the room more times than she could count, he ceased his pacing and turned to her.

'Mmmm. Twelve chests of silver? I suppose it could be worse.' He mused.

'How big are the chests?'

'Very big Daddy,' she answered.

'Have you seen the silver?' He asked as his eyes narrowed in suspicion.

'I have.' She lied.

'And just how big are the chests?' he asked again.

'The size of coffins, darling Daddy.'

'Oh well, it could have been worst.' He repeated.

'It could have been some penniless Irish peasant, or even (God forgive me) a bloody penniless bloody English peasant.'

'Do I have your permission then?' she asked in a demure way as she looked lovingly up at him.

'What if I say no?'

'Then I will still marry him anyway, and you will never see me again.'

'That leaves me with little choice then.' He said with a strained smile.

'Oh Father,' she purred. 'I knew you could not say no to me.'

'You will love him, for he is a lot like you in his ways.' She lied, as she threw her arms around his neck and smothered his pock marked face with kisses.

'Mmmm,' he huffed as he returned her embrace, happy that she had found a man at long last. Even though he was a bloody Englishman.

'What dowry shall I have?' she asked, knowing that now he had agreed that she was to be married. It would be the appropriate time to broach the subject of a dowry.

'DOWRY. DOWRY.' He roared, nearly deafening her.

'I shall give NO dowry to a damned Englishman.'

'He shall have my only daughter, and be thankful for that, for I shall not give a penny piece to be taken away to bloody England.'

'Oh Father, you are funny.' She giggled girlishly.

'He will not want money from you, for I have seen his fortune, or at least some of it, and he already has more silver than the whole of your own Kingdom and the Kingdoms of Kells and Trim put together.'

'Oh!' scoffed her father. 'Are you certain that you have seen all this silver?'

'Indeed I have,' she lied with a huff and a shake of her head, 'and he is paying each of his recruits a silver coin when they join him.'

King Mide rubbed his bristly grey chin in thought, but before he could speak, his daughter stroked the side of his face and purred.

'For my dowry, I would like you to give me one hundred men to join his army, and that would give you at least one hundred silver coins, which they would bring back to Navan when they return.'

'A HUNDRED. NEVER!' he roared.

'That would leave Navan defenceless against my enemies. 'NO. I say NO.' I cannot give you one hundred of my men. And who is to say that they WILL return.

Battle is a gamble, and the outcome of every single battle is in God's hands.'

'And you say that he a Christian?' he demanded.

'Yes Father.'

'Well that's something I suppose.' He said grudgingly.

'Still. One hundred of my men for a dowry is out of the question.'

What would happen if those bloody Mee's from Carin Tubber invaded us again?'

They slaughtered twenty of my finest warriors last time they raided us, and made off with over a hundred head of my cattle and God alone knows how many goats and sheep.'

'Well could you spare perhaps seventy five men?' she cooed.

'After all, I am a princess of the blood.'

'No.' was the adamant answer, as his hand automatically went up to stroke his chin yet again.

'I might. Just might be able to spare fifty men.' he said grudgingly.

'Fifty would be fine darling Daddy,' she said as she gave him another hug, for fifty men had been her target all along.

'You WILL equip them for me won't you Father?' she asked, but before he could answer, she continued.

'You know. Spears. Swords. Shields and leather war jackets?'

'Jesus Christ.' He swore. 'You will send me to a pauper's grave.'

The King turned away from his daughter, and walked slowly towards the dining table, which was groaning with all manner of food, and as he walked he was thinking for himself.

'Whilst those men are away, then this King will play.'

'I shall choose a few of them who have young wives, and I will invite those poor, lonely wives to dine with me from time to time.'

And I shall rid myself of a couple of noblemen who are becoming a nuisance.'

'They can be the Lords in charge of the warriors.'

'Then there is the daughter of the King of Louth. She is reputed to be a beauty, and is young enough to produce a son for me. Oh I have son's enough amongst the peasants, but that's not quite the same as a legitimate one.'

'The Good Lord alone knows how many little bastards I have produced after 30 years on the throne. I swear that at least a quarter of the youngsters in my kingdom look a bit like me.'

He smiled to himself as he picked up a well-cooked leg of a partridge and nibbled at it with the only two of his front teeth that remained.

CHAPTER 13

Aelnoth, Magnus and Oscar were reasonably pleased with the numbers of willing volunteers who had come forward during the last few weeks, as word had spread to the outlying towns, villages and farmsteads, swelling the numbers of new recruits of their army to over fifteen hundred men.

This number included some two hundred English veterans who had followed Earl Magnus into exile.

The new Irish recruits had been selected from over four thousand, who had wanted to join, but the three young Englishmen had chosen only those men who were either young or strong enough to undergo the sort of journey and battles, which the three men anticipated lay ahead of them.

On the last day of the Christian month of August (The month of the harvest) the sentries patrolling the palisade, sounded the alarm, bringing Aelnoth and his two friends to the walkway, where they were joined by crowds of warriors who were in varied states of dress and undress.

'What is it? Shouted Aelnoth, in order to make himself heard above the clamour that the unruly mob of warriors and citizens were making.

'There my Lord.' Said the sentry as he pointed in the direction of the few cottages that stood on the banks of the Liffey.

'An army, my Lord.' He said nervously.

Aelnoth stared at the banks of the Liffey and did indeed see an army.

'A pretty small army.' He scoffed.

'Can't be more than a hundred men.' he said with contempt.

'What on earth do they think they are going to do with that pitiful number of men?'

'Surely they cannot be thinking of attacking us?'

'Probably coming to join us.' Sniffed Magnus.

There was a long silence as the 'Army' trudged solemnly onwards.

'Look at their banners and their shields.' Said Magnus excitedly.

'It's Padraid and his brown shields.' He shouted.

Cheers and whoops of delight followed Magnus's statement, echoed out from the occupants of the walkway, who were jostled aside, as they were joined by crowds of people, who now thronged the walkway and the entrance of the gate, all expressing their delight that such a large band of famous Irish warriors had deemed to join this army, who they felt sure, could not help but defeat the Norman usurpers and regain England for the English.

Padraid and his men made an impressive sight as they neared the camp, marching three abreast through the cheering crowd and into the camp.

The Brown shields, which the warriors carried, were of a standard size, being round and slightly larger than the average English shield.

Each shield had an eagle painted in red, and each eagle held the boss of the shield in its claws.

Each of the warriors carried a spear, shield and knives, but a few also had two-handled battle swords, which they carried, strapped across their backs.

Several drums began to beat, and the drums were immediately joined by a dozen reed pipes, who were in turn accompanied by several of the men who carried the larger pipes made from the bladders of pigs, creating such a loud marching tune, that the watching crowds were soon clapping their hands and stamping their feet in unison with the music.

Padraid halted his men outside the walls, and within an hour there were neat lines of leather tents pitched in an exact square, with two guards positioned at each of the four corners of the square, who marched solemnly to and fro, as they patrolled the perimeters of their camp.

Padraid marched alone through the gates of Dublin, where the three Englishmen waited to greet him.

'Well met.' Exclaimed Aelnoth as he shook the right hand of the leader of the brown Shields.

'As promised.' Said Padraid as he moved to Oscar and Magnus.

'I have brought you one hundred of the finest warriors in the whole of Ireland to assist us in our cause.'

'They certainly look impressive' responded Magnus as they all looked towards the organised tented town that had sprung up in the meadow.

'Who are they?' asked Aelnoth as he pointed to a second body of men who had followed the Brownshields.

'It's your girlfriend.' Said Oscar in an almost nonchalant way.

'My girlfriend?' questioned the bemused Aelnoth.

'I don't have a girlfriend.' He added.

'There are none so blind as those who do not want to see.' Oscar said with a smile.

'Oh you mean Teresa?'

'Of course Teresa. Who else?'

'She is not my girlfriend,' said Aelnoth indignantly.

'She thinks she is.'

'Any-how, how can you see that it's Teresa?'

'I have far better eyesight and all I can see is a black crowd of what look like people.'

'I don't need to see her. I know it's her with a dowry.'

'What in hell are you on about?' said Aelnoth. 'Dowry indeed.'

'I haven't asked the girl to marry me, and therefore there is no Dowry.'

'You do not have to ask, for she will do the asking.' Said Oscar, with a faraway look in his strange coloured eyes as if even at this moment in time, he was gazing into the future.

The approaching crowd made their way around the newly tented town of the Brown Shields, and ambled through the gates, stopping a few yards short of Padraid, Aelnoth, Oscar and Magnus, who were slightly amused at this small horde of young warriors, for although the men appeared to be fully armed with spears, shields and body armour, they appeared to be without a leader.

They were also slightly amused that after the disciplined arrival of the Brown Shields, this latest gathering of Warriors was in stark contrast, and seemed to be nothing more than a mob of undisciplined young men.

There was movement from within the centre of the crowd, and the ranks broke to allow the diminutive figure of Teresa to walk to the front.

Walk is perhaps not the correct word to use. Strut or March would describe it more correctly, for she marched to the front of her fifty assembled warriors, and stood with her head held high as she peered directly into the eyes of Aelnoth.

Aelnoth returned her gaze, noting that this female who proudly stood in front of him was nothing like the grubby girl who he had saved from being slain by those tribesmen in central Wales, for she stood in front of him with her chin raised, dressed from head to foot in chain mail, which was ablaze with silver and gold etchings.

A huge golden buckle secured the wide silver belt, which girded her slender waist.

Her head was bare and her long auburn hair shone like gold.

'I have brought fifty of the best warriors of Navan to your cause, as a dowry for our wedding.' She said brazenly, as a smile flashed across her beautiful face, revealing a perfect set of white teeth.

Despite the fact that Oscar had told him that this would happen a few scant minutes before, he had considered the idea to be fanciful and wishful thinking, causing him to look down at the maiden with his mouth open in shock.

In fact the only thing that his mind could grasp was the fact that this young woman who stood before him, and who had just proposed marriage to him, had the most beautiful set of teeth that he had ever seen.

Magnus was grinning like a maniac, and savagely sent his elbow into the ribs of the dazed Aelnoth, bringing him back into the land of living.

'Well two swords.' He said, as his grin grew ever wider.

'Are you going to marry the girl?'

Aelnoth shook his head, and gazed at the lovely Teresa, who returned his gaze and smiled as she awaited his answer.

Aelnoth's brain was alive with so many things, and his mind was so confused that he thought for a moment, that he was going mad.

His brain told him that she was indeed a very beautiful woman, a very beautiful woman who just proposed marriage to him.

Which was a thing that should not have been done in this day and age, and yet she was a Princess who had brought fifty warriors with her as a dowry.

She was also the only child. (Well the only legitimate child) of a King, and with her would come a Kingdom. (Eventually.)

'Men would die to marry her for her beauty alone, would they not?' He asked himself.

'But then, men married for many different reasons.' He mused.

'Love. Lust. Wealth. Land. Sons or even daughters.'

'Companionship.'

'A good cook?

'Or merely someone who will care for them in their old age.'

196

'I have known peasants to marry to inherit a single field, or even a Bull, or a couple of cows.' He thought.

'What have I got to lose?' His brain asked him.

'Fifty warriors,' it told him.

'Do I love her?' It asked.

'Not really.'

'But you do lust after her?' It asked him.

'I do.' He admitted.

'But there are others who I have lusted after with far more vigour.'

'Ah, but they did not bring fifty warriors with them, or the promise of a Kingdom.'

'Damn it.' He thought.

'I suppose I will have to marry her.'

He looked down into her sparkling blue eyes and with a smile he said.

'Of course I will marry you.'

Her face broke into a radiant smile, and she leapt forward and flung her arms around his shoulders, stretching upwards to plant a long sensual kiss onto his lips.

Her warriors cheered and waved their shields and weapons in the air to show their approval, whilst Magnus and the two other Englishmen crowded around the couple, slapping them on the back, as they added their approval, for they too did not want to lose fifty good warriors.

The betrothal celebration that evening was long and noisy, with most of the warriors and the few ladies attending.

The celebrations ended in the early hours of the morning when the last warrior finally sank into the rushes which littered the floor, or else staggered off unsteadily and noisily to their sleeping quarters,

Aelnoth was one of the last to leave, and was escorted from the Hall by Magnus and Oscar, for although he had kept up with his companions drink by drink, he was not too sure if he was celebrating, or merely drowning his sorrows.

There was no sign of Ingrid that night, or the following day, as she had made a point of ignoring all manner of contact with anyone, other than the piebald pony, which she had recently purchased from a local farmer.

The following morning a steward roused Aelnoth from a deep sleep.

'Up. Up. My Lord. The King is here!!' Shouted the man.

'After several attempts, Aelnoth managed to sit on the side of his bed with his head in his hands, as his throbbing head attempted to register what the steward was shouting.

He ached all over; he retched up most of the beer, which he had consumed a few short hours ago.

Luckily, the steward was a bright individual and had anticipated the action, by catching most of the smelly liquefied residue in a large wooden bowl.

'What bloody King?' growled Aelnoth?

'Ireland has a bloody King in every bloody town and valley.' He snarled.

'THE King my Lord. King Diarmait. King of Leinster. My Lord,'

Despite his throbbing head, Aelnoth forced himself to stand, and eventually staggered over to the side of the room, where he plunged his face into a bowl of cold water, in an attempt to clear his throbbing hangover.

A little later, he walked manfully to the door and along the passageway, which led to the great hall.

Oscar, Magnus and Teresa were standing in a small group, whilst servants scurried hither and thither as they attempted to pile food and drink onto the table before King Diarmait arrived.

'You look like shit!' said Magnus as the pale-faced Aelnoth joined them.

'Never you mind my love.' Said Teresa soothingly, as she looped her arm around his.

'A bowl full of porridge will settle your belly before the King comes.'

In that, she was wrong, for just as she had finished speaking, a flurry of activity near the doorway bloomed into the King of Leinster, who swept into the room like an uprooted bush being blown about in a winter gale.

Diarmait was a huge man, who resembled a bear more than a man, for he wore a black bearskin over his shoulders, which draped down to his knees, causing his already gigantic frame to appear even bigger than it actually was, and although his jet black hair was windblown and matted, his neatly trimmed beard and his face contradicted the overall character of the man, for it was almost, but not quite, the face of a young man.

He had rosy cheeks, which shone above the carefully trimmed beard, and supported a small aquiline nose, which rose from between two blue eyes, which sparkled with intelligence.

'So you are the three Englishmen who are raising an army in my back yard are you?'

He said in a harsh voice, as his right hand sped to the elaborately carved hilt of his sword, which rested in an equally elaborate silver scabbard, hanging on a thick black belt, which circled his waist.

The six men who escorted him through the door were equally as large as their King, as well as being more fearsome, for each of the six bore the look of a killer.

The King held his left hand up for a second, causing his escort to halt, as he alone stepped to within a pace of the three young Englishmen.

His face broke into a smile, and his voice was quieter and more pleasant, as he asked.

'I suppose you are raising the men for me, but for the love of the saints, I know not where I shall use a force such as this.'

Aelnoth was the first of the three to recover his voice, and said in an almost timid voice, which was so unlike him, that his two companions hardly recognised his voice.

'Well. Not really my Lord.'

'We are recruiting them to take back to England, in order to win back our country from the Norman's.

'Oh Laddie. I know that. I was merely jesting,' as he gave Aelnoth a friendly slap on his shoulder.

'I have known your intentions long before you set foot in Leinster, and to be sure, I probably know the numbers and the calibre of your men better than you.'

'Come. Sup with me.' He said jovially, as he ushered the three Englishmen to the table, where he sat heavily on one of the benches, and immediately began to reach for food with one hand, whilst his other hand grasped a large goblet of wine, which he brought up to his lips and drank.

'I know you have a hundred of my Brown Shields, as well as a score or so from Navan, and that you are to marry young Teresa.'

He paused for a moment and winked at Aelnoth.

'Pity.' He said. 'I had my eye on her for one of my younger sons.'

'T'would have been a fair match, and would have brought my neighbour Navan a little closer to me, and that would be no mean thing, for the man is as slippery as an eel, so he his.'

'I hear she is a headstrong young lady, and I will be happy enough to see her married to you, rather than to one of Lord Mee's striplings, for that could set the whole of the west of Ireland against me.'

He chewed on the breast of a roasted partridge, which had been soaked in honey, and between mouthfuls and the occasional swig of his wine. He said.

'In fact, in order to show you my approval for your enterprise.'

'I shall furnish you with thirty ships to help you on your way, as well as one thousand good strong Irishmen to fight for you.'

'Oh they will not be my best men. For indeed, what sort of a King would I be if I were to give you my best warriors, and leave myself open to harm?' he spat out a small piece of gristle onto the rushes, which sent a couple of hounds rushing to the spot to gulp up the morsel.

'No.' he said merely. 'They will be ruffians and malcontents, as well as a half a dozen petty noblemen who are causing me a few problems, and thus. I will be well rid of them, and those few who are not slaughtered by the Normans, may well decide to stay in England, so that if you win. Or perhaps I should say. When you win, then they will no longer be my problem.'

'Indeed, they will be yours.' He said with a wide grin.

'My ships and my men do not come free.' He said seriously, as his goblet was refilled, and the glass hovered near his mouth.

'If you win.' He corrected himself again.

'When you win, I shall want Wales from Monmouth to Aberystwyth to consolidate the holdings I already own in Wales.'

'I. I will need to consult with my father, spluttered Magnus.

'For he will be the new King of England.'

'Ah. I tease you young man. Oh not about my demands, for they are genuine enough, to be sure.'

'Nay, lad.' He said as another broad grin crossed his unblemished face.

'I have already spoken to your father, and he has already agreed terms with me.'

'Where do you think he has been all this time?' But before the young man could answer, he continued.

'He has been with me, hunting in my forests and on the plains of Mayo.' he said merrily.

He laughed so much at his own cunning plan, which he nearly choked on the mouthful of food that he had been trying to swallow, causing one of his six bodyguards to rush to his King, and slap him on his back so hard that Aelnoth thought that the man might break his King's spine.

The King brought the food back up and spat it onto the rushes, causing the dogs to scamper over to the Kings side, where the food quickly disappeared yet again, down the largest dog's gullet.

He continued to cough and spit out the residue of his food as yet another commotion occurred at the doorway of the hall, and through the knot of men who were standing in the doorway, appeared none other than Earl Magnus himself, who was followed by his two huge Irish wolf hounds, and then by his two equally large bodyguards.

'What happened to you?' yelled the King at the top of his voice.

'Oh I lost the bloody boar,' snarled the Earl as he neared the King's table, where he immediately grabbed a roast partridge and commenced to take bites out of it, as he continued to speak with his mouth full.

'It was the biggest damned boar I have ever seen.' He announced.

'Gored one of my hounds so badly that I had to kill the poor old dog myself, and then the bloody boar disappeared into a patch of gorse that seemed to go on for miles.'

'We searched for him until bloody night-time, but never saw hide or hair of him again.'

'And I nearly lost my steed in one of your bloody peat bogs, which you Irish are so proud of, so we gave up and came back to feast with you.'

The Earl finally stopped chewing the mouthful of meat that he had in his mouth, and reached for a horn of ale, which he drained in one long swallow.

'Did you tell my son how many men and ships you would provide for our enterprise?'

Diarmait nodded. 'I did.' He said.

'And that I wanted half of Wales for my trouble.'

'Half,' spluttered the Earl.

'We only agreed on nigh on one third.' He said angrily.

'We agreed that all would be yours from the Sabrina to Aberaeron.'

'Aberystwyth.' Said Diarmait adamantly.

'Your son agreed.'

'Aberaeron.' Shouted the Earl loudly, as his right hand fled to the hilt of his sword.

'Ah to be sure. It was always Aberaeron.' Said Diarmait with a wan smile, as he touched the shoulder of the angry English Earl in a friendly way. And added with a more genuine smile.

'It was but a jest.'

'Aberaeron is fine.' He added.

'It will link up with the manors that I already hold in West Wales,' he added as the smile remained on his youthful looking face.

Earl Magnus glared at King Diarmait, knowing full well that the King had indeed been in earnest, and had tried to play himself and his son off against one another, in order to extend the already large holdings, which he held in Ireland, England and Wales, but he also realised that to argue or fight with Diarmait at this stage, over a small chunk of the a mostly uninhabited and worthless part of Wales, would bring his entire plans (or rather the entire plans of his son) to nought.

Earl Magnus also knew that the cunning King was bolstering the army with men and ships in order to protect his English and Welsh manors, for they both knew full well that if the Norman onslaught was not stopped, then the Irish Kings Manors would soon be absorbed into the ever-expanding Norman Kingdoms of England and Wales.

He held his ornate glass towards the King, and said in a voice that was loud enough to carry to the far corners of the Hall, and would thus be made evident to all the warriors and lords in the hall, that he had made a pact with their King.

'We are agreed then?'

'All the lands of Wales from Monmouth to Aberaeron will be yours for your help in our cause?'

King Diarmait knew that he had been out-manoeuvred and had no course other than to agree, or he would lose face, and be shamed as a breaker of oaths in front of his own Lords and warriors, so he stood to join the Earl and raised his own silver mounted drinking glass and with a forced smile, he clashed it against the Earls, thus sealing the bond between them.

It was at dawn on the first day of the new month, when their servants noisily entered their sleeping quarters and roused Aelnoth, Oscar and Magnus from their beds.

'My Lords. My Lords. Vikings. Vikings. Vikings.'

The three young men leapt out of their beds, dressing as speedily as they could, and rushed out into the bustling street, still half dressed, and armed with swords and shields, but they had not had sufficient time to don their mail shirts or helmets.

They skidded to a sliding halt on the muddy roadway as they realised that although there were more people about than was usual, the men who were abroad, did not seem to be in a panic, and were going about their normal duties without undue haste.

Aelnoth stopped a man who was ambling along with a goose under his arm.

'Where are the Vikings? He asked the man.

'Vikings?' the man said. 'What Vikings?'

'We were told that the Vikings had come, and yet no one seems to be alarmed.' He said to the man.

'Oh, the Vikings. You mean Bjorn.' He said with a wry smile.

'He arrived last night.'

'He's down by the Liffey.' He added, as he shook himself free of the hand, which Aelnoth had placed on his shoulder, and hurried away.

The three Englishmen replaced their swords into their scabbards, and walked leisurely down the roadway towards the river Liffey.

They had spent many an hour walking along the riverbank, where they had spoken to a number of seamen from the large fleet of merchant ships, which plied their trade along the coasts of Ireland, Wales and England, gleaning news about their homeland from the seamen who had been to England during the past few months.

During those months, they had not seen a single Viking longship on the Liffey.

This morning both sides of the Liffey seethed with activity, as the newly arrived Viking fleet vied with one another in their attempted to moor along the already overcrowded banks of the wide dark river.

CHAPTER 14

The diminutive figure of Bjorn was hidden by his sworn oathmen, as they approached the astonished Englishmen, but as the Northmen neared them, the large warriors halted a few paces from Aelnoth and his two friends, in order to allow Bjorn to emerge from their midst.

'Well,' said the small Viking Overlord, as a wide grin spread across his weathered face.

'I have brought a few of my Northern brethren to help us to conquer England.'

'What think you?'

'Very impressive,' answered Aelnoth.

'How many warriors have your brought?' He queried.

'Ah, you are young man who does not mince his words. I like that.' He said, and then he added.

'You remind me of myself when I was your age.'

'No messing about with flowery words.'

'Straight from the shoulder. I like that.' He repeated with a smile, but he still had not answered Aelnoth's question.

Aelnoth smiled back at the Lord of Dublin.

'So. How many?'

'Mmmm, perhaps a thousand. And then a few?' came the answer.

'A thousand?' queried Aelnoth, who was reasonably pleased with the addition of a thousand men to his small army, but from the numbers that he had assessed, when he had witnessed the hustle and bustle, which he had seen on the banks of the Liffey, he had surmised that Bjorn had brought at least twice that number.

'There seemed to be more than a thousand men here?' he queried.

'To be sure. You are a canny young man.' Said Bjorn.

205

'You are not wrong, for I have brought nigh on double that number with me from the northlands, but not all of them will be joining us in our conquest of England.' He said as he looked up into the young face of Aelnoth.

'I shall be keeping a few back here in Ireland.'

'Why?'

'Ah, there you go again. Straight from the shoulder.' He slapped the shoulder of the young Englishman playfully.

'A wise man does not put all of his eggs in one basket.' He said with a smile, and walked away. Thus closing the conversation.

'Have your men ready to sail by the next full moon.' He shouted over his shoulder as he merged back into a clutch of his oathmen, and disappeared into the crowds of Northmen who were assembling on the riverbanks.

On the ebb tide on the first morning after the full moon, a fleet of over eighty ships edged their way out of the mouth of the Liffey, and into the open sea, carrying almost four thousand warriors.

The fleet had no room for horses, other than the four horses, (two for hunting and two stallions for war) which Earl Magnus insisted must sail with the fleet.

The remaining longships, trading vessels and fishing boats were so crammed with warriors, that in many of the vessels, some men had space to sit but were unable to lie down during the entire voyage.

By dawn on the following day they could see the blurred coastline of south Wales, as a pleasant wind sent them gliding over an unusually calm sea.

The people of Bristol were alarmed to see the large fleet of mostly Viking longships appear off the headlands of the river Avon, and closed their gates long before the first of the invaders could reach the banks of the estuary.

The leaders of the Viking army sent a steward to the city under a flag of truce, but the Burgers of Bristol refused to see the envoy, due, it seemed to their distrust of the Anglo Irish and Viking army, or perhaps it was because of the harsh punishment, which had been meted out to other cities, who had opened their gates to enemies of the new King William.

Whatever the reason. The gates stayed firmly shut.

Scouting parties were sent into the surrounding countryside, scouring the prosperous lowlands for cattle, sheep, grain and horses, and after a siege that lasted for two weeks, the frustrated host boarded their ships, and sailed out into the wide estuary, and down the south-western coast of England.

After they had anchored their ships in the wide estuary of the river taw, the leaders gathered around a large fire as they waited for the side of an ox to cook.

Aelnoth sat alongside Oscar and Magnus, with the ever-present forms of Teresa who wore her shirt of chain mail sitting on one side of him, whilst the thin figure of Ingrid sat on the other side.

Earl Magnus sat by his son, and Diarmait chatted with Padraid of the Brown shields.

Bjorn sat apart, brooding, or so it seemed to Aelnoth, for he was still slightly suspicious of the Vikings true intentions.

Whilst Aelnoth was the youngest, and thus probably the least experienced in warfare of the leaders, he was becoming more and more frustrated that each of the different factions of the army appeared to have their own agenda, and not one of the leaders seemed to want to take overall control of the host.

He felt compelled to address his fellow leaders, and after a lot of consternation, he rose to his feet.

None of the other leaders appeared to notice that he had stood, and continued to speak to each other in voices that varied from loud to whispers.

'Friends.' He said loudly, but the talk continued.

He stooped and reached for his iron helmet, which he then banged his eating knife onto the helmet, causing the chatter to slowly stop.

'Friends.' He said again in a strong voice.

'As we are all assembled here. I think it would be a good idea for us to choose a leader, and to decide where and when we can meet our enemies and how we are going to beat them.

'Good idea young man.' Exclaimed Diarmait jovially.

'I suggest that since I am the King of Ireland, then I should command the army, and that I alone should decide on the army's strategy.'

'I agree.' Said Padraid in a loud voice.

'I have brought more men than any of you,' said Bjorn, 'and thus should be on equal footings with Diarmait, especially so, as I have left half of my men in Dublin to defend the city and the rest of southern Ireland.'

'We should have joint leadership.' He said in a loud voice.

'I should have some say in this matter.' Intervened Earl Magnus, 'since I shall be the new King of England,' he looked towards Diarmait, ' and it goes without saying that you shall still have your slice of Wales, and of course Devon and Cornwall, will go to you, my Good Bjorn,' as he nodded his head towards Bjorn.

Aelnoth feared that a serious argument was brewing, so he rose to his feet again and held his hands up in the air, in order to bring some semblance of calm to the meeting.

'Friends.' He said loudly. 'Friends, if we argue amongst ourselves. I fear that we may well all go on different paths, and if that happens, then the Normans will pick us off one at a time, like ripe plums in the autumn.'

The leaders ceased their banter and listened to the young Englishman, who continued.

'It is vital that we remain as one large army, for that is the only way that we can beat the Normans, who, as you all know, are well organised and are savage fighters.'

The men around the fire nodded and grunted their acknowledgment of the younger mans statement.

'I suggest that our army should have not one single leader, but should be guided by the Lords Bjorn, Diarmait and Earl Magnus, and that these three leaders must agree amongst themselves upon our strategy.'

'Where we lead our host? 'And when and where we meet our enemies. Hoping that it will be on ground of our own choosing and not theirs.'

'What think you?'

There were grunts and nods of approval from the assembled lords, but it was Padraid of the Brown Shields who rose to his feet.

'Young Aelnoth's words are good, and indeed he makes a lot of sense, for whilst we all have our own individual reasons for being here, unless we remain as a single coherent force, then it will be a foregone conclusion that in the long term, we would be overwhelmed by the Normans, who, as young Aelnoth says, would eliminated us one by one.'

He slowly looked around the small circle of leaders before he said.

'Is there anyone who does not agree with Aelnoth's suggestion?'

No one spoke.

'Then it is agreed?' he said.

'Agreed. Agreed. Agreed.' Came the mutterings from the assembled lords.

'Good.' Said Padraid.

'Then I suggest that we all take a slice or two of this beast, which looks to be roasted well enough to be eaten, and seal our agreement with another cup of this delicious ale.'

'Where is that boy?' he said loudly, and then shouted even louder.

'Boy. Boy. Come. Fill up our cups.'

'We have something to celebrate, and the good lord knows that with all this talking, my mouth is as dry as a grandmothers tit.'

Aelnoth and the other men left the three leaders, and went their separate ways.

As Aelnoth, Magnus and Oscar made their way through the encampment towards the area where their own men were camped, Aelnoth said to his two friends. 'I hope that those three can lead us to victory, but alas, I do have grave doubts.'

The other two grunted their agreement.

He added. 'Diarmait certainly has had enough experience of battle, but has he ever led a host of this size before?'

'My Father Magnus is an experienced warrior who fought at both the Battle of Stamford Bridge as well as Hastings.' Said Magnus aggressively, as he glared towards Aelnoth.

'He has already fought the Normans and will know how to beat them.'

'May I remind you,' said Magnus, 'that whilst we beat the Vikings at Stamford Bridge. The bloody Normans thrashed us at Hastings.'

'They had battle luck on their side,' said Oscar.

'If King Harold had not been so pig headed, and had waited for a few more days before he challenged the Normans, then we would have doubled our numbers, and the odds would have been in our favour.

'True. True.' Said Aelnoth thoughtfully, as he stroked his chin in an attempt to preventing himself from adding the question, which had been niggling away at his mind for more days than he cared to remember.

It seemed to him that Earl Magnus had so far taken more interest in inquiring which parts of England contained the best hunting, rather than the training of warriors, and practicing the strategy that would be needed to take England from the Normans, who, by all reports were growing stronger with each, and every day that passed.'

'Padraid and his Brown Shields seem to be good men.' Remarked Aelnoth, 'but Diarmait is the one who worries me most.'

'From what I have heard about him, he seems to be hungry for power, and he will tell lies, cheat, conspire and even kill to obtain power, for with power comes land, and with land comes money and Women.'

This remark was again followed by nods and grunts of approval as the three young Englishmen made their way to their individual leather tents, which had been erected by their personal servants.

As he crouched to enter his small leather tent, Aelnoth noticed that the calfskin tent, which belonged to Teresa, had been pitched next to his own tent, and as she lay half in and half out of her tent, he could see that her face was raised and she was watching him.

'When are we to be wed? She whispered.

'Soon.' Answered Aelnoth.

'As soon as we have beaten the Normans?' He added.

'Good night my love.' She cooed.

'Sleep well,' as she blew him a kiss.

'You too.' He mumbled as he made a half-hearted attempt to blow a kiss back to her.

He heard a snort from the other side of his tent, where he saw the thin figure of Ingrid, who had obviously heard their exchange of words, and as her white face met his own, she snorted again and turned her back on him, as she disappeared into her own small tent.

It seemed to be only a few minutes before the noise of the camp wakened him, despite the fact that he had had a good nights sleep, for he was a man who was usually a light sleeper, and he recalled that he had not been wakened once during the night, despite the noise that over four thousand men made from either snoring, talking in their sleep, or leaving their places to walk to the ablution pits, which each section of the army had dug for that particular purpose.

After a hasty bowl of steaming hot porridge, which was handed to him by the smiling Teresa, whilst Ingrid glared in anger at her, he met with Oscar and Magnus, who were in the process assembling a squad of fifty men, who they were arranging into a line of ten men long and five deep, forming a shieldwall.

As he joined them he remarked. 'They look reasonably good.'

'Looks aren't everything.' Came back the retort from Oscar.

'True.' Said Aelnoth.

'But we have already had them practice standing in a shieldwall time and time again, and this lot seem to have mastered it reasonably well.'

'That's not the reason for this last minute exercise.' Said Magnus, and before Aelnoth could ask the question. Why?' Magnus said. 'Oscar had one of his dreams last night.'

'Oh, What about?' asked Aelnoth.

'He saw our Shieldwall broken.'

'How? Horses? An arrow storm?'

'No,' was the glum reply.

'He says that his DREAM,' and he emphasised the word 'DREAM' did not actually tell him how, but he thinks that he saw 'AN AXEMAN.'

'The Normans do not usually employ axe-men; they rely on horses, armour and shields.' Said Aelnoth.

'AND discipline.' Said Magnus.

The group of warriors who had been assembled by Oscar were marched forward to face the shieldwall.

'Now remember,' shouted Magnus at the top of his voice.

'When the Normans.' He pointed to Oscar's group of men. 'Attack you. Keep together. Lock your shields just like you are doing now.'

'Do not break the line.'

'Do not rush forward, even if you see your enemy fall.'

'Do not run after him, even if you think he is beaten and is retreating, for it is an old trick to feint defeat, and then turn on your enemy, once he has left the safety of the shieldwall, and is isolated and vulnerable.'

'You men who are in the second, third and fourth lines. Jab your spears over the shoulders of your comrades.'

'Aim at the faces of your enemies. Jab them. Jab them.'

He thrust the spear, which he carried in his right hand forward, and screamed. Kill them.'

'And if the man in front of you falls. Step into his place and avenge him.'

'Kill the enemy, for if you do not kill him, he will surely kill you.'

'You can expect no mercy from these bloody Norman scum, for they are bred not to know the word.'

He was about to continue when he was interrupted by the sound of a horn, calling the men to assemble.

'Right you lot.' Shouted Magnus.

'Go to your assembly points NOW.'

As the warriors rushed to their own assembly points, the three Englishmen ran back to their tents in order to don their mail shirts, and collect their own war gear.

Each section of the army knew where they should assemble, but it took an enormous amount of time, hustle, bustle and shouting, before the army had finally settled into their separate positions.

Earl Magnus and his mixed English and Irishmen held the centre of the host.

Magnus and Oscar were on the right of Earl Magnus's sector, with Aelnoth stationed on the extreme left.

Teresa and her fifty dowry warriors (for that was what the rest of the army had named them) had merged to become part of Aelnoth's men.

King Diarmait and his one thousand men stood to the left of Earl Magnus, separated by Padraid and his Brown shields, who stood five deep behind their own small shieldwall.

Earl Magnus strode out in front of the assembled warriors and raised his hands in order to silence the noise that emanated from the host.

'Fellow warriors.' He shouted at the top of his voice, so that even those men who were on the fringes of the host could hear him.

'I have called you to arms this morning to inform you that our scouts have ridden far and wide, and have reported to me that they have found no trace of our enemy.'

A thin cheer came from an odd man here and there, which was speedily silence by the leaders nearest to them.

He held his right hand aloft again and waited until the assembly fell silent.

'This means that at the present time we are free to advance without fear of ambush, and I do assure you that I will continue to send more scouts even further afield, so that when we do meet our enemies, it will be at a time and a place of our own choosing.'

This announcement was followed by loud cheering from the warriors, thus having the intended effect on the moral of the men.

As soon as the cheering had died down, he said in a loud voice. 'We shall advance first thing in the morning, with my own warriors in the van, followed by King Diarmait, and then my son Magnus and his men.'

He walked as regally as possible to his fellow leaders, and bade them to dismiss their men, saying. 'As soon as we have broken our fast on the morrow, we will march towards the lands, which my family held near to the city of Bristol, and once we are there, I shall send a boat across to the island of Flatholme to rescue my mother and my sister Gunhild, whereupon I shall restore them to their rightful place.'

The following morning the army marched through the burg of Barnstaple, where some twenty-one men of various ages joined them.

The host tramped onward through the village of Pilton, camping as darkness overtook them, as they neared the Hamlet of Arlington.

More men joined them from Ilfracombe and the surrounding countryside as they made their way along the muddy roadway, which took them along the coast, past Lynmouth and Porlock, without a glimpse of a single Norman.

Local farmers told them that the few Normans, who had installed themselves in the farmsteads and villages along the fringes of the wastelands of Exmoor, had fled with their tails between their legs.

Oscar had been very quiet for the past three days, as he had trudged side by side with Aelnoth and Magnus.

He hardly uttering a single word, and only answering their cheerful banter with the odd nod or a grunt, which worried both Aelnoth and Magnus, for they could not see his face, merely the slits in his mask, which had been made for his eyes and his mouth.

'Something is amiss.' Said Aelnoth.

'Off-times I have seen him thus, and it has always been the harbinger of ill tidings.'

'It has been a hard time for him of late.' Remarked Aelnoth.

'He has had little or no sleep during the day, and yet he has still been quite active at night time, with his wanderings around the outskirts of the camps.'

'Aye,' answered Magnus.

'I was forgetting that he is a being of the night.' He added with a grimace.

They both glanced towards Oscar, who continued to trudge beside them in a sort of a trance, looking neither to his left, nor to his right, as he stared almost sightlessly with his strange coloured eyes, at the back of the man who walked in front of him.

Magnus looked towards Aelnoth and merely shrugged his shoulders as he continued to plod along the muddy roadway.

Aelnoth consoled himself when he thought of the numerous scouts, who the leaders had sent out in front of the army. Surely they would have spotted a Norman army, if indeed there was a Norman army out there. He mused to himself.

As soon as they had made camp that evening, Oscar immediately retired to his small leather tent where he snatched a few brief hours of much needed sleep.

He rose at midnight, and after a speedy meal of Luke-warm porridge, which his servant had left near the fire, he made his way over and around sleeping warriors.

Silently and unseen, he passed through the sentries who patrolled the outskirts of the camp.

To his left he could see a few lights from the small fishing village that was called Mine head.

In the moonlight he could also see a large number of warriors staggering back to camp, having spent the last few hours successfully draining Minhead's single Inn of its total stock of beer and home-made mead.

To his right there was nothing other than the desolation of Exmore, which faded into the distance, blocked by a range of hills that were locally known as the Brendon Hills.

All appeared to be peaceful and idealistic, with nought but the occasional scream of a fox and the chilling call of a nightjar to break the silence.

The eerie white form of a barn owl flew silently towards him and hovered a foot or so above his head.

He moved his head slightly and gazed up into the pitch black eyes of the bird, which showed no sign of alarm, as it stared down into the pink eyes of the strange human, almost as if he knew that this human was, like itself, a creature of the night.

The owl did not shift its gaze and continued to hover silently above Oscar's head, and then it suddenly let out a series of very loud screeches, which nearly deafened him, whereupon it turned its head towards the emptiness of Exmoor, not once, but twice, before it looked down intensely into Oscar's eyes, and as silently as it had hovered above him, it glided off in the direction of the desolate heathland.

Oscar trotted off after the owl, running through gorse-covered moorland, down valleys where the peat bogs were so wet, that his every step sank up to his ankles.

He sped through sparse stands of silver birch trees, halting after perhaps a couple of miles, when his messenger had suddenly disappeared.

The place where he had halted, contained a large outcrop of rocks, which were almost hidden by heather, high gorse bushes, and the odd tree, which had managed to survive the severe winter storms, which savaged this part of the south-west England.

Slightly out of breath, he walked over to the rocks, and scrambled up until he was in a position where he could look down into a wide valley below, and where, to his utter amazement, he saw a vast camp, which was alive with men and horses, illuminated by the flicker of numerous small fires.

The light from the fires hurt his eyes; temporary blinded him, causing him to look away and rub his eyes with the back of his glove.

He felt, rather than saw a presence behind him, but as he rose from his crouching position and turned, something crashed down on the back of his head sending him to the ground unconscious.

When he regained consciousness, he realised that he was sitting on the floor of a large white tent, with his hands firmly tied behind his back, which in turn were tied to the tent's main pole.

His black hood had been removed, and the light from the iron brazier caused him the pain that, although he was used to experiencing, still hurt his eyes.

Three men towered above him, and although he instantly recognised two of them as being Norman noblemen by their attire and their hairstyle, it was the third man who caused him to stare with his mouth open wide in astonishment, for the man was quite obviously not of European origin.

He had startlingly white curly hair, and his face was too round.

His lips were at least twice the size of any man he had ever seen, and his nose was flat, but although Oscar's mind unconsciously registered these facts.

The thing that had caused such confusion in the mind of Oscar was the fact that the man was quite obviously an Albino.

'Ah,' exclaimed one of the Noblemen, in a harsh sounding Norman French tongue.

'I see he is awake.'

He knelt down to be on the same level as his captive.

'Now we shall see what this spy can tell us.'

'Can you understand me Saxon? He snarled, causing Oscar to involuntary turn his face away from the man, whose breath stank of garlic and stale wine.

'I understand you Norman.' Answered Oscar.

'Ah, Good! Then perhaps you will be good enough to tell me what you were doing spying on our camp, and who sent you?' he snarled.

He turned his face towards the other Norman.

'You see, it speaks, and already he has told us that these invaders are not as stupid as you, my dear Rupert, think they are, for they also employ an Albino to do their night spying, just like we do.'

'Now! You pig. Tell me. How many men do you have?'

'How many horses?'

'How many Danes are there?'

Oscar looked away from the man and said nothing.

The man looked towards the Norman Albino and said, as he lightly slapped the face of his captive twice.

'He tells me that you have nigh on five thousand men. Is that true?' He snarled, as he looked towards the Albino.

Oscar did not answer.

'He also tells me that most of your rag-tag army are untried Irish peasants.'

'Is that true?'

'If that is what he said. What cause do you have to doubt him? Asked Oscar quietly, with a hint of sarcasm in his voice, as he forced himself to stare into the ice hard eyes of the Norman, which were mere two or three inches away from his own?

The Norman slapped the face of his captive again, before he rose to his feet and walked over to his companion.

'I shall leave Abdulla to question him. He is, after all one of the best 'Questioners' that I have ever known.'

'He will get something out of him.'

'Is it wise to rely on Abdulla my lord?' said the man so quietly, in order that Abdulla could not hear.

'Why not?'

'Well, my Lord. He is an Albino, and may have sympathy with a man of the same ilk.'

'Your fears are ill founded my friend,' said Earl Brian.

'He has served me faithfully these past five years, and never once has he given me cause to doubt him.'

'Besides.' He added.

'He is a Nubian, and has naught in common with these English peasants.'

'Come,' he said, as he slapped his second in command on the shoulder.

'Let us join our comrades at the table.'

'Tis already the early hours of the morning, and we have yet to sup.'

'Off you go Abdulla and get your tools of persuasion, and seek me out when you have gleaned the truth out of him.' He said amiably, as he escorted his comrade out of the tent.

Oscar was left alone, as Abdulla followed his master out of the tent.

Despite his struggle, the ropes that secured his hands to the tent pole had been tied by a man who knew his business, for there was not so much as a fraction of an inch of movement, which may have given him a smidgen of hope of freedom.

Nonetheless, with a lot of effort and more than a little pain, he did manage to slide the rope inch by inch up the pole, until he was standing.

He was stunned by the opulence of his surroundings, which were so unlike the small leather tents that he and the other leaders of the English army used, for the inside of this tent contained three expensive looking chests, a couple of chairs and a collapsible table.

There were expensive tapestries hanging on the sides of the tent, as well as ornate shields, swords, axes and spears.

The floor was covered with a number of sheepskin rugs, as well as a multi coloured exotic looking carpet.

'If they can carry this type of wealth to the battlefield, then their army is probably equipped in an equally expensive manner, and if that is the case, then how can we compete with wealth such as this?' He thought to himself.

His thoughts were rudely interrupted by the return of the Nubian Albino, who entered the tent, laden with an armful of iron and steel devices of torture.

The Nubian laid the metal instruments down on the table with a loud clatter, which jarred Oscar's already jumpy nerves.

'Do not look so afraid my friend,' said the Nubian.

'This is going to hurt you more than it is going to hurt me, and we must see a little blood. Must we not?' as his strange round face broke into a rare smile, revealing two rows of very white teeth (or what was left of two rows of perfectly white teeth,) for the top and the bottom fangs had been filed into a point.)

He walked over to the table and ran his fingers through his short white hair, as he pointed to one instrument and then to another, as if he was undecided which of these dangerous looking tools was going to be the tool of his choice.

'Ah, here we are.' He said as he picked up a tool resembling a sharpened pair of tongs.

He threw the tool back onto the table, with a clang, and turned again to Oscar, with a grin on his face.

'I jest.' He said, in broken English.

'I not torture a man like you?'

'We are the same, you and me.'

'I never see an Albino like me before.'

'I not harm you.'

He took a small phial out of his jacket. 'Drink.' He said quietly.

'What is it?' asked Oscar.

'Bit of this. Bit of that.'

'Will it kill me?'

'No. Not kill.'

'You sleep. Look dead.'

'Give time to get from camp.'

He placed the phial near Oscar's lips, and as Oscar opened his mouth he tipped the phial up.

As the rancid tasting potion seared down his throat, nearly choking him.

The burning sensation caused him to writhe in agony.

'What other choice do I have other than to trust you?' he gasped.

'Is so'? Answered Abdulla with a smile, which again revealed his filed teeth.

'This is nasty bit.' He scowled.

'Will hurt.'

'This hurt bit.' He added in his strange, guttural broken English.

Oscar felt drowsy and hardly felt as Abdulla snatched up a claw-like tool, which he had previously chosen, and raked it time and time again up and down, and across the face, neck and chest of his victim.

His left hand sped into the side of his jacket, and as if by magic, he brought out a year old chicken, which he slashed across the throat, and liberally sprinkled its blood over the face and chest of the now unconscious Oscar.

'There.' He said with satisfaction.

'No man not know alive.'

'Think dead.' He added to himself.

Earl Brian and his aide entered the tent a few minutes later and abruptly halted, as they saw a copious amount of blood, which covered his precious oriental carpet, and a prisoner, who's head lolled onto his bloody chest, as his body sagged against the ropes, which still held him tightly to the tent pole.

'Gods blood man. I did not tell you to kill him,' said Earl Brian in a loud voice.

He walked slowly over to the table to inspect Abdulla's instruments of torture, noting that several of them were covered in blood.

'I wanted him alive.' He said angrily.

'We may have learned more from him.'

'Still, he is dead, and only the good Lord himself can reverse that situation.'

'What did you glean from the spy?'

Abdulla hung his head and said mournfully. 'Not much.'

'They five thousand. Go Bristol.'

'Lot of Irish and Vikings.'

'That's what we thought.' Said Earl Brian thoughtfully.

'Still it is good that our suspicions have been confirmed.'

'We must be up and on the march by dawn.'

'What I do with body?' asked Abdulla.

'Oh, dump it somewhere.'

'Burn it. Bury it.'

'I don't give a damn what you do with it, just get this offal out of my quarters.'

Abdulla immediately walked to the doorway of the tent and said in a loud voice to one of the guards.

'Fetch horse. Help get body away.'

The guard brought his right fist up to his forehead to acknowledge the order and turned to obey.

To Abdulla, it seemed to be an age before the guard returned with a horse, but in truth it was probably no more than a quarter of the hour by the sand clock.

'Help get him on.'

'I not carry damn spy through camp alone.'

The guard took the so called spy's shoulders, whilst Abdulla lifted his feet and together they carried Oscar out of the tent and heaved his body over the saddle, whereupon Abdulla reached under the horse and with a leather strap, he tied the hands and feet tightly, so that the body would not slip off.

He casually led the horse through the camp; hailing a man here and there and answering the odd question. Laughing at the occasional lewd jest that some of the Norman warriors made towards him and the body, for he had become immune to words like, Freak. Demon and other insults.

Eventually, he passed the empty space between the camp and the guards, and led the horse up into the high gorse bushes, leading him past the rocks where he had originally captured Oscar.

He continued to lead the horse for another quarter of a mile, before he halted in a small hollow in the heathland, where he cut the thong, which held Oscar to the horse and pulled him onto the ground, where Oscar lay silent and apparently dead.

It was only after the complete contents of his canteen had been splashed over Oscar's face, and Abdulla had slapped the cheeks of Oscar several times, that a flicker of life returned to the prone figure of his fellow Albino.

The eyelids flickered a number of times before they remained open, to reveal the pink eyes of the drugged man, whose hands immediately flew up to his eyes, for without realising it, Abdulla had failed to realise that dawn was beginning to break, and the weak sun was shining directly into Oscars eyes.

'Bugger,' swore Abdulla, which was the only Norman swear word that he knew.

'Sorry. I no think,' and he rose to rummage through his personal bag that hung from the saddle.

'Ah.' He said, as he pulled two dark leather hoods out of the bag and walked over to Oscar.

'One for you and me.' He said quietly as he commenced to place the hood over his head and downwards so that it covered the whole of his head, except for four small holes that had been left for his mouth, nose and his two eyes.

Over the eyeholes, the maker of the hood had glued inch long strands of horsehair, in order to give Abdulla as much protection as possible from bright lights.

He then stooped down by Oscar and helped him to don his hood.

'You feel good now?' he asked.

'Better. I think. But my head throbs like I have been kicked by a mule.'

'Drug gives headache.' Said Abdulla.

'How Hood?' He asked.

'Bloody wonderful.' Oscar lied, as he attempted to rise into a sitting position.

After his second attempt he was more or less upright, and he retched and retched, bringing up every scrap of food that he had eaten over the past twenty-four hours.

'Me help.' Said Abdulla as he grabbed Oscar's arms and heaved him up.

After a short time, Oscar rose unsteadily to his feet.

'Why did you help me? He asked.

'Spirits say Help.' was the reply.

'I with Normans. Me slave. Give me house. Food. Cloths. Slave-girls.'

'Me still slave.'

He scratched his inch long curly white hair through his hood, and looked into the pink eyes of Oscar, with eyes of the same hue.

223

He continued. 'Never seen another Albino.'

'Could not kill.'

'Love at first sight.' Quipped Oscar, whose head was beginning to clear, as he made a half-hearted attempt to make light of the situation.

Abdulla's reaction to Oscar's remark, struck Oscar into silence. For Abdulla's face revealed that the man really did have deep feelings for his fellow Albino.

'We should go and warn my friends.' Said Oscar.

'You.' He pointed. 'Not fit to travel' said Abdulla.

'I give strong drugs. To look real.' He added almost apologetically.

'I must cut. Make look real. Or not believe.'

'Forgive?'

'There is nought to forgive my friend.'

'I shall forever be in your debt, for there is no doubt that they would have killed me, and I suspect that it would not have been a quick death.'

'Come.' Said Abdulla.

'Me help you up on horse. I lead way.'

Once he was in the saddle, Oscar felt a little better, although his head was still spinning, and his stomach ached so much that he felt that he was going to retch again, but by sheer willpower, he managed to stay upright, and held onto the reins as if his very life depended on it.

With Abdul leading the horse, they made their way up and out of the small hollow, but as they neared the crest, Abdulla suddenly flung his hand out and crouched down.

'Back. Back.' He hissed as he pulled on the reins, forcing the horse to retrace its steps a few yards backwards.

'What is it?' asked Oscar groggily.

'Norman.' Was the reply.

'Come.' Said Abdulla, as he wrenched the reins of the horse, forcing the beast down the slope towards a small, steep indention in the dell, which was overgrown and sheltered by several large gorse bushes.

The two men urged the horse close to the bank, into a position where they would not be seen by anyone, other than the very curious, hoping that the Norman army, who were passing less than one hundred yards away, would not see them.

After a long wait, the noise of the passing army and their equipment abated, and eventually faded into the distance, thus allowing the quiet of the moorland to resume to its natural serenity.

The two Albino's crept slowly to the top of the dell, and once Oscar had snatched up a couple of handfuls of dry bracken, which he placed on top of the hoods of both Abdulla and himself, in order to camouflage the outlines of their heads.

They carefully lifted their heads over the ridge, in the hope that no Norman stragglers or scouts remained.

'All gone,' said Abdulla, stating the obvious, for there was neither sight nor sound of the Norman host that had passed, a few brief minutes ago.

'Thank the good Lord for that.' Sighed Oscar.

'Now we must make haste to my friends and inform them of what we know,' he added.

CHAPTER 15

Despite the fact that it had been two days since Oscar had left, the camp had not moved, apart from seeming to be less crowded than he remembered.

The only other thing that appeared to have changed was that it was much dirtier and stank so much, that a blind man on a donkey could have located it, by smell alone.

In order to prove his identity, the guards forced Oscar to remove his hood, and once the hood had been removed, they instantly recognised him, and in their excitement at seeing him again, they shouted at the top of their voices. 'Oscar is here. Oscar is here.'

For the camp had been abuzz with the news that their famous Albino.

The man who could see in the dark, and who they thought had either deserted them, or had been killed.

The guards completely forgot to ask for the identity of his companion, and escorted both of them through the growing throng of warriors.

The growing noise made by the warriors, caused Diarmait, Bjorn and Padraid to leave the table where they had been sitting, and shoulder their way through the crowd, where they found the younger Magnus and Aelnoth already joyously greeting Oscar and his still hooded companion.

'Where the Devil have you been? Exclaimed Aelnoth as he slapped Oscar on the shoulder in delight.

'We thought you had got lost or had been slain or something.'

Oscar, who was pulling his hood over his head, held his hand up to the crowd and shouted loudly in order for his voice to be heard over the clamour that the warriors were making.

'Quiet. Quiet.' He shouted.

'You are making so much noise that our enemies will hear you, and think you are attacking them.'

His remark caused the few men who heard his words to laugh, but they too turned to face the crowd and held their hands in the air so that the noise slowly abated enough to allow Oscar to speak.

'My friends,' he said loudly.

'Thank you for your warm welcome.'

'I had no idea that I was so popular, but I can assure you that all is well with me.'

'I had a slight mishap out there on the moorland, and my friend here saved my life, so I want you all to know him and show him the respect that he deserves.

He then turned to Abdulla and said. 'Take your hood off, or they will not know you.'

Abdulla removed the hood, causing cries and gasps of alarm, with many men crossing themselves.

'By Odin's balls,' shouted one of the Vikings, who was obviously still a believer in the old Gods.

'It is Loki. The trickster. The wearer of the mask.'

'Gods blood.' Exclaimed Bjorn. 'I cannot believe my eyes.'

'He is another Albino.' He said with alarm in his voice.

'He is indeed.' Said Oscar, 'and he is another man who can see in the dark.'

'Just how lucky can we be?' He added.

This remark caused a snicker or two from the crowd, and the mood altered from one of fear, to one of elation, as the men cheered and clapped their hands in joy.

After a little while, Oscar said quietly to Diarmait. 'Call the other leaders together.'

'I have news that you may find disturbing.'

When the leaders assembled in Diarmat's tent, Oscar said. 'I was captured by a man who was a scout for the Norman army, and my friend Abdulla saved my life.

'Normans!! Exclaimed Diarmait.

'You mean to tell us that there is a Norman army near?'

'I am, and they know our numbers, and that we are heading for Bristol.'

'Horse manure and cow shit.' Said Bjorn angrily as he spat on the floor in disgust.

'How did our scouts not locate a whole bloody army?'

'That puts us at a severe disadvantage.' He added.

'Why,' asked Aelnoth?

'Well. We have lost the element of surprise.' Answered Bjorn.

'Oh. They were always going to know that we had landed, and pretty well what part of the country we were in.' said Aelnoth.

'I think that we still have an advantage, because they do not know, that we know that they are here, and now that we do know about them, we must expect that they will probably, either try to catch us on the march, or try to ambush us, and attempt to bring us to battle at a place of their choosing.'

The leaders nodded at the knowledge and reasoning of the youngster.

'It's up to us to make sure that they do none of those things, and with these two scouts who can both see in the dark, then we have a good chance to turn the tables on them, and either catch THEM on the march, or bring them to battle at a place where we will have the advantage.'

'You speak well my friend.' Said Diarmait.

'But we would do well to remember that Oscar here, can see in the dark, and yet he was captured.

'What I failed to tell you.' Intervened Oscar.

'Was that the man who captured me was non other than my friend here, Abdulla.'

'Are you telling me that it was he who captured you? And yet it was also him who saved you?'

'I am indeed.'

'Mmm, said Bjorn. 'Odd. Why would he do such a strange thing?'

'Aye, odd it is, but that is how it was.'

'Why?' Reiterated Bjorn stubbornly, for in his suspicious mind, the word 'SPY'? Screamed at him.

'Why what?'

'Well, why did he save you, when he was a spy for the Normans?'

'Because he is an Albino.' Said Oscar.

'And I have never seen another like me.'

'Neither have any of us, I'll warrant.' Said Bjorn, as the simple logic of the explanation drove the 'spy' word from his brain.

The other men in the tent nodded and grunted, thus accepting the situation.

Diarmait moved over to the table and studied a rough map.

'We are here.' He stabbed his finger to a point on the map where he thought his army was camped.

'To the left we have the sea, whilst to our right we have the uncharted moorland of Exmoor, which more or less blocks us either way.'

'We could, of course return to our ships, and sail towards Bristol or the south-eastern coast of England, but that would look like we are retreating from our unseen enemy, and the men may look upon it as a defeat, and lose heart.'

'But the weather has already turned, and we could get caught in the estuary, and if we are caught there, we could easily lose our ships and our lives.'

'But where are the Normans?' asked Padraid of the Brownshields.

'Indeed?'

'That is what we need to find out,' said Diarmait.

'How many horses do we have?' He asked.

'Not really sure.' Said Earl Magnus. 'I have four. But I will not be using my two stallions for mere scouting.'

'They are much too valuable for that.' He said loftily.

'Three of my men own horses, and I expect that there are probably a dozen or more in the rest of the host.'

'That's maybe fifteen or twenty,' said Diarmait optimistically.

'Right, my friends, I need you to provide me with enough horsemen to ride these horses, and have them ride out in twos, at least five miles ahead of us.'

'Tell them to ride so that they can see the next two riders both to their left and to their right, and when they see any sign of the enemy, then one of the horsemen must ride back as speedily as they can, in order to give us enough time to form up into our battle lines.'

'The remaining riders must stay and keep the enemy in sight, and when they form up into their battle formation, then that is the time for the remaining horsemen to rejoin us.'

'Is that clear?'

'Aye, Aye they all chorused as they hastened to leave the tent.

Within the hour the army was on the move, tramping out of the stinking camp, past fires, which still burnt, and the heaps of rubbish that an army usually leaves, when it breaks camp.

The horsemen ranged ahead of the army, who trudged in their individual groups along the muddy roadway, up and along the coast road towards Bristol.

The host had covered some eleven miles on the first day, with no sighting of the enemy, but around noon on the second day, several horsemen could be seen lashing their mounts as they galloped back towards the marching men.

Two of the horsemen skidded to a halt at the same time in a shower of mud, a few yards from Earl Magnus.

They both leapt to the ground and knelt before the Earl.

'We have found them my Lord.' Panted one of the men.

'Obviously.' Said the Earl snootily.

'Where? You idiot.'

'Are they on the next rise or ten bloody miles away?'

'Quickly, you stupid Oaf. Where in the name of hell are they?

'My Lord.' Said the second man in a more controlled manner.

'They are about a mile, and then perhaps a half mile further.

Arrayed on a rise.'

'Waiting for us.'

'Indeed.' Snorted the Earl.

'Ride down the line and have the leaders attend me here.'

The man placed his fist on his forehead in acknowledgment, and leapt into the saddle, spurring his still sweating mount down the roadway.

After a brief meeting, it was agreed that the army should march to a point some three quarters of a mile further up the roadway, where the scouts informed them; they would find a round hillock, bordered by a small stream, which gurgled along a dip in the landscape, between the hillock and the Norman army.

The leaders hurried back to their particular sections of the army, in order to urge their warriors along the roadway and up the small hillock, where, after a lot of cussing and shouting, the army eventually formed up to face their enemies, perhaps an hour on the sand clock, before dusk.

'Tis a little late in the day to start a battle.' Remarked Earl Magnus.

'Indeed it is.' Answered Bjorn.

'But I think we should remain at our posts a little while longer.'

'These Normans are masters at trickery, and a man can never know for certain what the devils will come up with.'

By nightfall there was no sign of movement in the Norman camp, and Earl Magnus ordered the army to make camp.

He sent one hundred and fifty men down to the outskirts of the camp, and ordered them to halt perhaps one hundred paces before they reached the bottom of the hillock, where they were told to form a line around the entire hillock, and stand guard.

Oscar and Abdulla left soon after midnight, and made their way silently through the heathland to the rear of the Norman camp, where they paused for a while to ensure that they knew the true positions of the sentries who patrolled the perimeter.

The sentries in that particular sector patrolled an area of perhaps one hundred yards each, before they met another patrolling sentry, and retraced their steps to their original position.

On each occasion that they met, they exchanged a few words, and on the odd occasion paused for several minutes for a short chat.

'I'll take the one on my side when he reaches the half way point of his walk and you take the one on your side at the same time.' Said Oscar.

'And then they will be about two hundred yards apart, and if one of them should make a sound then it will be unlikely that the others will hear him.'

Abdulla nodded and whispered. 'I make no noise,' before he slipped silently away on his mission.

Both sentries had their throats cut within seconds of each other without making a sound, thus allowing the two Albinos to creep silently into the sleeping camp.

Abdulla led the way through the throng of sleeping men, towards the centre of the camp, past fires where an odd man here and there sat by a fire.

'The Lords always in middle, we find them.' He whispered.

'I long time with them.'

'Know their ways.'

'Come. Follow.' He said quietly.

'With a bit of luck we might be able to cut the head off this snake and save a lot of good men's lives.' Said Oscar.

A little later Abdulla halted, and pointed towards a tent that was at least ten times larger than the small tents of the common warriors.

'Two sentries.' Whispered Oscar quietly.

'Two we see.' Answered Abdulla.

'More in tent.' He added.

'That could make it tricky.' Remarked Oscar.

'Still, we have come this far, so we have got to give it a go.'

'You stay. Me go,' and before Oscar had time to object, Abdulla stood, and made his way towards the camp.

Abdulla took the bold approach and walked bravely up towards the sentries.

'Gods blood.' Exclaimed the elder of the two sentries.

'It's the Albino. I thought he was dead.'

'Nah,' answered the other who was the kind of a man who you would not pick a fight with in a Tavern. 'I heard he had deserted.'

'What do you want'? Snarled the elder sentry?

'I come see Earl Brian.' Answered Abdulla.

'You are a dirty traitor.' Accused one of the guards.

'I no traitor. I leave. I come back.' Said Abdulla.

'Returned, my big fat ass.' Hissed the sentry.

'You are a bloody traitor.

'Grab him,' and before Abdulla could move, the spear point of the younger man pricked the skin close to Abdulla's Adams apple.

The elder sentry took a pace backwards and poked his head through the flap of the doorway and beckoned the two sentries who were inside the tent, to join him.

'Tie up this traitor.' He snarled quietly, 'and we shall see what the Earl has to say in the morning.'

The two brawny guards grabbed Abdulla's arms and held him fast, whilst the youngest of the four guards went into the tent to find a length of rope.

One of the guards who held Abdulla let out a scream, as Oscar's sword entered his back and pierced his heart, causing the man to release his hold on his prisoner, as he collapsed in a heap.

With his one arm released, Abdulla snatched his knife out of his belt and plunged it into the other guard who held him, causing him to scream with pain and clutch his stomach as he staggered away.

The youngest of the sentries slashed his spear at Abdulla, catching him on the side of his head, and sending him reeling away with a savage pain, which shot through his star spangled brain.

The third man now rushed out of the tent carrying a length of cord in one hand, and a spear in the other, and attacked the two would be assassins, shouting at the top of his voice. 'Alarm. Alarm. We are attacked.'

The two Albino's glanced at each other in alarm, knowing that their plan had been thwarted.

'Quick.' Shouted Oscar. 'Run.' And he stepped away from the two Norman sentries, turning on his heel and raced away, closely followed by his Nubian friend.

Fortunately the guards shouts of alarm had not yet reached the outer perimeter of the camp, as the two men ran through and over the sleeping warriors, passing a shocked sentry, as Oscar crashed into him, sending the man tumbling in a heap, as they ran as fast as they could into the blessed darkness.

They stopped in order to allow their sensitive eyes to adjust to the darkness, leaving the Norman camp in turmoil, as the Norman warriors were being wakened from their slumbers by the alarm.

'At least we woke the beggars up.' Grumbled Oscar, but he was, nonetheless angry that they had failed in their purpose to slay any of the Norman leaders.

'Aye,' answered Abdulla.

'No much sleep for night. They tired in morning,'

They passed silently through their own sentries and returned to their own small leather tents in order to get a little sleep, in readiness for the battle that both sides seemed intent upon staging on the coming day.

The blowing of horns and the shouts of men wakened Aelnoth long before dawn, causing him to think that the camp had been attacked, but when he rushed out of his tent with sword and shield, he realised that there had been no attack and that the warriors were being roused from their slumbers earlier than usual, on the orders of Earl Magnus, who wanted his men to be up and ready, just in case the Normans had an early attack on their minds.

After the scouts had reported to the Earl that the enemy had not stirred, he ordered the men to eat, drink and attend to their bodily functions, and look to their equipment, in readiness for the coming battle.

Aelnoth met with Magnus the younger and Oscar, who was, as usual, closely followed by his new friend Abdulla.

'What happened to you two last night?' he asked Magnus.

'Oh, we went on a little fishing expedition.' Came the answer as he turned his head and winked at Abdulla.

'Did you catch anything?'

'We very nearly caught a spear or two.' Answered Oscar.

'How come?'

'Well, we went into the Norman camp with the intention of slaying Earl Brian and perhaps a few others of his main men, but nearly got caught, and were lucky to get away with our lives.'

'Got a few guards and woke the buggers up though.' Growled Oscar.

Their banter was interrupted by a messenger, who ran through the camp and skidded to a halt before Earl Magnus who was in the process of joining his son.

'My Lord,' gasped the messenger.

'The enemy are massing.'

'Christ's blood.' Spluttered Earl Magnus.

'Here we are chatting like a gaggle of fishwives, whilst these Norman bastards are about to steal the march on us.'

'Sound the horns.' He shouted at the top of his voice, and within a few seconds the horns and the drums called the army to arms.

It took much longer than Aelnoth would have liked before the army had sorted itself out, and were assembled in their allotted places on the brow of the hillock, with Earl Magnus and his men taking the centre position of the army, whilst Diarmait and his men from Leinster stood on the Earls left.

The one hundred Brown Shields of Padraid stood between the men of Leinster and Earl Magnus, forming a solid, disciplined shieldwall some five men deep.

Aelnoth, Magnus and Oscar and their warriors held the right hand side of the host.

Squeezed next to Aelnoth was Teresa with her fifty dowry-men, whilst Bjorn and his Viking warriors stood to the right of him.

As soon as he had wakened, he had ordered Ingrid to retreat to the rear of the army, and to remain with the baggage animals and their guards, until he personally returned to fetch her.

Aelnoth strode out before his assembled men, and held his hand up in order to silence the nervous laughter and chatter that emitted from them.

'Men.' he said in a voice that he hoped would be loud enough for every man to hear.

'To-day we shall put into practice all the drills, and the skills that myself and your other leaders have tried to drill into you.'

'Remember all that you have learned over the past few weeks.'

'The enemy there and he turned and pointed his sword to the assembled Norman army that stood a mere four hundred yards away.

'They are merely men. Like you.'

'They can bleed. They can die.'

'They have been feeding on the fat of the land.'
'They have not been training hard like you.' He lied.
'They are looking across this valley, and are probably pissing themselves with fear.'
'Be brave.' He bellowed.
'Remember. Keep in the shieldwall.'
'If they turn tail and run. Do NOT chase them, for if you do, you will be open to their spears and will probably be slain.'
'Stay in the shieldwall.'
'Prod the buggers with your spears and keep them at arms length, but DO NOT leave the safety of the shieldwall.'
'Shove your bloody spears into their eyes.'
'You men who have practiced shoving your spears under the shieldwall. Don't forget the lessons you have learned.'
'Stab at their legs and bring them down. Then your fellow warriors can finish them off.'
'Remember. These bloody Normans don't even trust their own kinfolk.'
'They carry their gold with them.'
'After we have won. We shall all be rich men.'
'Show them no mercy.'
'Show them your bravery.'
'WE CAN BEAT THEM.'
'WE WILL BEAT THEM.
'KILL THEM.' He screamed at the top of his voice.
The men responded, and roared their approval.
'Kill them. Kill them. Kill them.' They screamed.

Their screams seemed to waken the rest of the army, who echoed the screams with screams and shouts of their own, until the whole army was hooting, bellowing and crashing their weapons onto their shields, filling the valleys and the hills with so much noise, that it echoed across the hills and moorlands, sending flocks of lapwings and skylarks squawking into the air.

Lapwings and skylarks were not the only beings that were roused by the noise, for the packed ranks of the Norman army, who had been more or less quiet, stirred as if a sudden and violent hailstorm had swept into them.

Men suddenly strode out in front of the army, causing the whole of the Norman host to move slowly forward, and down the slope towards the English/Irish and Vikings.

'Good.' Exclaimed Aelnoth loudly.

'That is what I hoped might happen. Now they will have to attack us uphill, and we shall have the higher ground.'

Above the hubbub of the army, he heard Earl Magnus shout. 'Archers. Are you ready?'

'Ready.' Shouted the Archers.

'Spearmen. Are you ready? He roared.

'Ready.' Answered the spearmen, who stood in the innermost ranks, behind the tried and tested warriors who inhabited the two front ranks of the shieldwall.

CHAPTER 16

The Norman host made their way down the slope and over the stream, only breaking their solid ranks to avoid the thickest and highest of the gorse bushes, which peppered the hillside.

The warriors in the army of Earl Magnus watched silently as the heavily armoured foot soldiers continued to trudge up the slope towards them, causing many of the Irishmen who had not seen battle before, to step back and look over their shoulders for a way to flee.

The Normans stopped short of the English Host in order to adjust their lines, which was probably a mistake, because as the men of Earl Magnus's army saw them stop, they ceased being cowards and became warriors again, causing their shieldwall to stiffen, as they waited for their enemies to close the remaining fifty or so yards, which separated the two sides.

'Archers. Loose.' Bellowed Earl Magnus and the archers loosed their shafts over the heads of their fellow warriors, so that their shafts fell like a hailstorm upon their enemies, who strove forward manfully in order to reach the shieldwall.

The arrows were joined by the heavy war spears that were hurled over the shieldwall into the packed Normans, who held their shields aloft in order to protect themselves from the lethal hailstorm.

Most of the spears and arrows hit the shields, but many flew through the gaps, so that a great many of the warriors in the leading ranks fell dead or wounded, leaving the second and third ranks open to the deluge, which continued to fall upon them.

The Normans paused their advance for a brief moment, before they continued to trudge up the hillside, until they neared the ranks of their enemies, and as the arrow and spear storm ceased, they were allowed to ply the trade of hack and thrust, causing their enemies, who were fresh from the training fields to waver, unused as they were to the sight of their fellow warriors blood splattering them, as their friends reeled and fell around them.

Shields clashed loudly against shields, as men pushed and shoved, and swung their swords and axes, whilst their fellow warriors who were behind them, prodded their spears over the shoulders of the man in front of them, and into the faces of their enemies.

Aelnoth found himself confronted by swarthy-faced giant, who immediately swung his axe over Aelnoth's shield with the intention of hooking his axe over the shield and pulling it away from him, which would leave Aelnoth's chest open to a spear thrust from one of the giant's fellow warriors.

Aelnoth thrust his knee into the base of his shield in order to counter the move, whilst at the same time he thrust his sword forward, only to find it blocked by the giants own shield, as he and his opponent heaved and grunted, as each man tried to get the upper hand.

The giant was an experienced warrior, who, from the scars on his face and his sword arm, bore proof that he had stood in a shieldwall on more than one occasion.

Aelnoth could smell garlic and wine on the man's breath, and the man's face grimaced, as if he had swallowed a nest full of wasps, as he hacked and thrust at Aelnoth.

The giant's raw strength was proving too much for Aelnoth, and he felt himself being forced, inch-by-inch backwards, into the man behind him.

The battle madness had yet to come upon Aelnoth, for his mind told him that this giant of a man was probably the 'Axe-man' who Oscar had seen in his dream, and if he were that particular man, then he would be the man who would break Aelnoth's shieldwall.

And yet, despite the massive strength of this gigantic warrior, Aelnoth's strength and skill had so far countered everything that the giant had thrown at him.

Relief came from an unexpected quarter, as the man who stood behind Aelnoth thrust his spear over Aelnoth's shoulder, and the spear glanced off the side of the giant's helmet, causing him to take a step backwards.

Aelnoth sent the boss of his shield crashing into the giants shield, whilst at the same time he slashed his sword downwards onto his opponents shoulder, breaking the mans shoulder bone and sending him backwards, where he staggered a few steps before he fell backwards into the ranks behind him.

A sword sped towards Aelnoth's head, swung by a man who had stepped into the breach, which had been left by the wounded giant.

Aelnoth raised his shield to protect himself, and an instant later the sword crashed down into his shield, sending flashes of pain down his arm and into his shoulder, he knelt down on one knee, behind his shield and thrust his sword under the mans mail shirt and up through his belly and into his heart.

He twisted the sword and wrenched it out, a mere second before an old gnarled warrior literally stepped over the dying man, and thrust his spear towards Aelnoth's face.

Aelnoth felt the razor sharp, leaf shaped spear graze his face, and stepped forward suddenly, head butting the man and sending him reeling backwards.

As the man fell away, Aelnoth glanced along the line of the shieldwall, where he saw that the Brown Shields had not only withstood the Norman charge, but were actually advancing in a wedge formation, down into the very heart of the Norman army.

'Blast the arrogant fools.' He cursed.

'They have left the men on the left and the right of them with a gap to fill, and they are too timid and inexperienced to do so.'

Nonetheless, Irish and English warriors were rushing forward in an attempt to fill the gap that had been left by the Brown Shields, but only managed to fill the hole with a shieldwall, which was a mere two men deep.'

The Normans crashed into them like a tidal wave, sending man after man reeling backwards, either dead or wounded, creating an ever-widening hole in the centre of the army.

Aelnoth could do nought but look as the hole widened ever further, as more and more Norman warriors poured through the gap, slaying men in their dozens, as they cleaved their way into, and through the very centre of his army.

Aelnoth fought with desperate courage, slaying the man in front of him, only to be confronted with a fresh warrior, who seemed to appear almost as soon as the slain man had fallen away.

His arm ached. His face and body was painted red with other men's blood.

A cursing Norman, whose spittle dribbled down his grey beard like an ox at the plough, stood in front of him and thrust his spear into the centre of Aelnoth's shield, but Aelnoth took the jarring blow on the side of his shield, and slashed at the legs of his assailant, only to be thwarted by the rim of the mans kite shaped shield.

He immediately switched his attack to the mans head, and struck him on the side of his neck, just below his helmet, which was one of the few parts of the Normans that was unprotected, (thus it was their most vulnerable spot,) and sent the man to the ground in a pool of blood.

He dared to glance for a brief second along the line of his shieldwall again, and was dismayed to see that the Brownshields had been completely surrounded by the Normans, and although they were still in a wedge formation, and were still fighting savagely amongst the litter of slain enemies, they were now much fewer in number.

His own men. The men who he and his friends had recruited and trained were nowhere to be seen, other than the heaps of dead and wounded, which were strewn over the hillside, and he assumed that those were the bodies of the men in whom he had placed so much faith.

A few bunches of warriors still fought for their lives, but they were fighting a losing battle, for with a few exceptions, they were completely encircled by their more heavily armoured opponents, who now also had the advantage of numbers and were cutting men down almost at will.

The army, or what was left of it, began to run, and as Aelnoth glanced quickly at them, their retreat reminding him of clouds of dry leaves being scattered by an autumn wind.

He saw that his defeated warriors were being chased by their ironclad foes, who were racing after them and hacking at their unprotected backs.

He could see no sign of Earl Magnus.

Aelnoth felt a tug on his arm, and spun around to face another foeman, but saw the haggard and blood strewn face of Teresa staring up at him.

'My Lord.' She gasped.

'All is lost. We must escape.' As she tugged again on his sleeve.

'All my men have been slain, and the Brown Shields have been overwhelmed, but Lord Bjorn and his Vikings are still standing.' She said, as her blue eyes gazed up at him, imploring him to join her and help her to fight their way towards the Northmen.

Aelnoth looked towards Bjorn and his Vikings, who were fighting off hundreds of Normans, but he was relieved to see that they still held their formation behind a shieldwall that still looked to be at least four or five men deep.

'Follow me.' He shouted, as he grabbed Teresa by her shoulder and pulled her after him, as he hacked his way towards Magnus, who was fighting off two Norman spearmen.

Magnus's attackers were attempting to manoeuvre themselves into a position where they could attack him from both the front and rear at the same time.

Aelnoth crashed into the nearest spearman who had his back to him, and sliced through the man's neck with his sword.

The second man, who, a few seconds ago, had been confident that he and his friend would soon slay this nobleman, and strip him of his sword and his wealth, was so shocked by the sudden reversal of the situation, that he just stood, with his spear held forward and his shield down, leaving the top part of his body open to attack.

A very relieved Magnus shook the man out of his dilemma with a savage slash to the mans neck.

'My thanks to you. Two swords.' He gasped.

'I thought those two buggers had me.'

Aelnoth suddenly realised that in the heat of the battle, he had not actually drawn his second sword and shook his head in amazement.

'Come.' Shouted Aelnoth.

'I'm making for Bjorn.' And pointed to the right of the mound where Bjorn and his Northmen were still battling with the hordes of Norman warriors, who were still struggling up the hill in ever growing numbers towards the Northmen.

'I'm with you.' Shouted Magnus.

'Have you seen my father? The earl Magnus.' He asked.

'No.' answered Aelnoth with a shake of his head.

'I haven't seen Oscar or Abdulla either.' He added.

As Aelnoth, Magnus and Teresa fought their way towards the Vikings, his mind seemed to speak to him. Not of battle as such, but of the way that he had heard

Poets talk of the wonders of battle, when he had been in the Hall of his father, on the many occasions that his father had hosted English noblemen.

The Poets tell of the glory of battle, but few Poets have ever held a shield in a shieldwall. His brain told him.

Few Poets have ever slain a man, unless it was by poison or by other devious means.

Even fewer Poets know that when you get a mans blood under your fingernails. The only way to remove it is to scrape it out with a knife.

They tell of a warriors bravery, and sing about the glory of his deeds, and of the giants who he has slain, but Aelnoth and the few survivors from the centre of their host, saw little glory, as they hacked their way through the Normans, accompanied by a dwindling number of survivors from their own army, who still fought to the death against the superior numbers, and better trained and better armed Normans.

Their blades were not gleaming, as the Poets say.

They were dull with blood and gore.

Their spears did not shine, as the Poets say.

They were bloody and bent, from the times that they had been thrust against the metal helmets and the bosses of the shields, which they had failed to penetrate.

Those craven Poets had never stood in a shieldwall and smelt the sweat, piss and shit of his own and other warriors, who cursed and heaved as they strove to slaughter one another.

Eleven Normans barred their way, forming a small shieldwall in order to prevent Aelnoth's small group from joining the Northmen.

Aelnoth noted that three other survivors had joined his small band, making their numbers up to six, as they neared the Normans.

'Let's go around the sods.' Said Magnus, but as they made their way to the left, the Norman shieldwall moved to the left and barred the way.

'Seems not.' Said Aelnoth.

'Their loss.' Shouted Magnus, as he crouched into a fighting position and prepared to charge the line.

'The six of us must take on the two on our right.' Shouted Aelnoth.

'That way, the other sods will try to encircle us, and we can take them out, one by one.' He added.

'Hope you are right.' Said Magnus as he moved to join the rest of the group.

In the meantime. Teresa had picked up one of the many spears that lay scattered over the battlefield, and without saying a word, she suddenly flung the spear, which sped unerringly straight into the forehead of the man who held the centre position of the shieldwall, flinging the already dead man backwards and thus shattering the seemingly unshatterable Norman shieldwall.

'Hells bells,' said the startled Aelnoth as he leapt forward.

'Where in Gods name did you learn to throw a spear like that?'

'In the bogs of Ireland. Where else?' She said with a smile crossing her blood-smeared face.

'Let's get the rest of the buggers,' shouted Aelnoth.

'Before more of their friends join 'em.'

As one, they crashed into the shattered shieldwall, sending two men to the ground, and the survivors backwards, and into the main body of Normans who were still assailing the Viking shieldwall.

Aelnoth and his men followed the survivors into the backs of the Normans, who were still facing the Vikings, and who now found themselves attacked from their rear, and as they speedily turned to face their attackers, they found themselves assaulted from both their front and from the rear, by large bands of Vikings who had left their shieldwall, and hacked into the unprotected backs of their Norman enemies, whilst Aelnoth and his band of fugitives hacked at them from their front, sending man after man to the ground, dead or wounded.

Almost as if someone had issued an order, the Norman attack faltered and then ceased altogether, as they retreated and ran out of range of the Northmen's spears and arrows, which still flew from the Viking ranks.

'Run you bastards, Run.' Laughed Aelnoth, but as a jubilant Teresa flung her arms around his neck, she heard him swear.

'Damn and Blast.' He said so loud that he nearly deafened her.

'What's wrong my Love,' she said happily.

'We beat them didn't we? And now we can escape with Bjorn and his Northmen.'

She kissed him on his bloodied and sweaty face, before she dropped to the ground and turned to gaze in the direction that he was staring.

'Oh my God.' She exclaimed.

'They have released their horsemen.' And stared almost in disbelief as hundreds of mounted warriors poured over the brow of the hill, in a seemingly never-ending torrent of iron-clad horsemen.

'Quick.' Shouted Aelnoth.

'Run for your lives.'

'Get behind the shieldwall. It's the only chance we have.'

They reached Bjorn and his Northmen a few short minutes before several hundred horsemen skidded to a halt a few feet short of Bjorn's shieldwall, and the fugitives gasped for breath as they watched the riders veer away, for their steeds had balked at charging into the thick hedge of spears, which protruded from the solid lines of the disciplined and experienced Vikings.

By Freya's tits, that was a close run thing.' Gasped one of the men who had joined Aelnoth and his friends.

Showers of spears and arrows flew from the inner ranks of the Vikings, clattering like hailstones on the iron helmets and shields of their foemen, sending a number of horses and men screaming to the ground, and forcing the rest of the horsemen to urge their expensive mounts backwards, out of range, and causing at least half of their number to ride off in order to find easier prey, where they joined the bulk of the Norman horse warriors, who cheered and hollered with delight, as they rode amongst the fleeing army, spearing the running men and slashing down with their swords at the unprotected necks of the defeated English and Irish warriors.

'Now my Brothers.' Shouted Bjorn to his men.

'Keep that shieldwall solid and follow me back down the road to where we left the ships.'

Aelnoth said quietly to Magnus. 'Great idea, but does he realise that it is at least eighteen or twenty miles to the Taw?'

Magnus nodded. 'At least.' He agreed, 'and I'll warrant that those horse warriors will cut us to pieces long before then.' He said glumly.

'Maybe so, but something tells me that we will board the ships.' Said Aelnoth. '

'I'm not so sure that they will want to risk losing their precious horses just to add us few to their tally.'

'We shall see.' Said Magnus glumly.

Dusk came slowly to the solid column of Vikings, and the few English and Irish survivors who had managed to join them, as they slowly retreated through the dead and dying on the battlefield, onto the roadway, whereupon they trudged for most of the night, until they were forced to stop through weariness, and the needs of the wounded, who had been falling by the wayside during the long hours of darkness.

They camped for a few hours on a high point, which gave them at least some sort of protection, and although a number of enemy horsemen ventured to within a hundred yards of the sentries, none attacked.

Bjorn had them on the march before dawn, but their progress along the muddy roadway was painfully slow, due to the large numbers of wounded, who needed either to be carried on hastily made stretchers, or helped along by their comrades.

Aelnoth and Magnus trudged alongside Bjorn, as the three of them herded the stragglers along, as fast as they could.

'How far is it to the Taw? Asked Magnus.

'Not really sure.' Said Bjorn with a worried look, as he stared into the distance as if he expected to see more of the Norman horsemen, who had been harrying them on the yesterday.

'Can't be too far now.' Said Aelnoth.

'I remember that crag over there,' and pointed to a cluster of rocks, which studded the moorland some half a mile away.

'I think the river is in the next valley, just after we pass the village of Braunton, and I think that is Braunton over yonder.' He nodded towards a cluster of cottages that appeared over the rise.

Braunton was a ghost town, with no sign of man or beast, as the remains of the defeated army hurried as fast as they were able, past the silent cottages.

They trudged further along the muddy road, and as the for-front of the men reached the top of the rise, they let out a weak cheer as they spotted their longships moored along the banks of the river Taw.

'Not far now.' Said Magnus cheerfully, but no sooner had he spoken, than a thin wail went out from the weary men, as several hundred horsemen appeared on the horizon some three quarters of a mile away.

'Hurry.' Shouted Bjorn. 'Or the horsemen will be on you.'

The few remaining captains of the longships echoed his words, and they pushed and shoved their men down the slope towards the river Taw, and the safety of their ships.

A few of the men had boarded the first three longships when the Norman horsemen crashed into the packed, panicking Vikings, who were more interested in boarding their ships than turning to fight the advancing horsemen, so that within a few brief moments, the horsemen were inside the Viking throng, hacking and thrusting at will, as the Northmen tried in vain to avoid their bloodied blades.

'Slay the Horses.' Shouted Aelnoth, who was now almost within reach of a spear thrust from the nearest horseman, who was wielding his bloodied spear with vigour, and had a savage smile on his face, as he searched for the man who he would slay next.

His gleaming eyes fell upon Aelnoth, and he spurred his horse forward to make the killing blow, but Aelnoth two swords, drew both of his swords and stepped forward to meet the Norman, as a strange calmness came over his entire body, as he recalled a saying, which his father Edric had said to him on more than one occasion.

His Father had said. 'If your sword is too short, then take a step forward,' and with a silly smile on his young face, that is exactly what he did.

He took a pace forward, and ducking under the spear, which the Norman had thrust at him.

With his left hand, he plunged his sword deep into the belly of the Stallion, and as the horse reared and squealed in pain, he brought the sword, which he held in his right hand down, and sliced through the leg of the Norman, causing the man to cry out in pain, as horse, rider and leg fell in a heap into the path of another horseman.

Aelnoth scooped up the fallen Norman's spear and hurled it with such force that it entered the belly of the following Normans horse, stopping the horse's forward motion, as if it had ridden into a stone wall, and causing it's rider to topple over the horse's head, whereupon Aelnoth simply brought his sword down and sliced the man's head off his shoulders.

Many of the Vikings watched in awe as Aelnoth continued to slay horseman after horseman, causing men to rally, and find their own courage return, and they and a dozen other men leapt forward to join him in his spree of murderous destruction.

Magnus joined Aelnoth and the growing number of men who were joining him, fighting a savage rear guard action, holding off the remaining Normans who, seeing these savages kill horse and horsemen alike, wavered and backed their stallions out of range, thus allowing a large number of Vikings to board their longships.

Aelnoth and his men slowly backed towards the last remaining longship, fighting and slaying the final Norman who led his horse into the shallow water, in a futile attempt to prevent the last few men from finding sanctuary aboard their ships.

Magnus and Aelnoth were the final men to board the last ship, which left the muddy banks of the Taw, dodging the final spears, which were hurled at them, as they heaved themselves up, out of the muddy water, and onto the comparative safety of the ship.

Aelnoth looked around at the bloodied and weary men who sat on the benches and storage crates, or lay on the deck of the ship, as it drifted slowly with the flow of the river.

He breathed a sigh of relief as he saw the frail figure of Ingrid, whose tear streaked face shone out like a beacon amongst the ragged and blood soaked Vikings.

'Where is Teresa?' he asked.

'I haven't seen her since we broke camp this morning.' Answered Magnus.

'Hell's bells.' Swore Aelnoth.

'I hope to God that she is not slain.'

'Me too.' Said Magnus. She was a lovely girl. Gutsy too.'

'Never did see a woman who could throw a spear like that.' He mused with a shake of his head.

'We have also lost Oscar. And his friend Abdulla.'

'A sad day.' Growled Magnus.

Then he added. 'To say nothing of losing the battle.'

He shook his head in disgust and spat into the river. 'And we now have little or no chance of winning back England from these bloody Norman pigs.'

'The bastards sure know how to fight.'

'Indeed they do.' Answered Aelnoth.

'They cut through our shieldwall like a bloody hot knife through butter.'

'Damn and Blast them.'

'May they burn in Hell?' Said Magnus, as he hawked and spat another goblet of bloodied phlegm into the river.

The Captain who held the rudder shouted. 'Who goes there?' causing the two Englishmen to look up and see another longship coming alongside their own ship.

'Is that you Volund with my ship, The Walrus?' shouted a rough voice,

'It is my lord.' Shouted the Captain.

'How many men do you have?' Came a voice that they recognised to be that of Bjorn.

'About sixty or seventy.' The reply was shouted across.

'Including two Englishmen.' Said the Captain as an afterthought.

'Of any Note?' he was asked.

'Don't know, but they are good fighters.' Was the answer, as the Captain turned towards Aelnoth and Magnus?

He turned to the two Englishmen and asked in a surly voice. 'Who are you?'

'I am the Lord Magnus, you Oaf,' snapped Magnus, 'and my friend here is the Lord Aelnoth, and we are Lords in our own right, you thick headed Viking.'

'They say they are named Magnus and Aelnoth.' Bellowed Captain Volund almost nonchantly across to the other longship.

'And they claim to be Lords of somewhere or other, although I have never heard of them.'

'Well I have, you stupid man.' Called the voice across the gap, which had narrowed to a couple of feet between the two ships.

While this banter had been going on, the ships were being tied together, and as soon as the ropes had been made secure and a plank stretched across the gap, the small figure of Bjorn stepped across the plank, and landed lightly into the deck of 'The Walrus'.

He was already in one of the blackest moods of his life.

Furious at the defeat that he and his fellow warriors had just suffered, and equally annoyed that he would now not be blessed with the silver and land that he had anticipated would be his, after he had thrashed the Normans.

He was livid that his enemies had defeated his Vikings, who he had thought to be the finest warriors in Europe.

He was furious because of the ships he had lost, and he was absolutely raging, as he had just witnessed the slaughter of a sizable portion of his Viking host on the banks of the Taw.

He found it difficult to accept that he had lost so many of his ships, which had been abandoned at their moorings along the river, where several were burning, whilst the remaining ships had been captured by the jubilant Normans, who screamed and hooted at their victory, as they looted the bodies of the fallen Vikings, and danced like maniacs on the decks of their newly acquired longships.

He needed to vent the rage out of his system one way or another, and yet his logical brain told him that his dearth of Captains and ships had already reached a critical point.

The first thing he did was stalk up to the Captain and slap him twice on both sides of his face.

'You bloody dimwit.'

'If it hadn't been for these two Englishmen, who are, in my opinion, the finest warriors I have ever seen in my entire life. You and probably the rest of us would now be lying dead with our slain comrades on yonder river bank.'

He slapped him yet again, not once, but twice, as if he needed to emphasise the point he was trying to make.

'They.' He pointed towards Aelnoth and Magnus.

'THEY tackled those bloody Norman horsemen, and prevented them from killing the bloody lot of us. YOU STUPID MAN.'

The Captain hung his head, as his Lord and master continued to harangue him.

'If you were not such a good Captain. My good Volund. I would ban you from ever setting foot on one of my ships for the rest of your life.'

'As it is. I seem to have lost over half of my Captains, so you can thank your lucky stars that I shall relent, and allow you to continue to be one of my Captain's, but I want you to understand this. You are to treat those two men like royalty.'

'LIKE BLOODY ROYALTY.' He shouted at the top of his voice.

'DO YOU UNDERSTAND? LIKE BLOODY ROYALTY.' He shouted loudly into the face of the Captain, who stood at least twelve inches taller than his master.

'Aye. My Lord Bjorn.' Said the Captain glumly, for although he knew that he had unintentionally slighted the two Englishmen. He also felt that his Lord was treating him rather unfairly, in disciplining him in front of his crew.

'Still.' He thought to himself. 'I am still the Captain of 'The Walrus,' and although I have never before set eyes on half of these men, who have found sanctuary on my longship, I am still their bloody Captain.'

'Except for those two bloody Englishmen.' He mused silently to himself.

Volund was a very experienced Captain, and was usually a good judge of men.

He could unerringly pick out a good oarsman from a crowd of near-do-wells.

He was big and ugly enough to handle a crew of savage warriors, and able get the most belligerent of men to follow his orders.

But, he also knew the reputation of this small man, to whom every Viking who entered the port of Dublin, as well as those who had settled in that part of Ireland where he held sway, owed him allegiance.

He knew of men. Big men. Savage men, who had crossed Bjorn, and although he had not personally witnessed their demise, he and most of the Viking world knew that those men were either no more, or had turned up with missing arms and legs.

He recalled the popular Norse saying. 'Beware of the wrath of a quiet man.'

Volund was a large powerful man, bred from large powerful men, for men needed to be so if they were to survive where he was born, in the far north of Norway, for it is a land that is the haunt of trolls and Valkyries, who are the maidens who dwell on the mountains of ice and escort slain warriors to Valhalla.

'They will be busy today.' His agile mind told him, almost forcing a smile out of his weather-beaten face.

Lord Bjorn, who was speaking to him in a more civil manner, interrupted his thoughts.

'My own longship is undermanned, and yours seems to be carrying too many men, so I suggest that I take a dozen of your men over to my ship.' He said, as he stepped away and ushered the men across the plank that had been placed between the two ships.

He turned towards the two Englishmen and said. 'I am eternally grateful for your bravery back there on the shore.'

He gripped the right hand of both Aelnoth and Magnus, and shook each hand with vigour and friendliness, saying. 'You two men saved what is left of my army, and we few here, aboard these ships give thanks to the Gods for your valour and to your bravery.'

'I will give orders to each Captain of the twenty-one ships to drink to your health.'

'Twenty-three,' said Aelnoth before he realised what he was saying to this leader of men.

'I beg your pardon?' said Bjorn, who was slightly shocked that such a young man should correct him.

'My apologies, my Lord,' stuttered Aelnoth.

'It is a bad habit, which I have inherited from my sire. The Lord Edric.'

'Both he and myself seem to have a habit of counting things. Men. Horses. Sheep. Birds in the sky. Everything.'

'So,' he nodded his head to the ships that awaited Bjorn's orders; 'Twenty three.'

Bjorn turned from him and slowly counted the ships, which were afloat in the estuary.

He eventually turned back towards Aelnoth and turned back towards him with a smile on his face.

'By Odin's balls. You are correct. There are twenty-three.'

But then his face became very serious again, as he realised that only twenty-three ships and their crews remained out of the huge fleet of eighty ships, which had left Ireland a few short weeks ago.

As the last of the men crossed to Lord Bjorn's ship, two figures emerged from the cluster of men who were milling about, as the new men looked for a rowing bench to sit on.

The two men stepped on the plank and crossed over to Captain Volund's ship.

'Are my eyes deceiving me?' exclaimed Aelnoth, 'or am I seeing the ghosts of our dead friends, Oscar and Abdulla?'

'We are no ghosts.' Uttered the first man as he removed his hood to reveal the smiling face of Oscar.

The two men embraced Aelnoth and Magnus over the small body of Ingrid who was standing next to Aelnoth, causing Aelnoth to experience a feeling of emotion that he had not felt since the disappearance of his Father Edric, many years ago.

'All four together again.' Shouted Magnus with glee, as a silly grin crossed his dirty, bloodstained face.

'Five.' Piped up the muffled voice from Ingrid, as she reluctantly untangled herself from Aelnoth's body.

The Captain and the helmsman steered the longship towards the mouth of the estuary, as they followed the small fleet of Viking ships in the wake of 'The Dragon,' which of course was Bjorn's personal ship, being the largest ship in the fleet.

The hurried flow of the river and the stiff breeze sped the ships down the estuary, which gave the crew a little time to familiarise themselves with their new shipmates, causing much banter and laughter from the men, who, despite their cuts and bruises, now considered themselves to have ' Battle luck.' Having survived the battle, and happy to be sailing merrily away from the carnage, which they had just experienced.

Aelnoth, Magnus, Oscar Abdulla and Ingrid sat on the deck near the helm, telling of their individual adventures since they had been parted, when the shield wall of their ill-fated army had been shattered.

CHAPTER 17

Bjorn led his fleet across Bideford Bay and around the point of Hartland, where the fair wind that had sped them thus far on their way, deserted them; turning into a squall which told the experienced seamen that more severe weather was on the way.

Aboard the Walrus, Aelnoth turned his worried face towards Volund, 'Don't worry,' Volund shouted.

'I know this coast well enough. I will find a sheltered cove, where we can spend the night ashore.'

Despite the gallant Captain's seamanship, the Walrus was driven past the cove where Volund had intended to shelter, the seas being too turbulent for him to attempt to beach the ship.

'We will just have to ride the storm out, and hope for the best.'

'Half sail.' He shouted, 'Or we will lose the mast.' And half a dozen men hauled the sail down, before they returned to their benches, where the rest of the men were struggling with the oars in an attempt to keep the ship on an even keel.

The remaining crew members were bailing water out of the bilge, with anything that would hold water.

Aelnoth raised his hand to cover his eyes as he stared into the gloom, in order to see how the rest of the fleet were faring, but could only make out four ships, and those were a long way off.

Oscar and Abdulla were bailing water with their helmets, whilst Magnus was helping a wounded man with his oar, as they struggled to keep the oar in the water.

Ingrid sat huddled near the tiller, drenched and shivering with fear.

The Sagas tell us of the wonders of the sea. Of Whales and sea monsters, and of the glory of the sunset, but they do not speak of seasickness, thought Oscar, as he puked up little more than sticky bile, making him afraid that if he puked any more, he would heave up his very insides into the churning sea

Aelnoth sat behind Magnus to help with the oars. 'Bloody weather.' He shouted.

'God must be angry with us, for he has allowed our army to be defeated, only to save us, and then drown us.' He gasped one of the larger waves crashed against the side of the ship to splatter his face with ice-cold seawater.

'Whose God?' shouted Magnus over his shoulder? 'Yours or mine?'

Aelnoth's soaked face broke into a smile, for he had forgotten that Magnus was a believer in the old Northern Gods of Woden, Thor and the other Gods, whose names he could not recall.

The gale drove the Walrus south, as the men struggled to prevent the ship from being swamped by seawater.

Volund had experienced many storms in his life, but none more ferocious than this, as he steered the Walrus with uncanny skill between the churning rocks of the Scilly Isles and the mainland, allowing the raging sea to drive his beloved ship relentlessly southwards.

After two days of constant struggle, all of the men were weary and exhausted through constant strain and the lack of sleep.

The wind slowly dropped from a gale into a stiff blow, which continued to drive them onwards, allowing the weary, soaked and tired men to haul in their oars, and flop onto the deck and benches for a much needed rest, whilst Volund and the men who had held the tiller throughout the previous night were relieved by fresh men, who could do nought but allow the wind to drive the ship ever southwards.

The Captain ordered the sail to be raised.

'Make sure you get as much water out of it before you haul it aloft.' He ordered. 'Or the weight will capsize us.' And after following his orders, the still saturated sail flapped lazily as the heavy sail allowed its remaining copious amounts of seawater to drain onto the deck, drenching the already wet men, causing them to curse and move to the front and the aft of the longship until the sail began to dry out a little, and filled, sending the ship skipping across the still turbulent sea.

'I can not see any of the other ships.' Said Aelnoth to the Captain.

'No.' He answered gloomily.

'They are likely to be on the rocks or at the bottom of the sea.'

By nightfall both the sail and the crew had dried out.

The latter rested, with filled bellies of cold beer and dry, salty meat, and the sail was filled with the stiff wind, which still blew savagely from the north.

'Don't like this,' muttered Volund, as his eyes strained into the growing gloom.

'Don't know where we are, or where land is.' He uttered grumpily.

'Tis much warmer though, so we could be somewhere off the coast of Frankia or even Spain.' He added as an afterthought.

'Down Sail.' He ordered.

'We don't want to hit any rocks in the night.'

'Out oars, and you can warm yourselves up a bit, with an hour or two of rowing.'

'If any of you who have better hearing than me, and think that you can hear the sound of the sea lapping against the shore or the rocks, then for Gods sake shout.'

'I've been on the tiller for more than two days, so I'm off to snatch an hour's sleep.'

He handed the tiller over to the helmsman, and walked unsteadily towards the small leather tent, which served as the Captains quarters.

He groaned aloud as he stooped down to enter the small tent, and as he settled down under his still wet bedding, he shouted. 'Don't forget to rouse me if you hear or see anything.'

It appeared to him that he had only just closed his eyes, but in fact it was nigh on five hours later, when a rough hand shook him awake.

'Captain. Captain.' The voice repeated, as Volund shook his head a couple of times in order to clear his head.

His bleary eyes recognised the young anxious face of Aelnoth who was leaning over him.

'Captain.' Aelnoth repeated. 'We have sighted land.'

Volund struggled up from the low tent, and walked slowly to the prow of the longship, where he could see a dim outline of land stretching to the aft of the ship.

'Helmsman.' He shouted.

'Steer aft and we shall see what manner of land is yonder.'

Aelnoth sighed aloud with relief as they neared the coast, for in truth he had been ill at ease since the storm had forced them off course, and especially so, when he had found that the rest of Bjorn's fleet had disappeared, leaving this small and vulnerable longship alone in this seemingly endless expense of Empty Ocean.

Ingrid joined him and Clung onto his arm, as they both stared at the dull grey outline of the land in the distance.

Magnus, Oscar and his constant companion Abdulla, followed Aelnoth and Ingrid as they made their way to the prow, where Volund was deep in conversation with one of his crewmen, as they both stared at the land, which was now no more than a quarter of a mile away.

'Do you know what land it is?' asked Aelnoth.

'Not really.' Came the solemn answer from the Captain.

'I think it could be Spain, but we won't know for certain until I can spot a bit of the shoreline that I recognise, or until we can speak with the people of the area.'

'I can see no sign of habitation?' Queried Aelnoth.

'Oh. If this Spain, or even Frankia, you will see no villages along the coast.'

'Why is that?' asked Aelnoth.

'Northmen and Barbary Pirates have been raiding these coasts for the last five hundred years, so all the townships and villages have either been destroyed, or are hidden from the eyes of the likes of me and you.'

Said the Captain with a grim smirk that split his weathered face.

Volund skilfully steered the Walrus into a small cove, where he beached the craft on a small strand of shingle, below white cliffs, which were topped by thick windblown shrubs.

After enjoying barbecued fish and the last of the stale beer, the weary crew gathered around the three small fires, and enjoyed the first good nights sleep since they had battled with the Normans, what seemed to be a lifetime ago.

In the morning Volund called Aelnoth and his friends over to join him.

'I am not really sure what land we are in.' he said grimly, 'but whether it is Spain or Frankia matters little.'

'What does matter now, is where we go from here.'

He paused for a moment before he continued.

'When the wind changes we could retrace our steps, so to speak, and sail north, either to England, Ireland or even to Scandinavia.'

'Like drowned rats returning to their nests in defeat.' Spat Aelnoth.

'I think that to return to England would merely land us into the hands of the Normans, who would surely have us slain.' Ventured Magnus.

'Aye,' said Oscar.

'They have become too powerful, and are much too strong for us to tackle now.'

'We have gained nought from our ventures.' Interrupted Volund.

'So I suggest that we go 'A-Viking' along the coast of the warm sea.'

'I have heard that the Emperor of Micklegard needs Northmen.' He added

'Micklegard.' Exclaimed Oscar.

'Where in the name of Hell is Micklegard?'

'I see that you have not yet been A-Viking.' Said Volund with a smile.

'Micklegard is what we Northmen call Byzantium, or even Constantinople, and the Emperor will have no guards other than men of the north for his personal bodyguard.'

'They are called the Varangian Guard, and are the finest and fiercest warriors in the world.'

'He used to recruit only from Sweden, Denmark and Iceland, but I hear that since the Normans conquered England, at least a quarter of his bodyguard are Englishmen, who prefer exile rather than live under the Norman yoke.'

'Why doesn't he use his own warriors?' asked Magnus.

'He doesn't trust 'em.' Came the quick answer.

'I don't blame him either.' He added.

'They are a shifty lot, and I would advise you not to put too much trust in them either.'

'Haven't you heard the old story of 'Beware of Greeks bearing gifts?''

'Aelnoth ignored his remark and asked, 'why should we fight for this foreign Emperor?'

'We may as well go home to England and die there, AND take a few of those Norman bastards to hell with us.'

'I will tell you why we should fight for the Emperor,' said Volund.

'He is one of the richest men in the world, and he pays his personal guard with more gold and jewels than you could imagine.'

He continued as he held his hands out wide as he said. 'I have seen men return from Micklegard with more gold, and more treasure than a strong man can carry.'

'And.' He continued. 'It is their law than when an Emperor dies, then his Varangian guard, in other words, 'US,' have the right to loot his treasurery, and take away as much gold and precious stones as we wish.'

'Let us hope the old bugger dies sooner rather than later.' Said Oscar.

'Do you think he will accept us? Asked Magnus.

'Well.' Answered Volund. 'It is true that he does not accept all Northmen who want to join, but I do have a friend of a friend, who left Norway four or five of years ago, and who is, if what I have heard is true, now a man of a high rank within the Varangians, so I think that we have a very good chance of being accepted.'

'How far is it to Micklegard?' asked Aelnoth in a serious tone.

'Well, since I am not really sure exactly where we are, it is hard to say how far it is, but if we can follow this coastline south and then turn east into the inland sea, which is called 'The Mediterranean,' it will probably take us perhaps three or four weeks, depending on the winds and the weather,' he added.

The men who had been on sentry duty for the latter part of the night, joined the main body of men, and ate a hasty breakfast of dried herrings, being the staple food, which most longships kept in salted barrels.

As soon as the last of the men had finished eating, they helped their fellow warriors to push the longship off the shingled beach, and into the sea.

The rowers pulled on their oars, sending the Walrus skimming over the silver sea.

Oscar sat on the deck, and took out the small leather case in which he kept, what he called, 'his magic stones,' and emptied them onto the deck.

Aelnoth looked towards Magnus and Abdulla and shook his head.

'Here we go again.' He said.

'He seems to bring out the runes every day. Must be worried about something.'

'True.' Answered Magnus, 'but each time I ask him, he will not tell me. He just looks at me with a blank face and turns away.

'Today different.' Said Abdulla.

'Why do you say that?' asked Aelnoth.

'See face.' Answered Abdulla in his strange accent.

Oscar seemed not to notice them as he continued to stare at the runes for such a long time, that his three companions became bored, and began to chat amongst themselves, as they gazed at the coastline, which was a few hundred yards distant, and seemed to be dull and unchanging, with no sign of human habitation.

Suddenly a low moan came from their friend who sat on the deck, and who flung both of his arms out before him, whilst the low moaning continued to emit from his open, dribbling mouth.

'I see the widows spinning their threads.' He said in a high-pitched voice that sounded more like the voice of a young girl than his own normal voice.

'I see the three Norns again.' He said.

'They are the same as before.'

'They are at a loom, and are weaving the destinies of men.'

'They stare at me, but they have no faces.'

'Four men stand on a hill.'

'I see war. Burning cities.'

'Sinking ships. Death and devastation.'

'I see the face of a wolf. A wolf.' He repeated

'It is the same wolf that I have seen before.'

'It has the hand of a man in its mouth.'

'It is in a tree.'

'It is smiling at me, but it is not the smile of a wolf.'

'Neither is it the smile of a man.'

'Ah! It is the smile of a woman.'

'A beautiful woman.'

His three friends leaned over him as he continued to mumble incoherently in the voice of a young girl, but his words became jumbled, and seemed to be in a language that they did not know, until he became silent.

And then his body was wracked with shivers and he fell full length onto the deck where he lay apparently asleep.

'Bullshit. It's all bullshit. I've heard this rubbish before.' Said Magnus scornfully.

'A bloody wolf in a bloody tree.' He sneered.

'Priests and soothsayers can often misinterpret the will of the gods.' Muttered Aelnoth.

'I don't believe a word of it.' Growled Magnus, as he gazed at the passing coastline.

'Ship.' Shouted one of the crew.

'Where away?' shouted the Captain.

'Yonder,' shouted the man, as he pointed to an area some half a mile away, where a small fishing vessel bobbed up and down in the swell.

'Steer to the port.' Ordered the Captain.

'Make for yon boat.'

The Helmsman adjusted the rudder and the longship skidded through the water like a flying fish towards the small fishing boat.

The fisherman had seen the longship, and had already hoisted his small sail and was attempting to reach the shore before he was caught.

His small fishing boat was overhauled within the space of a few minutes and bobbed up and down, alongside the much larger longship.

The terrified man gazed up at the fifty seven savage looking men, who stared down at him from the strange craft, which had forced him to cease his futile effort to outrun them.

'What are you?' shouted Volund. 'Espania? Franks?'

The mans normally brown face blanched into a mask of horror, as he tried to understand what this hairy savage was shouting, and although his mouth opened several times, no words came from its dry interior, as he continued to gape up at the men who, he was certain, would slay him and steal his cherished fishing boat, as well as the four baskets of fish, which had taken him most of the day to catch.

'I try.' Said Abdulla as he eased his way through the crowd of men who stood along the side of the ship.

He then proceeded to shout across to the man in at least two languages that the rest of the crew did not understand, although Aelnoth did manage to make out the word 'Mediterranean.' Amongst the jumble of words that Abdulla said.

Abdul turned to the Captain who was standing by Aelnoth and Magnus and said. 'I not really understand. He from a people I not know.'

'When I say Mediterranean, he nodded his head to the south.

'We go that way.'

'Let him go?' he questioned.
'Why not.' Said Volund.
'I doubt he has ever travelled further than the edge of this bay and would be of little use to us.'
'We could sell him as a slave.' Suggested one of the men.
'When and where?' asked the Captain?
'And in the meantime he would be just another mouth to feed, and we have little enough food for ourselves, until we can make landfall and get some more.'
'There is fish in his baskets.' Ventured Aelnoth.
'Good thinking.' Said Volund.
'Grab those baskets of fish and send him on his way.' He ordered.
Volund steered the ship into a secluded cove, where the crew cooked the fish over open fires, and enjoyed a good night's sleep with full bellies, washed down with fresh water from a nearby stream.
The following morning Volund sent half a dozen men out to hunt for game.
'Report back to us if you do see any towns or villages, and make sure that they don't see you, and follow you back here.'
'The last thing we want is a horde of howling foreigners charging down those dunes towards us.'
The men returned carrying a sparse assortment of game, which varied from sparrows and robins to one small half grown deer, which was of a breed that none of the men had ever encountered before.
'I am sure it will taste just as good as a red deer from home.' Said Magnus, as the hunter dumped it onto the ground with the rest of the catch.
'We will put them all in the pot together when we make camp this nightfall.' Said the Captain. 'But now it is time to set sail.'
'The wind is fair and we should be on our way.'
The crew followed his example and boarded the ship.
Four of the men helped the rowers by pushing it off the sandy beach.
Volund noticed a change in the sea by mid-morning.

'The waves are different.' He remarked to the helmsman, who stood alongside him.

'Indeed.' Answered the man who was noted for his dull demeanour and his lack of conversation.

'And over yonder.' Said Volund, as he pointed towards the sea some half a mile ahead of them.

'The colour of the sea is changing.'

This remark caused a mere grunt from the helmsman, who was probably one of the few men amongst the crew who had not slept well, and was growing weary from standing at the helm for all of the morning, and was becoming resentful that he had not been relieved several hours ago.

'We are nearing the mouth of the Mediterranean,' said the Captain in a loud voice so that the men at the bow of the ship would be able to hear him.

A thin cheer came from the crew, as they envisaged sailing happily on the warm friendly sea.

By nightfall they still had not reached the mouth of the Mediterranean, and were forced to spend another night on a windy beach, where a cold wind blew so wildly that it was only after great difficulty they managed to kindle a fire, in order to boil the stew that they had been looking forward to for most of the day.

By dawn, the wind had died down to a gentle breeze, cheering the men, who thought that the hard day of rowing and the struggle that they had expected, now looked unlikely, hoping that the gentle breeze would allow them to sit on their benches and storage chests, and watch the coastline pass by, as the sail took them effortlessly towards, and into the Mediterranean.

'There it is.' Shouted Volund, as he pointed ahead.

'What is?' asked Magnus as he stood up to stare into the distance.

'I can see nought but more bloody ocean.' He said disgustingly.

'It's the Mediterranean you silly sod,' said Aelnoth.

'Or, to be more honest. It is the entrance into the Mediterranean.'

'Out oars.' Shouted Volund.

'Damn and blast.' Swore one of the seamen. 'Here we go again.'

'They don't call you Grimvald the Groaner for nothing, said his bench mate.

'Grimvald merely gave Rugalf a sour look, for although Grimvald was an experienced warrior, and a copious slayer of men, who had stood in the shieldwall more than four times, there were times that he silently admitted to himself, that he was a man who found fault with most things, and with most men.

Grimvald knew that Rugalf was also a savage and merciless killer, and was probably one of the finest warrior's on board, although he surmised. 'I have not seen the skills of some of these new men, especially those three Englishmen and their hooded Nubian.'

'Don't start rowing yet lads.' Shouted Captain Volund as he interrupted their banter.

'Wait till I tell you.'

'The tide is right, so we might just be able to sail her in, but I have been this way twice before, and I know that entering this inland sea can be tricky, so steady as she goes, and wait on my word.'

Volund and his helmsman heaved on the rudder, as they attempted to steer the ship into the centre of the stream of water that was rushing into the Mediterranean faster than a man on a galloping horse.

'Row now lads.' He shouted.

'Keep your strokes steady and in a few minutes we will be in the centre, and the incoming tide will take us in.'

Almost as soon as he had finished speaking, the tidal surge took hold of the craft, and sped her through the channel faster than most of the men could believe that a ship could travel.

They rested on their oars and stared in wonder as they entered the warm inland sea, which no more than three of the crew had previously seen.

'God's blood.' Exclaimed Aelnoth, as the ship slowed down.

'That really was unbelievable.'

'By Odin's sacred balls,' said Magnus.

'I cannot believe that a ship could go so fast.'

'It was as if the Valkyries themselves were escorting us into Valhalla.'

'Bloody heathen.' Said Aelnoth, half in-joke, as he slapped his friend lightly on his shoulder.

'Maybe I am,' answered Magnus.

'But does your Christ God have beautiful maidens to escort you to your Heaven, when you fall in battle?'

'We have Angels with harps to escort us.' Said Aelnoth adamantly.

'Bloody harps,' said his friend in disgust.

'Our Valkyries sing battle songs to us, as we go to Valhalla.

Aelnoth merely nodded and turned away, for he had been here before with his friend, and knew full well that Magnus was a dyed in the wool believer in the old Gods, and had reached the decision long ago that his friend would never change.

'Captain,' shouted one of the men. 'Two ships over there.'

'Where?' asked Volund?

'Over yonder.' Answered the man, as he pointed to the eastern shore.

'My God, you have good eyesight,' said the Captain as he shaded his eyes from the sun, and screwed he eyes up in an attempt to see the ships.

'My eyes are not as young as yours.' He said, as he turned towards Aelnoth.

'Can you see them?' he asked.

Aelnoth stared to the east into the haze where he could just make out two ships, which appeared to be heading towards them.

'I see them.' He said quietly. 'And they seem to be heading for us.'

'By Freya's sacred tits.' Swore Volund.

'I think they could be Barbary pirates.'

'They inhabit the eastern shore of the Med, and prey on unsuspecting seaman passing through the straits.'

'They could have a bit of a shock when they prey on us.' Said Aelnoth as his right hand went down to his sword.

'Don't be too sure of that,' shouted the Captain.

'They are savage buggers and they show no mercy.'

'Man the Oars lads.' Shouted the Captain.

'Let us try to outrun them, and if we can't outrun them, then we could have a bit of a fight on our hands.'

Despite the fact that each oarsman was straining on his oar and the sail was full, the two boats were gaining on the longship.

'Steer to the shore,' ordered Volund. 'It doesn't look like we can out run them.'

They were less than two hundred yards from the shore when the first ship reached them, and begun showering the longship with clouds of arrows, which zipped through the sail and slammed into the men's shields as well as the decks and the mast.

Two arrows found a human target, as one thudded into the thigh of one of the men, whilst another sliced through one man's throat, sending him to the deck in a spouting, frothy pool of blood.

No less than four arrows embedded themselves in Aelnoth's shield, but the arrows failed to penetrate through the thick boiled bull-leather.

When the arrow storm had ceased, he brushed the arrows off his shield with his Saex, and as the arrows fell around his feet, he thought to himself, that if these arrows had been made of good English oak or ash, instead of what looked like reed, they would probably have slain him and many more of his shipmates.

'Repel Boarders.' Yelled Volund, as a wave of pirates seethed over the bows and into the Viking ship, causing the Vikings to charge into them with Axe, Spear, and Sword, thrusting and hacking at these heathens who had dared to attack a Viking longship.

Vikings and Pirates fell dead, or reeled back wounded from the fierce melee that ensued, with no side yielding or winning.

Aelnoth and his three friends just happened to be to the rear of their fellow warriors, and as yet, had taken no part in the fighting, as four or five men stood between them and their foes.

The sea caused the rear of the Pirate vessel to swing around and crash into the longship.

'Follow me.' Roared Aelnoth, and without looking to see if his friends had heard him above the noise and screams of those who were fighting a few yards away, he leapt over the side, and landed on the steering platform of the Pirate ship, where a startled helmsman jumped back in alarm to see this long haired youth appear, apparently from nowhere.

The man had no time to draw his weapon as Aelnoth slashed one of his two swords down through the mans neck, sending him backwards into the foaming sea.

Aelnoth turned towards the crowded forward part of the ship, where a crowd of Pirates were battling with the Vikings, and had their backs towards Aelnoth and his three friends who had just joined him.

'Let's go.' Screamed Aelnoth at the top of his voice as he raced the twenty or so paces across the deck, and commenced to thrust and slice, like a windmill in a gale, into the startled Pirates.

Many of the Pirates saw their comrades falling, and turned to face their new enemies who numbered a mere four men, causing at least a score of them to attack Aelnoth and his friends, whilst the rest of the Pirate crew continued to assail the main body of Vikings, who were still battling to repel those Pirates who had boarded their longship.

A swarthy Giant of a man, who appeared to be the Pirates leader, shouted a string of words at his men, as he turned towards Aelnoth, and with a leering smile, which crossed his pockmarked face, he ushered the twenty or so Pirates who were with him forward, sending them crashing into the four Englishmen, only to be met with a small four man wall of shields and a gleam of weapons, which immediately sent three of them backwards, either dead or wounded.

The Giant literally pushed a number of his men out of the way so violently, that one of them was thrown so hard against the low planking that he toppled overboard with a dull splash and disappeared beneath the waves.

The Giant strode arrogantly towards Aelnoth, who was the nearest of the four boarders.

The man had a small round shield in his left hand; whilst in his right hand he held a long curved sword, which was of a style that was alien to Aelnoth.

The giant slashed at Aelnoth, causing Aelnoth to lean backwards as the savage looking sword whistled past his face, allowing Aelnoth to slash the sword in his right hand towards his enemy's waist, but his own slash was easily blocked by his opponents' small shield.

Aelnoth took a step backwards just in time to avoid a backhanded slash from the curved weapon, and allowed the weapon to continue harmlessly on its journey.

He stabbed forward with the shorter sword in his left hand into the belly of his foe, only to jolt his arm, as his sword met the chain mail, which the Giant wore beneath the grubby white smock that covered him from neck to ankle.

His three friends and a small crowd of Pirates watched the contest, emitting shouts of encouragement from the Englishmen, and hoots of laughter from the Pirates, who, from their joyous merriment, must have seen their leader in action on numerous occasions, and fully expected him to slaughter this boy within the next few cuts of the huge sword, which he handled like a lightweight toy.

Aelnoth realised that despite the weight that his opponent carried, he was obviously an experienced and agile fighter, who was not only used to dictating a fight, but also confident of winning, for this contest had already outlasted most of the contests that Aelnoth had ever been in, or indeed longer than any contest that he had ever seen.

The Pirate's face still held the same silly, sneering smile that he had started contest with.

Aelnoth whirled both of his swords in a way that was familiar to him, and a way that usually caused panic or confusion in most of the men he had met thus far, but this Giant of a Captain blocked every move, and slipped almost casually away from the few cuts, which he knew he would be unable to block.

Aelnoth noticed that the Pirates face had suddenly changed, as he raised his curved sword and brought it down towards his opponent's head with the speed of an eagle.

Aelnoth caught the blow not on his head, but on the edge of his raised Saex, jarring his arm so badly that bolts of pain shot through his arm and shoulder, causing him to retreat a pace in order for his arm to regain some of its strength.

The power of the blow caused Aelnoth down onto his knees, but as he did so, he slashed at the ankles of his enemy, slicing through one leg completely, and half way through the other.

The Giant screamed in agony, as his sword and shield dropped to the floor, followed by the Giant himself, who crashed onto the deck, and rolled in excruciating pain as he tried to stem the blood that gushed from his wounds.

Aelnoth stopped the screaming as he stepped forward and decapitated him.

He stooped and held the head in the air, as the dead mans blood cascaded onto the deck.

The Pirates wailed in alarm and dropped to their knees in surrender.

'Christ's alive.' Exclaimed Magnus.

'Never seen anything like that before.'

'Forget that,' panted Aelnoth.

'What shall we do with these buggers?'

'And that lot there?' questioned Oscar as he nodded towards the rest of the pirate crew who had also witnessed their leaders death, and had joined their fellow pirates on their knees.

'Christ's blood.' Said the bemused Magnus, who gazed at his youthful friend in awe.

'I thought you believed in Thor and Odin.' said Aelnoth.

'A slip of the tongue, dear boy. A slip of the tongue.' Repeated the red faced Magnus with an apologetic smile.

'Nonetheless,' said Aelnoth.

'What are we going to do with them? Their second ship is getting dangerously close.'

'Ask Volund; He's the bloody Captain of this ship. Not me.'

Aelnoth rushed to Volund. 'What shall we do with these prisoners?'

'That other bloody ship is nigh upon us.'

'I don't bloody well know. You are the Lord of war, or so Bjorn has led me to believe, so you decide, but you had better decide quickly, unless you want to be chin deep in pirates again.'

After a moments thought, and a stroke of his sparse beard.

'Disarm the sods, he shouted, 'and throw all their weapons onto the deck of our ship, and I'll show you what to do with 'em.'

The pirates were quickly disarmed and their weapons thrown into the deck of the longship, whilst all the pirates were ushered to the aft of their own ship.

Aelnoth ordered all the Vikings onto their longship, causing the pirates to think that they were about to be released and allowed to sail away unharmed, but their smiles turned to tears and pleadings, as they saw Aelnoth raise a hastily borrowed English axe, and split a hole in the bottom of their ship, large enough to drive a small cart through.

He threw the axe back into the longship and quickly leapt over, leaving the wailing pirates rushing towards the hole, which was already gushing water at an alarming rate.

'I think that the other ship will have no alternative other than to rescue their mates, and that will be the end of that.' He said, as he plonked his rear-end onto a storage crate, and attempted to wipe some of the blood off his hands and face.

As they rowed away, Aelnoth sighed with relief as he saw that his prediction had been correct, for the sinking ship was already settling in the water, leaving shouting and screaming pirates pleading and fighting with each other, in their attempt to get on board the second ship, that had, as he had predicted, ceased its pursuit, and was attempting to get alongside the sinking vessel, which was wallowing in the swell, as the pirates threw ropes across to their floundering comrades in their attempt to rescue them, before their heavy chain mail shirts dragged them to a watery grave.

'Down oars.' Shouted the Captain.

'Tend to the wounded,' he added, 'and let the sail do the work.'

With groans and sighs of relief, the men shipped their oars and began to see to their wounds.

'How many men did we lose?' asked Aelnoth.

'Three,' answered Magnus, 'and I don't think he will last long.' He added as he nodded towards a man who was being comforted by one of the older men.

'Took a spear through his gut, so it don't look good.'

Aelnoth shook his head in sympathy, and gazed along the ship, where he saw that many, if not all of the crew had sustained some sort of injury, and were all busy splashing fresh sea water over their wounds before they were bandaged.

'It looks like you could do with a bit of help from that wound on your arm.' He said to Magnus.

'Sit here and let me stem the flow of blood or you will be joining him on his way to Valhalla.'

'You mean Heaven,' answered Magnus with a smile as he wearily sat on a bench.

Abdulla and Oscar made their way through the middle of the ship to join them.

Both had cuts and bruises, but seemed to be in high spirits.

'Scimitar?' Asked Abdulla, who pointed to a long slash that oozed blood from Aelnoth's left arm?

'What?' said Aelnoth?

'Scimitar.' Repeated the Nubian.

'What the hell's that?' Growled Aelnoth, who ached from head to foot from the cuts and bruises that he had received during the battle.

'Scimitar. Bent sword,' said Abdulla, as he gestured the curved sword that the pirate captain wielded with such skill.

'Oh. That's what they call it. Is it?' answered Aelnoth as he realised that the curved swords that the pirates had used, were called Scimitar's.'

'Bloody dangerous thing.' He exclaimed with a grimace.

'Most weapons are.' Said Magnus with a smile as he flexed his injured arm.

'Thanks' he said to Aelnoth. 'Should be as right as rain in a few days time,' but he let out another groan as he stretched his arm just a little too far, causing spasms of pain to shoot up his arm and into his shoulder.

As the sun was beginning to disappear over the horizon, Volund steered the Walrus past a small island in order to reach a much larger stretch of land, which shimmered in the sea a few miles to the larboard.

'If my seamanship is correct,' he mumbled. 'That should be the island of Majorca, and if it is, then we should find a safe anchorage in the bay of Palma.'

'Mind you.' He added.

'I have only been there once before, and it was a friendly enough place then. I just hope it still is, for we sorely need to rest a while and fill up our water barrels, and we are nigh out of food.'

The bay of Palma was wide, placid, and the bluest sea that Aelnoth had ever seen.

'How can it be so blue?' he said in amazement.

'No idea,' answered Magnus, 'strange though,' he added.

'Because when you get a bucketful of the stuff, or scoop it up in your hands, it just looks like clear water from a normal mountain stream and yet here it is. As blue as the sky.'

'And undrinkable.' Said Aelnoth quietly.

'It certainly is.' Answered Magnus as he gazed across the bay towards the land.

Volund beached the longship at least a quarter of a mile from the small settlement of Palma.

'Better safe than sorry.' He remarked.

'I suggest that at least half of the men should stay here to defend the ship, whilst you and the rest of the men make your way to the village and see if the natives are friendly.'

'Will you be coming with us?' asked Aelnoth.

'I think it best that I stay here with the ship, just in case we need to make a hasty getaway.' Said Volund.

CHAPTER 18

Led by Aelnoth and Abdulla, they walked quietly into the silent assortment of stone houses and shacks, which made up the village of Palma.

'The place seems to be deserted.' Remarked Aelnoth.

'See!' said Abdulla, who pointed to a small fire, which contained a steaming copper pot, some fifteen or twenty feet away.

'They here.' He said in a quiet voice.

'Lower your weapons.' Said Aelnoth in a loud voice, as he sheathed his long sword and lowered his shield.

The sun blazed down on the silent village, as his eyes fell upon a thin dog that stretched in the shade of one of the stone houses, and the eyes of two scrawny cats followed him as he walked slowly up the dusty street, which seemed to be the main thoroughfare of the village.

'You men wait here.' He said to the Vikings, who seemed to be even more uncomfortable than he was at the eerie silence of the place.

'Abdulla and me will see if we can find anyone here.'

Followed by the hooded Nubian, he approached the door of the nearest house, and to his astonishment, the door was not only unlocked, but it was actually swinging in the breeze.

He pushed the door and as he took a step inside the darkened room he shouted in a pleasant voice. 'Hello. Hello. Is anyone here?'

His voice seemed to echo in the empty room, but the only response it brought was a slight squeak, as the door moved in the wind.

'They not know words.' Said Abdulla.

'I try.' And he shouted in a loud, but soothing voice a string of words that made no sense to Aelnoth and seemed to him, to be total gobblygook.

There seemed to be no reply from the seemingly empty house, and they were about to leave and try elsewhere, when the muffled sound of a child crying came from within the building.

'Stay close to me,' said Aelnoth as he stepped into the doorway, only to find the strong hand of Abdulla on his shoulder, preventing him from entering.

'I go first,' he said.

'See in dark better.' He said as he stepped in front of Aelnoth.

'You follow,' he added as he entered the darkened room.

Aelnoth slung his Fathers old shield around so that it protected his back and with his left hand on the shoulder of Abdulla, he followed his friend into the room.

They moved carefully from the room, through a doorway, and into a second room, which was even darker than the first, with no sign of a window or doorway that would allow the slightest glimmer of light into the room.

'Is here,' he heard Abdulla say, and although Aelnoth's own eyes had adjusted a little to the darkness, he could see nothing, and felt that the stifling heat and the blackness of the room had taken him into the very belly of hell, causing trickles of perspiration to run down his forehead, and into his eyes.

Abdulla spoke again, and his soothing voice eventually caused a mumbled response, which seemed to come from the floor in front of them.

'They Frightened.' He said.

'Me not know much language, but they 'fraid of us.'

'They.' Said Aelnoth. I can't see anyone. How many are they?'

'Man. Woman. Two Childs.' Said Abdulla.

'Try to get them to come out in the open.' Asked Aelnoth.

'I try. You go.' Was the quiet answer from the Nubian?

Aelnoth fumbled his way through the darkened room and out into the bright sunlight, waiting in the shade for some time before his own eyes adjusted to the brightness.

After a long wait, the hooded Nubian emerged through the doorway, and as he shaded his sensitive eyes against the glaring sunlight, he ushered a small thin man, who was followed by either his wife or perhaps his daughter, who held a small child in her arms.

'Woman say she find more men.' said Abdulla, and gently touched the woman on her shoulder, indicating that it was safe to move away from his protection and pass through this group of fair haired, bearded savages.

A short while later she returned, accompanied by two old men, and the trio hesitatingly walked towards the Nubian, who seemed to be the only man amongst these fair-haired savages who she could trust.

After a long conversation, which none of the Vikings could understand?

Abdulla turned to the crowd and said. 'Ships come. Take men to row.'

One of the old men intervened and said in a tongue that Abdulla could understand. 'It was the fleet of the Emperor who took all the young men into slavery to serve on his ships. Only us two old men and six of the younger ones who were up in the hills managed to escape.'

'Never mind that.' Snapped the angry voice of Grimvald the groaner.

277

'Ask the silly old goat where we are.'

'Oh. I know already.' Answered Abdulla. 'We in Frankia.'

'Don't be stupid,' growled Grimvald.

'We were in Frankia a week ago, and we have entered this inland sea since then, so how in the world can we still be in Frankia?'

'Still Frankia,' answered the hooded Nubian. 'Frankia big. Go this far.'

'Balls;' spat Grimvald. 'Can't be Frankia. We are bloody well lost, 'aint we?'

'We in bay of Saint-Maxime,' said Abdulla. 'Frankia.' He reiterated with a snort.

'How far are we from Micklegard?' asked Aelnoth.

'I ask.' said Abdulla as he turned towards the two old men, who he entered into a long, drawn out conversation that only he and the two men could understand.

The Northmen were beginning to get bored standing around in the heat, watching the three men who seem to have reached a critical stage in the negotiations, when the two old men had begun to stamp their feet and wave their arms in the air.

'Kill the silly old buggers,' snarled Rugalf the savage, 'and let us loot the bloody place and be on our way. They probab.' But he was interrupted when Abdulla turned and held his hand up to speak.

'Men once warriors for Emperor.' He said slowly.

'Micklegard maybe two week sail.'

'What about food and water?' asked Aelnoth as he tried to steer the conversation back to the reason that they had entered the village in the first place.

'Plenty water.' Said Abdulla as he pointed to a dip in the low hills that surrounded the village. 'River.'

'Food! Only fish.' He added.

The men who had virtually lived on dried fish, salted fish and fresh fish for many days, groaned aloud as they heard the word 'Fish.'

'What about them goats?' snarled Rugalf? As he nodded his head towards a distant hill, where a small herd of goats had just begun to trickle over the top of the hill.

Abdulla looked at the hillside and turned back to face the two men, with whom he conversed, and then after another long tirade of unpronounceable words, he turned back to the Northmen and announced.

'Men say, only sell twenty goats for gold.'

'Gold!' exclaimed Rugalf vehemently.

'Who the shit has gold? I haven't got any gold.'

'We are the bloody survivors from two bloody battles, and were lucky to escape with our bloody lives. Tell the silly old fools that we ain't got no gold, and we will take their bloody scrawny goats whether they like it or not.'

'See if they will take silver for the goats?' asked Aelnoth.

'How come you've got silver when the rest of us are penniless? Snarled Rugalf, as he walked to within a foot of Aelnoth and towered above him, as his ugly face and his stale breath pushed into the face of the young Englishman.

'Tis the last of the silver that I received in Ireland, for taking the Godwinson treasure back to Earl Magnus.' Answered Aelnoth, as he stared back into the bloodshot eyes of 'Rugalf the savage.'

He stepped back a pace and undid the straps of his leather tunic to reveal a thick calfskin belt that girdled his waist.

Rather reluctantly, he knelt to the ground and after a lot of fumbling as he tried to untie the stiff leather, salt encrusted fastenings; he emptied its contents on the ground, until the growing pile of silver drew gasps of awe from the watching Vikings.

The two old men also stared down in amazement at the large pile of silver, and it was clear to Aelnoth by their faces that there was enough silver in the pile to purchase more goats that the village of Palma possessed.

Grimvald the groaner had also seen the look on the faces of the two old men and growled as a rare smile crossed his grubby face.

'It seems that we will be dining on roast goat tonight lads.'

Aelnoth sealed the deal with a shake of the hand, as the smiling old villagers scooped up half of the pile of silver, for Aelnoth was adamant that that was more than enough to pay for a few scrawny goats.

They left almost half of the flock of goats with the village, and drove the rest along the beach towards the ship, where they were greeted by their cheering shipmates who made so much noise that the goats scattered in all directions, and were chased by the happy, noisy Vikings.

At least four of the flock disappeared, never to be seen again, although Aelnoth knew that the four escapees would probably rejoin their kin, who were in the process of being driven into their night quarters by a small crowd of village children.

Accompanied by the small flock of noisy goats and ample water in the water barrels, plus a friendly wind and a calm sea, they glided past the rocky island of Malta and the tip of Italy without further encounters from unfriendly ships.

They passed the island of Crete and into the sea of Greece, through a sea that contained so many islands that Aelnoth found it difficult to comprehend.

Nonetheless, Volund steered the longship unerringly through the gaps between the islands with such skill that Aelnoth silently thanked God that fortune had favoured them with such a skilled seaman, especially so, as they passed though channels, which were so narrow, that in places he felt that he could touch the rocks that they glided silently passed.

It was here that they began to see fishing vessels and trading ships, plying their trade between the islands.

A huge warship, which contained no less than three banks of oars, whooshed past them as if they were standing still, making the feared Vikings feel like dwarfs, as they stared up at the armed warriors, who in turn were staring back down at them.

More and more ships appeared as they neared what looked like the mainland, until Volund ordered the sail to be lowered and the oars out, in order to continue their journey through the mass of shipping.

'There she is.' Said Volund in a loud voice as he pointed to the shore.

'Good God.' Exclaimed Aelnoth, as he looked through the channel, which led to the city of Constantinople.

'Now that is impressive.' He said as his eyes attempted to take in the vast walls, which circled the huge city, noting that the walls contained a solid stone tower every hundred yards.

'The city is built on seven hills.' Said Volund, to the astonished young man.

'And the walls are fifty feet high and over seven miles long.'

'It seems to have changed little since I was last here.' He muttered almost to himself.

'And how long is that?' asked Aelnoth in an awed voice, for he had long thought that this captain, despite his aloofness and obvious dislike of the three Englishmen, was a much travelled and a rather extraordinary man.

'Ten. No. It must be eleven years since I left.'

'I was nought but a boy then. Perhaps your age, and that would make me thirty. No, I must be thirty-one or even thirty-two. I'm not really sure.' He said as he scratched his tangled, unwashed, greasy hair.

'How old are you?' he asked Aelnoth, which was perhaps the most friendly sentence he had ever uttered to him.

'Eighteen.'

'Loki must have some great jest in mind for you, to have brought you here at such a young age.' He said as a rare smile crossed his weather-beaten face.

'Ha!' he shouted aloud. 'They must have seen us.'

'Who's seen us?' asked Aelnoth.

'The cities sea patrol.' He said.

'They do not like to see dragon ships in their waters.'

'Dismantle the dragons head.' He ordered, and a group of men leapt forward and hammered out the wooden dowels, which held the head in place, on the raised prow of the longship.

'Good!' exclaimed Volund.

'That ought to tell them that we are not a war-ship, but that we are mere northern traders.'

'Traders in war.' Said some wit from amongst the crew, causing a chuckle here and there.

The four ships were laden with armed men, and flew over the water towards them with such skill that belied their wide bellies and their single sail, which was draped in the shape of a triangle in brilliant gold and blue colours.

Two of the ships stopped on both sides of the longship, and an eerie silence descended on all five ships, as the warriors on all of the ships held their shields high and glared across the narrow space of calm water, which divided them.

'Norsemen?' said a loud voice from one of the ships.

'Ja,' bellowed Volund.

'Is the white wizard with you?'

'We are all white and I am a bit of a wizard with this spear I am holding.' Shouted Volund half in jest, for not once when he had lived in Constantinople, had he been spoken to in such a rude manner, especially by a man from the north.

'And if you do not answer my question QUICKLY, you will find that spear imbedded in your own guts.'

'I shall only ask you one more time.' He shouted. 'IS THE WHITE WIZARD WITH YOU?'

Aelnoth could see that the captain was beginning to go red with rage at the unseen man's tone, and fearing that Volund's anger may cause him to do something rash, notwithstanding the fact that they were in a hostile situation and outnumbered by about ten to one.

Aelnoth shouted 'We have a wizard with us, although he may not be the man you seek.'

'Let him step forward?' came the order.

Aelnoth held his left hand out and beckoned Oscar to join him at the side of the ship.

'Remove the man's mask.' Ordered the voice.

'His eyes are sensitive to the sunlight, and he will not take off the hood.'

A single arrow suddenly appeared an inch from Aelnoth's hand, which had been placed on the side of the longship.

'REMOVE THE HOOD.' Ordered the voice.

'I shall ask him to take off his hood.' Shouted Aelnoth.

'But if he does, he will probably cast a spell on you, and you will die a lingering death within the month.'

'I have seen it happen on more than one occasion.' He lied.

He turned to Oscar and said quietly. 'Pretend you are about to take your hood off.'

Oscar began to remove his hood, grunting as he prised the clinging leather up over his chin and up to the top of his cheeks.

'That's enough,' shouted the voice.

'I can see that he is the man we seek.'

'Follow me into the harbour.' He shouted, as the captain of his ship skilfully sent his ship gliding away and around in a half circle to lead the small flotilla towards the entrance of the harbour.

'God's blood.' That was strange,' remarked Aelnoth.

'Never seen anything like that in my life,' said Volund.

'They usually welcome warriors from the north with open arms.'

'Can't get too many of us.' He added.

Aelnoth noticed that the massive iron chain, which had been linked across the harbour to exclude any undesirable ships from entering the port, had been withdrawn, and was stacked onto two of the four ships, which were anchored in strategic intervals across the mouth of the harbour.

'Strange.' Said Volund quietly.

'What is?' asked Aelnoth, who stood alongside the captain.

'Well,' he said as he ran his rough hand through his grubby beard.

'They are not leading us into the main harbour.'

'In fact, it looks like we are heading for the Palace.'

'The Palace. You mean we might see the Emperor himself? He asked.

'Indeed you might.' Answered the Captain.

'And if your friend there doesn't perform correctly,' as he nodded towards Oscar.

'The Emperor might be the last thing you will ever see on this earth.'

The ship, which contained 'the voice', docked on one side of a small stone jetty, whilst the other escort ships stood out to sea.

Volund, pre-empting any order from 'the voice,' steered the Walrus to the other side of the same jetty, ordering two of the men to jump onto the jetty, in order to secure the ship to one of the huge wooden posts that had been placed there for that particular purpose.

'Leave the crew aboard and follow me with the Wizard and his three companions.' Said the voice.

Volund, Magnus, Oscar, Aelnoth and Ingrid, who rarely left his side, stepped onto the jetty, and were immediately surrounded by at least twenty armed guards.

'What about Abdulla.' Shouted Oscar.

'Abdulla must come too. I will not go without Abdulla.' He shouted at the top of his voice, and was on the point of jumping back onto the longship, when the voice said. 'What's all the fuss?'

The guards parted to reveal a wizened old man with a long white beard, and hair of the same hue, seated on a sedan, which was carried by four large black men, who were dressed in the most vividly coloured attire that the Vikings had ever seen.

'He will not come without his friend.' Said Aelnoth in a quiet voice.

'Will he not then?' said the old man.

'Oh well! I suppose one more man will make little difference.'

'Bring him along.'

Abdulla emerged from the crowd of Northmen, and jumped nimbly onto the jetty to join his friends.

'Christ's blood.' Exclaimed the old man.

'Another man in a hood.'

'What ails you northern heathens?'

'Are your faces so ugly that you deign to be seen by normal men?'

None of the five answered, but merely exchanged strange looks, and raised eyebrows in anticipation of what was likely to happen when the Emperor ordered the masks to be removed. As they suspected he surely would.

'Leave your weapons.' Ordered the man on the sedan.

They reluctantly obliged, and the clatter of iron striking iron rang out in the breeze, as they threw their weapons onto the stone jetty.

As they walked towards a large iron studded door, which appeared to be the only exit from the jetty, the old man looked up towards Aelnoth, who was the nearest to him, and said in an unexpectedly quiet and refined voice.

'I am called Leif the Norseman, although I originally came from Iceland.'

'I thought that you were one of us,' answered Aelnoth.

'No one who is not from the north can speak our tongue so readily, although I must say that the rest of these warriors also have the look of colder climes about them.

'Indeed,' said Leif. 'They are Varangians.'

As they reached the door he said. 'Halt.' And the party of guards and their charges halted before the door.

The huge door swung open, and four men, who, by their hair colouring, which varied from blond to brown hair, and their fair complexions, proclaimed to the newcomers that these men too could be none other than Northmen.

The men strode forward and lifted the sedan, which they then carried boldly through the open doorway.

Aelnoth and his friends followed, and were met by ten heavily armed men.

'These men are all of the Emperors Varangian Guard.' Said Leif with a hint of pride in his voice.

'The Emperor will trust no man of the south to attend him, and only warriors from the north are allowed into the Varangians.'

The stern faces of the Guards cracked into smiles, and as they escorted Aelnoth and his friends through a maze of passages and rooms, which were filled with dusty statues and busts of famous men, the guards bombarded the newcomers with questions of their homelands.

'There will be time enough for your questions.' Snapped Leif with authority, causing the Guards to reluctantly hold their tongues, and continue to march solemnly through the dim passages and huge silent rooms.

'That is of course.' Added Leif. 'If these new friends of ours do not upset the Emperor, for it has long been foretold that a White Wizard would come from the northlands, and help us to cure the ills of the Empire.'

'Let us hope that he can.' Mumbled one of the Guards.

Slowly the passages became lighter. The rooms were cleaner, and were crammed with tables and chairs of gilt, upon which lay gold and silver ornaments of exquisite workmanship and beauty.

The walls were covered with huge, colourful tapestries, depicting scenes of battles long past, as well as scenes of the hunting of deer, wild boar and other huge animals, which were unfamiliar to the Northmen.

Although they had caught fleeting glimpses of servants or slaves in the distance, they had not yet seen any-one of note, until the guards flung open two large doors to reveal a brilliantly lit room, which seemed to be full of people.

Despite the number of people in the room, who were either sitting or standing along the sides of the room, not a sound emitted from the assembled congregation.

At the far end of the room was a raised platform, containing a single large and ornate golden chair.

A man in a white robe sat on the chair and rested his head on his hand, whilst his elbow lay upon the side of the chair.

'Obviously the Emperor.' Said Aelnoth, trying to sound nonchalant and unimpressed. Both of which were untrue.

'By Odin's sacred balls, I hope Oscar can convince the old bastard that he is this bloody White Wizard, who they seem to think he is.' Said Magnus.

Aelnoth felt a nudge in the small of his back and looked around to see one of the Varangian Guardsmen prodding him forward with the butt of his spear.

'Your turn my friend.' He said with a grin.

'Try to impress him or you and I may never meet again.'

Aelnoth, Magnus, Oscar and Abdulla walked slowly through the centre of the silent room towards the Emperor.

Aelnoth glanced toward Oscar, and although he could not see his face, he did notice that his hands were clenched into a fist, and he seemed to be a little unsteady as he walked forward, for he seemed to sway just a little, tempting Aelnoth to lay a hand on his friend in order to steady him.

Leif had mysteriously vanished. Presumably carried away by his attendants.

They were halted a spears-length away from the bottom of the marble steps, which rose towards the Emperor's throne.

Aelnoth glanced up towards the Emperor, and was startled to see that he was not the old man who he had envisaged, but was a fresh-faced young man of perhaps twenty-five summers.

'Remove your hoods.' Ordered the Emperor in a totally unexpected deep voice from such a young man.

Both Oscar and Abdulla pulled the tight fitting leather hoods up and off their heads.

Gasps and shouts came from the otherwise silent audience.

The Emperor's hand flew to his mouth in shock, but he quickly recovered his aura of royalty, and held his hand up for silence.

'Ah, I see the reason why you were reluctant to remove your hoods, and although I have not seen an Albino before, I have read about them in the Holy Scriptures, thus I know of them, and that I have nothing to fear from you.'

'Or have I?' he added quietly.

'Bring the Oracle.' He said, and one of the men who had been standing to the side of his dais, immediately left the room.

'Sit.' He ordered, and closed his eyes and rested his head in his hands, as if he was contemplating some difficult decision.

The four men looked around the room for a seat, but there was not a single seat in the room, so Aelnoth took the lead, and sat on the bottom step of the Emperor's dais.

His three friends joined him and sat on the cool steps with him.

'What are we supposed to do now?' whispered Magnus.

'Sit here like idiots with the rest of these silent lackeys?'

'They are silent because I have ordered it so.' Came a voice from the throne that was just loud enough for them to hear.

All four heads turned towards the Emperor whose head still rested in his hands as though he was asleep.

'Is it true that you Albino's can see in the dark?' he asked.

The question was so unexpected, that for a long moment no one answered, until Oscar gathered his wits and said in the strongest and most civil voice, which he could muster.

'We see well in twilight and on what a man would call a normal night, your Highness, but not that well, if the night is pitch black.'

As if he was satisfied with the answer, he nodded and asked.

'I can see that one of you is a Nubian, but which one of you is the White Witch?'

Before they could answer, a door at the end of the Hall was flung open, and four men of the Varangian Guard ushered in a small figure, which dragged its left foot across the marble floor, in an attempt to keep up with the long strides of the northern Guards, as they approached the Emperor.

The small figure was leaning heavily on a long stick, and as the four Varangians halted, the small figure continued its approach.

Aelnoth thought that he recognised the figure as being an old woman, but then he shook his head in annoyance, for he knew that he was mistaken, as there was no way that he could possibly have seen her before.

She was dressed in a black cape, which not only covered her head, but also reached the marble floor and dragged along the floor, where it brushed along the floor as the woman continued to approach the Emperor.

Plonk went the stick, followed by a slow step, that itself was followed by the sound of the other leg, as it was dragged forward.

The woman neither knelt or bowed her head before the Emperor, she merely looked up at him with eyes that were as black as night, as they sparkled from either side of a nose that was so hooked that it looked like it had been stamped on by a very heavy horse.

This little old woman seemed to captivate Aelnoth, and he noticed that the Emperor himself also seemed to be in awe of her.

Whilst Aelnoth was intrigued by the woman, he was equally intrigued by the staff, which the woman leant upon, for although the wood itself was black, a golden snake had been carved upon it, causing the snake to encircle the staff until its head protruded at the top, with its mouth wide open, with its white fangs bared, as if it was about to strike, and whilst that in itself was awe inspiring, the blood red eyes of the serpent were so realistic that it made the snake look alive.

The silence of the crowded room was broken by the voice of the Emperor who said in a rather shaky voice.

'Is this the White Wizard that you have seen in your dreams?'

Without taking her eyes off the Emperor, the old woman said in a voice that crackled like an old piece of parchment.

'It is he.'

'Come forward.' Said the Emperor as he indicated Oscar to mount the steps towards him.

'I would study you in more detail.'

Oscar took a step forward and began to mount the steps, but was frozen into immobility as the crone screeched loudly.

'No!! Not him.'

CHAPTER 19

The Emperor was as shocked as the rest of the people in the room, for they had all assumed that the White Albino was The White Wizard.

The Emperors knuckles showed white, as he held the sides of his throne in anger, and he snapped. 'Who then?'

'The young one is the one you seek.' Cackled the crone, as if it was all one big joke.

'He is the one.' She said again as she pointed one of her crooked fingers towards Aelnoth.

A shocked Aelnoth stared in amazement at the crone with an open mouth, but failed to utter a single word at this unexpected turn of events.

The Emperor was also speechless, as he and the rest of the occupants of the room stared at this beardless young man who, hereto, no-one had given a second glance, as all of their attention had been on the two white haired Albinos'.

'I, I am no Wizard.' Stammered Aelnoth.

'I am merely a young man who has been dispossessed of his homeland and I have come here to find succour, and to serve in the Varangian guard.

He stared down at the old woman, who in turn was staring back at him with those black eyes, which seemed to emit a dark radiance that drilled into his head.

'He is the one.' She reiterated.

'Although he does not yet know it, for he has not yet reached his full power.

No other person in the huge hall uttered a single word, except for one of the robed figures in a corner of the room, who started to cough, and then he held his hand to his throat and collapsed into a heap on-to the marble floor.

The Emperor broke the silence that followed the thud, which the man had made when he hit the floor.

'Is he dead?' He asked, and one of the men who was nearest to him stooped down, and placed his hand on the man's pulse.

'He is my Lord.' Said the man as he rose and bowed his head towards the Emperor.

'Good!' exclaimed the Emperor.

'He was one of the most devious conspirator's in my court, and I have long wished him dead.'

'Is this your doing?' he said in a sinister voice as he looked down towards Aelnoth.

'It is not my Lord.' Answered Aelnoth in a firm voice.

'I think it was.' Hissed the Emperor.

'No matter.' He added.

'It is done and cannot be undone.'

'Take him away and have his body burned, and cast his ashes into the sea.' He ordered.

'How are you called?' he said, as he returned his gaze towards Aelnoth.

'I am Aelnoth Edricson, from the borderlands of England, where my father was a Lord of that place, and a warrior of some note.' Said Aelnoth, speaking as coolly as he could.

'His Mother was a Queen of the woodland sprites, who had powers that were beyond my own feeble dabbling's.' Uttered the squeaky voice of the old hag.

'How in God's name did you know that?' asked a shocked Aelnoth.

'And has he inherited some of his mothers magic?' asked the Emperor.

'It would seem so your majesty,' answered the Hag.

'I will take him with me and find the true worth of this young 'White Wizard,' she added, as she turned, and without asking permission from the young Emperor, she took the left hand of the still confused Aelnoth, and led him like an errant schoolboy across the centre of the room, and through the silent audience to the door.

The four Varangian Guards escorted Aelnoth and the old woman through a courtyard, which was full of noisy people, who all seemed to be holding what looked like partitions, and who continued their talking and arguing, as they reluctantly moved aside to make way for the silent Varangians, who shoved the few people, who had failed to see their approach, out of the way.

The Guards left as the old woman entered a large, unpainted door that led into a sunlit courtyard, where she was greeted by a very large, gnarled old man of perhaps fifty summers, who bowed his head to her.

'My apologies lady. I had not expected you to return so soon.'

'You should be on the gate.' Snapped the old lady, in a voice of authority.

'Can I smell wine on your breath?'

'If it is so, then you will find yourself back on the slave block.' She snarled as her coal black eyes glared up at the quivering man.

She led Aelnoth across the cobble-stoned courtyard, and entered through a door, which was so low that Aelnoth had to crouch to enter, and once he had done so, he found himself in a large room, which was cluttered with all manner of things, including metal pots and pans, which simmered over small fires.

She halted near one of the pots and lifted its lid to smell the foul odour that emitted from it, without making a comment as to whether or not the contents of the brew were to her liking or not.

She turned towards Aelnoth and indicated that he should sit on one of the two chairs, which lay near a small table that was so full of things that Aelnoth thought that if one more item was placed upon it, it would surely collapse.

'Sit.' She said in an almost friendly manner.

As he sat she said. 'I am called 'Agio.' At least, that is what you may call me, but I dare say that my enemies, and I have many of them, would call me by other names.'

'Some of which I would not repeat in genteel company.'

'I am what you Northern barbarians would call a 'Soothsayer, or a Sage, and I am in the service of the Emperor, as was my mother before me, and her mother before that.'

She suddenly turned her head and screamed at the top of her voice. 'Wine.'

'I have served this young Emperor since his birth, and before that, I served his father, and his father before him.

'I have seen the empire of Constantinople through times of greatness and disasters, but since the latter days of this Emperor's father, the greatness of the empire has been eroded by raiders from Armenia, Scythia and Lydia, who are themselves being driven south by great numbers of nomadic raiders from the east.'

She paused as a young maiden entered the room carrying a silver tray, which contained two exquisitely shaped glasses and a large silver jug filled with red wine.

The dark haired girl filled the two glasses with wine and left without a word.

Both Agio and Aelnoth lifted their glasses to drink, but before doing so, Aelnoth gently touch the glass of Agio with his own glass before he raised t to his mouth to drink.

'Ah, you Northern barbarians.' She exclaimed with a sly grin.

'Do you really think that clashing your drinking vessels together will chase away the evil spirits that dwell in them?'

'How do you know so much about our customs?' asked Aelnoth.

'By the Gods,' she said as she relished her drink.

'I have seen you northern Varangians come and go over more years than I care to remember, and I can speak many of your languages better than my own. However. I digress. Where was I?'

She took another sip of her wine and smacked her thin lips.

'Ah yes. The Armenians and Scythians, and the Lydian's.'

'Well, our armies are slowly being whittled away by these savages.'

Now we have to contend with the Seljuk Turks, who have always traded with us in peace, but a man called Tughril has risen from amongst their ranks, and has proclaimed himself to be their leader.'

'He calls himself, 'The Sultan Tughril, beloved by God.'

Hence the Holy Empire of Constantinople is being eaten away, and eroded by these enemies.'

'Our city and our Empire are like a great palace, which is being destroyed by termites, and is falling in upon itself.'

Aelnoth nodded, and took another sip of the most delicious wine that he had ever tasted, as he tried to digest the news that Agio had just revealed.

'And how do I fit into the scheme of things?' He asked.

'I am merely a young man of eighteen summers, and despite what you may think. I am not a Wizard, and the only miracle I have performed to date, is to arrive here with my skin intact.'

'I really do not know what I am doing here.'

'Your path was chosen long ago.' She said in a quiet voice.

'And everything that has happened to you thus far has been merely a small step in your life that has led you here, to us.

'You have been led here by the Gods.' She hissed.

'To this very room, at this precise moment in time.'

'The past is the key to the future.'

'It cannot be altered any more than a man's true destiny can be altered.'

'What has been ordained to happen? WIILL happen, and we have waited for you for many, many years.'

'The first thing you must do is to learn our language. For you cannot lead an army of warriors who cannot understand you.'

'Lead an army,' said the shocked youngster.

'I have only been in one battle, and even then, we were defeated.'

'I was merely one warrior amongst thousands.'

She totally ignored him and said. 'I shall arrange for tutors to teach you our tongue, and the ways of our nation.'

'I shall also allot a tutor for a number of the Varangian guards, who will teach them the basics of our language, for although many of them have been in Constantinople for many years, most of them speak their own heathen tongue, and have made scant effort to learn the language of the Greeks, other than to ask how much a tankard of wine is, or the price of a Whore.'

She emptied her glass and rose from her chair with the help of the table and her golden staff.

'I would like my sister Ingrid to live here with me.' He said.

'Ah, your sister.' She said quietly.

'Of course we both know that she is not really your sister. Do we not?'

'But who am I to deny you your pleasures?'

'I shall have her brought here, but if she diverts you from your studies, she will, just as easily be removed.' She hissed.

'Come.' She said.

'It is time to show you to your quarters,' and rang a small bell, which sounded like a cowbell that he had oftimes heard being rung in the valley pastures at Wentnor, but much more genteel.

The dark haired slave girl instantly appeared at the door, and crossed the room towards her mistress, where she stood with her hands folded across her front and her head bowed.

'Take my Lord Aelnoth to his quarters and bathe him.' She ordered, and the girl made a slight courtesy and turned to lead Aelnoth out of the room.

'Prepare a bed in one of the spare rooms in Lord Aelnoth's quarters for his sister.' She ordered.

As Aelnoth turned to follow the girl, Agio said in a loud voice.

'And make sure that you bathe him before he goes to bed.'

'He smells like rancid goats milk.'

Like most Englishmen of the age, Aelnoth was not a man who bathed on a regular basis. Certainly, he may have scrubbed the grime off his body during a warm day during the English springtime.

And during the summer, he also may have swam naked in the stream that had cascaded near his home, but the steaming hot, scented pool, into which he was eventually coaxed, was a very new experience for him.

As he lay on his back in the shallow pool, he sighed with pleasure and felt reborn, although he did object to the semi naked slave girl showering him with perfumed water, and washing his hair and his beard, admitting silently to himself, that once the deed had been done, that he did feel totally invigorated, and ready to face whatever this strange woman named Agio had in store for him.

At dawn on the following morning, his day began with a breakfast, which could only be described as sumptuous, for it consisted of freshly baked bread and delicious meats, of a kind that he had never before tasted, washed down with weak wine, which he suspected had been watered down in order to avoid intoxication.

After he had broken his fast, he followed Agio into the courtyard, where her gigantic servant stood in the centre of the courtyard with his arms crossed, as if he was guarding the small pile of weapons, which lay on a stone table in front of him.

'This is my servant Abbi,' she said.

'He is a Lydian, who was taken in battle, but for the love of God, I know not who captured him, for he is the most formidable warrior I have ever seen.'

She turned towards the slave and reached up to pat him gently on his huge chest.

Abbi looked down to his mistress with a look of pure love, which rather intrigued Aelnoth, for it was not a look that he had ever seen a slave bestow upon his owner.

'I think he was probably knocked unconscious in the battle.'

'Perhaps from a slingshot, for the Greek slingers are renowned for their skill with the sling throughout the known world.' She explained.

'I've never heard of them.' Aelnoth thought silently to himself.

'The problem is that although his captors chained him, they found that they could not control him, so they cut out his tongue. Thus, I have never been able to find out much about him.'

'Nonetheless. I love the ugly brute, and indeed I really do think that the feeling is mutual.'

'Abbi will train with you for four hours by the sand clock each morning, and after you have bathed and eaten, I will arrange for you to meet with some of the Emperors generals, as well as some people who know about warfare and tactics.'

'These will be men who have experienced defeats as well as some successes upon the battlefield.'

'You and I will then spend a few hours together before and after our evening meal.'

She was about to hobble away with the aid of her golden staff, when she suddenly stopped, turned to him and said. 'I must be getting forgetful in my old age, for I have failed to inform you that I have employed a number of additional Armenian guards to keep you safe, for although you may not realise it, everyone from Noblemen and their ladies, down to the meanest of our street beggars are talking about 'The White Wizard,' so word is certainly winging its way towards our enemies, who will, no doubt, employ assassins to eliminate you.'

'Why not get a dozen of the Varangian Guard to keep us safe? He asked.

'They are supposed to be the best of the best, and I could speak with them in the language of the North.'

'Ah,' she said with a sad smile that cracked her wrinkled face.

'That is exactly why I have not chosen the Varangians.'

'As I have already told you. You must learn the language of Greece, for that is the most widely tongue used in our empire.'

'I do speak Latin.' He offered with a weak smile.

'Christ alive.' She said with genuine shock.

'You northern barbarians never cease to astound me.'

She turned away from him, and he was sure he heard her chuckling as she hobbled her way across the courtyard.

Aelnoth walked the few paces back to Abbi, whose gaping, empty mouth grinned at him, as he held out a long spear and a shield.

Aelnoth took the spear and shield from the giant, finding the spear much lighter than an English spear.

The shield was also unfamiliar to him, for it was about half the size of an English shield, and although it was made of metal, instead of wood and boiled leather, it weighed much the same as his fathers' old shield, which still lay against the wall in his new sleeping quarters.

Suddenly the large, slow moving slave turned into a gifted and savage warrior, as he moved with the speed and agility of a man half his age, and almost miraculously appearing in front of Aelnoth so quickly, that his spear clanged noisily against Aelnoth's shield, as Aelnoth's automatic reaction raised his own shield just in time to prevent the giant's spear from piercing his left shoulder.

Aelnoth took a pace backwards and eyed his opponent with renewed respect.

He then decided that the best form of defence was attack, and took the fight to the giant, thrusting at his left, right, centre, and slashing upwards towards his head before he stooped and thrust his heavy spear at the giant's unprotected legs.

His spear grazed his opponent's right ankle causing the giant to nimbly hop backwards, as the man's grinning face altered to become the face of a more serious man.

Aelnoth thought that his mouth formed the word 'Good,' but he was immediately forced backwards, as the giant launched a series of attacks with both his spear and his shield, until with one enormous lunge, he clashed his shield into Aelnoth's own shield with such force that it flung the young Englishman backwards and onto the ground, where he lay dazed for a brief moment, and as his eyes cleared he found himself staring up into the giant's grinning face, and felt the prick of his spear under his chin.

Abbi removed his spear and held out a hand, which was clasped by Aelnoth's own hand, as the slave hauled him up onto his feet with an effortless heave.

The rest of the morning was spent in further spear and shield exercises that left both of Aelnoth's arms practically numb with exertion, and his legs shaking like jelly, whilst the still grinning giant seemed to be untouched with fatigue, as he gathered up the small pile of weapons, and took them back from whence they had come.

Aelnoth sighed with relief as he eased his aching body into the warm bath that the servants had prepared for him.

The slave girl began to rub a sponge over his shoulders and down his back, easing his aching muscles and causing him to say in his native tongue.

'Christ alive that feels good.'

The girl recognised the word 'Christ.' and said in Latin.

'Serves you right you dirty great barbarian.' Words that she believed that he did not understand, and when he answered in the same tongue. 'Why is that?'

The shock almost caused her to fall into the bath with him.

'Forgive me my lord.' She exclaimed as her hand went up to her mouth as if she could push the words back into her mouth.

'I didn't mean it my lord,' she said, as tears began to cascade down her face, for she feared that if this barbarian were to inform her mistress of her impudence, Agio would either have her whipped, or send her to the slave market, where she would be sold to some lecherous old thug, who would be free to impregnate her with a dozen of his own brats, before she became too old to bear him further children, whereupon she would be thrown out onto the street.

'I spoke without thinking my Lord.'

'Please forgive me.' She pleaded.

'Forget it.' Said Aelnoth with a smile, for he was quite pleased that he had found someone with whom he could at least have a conversation with, albeit in a language that was not his own.

'How are you called?'

'Nike.' Said the girl quietly, for she was hugely relieved that this barbarian seemed to have forgotten her insulting remark.

'Strange name?'

'My father named me after 'Nike' who is the Greek Goddess of Victory.' She said as she raised her chin a little, indicating her pride of bearing the name of a Goddess.

'So, you are Greek?'

'I am my Lord, or at least I was, before I became a slave.'

'How did that happen?'

'It is a long story my lord,' said Nike.

'My Father was a very rich merchant, dealing in silks and other things, but he was cheated by a man who he called 'a friend,' and our whole family were forced into slavery, to pay some off the debts we owed.'

'So you obviously speak Greek as well as Latin,' said Aelnoth, stating the obvious.

'I do my lord, and a little Armenian.'

'Good! I will have you teach me to speak Greek.'

'For instance. What is Greek for this? Water?'

'Hudor' she said, and he repeated. 'Hudor,' and so his first lesson in Greek began.

It was a lesson that was followed each morning after he had battled with Abbi, strengthening his entire body and enhancing his already considerable skill with all of the weapons from both the east, and north of Europe.

His skill with weapons, coupled with the knowledge, which he learned from Nike, and Agio's scholars, soon made him a man to be reckoned with, eventually earning him respect and admiration by young warriors and old generals alike.

One of the Varangian guards escorted Ingrid into his quarters late one sultry hot afternoon, and when the girl saw him, she ran the few steps across the room and flung her arms around his neck and gasped. 'No one told me where they were taking me; they just arrived and told me to collect my things and follow them.'

'I can't tell you how relieved I am to see you, she said.

'Where do I sleep?'

She seemed a little disappointed when Aelnoth led her to her room that was across the courtyard from his own quarters, but as soon as she saw the rich furnishings, she cheered up and became her perky, happy self again.

He left her and immediately made his way to the servant's quarters where he found Nike busy in the small kitchen.

'Nike,' he said in the manner of a master speaking to his servant.

'My sister Ingrid has just joined us, and I want you to make a point of looking after her.'

'Make sure that she fits in and comes to no harm, and if she wants to go out into the city, make sure that she is escorted either by Abbi or a couple of the guards.'

'Yes master,' she said.

'I will look after her.' Pleased that her master had given her the task of looking after his sister, as it would give her more time away from other duties, such as cooking and cleaning, besides, she was eager to meet his sister and find out what sort of people these northern women were.

Aelnoth's grasp of the language astonished Agio, who was delighted with the speed of his progress, although he continued to deny that he was 'The White Wizard,' and his inaptitude for her teachings of Witchcraft, frustrated her so much that she began to consume more red wine than she had ever drunk in her long, long life.

Aelnoth's arms and legs strengthened so much, that after the each training session with Abbi, after beating him in most, if not all of their mock battles, he looked forward to the warm baths and the long massage, which Nike gave.

After one particularly long and gruelling session with Abbi, he rested his aching body on his couch, for what was going to be a few brief minutes rest, but in fact turned out to be more like a hour.

As he was waking, his half opened eyes gazed through the half open doorway, where he saw one of Agio's serving girls standing by a small table.

His suspicious were aroused as he noticed that she was emptying a small phial of white powder into a decanter.

It was a decanter, which he had seen before, when the girl had entered Agio's quarters with food and wine.

The girl glanced around, and as her eyes fell upon the prone figure of Aelnoth, they remained on him for a few brief seconds before she looked away, and continued to look around in a suspicious manner.

She took up the tray and left the room.

Aelnoth rose speedily from his couch, and followed the serving girl, as she made her way through the passageways and rooms, which led to the sleeping quarters of her mistress.

The girl tapped the door of Agio's quarters and entered, making her way towards the low couch where her mistress was taking her afternoon nap.

She placed the tray on a small table beside the couch, and turned to leave the room.

Aelnoth met her in the doorway and prevented her from leaving.

'What did you put in your mistresses drink?' he asked quietly.

'Nothing my lord,' answered the girl as she lifted her chin defiantly and looked up into his icy blue eyes.

'Come.' He said sternly.

'We shall see,' as he grabbed her hand and led her over towards Agio, who had been wakened by their voices, and who now sat up upon the couch, looking at them as they approached.

'What is all this about?' she said angrily.

'What are you doing in my sleeping quarters?' She spat.

'I have had men garrotted for less.'

'You will not garrotte me.' Said Aelnoth confidently.

'Why not?' she snarled.

'Do you think I would not dare, because you are called 'The White Wizard?'

'That name will not save you?'

'Oh I think it will,' answered Aelnoth.

'Pah.' She spat.

'I have favoured you for far too long, and have seen nought for my troubles.'

'The Empire is still teetering on the verge of collapse, and the Emperor himself is losing his patience with you.'

'He is beginning to think that you are nought but a fraud.'

'I too am worried, for you have performed no miracles since you got here.'

Aelnoth merely smiled and ignored her quip.

'Here.' He said, as he stooped forward and poured out a glassful of wine from the decanter.

'Drink this and all of your worries will fade away and he thrust the glass of wine into her hand.

She raised the glass to her lips and looked up to him, only to see him gazing down at her, and shaking his head.

'What?' She asked hesitantly.

'What?' She repeated.

Suddenly, she seemed to comprehend what he was indicating, and she looked at the glass of wine, and then back upwards into his face, causing her own wrinkled face to grimace, as her almost toothless mouth opened, and without saying a word she flung the glass and its contents across the room in disgust.

'Poison?' she spat.

'Well,' said Aelnoth.

'I'm not really sure, but I did see this wench pour some white powder into the decanter.'

'Did you indeed?'

'In that case,' she said as she rose from the couch with a loud groan, and the help of her stick.

'We have a ready made taster, do we not?' and hobbled the few paces to the table where her shaky hand filled a second glass with the suspect wine.

'Drink.' She demanded as she thrust the glass of wine towards the quivering girl.

The girl attempted to retreat and shook her head, but was held firm by the strong hands of Aelnoth.

'Just give her a sip.' Said Aelnoth.

'Not enough to kill her, but just enough to make her sick.' He added in his innocence.

'A sip could kill.' Snarled the old woman.

'No,' she spat. 'I would have swallowed the full glassful, and so will she.'

'Hold her still.' She demanded, and much against his better nature, or perhaps it was from the genuine dread that he felt for this ancient hag, caused him to hold the girls head still as Agio held the servant's nose.

After a few moments her mouth opened as she gasped for air, and Agio quickly emptied the wine into the girl's open mouth.

The girl coughed and spluttered, but her mouth was held shut by the surprisingly firm hold of the old woman, who waited until she saw the girl swallow before she removed her hand, and allowed the girls mouth to open, where a dribble of the residue of the wine, which she had failed to swallow, oozed out of the corners of her mouth.

'Now we shall wait and see.' Said Agio as she sat down on the couch.

'We shall see what we shall see.'

'Sit her down there.' She ordered, as she nodded her head towards a chair.

Aelnoth guided the sobbing girl to the chair, where she sat and ran her hands frantically through her long dark hair.

'Who ordered you to poison me?' demanded Agio.

The girl did not even look up or answer the question. She merely continued to run her fingers through her hair, and pull at strands of hair as if she was attempting to wrench the poison out of her head.

'What did they promise you?' said Agio in as kind a voice as she could muster.

'Was it Gold? Silver?'

'A rich husband? Land?'

'Did they offer you your freedom?'

That particular question appeared to have found its target, for the girl ceased wrenching at her hair for a moment, and looked up into the wrinkled face of her intended victim.

'Stupid girl.' Said Agio in a tired voice.

'Freedom would have been yours once your beauty had faded, like all the other girls who have preceded you.'

The girl looked at her mistress again as if she disbelieved what Agio had said.

'Tis true.' Said Agio.

'Why do you think there are no old and haggard women in my household?' she asked, and then added with a smile. 'Except me.'

The girl shuddered and her hand flew to her stomach and she groaned.

A moment later she was on the floor, writhing in agony and groaning aloud, with an occasional word emitting from her swollen throat.

'It.' She gasped. 'It was Elg.' but failed to utter anything, which they could comprehend, as her throat rattled and she lay still.

'Did you hear what she said?' demanded Agio.

'Your ears are younger than mine.'

'It sounded like Elg' something or other.' Answered Aelnoth.

'Arrg,' she growled. I know a dozen lords and princes who sound like that.'

'It could be any one of them.'

'Pity,' said Agio.

'I quite liked the girl.'

'Still, you did save my life, and for that, I am eternally grateful.'

'Time for something to eat, and a fresh jug of good wine.' She added as she shuffled towards the door in order to commence her duties, as if the death of a young girl and an attempt on her life had never happened.

'One that is not poisoned.' She said loudly as she passed through the door.

During the following days and weeks, many prominent members of the council, as well as a number of wealthy merchants whose names contained something like 'Elg,' died in mysterious circumstances.

One leading member of the council, who was a young vocal and ambitious man, and who was in surprisingly good health, suddenly collapsed from a heart attack and died on the floor of the council building, before a host of his horrified colleagues.

A wealthy merchant slipped off the quayside near his warehouse, where he had walked a thousand times before, and disappeared into the bay, never to be seen again,

Another cantankerous old senator was found in bed by his servant in the embrace of a five-foot long cobra.

Other men disappeared or resigned from their posts, and fled to their villas in the country, where they enjoyed the fruits of their labour in the pleasant groves of their vineyards and olive orchards.

Aelnoth's training with Abbi continued, and with each passing day he became more proficient with the eastern weapons, finding that the curved scimitar was far more effective than the straight English sword, especially when it was used by a man riding on the back of a horse, for the curve seemed to inflict far more damage on the sacks in the training field, which had been set upon stakes to resemble men.

However, perhaps it was due to stubbornness or perhaps merely his preference, he continued to favour his own Saex and long-sword.

Some of the weapons were far more sophisticated than the northern European weapons, as well as being more pliable; seldom breaking and he found that they could be sharpened to a finer edge.

He now habitually beat the frustrated Abbi without too much of an effort.

Each day, his conversions with the Generals and tacticians became easier and easier, as he listened to them speaking Greek, (sometimes with a more broad and foreign accent than his own,) for most of them had originated from the conquered peoples, who made up the mosaic pattern of the empire.

Several months into his education, he thought that it was time for him to speak about some of the more recent successes and failures of the Empires battles.

Many of the generals claimed to be the main contributor of the rare victories, whilst all of them blamed other men or difficult circumstances for their defeats.

'It appears to me.' He said to an assembly of aged Generals.

'That most of your successful battles have been against Armenian and Lydian tribesmen, whilst the people who defeat you time and time again, and who seem to occupy more and more of your cities and territory, are the Seljuk Turks.'

'Why is that?' he asked solemnly as he looked at each of the five old Generals in turn.

The Generals all seemed to speak at the same time, offering excuses and reasons that had caused their squadrons and armies to be defeated.

He held his hand up for silence, which was eventually granted as the last two Generals fell silent.

'I will tell you why.' He said grimly.

'The Seljuk Turks are both cavalry and archers.'

'In other words they are bowmen on a horse.'

'From what I have heard here in this room over the past weeks, is that whenever you meet them, they shower your warriors with arrows until they have run out of arrows, and then they return to their camp, or to their baggage carts to replenish their supply of arrows from their seemingly endless supply, and return to decimate your ranks even further.'

'In other words your warriors have little option other than to cower behind their shields while your enemies decimate your ranks, until the survivors are forced to flee for their lives, only to be ridden down and slain by these horse-archers.'

'You obviously have archers.'

'Why do you not match them with your own archers?'

Once again the Generals answered him all at the same time, until one of the most senior amongst them rose to his feet and held his hand aloft for silence.

'Of course we have archers.' He said indignantly.

'And bloody good ones at that, but they are no match for the Turks.'

'For every arrow that we launched towards them. They launch two or even three at us, and they are galloping around on those blasted ponies of theirs, hanging on the far side of the damned things, so that we can't hit them.'

He sat down with a plonk and crossed his arms across his chest, as he glared angrily at this young northerner upstart, who dared to criticise his warriors and his tactics.

Aelnoth ignored the old Generals glares and asked.

'How many units of Cavalry do we have?'

Blank faces answered his question, causing him to surmise that none of those present knew the numbers.

After glancing at his colleagues, the same old General stood and said, 'I know that the Emperor has one thousand horsemen in and around the city, and they patrol the neighbourhood in order to assure the people that all is well.'

'He also has cavalry patrolling our boarders with Armenia, Egypt and Palestine, as well as others that I do not know about, but I have no idea as to their numbers.'

'Only the Emperor himself can answer that question,' said the white haired General, 'and I do not propose to question him on the matter.'

'I am much too fond of my head to be that stupid.' He said with a chuckle, as he sat down on his ornately carved chair.

That very evening, Aelnoth asked Agio if she would arrange for him to have an audience with the Emperor.

'Is it important?' she asked.

'Very.' He answered.

'In fact it is extremely important, and could be so important that unless I see him, and obtain the authority from him, to allow me to raise an army of horse archers, along the same lines as the Seljuk Turks, he could end up losing his Palace, his City and his entire Empire.'

CHAPTER 20

Aelnoth was forced to wait a frustrating three days before he was granted an audience with the Emperor, and when he was eventually allowed into his presence, Aelnoth was just one of a long line of petitioners waiting to see him.

After shuffling forward for half of the morning, it was finally his turn to speak to the young Emperor.

'Ah! Exclaimed the Emperor. 'The White Wizard,' or rather the young man who is adamant in his denial that he is NOT 'The White Wizard,' and who has yet to perform a single act that is at all out of the ordinary.'

'Why is that?' he spat rather angrily.

'Your highness,' he said as he bowed his head towards the Emperor.

'I need to speak to you in private.

'Why so? You are amongst friends in my court.' Said the Emperor haughtily.

Aelnoth spoke boldly. 'Your majesty, I am sure that most of your nobles are trustworthy and loyal men, but if only one of these men present can be persuaded to take gold, land or a position that he aspires to, for a snippet of information, which could cause you damage, then if that single man hears what I have to say to you, he alone could cause the destruction of your Empire.'

The Emperor looked almost casually around the room, which was crowded with two hundred or more of Nobles, petitioners and their servants.

His eyes rested on a single individual here and there, before his eyes continued their survey of the room.

'Your advice is sound, for I have nearly forgotten about the White Wizard who has been sent to protect us from adversity.'

'The business of state is pressing, you know.' He added almost apologetically voice.

'Leave us.' He said loudly.

The congregation stared at one another in amazement at the order, for it had long been the tradition that this particular day of the month had always been set aside as a day for the people, and a day when the Emperor listened to, and settled many of the petitioner's disputes.

'Clear the room.' He said in a loud voice.

The men of the Varangian Guard moved from their positions in front of the Emperor and from the two doorways of the great Hall, and ushered the crowd of grumbling Petitioners, Lords and their Ladies, and the host of their servants, out of the room.

After a short wait, the room was finally emptied except from the ten Varangians who stood by the far door.

'Wait there.' Ordered the Emperor.

'Now what is so important that you have demanded a private audience with me?'

'May I approach closer your majesty, for even Northmen can be corrupted'?

The Emperor nodded, and beckoned Aelnoth up the steps towards the throne.

Aelnoth spoke quietly so that there was no possibility of being overheard.

'To be blunt your highness.' Said Aelnoth.

'There is no other way to broach a subject, which is so important, that it must be for your ears only.'

'Well. Spit it out.' Snapped the young Emperor.

Aelnoth hesitated for a moment, and said quietly, as he looked into the green eyes of this young Emperor.

'If I am to save you, your city and your Empire, I need to have access not only to your treasury, and I also need to have a free hand to recruit and train an army, not only of foot soldiers, but also of horsemen who can outride and outshoot your enemies.

This new army must also be strong enough to defeat your enemies, who will invade your Empire with an army of untold numbers in two years time.'

Aelnoth himself did not know where the figure of, 'Two years,' had came from, for it had appeared in his mind at the same moment that he had uttered the words.

Although the Emperor was shocked by the demand, it seemed to Aelnoth that he was not as outraged as he should have been, and he suspected that despite the Emperors young age, Aelnoth felt that the Emperor's large network of spies and informers had already informed him of the potential perils, which threatened his crumbling Empire.

'How much of my treasury do you need?' he asked.

Aelnoth was nonplussed, for he had fully expected the Emperor to rant and rave, but the Emperor merely rested his elbow on the edge of his throne and looked down thoughtfully at Aelnoth.

Nonetheless, he answered the Emperors question.

'I really don't know,' he said, 'but I suspect it will be a lot.'

'I will put one thousand of my horsemen at your disposal.' He offered.

'Ah,' thought Aelnoth.

'He does know of my mission,' and a slight smile crossed his face.

The Emperor also saw the smile, and he rose from his throne and regally walked down the two remaining steps towards Aelnoth.

'You have probably guessed that I did have some inkling of your demands, and have already given them much thought, and before you ask. I have not discussed the situation with any of my advisors.'

'Not even the Keeper of my treasury,' He added.

'For he is a Jew, and as he is one of the conquered peoples who hold allegiance to me, it would have been unwise of me to do so.'

'Do you not agree?' he said as a tired smile crossed his young face.

'Indeed I do your Highness.'

'Bring me the Keeper of my Treasury.' He shouted at the Varangians who were still standing in a group near the door.

Whilst they were waiting for the arrival of the Keeper of the Treasury, they spoke about Constantinople and of its satellite dominions who paid tithes and taxes to the Emperor in return for his protection, and the Emperor was fully aware that due to the ever increasing raids of barbarians from outside the Empire, the steady erosion of his armies, their manpower and strategic positions was continuing at an ever increasing pace, draining him of his warriors, citizens and income.

He rubbed his neatly trimmed beard, as he explained that many of the dominions had ceased paying their taxes, whilst others were becoming more and more in arrears with their payments, resulting in an ever depleting amount of silver and gold going into his treasury.

The door opened to admit two men of the Varangian Guard, who towered over a small, white haired old man who was dressed from head to toe in black.

'Ha, here you are,' exclaimed the Emperor, and as the man slowly approached.

'Joseph.' He said.

'This is Aelnoth. 'The White Wizard and the man tentatively held his hand out to be shaken by Aelnoth.

'Aelnoth is from the North and has been sent to help us.'

Aelnoth shook the man's hand, and as he withdrew his hand he felt that he had just held a wet fish.

'He is to have free access to the treasury.'

'Is that understood?'

'Free access my Lord?' Asked the treasurer in a voice that questioned whether or not he really had heard the Emperor say such blasphemous words.

'Free access?'

'Indeed.'

'To everything my Lord?'

'Everything. Gold. Silver. Coin. Everything.'

'But my Lord, How will I pay the servants? The court?'

'Let them wait.'

'Wait. Your Highness. How?'

'Make promises. Excuses. Say the money has been delayed.'

'Anything. Just do not pay them in full until I say so.'

'Anyway, we should be all right for a few months. Should we not?' He added.

'If you say so my Lord.' Answered the treasurer, and his already sour face became even sourer, as he backed away a few paces, before he turned and shuffled towards the door.

'You had better go with him to the Treasury.' Said the Emperor as he smiled towards the Englishman; causing Aelnoth to realize that the old Treasurer had expected Aelnoth to follow him.

He made a speedy bow to the Emperor, and thanked him, before he dashed off in order to catch up with the Treasurer.

As he left the room he caught a glimpse of the Treasurer, who was in the act of turning off the corridor and entering a door on the right hand side.

Aelnoth ran down the corridor where he caught up with the little man, who was in the process of passing two Varangian Guards, where he began to descend a set of wide stone steps.

'Is this the way to the treasury? Asked Aelnoth.

The Treasurer merely looked towards Aelnoth with an odd look on his wrinkled face, and deigned to answer such a silly question.

After walking along two other corridors, and passing four more Guards, the duo reached a huge iron studded door, which was guarded by another brace of stern faced Varangians.

They obviously knew the Treasurer, for they moved from the centre of the door to allow the Treasurer and Aelnoth access.

The old Treasurer delved into the folds of his cloak to produce a large iron key, which he fumbled with, as he attempted to insert it into the lock.

One of the Guards said. 'Well by Thor's tentacles, if it isn't 'Aelnoth. The White Wizard.'

'Didn't recognise you at first in this dim corridor.'

'How are things going for you Aelnoth two swords?' Asked the Guard.

'Fine thanks. And yourself?'

'Bored,' answered the guard who seemed pleased, either at a slight relief from the boredom, which both of the Guards experienced whilst standing guard on a door in a dull corridor for hours on end, or perhaps it was that when he got off duty, he would be able to boast to his fellow warriors that the famous White Wizard 'Aelnoth' had crossed his path and had actually spoken to him, and that alone should earn him at least a couple of flagons of wine this evening.

Aelnoth followed the Treasurer into the dark room, which was suddenly lightened, as the Treasurer moved across the room, and began to light several of the oil lamps, which were positioned at strategic points along the walls.

The room itself consisted of a number of smaller rooms, which had been constructed along one side of the wall, and stretched away into the darkness.

The Treasurer continued to walk into the darkness, carrying one of the oil lamps, which lit up more and more of the treasurery as made his way forward.

'All of these booths used to be full of gold and silver in his fathers day,' said the old man.

'But since the young Emperor took over, I have been paying out more money than we are taking in.'

'Can't go on like this.' He said grumpily as he shook his head.

Both men came to a halt about a third of a way along the vault, as the Treasurer shone his lamp into one of the rooms, revealing a huge pile of silver, which reached from the floor to the ceiling, and sparkled in the lamplight.

'Most of the gold is gone.' Said the old man.

'Only this silver is left.'

'And are all those rooms up there full of silver?' asked Aelnoth as he pointed into the darkness to where he surmised the end of the vault would be.

'Oh yes.' Answered the Chancellor.

'Will it be enough?' he asked.

'It will have to be.' Answered a pleased Aelnoth, for although he could not really see the far end of the vault; he surmised that the few rooms that were within his vision should be more than enough to enable him to carry out his plans.

'I shall need access to the vault.' Stated Aelnoth.

'I spend all of my waking hours down here. Writing in the ledgers,' said the chancellor, as they walked back towards a large desk that was covered in parchments.

'I will instruct the Guards to allow you to pass.'

'And what if I need money in a hurry at midnight, or at some ungodly hour in the morning?' asked Aelnoth.

'Then the guards will escort you to my sleeping quarters.'

'They are not far, and I will open the vault for you.'

The Chancellor sat down on a well-worn chair, and commenced to study a parchment.

Aelnoth left the room and spoke a few friendly words with the two guards, before he retraced his steps along the passageways and out into the sunlight.

The blazing sun temporarily dazzled him, causing him to think of his two Albino friends, and he wondered how they were coping, not only with the heat, but also with the almost eternal sunlight.

During the following days and weeks, he commissioned four merchant ships, with an escort of three fighting galleys to sail to Spain, with orders to scour the countryside for ready-made longbows, and logs of yew, which were commodities that Spain had in abundance,

He gave the captains strict orders to fill their holds with Longbows and yew wood, and return to Constantinople at their earliest opportunity.

He sent over one hundred, ten men troops of horsemen, across the borders into all of the satellites nations, with orders to recruit horsemen and archers.

Authorising them to promise citizenship for life to all who rallied to his call, as well as a purse of silver and a plot of fertile land where they could settle, and live free of tax for the rest of their lives.

CHAPTER 21

Aelnoth ordered his recruiting parties to scour the teeming streets of the city, with orders to recruit any strong young men for the army.

'With direct orders from the Emperor,' he said, tongue in cheek.

The standing army was not immune from his long reach, and those thousands of men who seemed to be whiling away their time, waiting for retirement on useless checkpoint duties, or rolling dice' in remote and almost forgotten garrisons, were recalled to Constantinople, and billeted in the new city of tents, which had been erected on the rolling hills that surrounded the city.

As soon as these men began to arrive at their allotted check-points, they were assigned to new units, which were led by either veterans, or one of the growing numbers of promising young men who Aelnoth had promoted.

Aelnoth ordered that these new units were to be peppered by the pick of the Varangians, whose duty it was, to provide weapon training and discipline into these raw recruits.

These Northmen were renowned for their loyalty, as well as their prowess in battle, and were readily accepted by most of the new arrivals, but the variance of nationality, age groupings; and experience did cause some unrest.

This unrest was speedily stamped upon, and after a dozen or more public floggings and a couple of executions, the unrest faded away, and the new and old warriors settled into their assigned duties.

The Varangians found it very difficult to drill disciple into warriors who were renowned, and indeed proud of their bravery and individualism, but after a lot of cajoling, flattery and training, these men eventually fell under the spell of the battle hardened Varangians.

Thankfully, a large number of the recruits excelled in horsemanship as well as marksmanship.

Some six weeks later, when Aelnoth had been riding outside the city, he had met an archer who was on his way to join the Emperors new army, and he noticed that the man carried a large and unusual bow, which hung across one side of his horse in a deerskin bag.

Across the opposite side of his horse lay a similar bag, and that bag was filled to the brim with arrows that were at least six feet long.

After a brief introduction and a little friendly banter, the archer was persuaded to demonstrate his prowess with the bow, and much to Aelnoth's surprise, the man took off his riding boots and replaced them with soft leather boots.

He then lay on the ground, whereupon he rested the body of the bow on the soles of his feet, placed an arrow in the string, and using both of his hands, he stretched the bowstring back to his chin and loosed his shaft.

The six foot long arrow shot away with such speed, that the eagle-eyed Aelnoth lost sight of it, as it disappeared into the distance.

The astounded Aelnoth rode alongside the man as they went to retrieve the shaft, and when they eventually found it, the huge arrow had covered a distance of nearly three times the length that a good English archer could cover with his longbow.

'How are you called?' asked Aelnoth.

'I am called 'Hallandor the bowman.' Said the man, proudly.

'Hallandor,' repeated Aelnoth.

'And tell me Hallandor, where are you from?'

'Scythia.'

'Then I shall call you Hallandor the Scythian.' Said Aelnoth.

'Not only will I accept you into the Emperor's new army.' Said Aelnoth to the Scythian, 'but I will make you a Commander of as many squadrons of archers who you can train to use a big bow like that.'

'I am sure that you can find men for me to train.' Said Hallandor.

'But I doubt that you will find any bows like mine in Constantinople.'

'Then I suggest that we meet with the royal bow-makers, and you can tell them what type of wood you need, and instruct them how to make your bows.'

'They are skilled men, and I am sure that with your help, they will be able to provide us with a goodly number of bows before we march.'

Aelnoth installed Hallandor in comfortable quarters before he introduced him to the Royal bow-makers, ordering them to follow the instructions, which the Scythian gave them, and to recruit as many apprentices as they needed, in order that they could construct fifty Scythian bows each and every month.

He stressed to the bow-makers that these new bows would make the difference between victory and defeat, should the Emperor go to war.

He then took the Scythian to the street of arrow-makers with similar orders, threatening dire consequences to any who failed to make their quota of one thousand, six-foot long arrows each month.

Again and again he stressed the importance of the arrows, telling each arrow-maker in turn, that if war did break out, and the Emperor was defeated though lack of arrows, then the city would be put to the torch, and they, along with their families and the rest of the citizens would all be put to the sword.

His message appeared to have been understood, as dark shadows of terror crossed the faces of the makers of arrows.

Aelnoth visited the street of arrow makers a number of times during the following months in order to inspect their work.

He delved to the very bottom layer of arrows, which lay in the large wicker boxes, where the arrows had been carefully stored, and scrutinising each shaft in detail, trying, in vain to wrench the iron heads off the shafts, in order to assure himself that they were strong and sharp, for he had heard rumours that many of the families who made their living by producing arrows for the Emperor's army, employed slaves and children in order to reach their quota's, and although he inspected a large number of the boxes, he found all of the arrows to be of excellent quality.

The Bow makers were not progressing so well, as only a small part of the assignment of Spanish Yew had arrived in one single ship.

The Bow-makers had constructed a large number of bows from local wood, but had run out of that source over a week ago, causing many of them to sit idly around their small fires, drinking the local brew of what passed for wine.

The two transport ships finally arrived from Spain, laden not only with logs of yew wood, but one of the Captains had managed to purchase over two thousand ready made bows, which gave Aelnoth hope that by the end of the following two or three months, his newly formed army would not only be sufficiently trained to take to the field, but they should also be supplied with nearly ten thousand archers, which consisted of seven thousand ordinary archers, plus three thousand archers who had been trained by Hallandor the Scythian.

* * *

It was the largest and the best supplied army that had left the city of Constantinople for more than one hundred years.

Aelnoth led the first division, behind a screen of one hundred scouts, who were sent ahead on some of the finest horses that the still rich city could provide.

Two thousand mounted spearmen rode behind the first division, resplendent in their white flowing robes as they proudly rode their large Spanish stallions through the crowded streets.

Magnus headed the second division, whilst Oscar led the third.

Each division consisting of ten thousand infantry intermingled with squads of trained archers.

Each of the three Englishmen was accompanied by a host of generals, servants and advisors, who supposedly knew the areas through which they would be travelling.

The huge baggage train was strung out in a long column of carts, carried crates of arrows, vast amounts of food, water and fodder for the animals.

They, in turn were followed the main body of the army, who were protected by an escort of two thousand mounted lancers.

The six thousand horse archers had been recruited and trained in a secluded area some twenty-five miles away from the prying eyes of Constantinople's citizens.

Aelnoth had ordered these horse archers to stay at least five miles behind the baggage train, and to hide themselves during the daylight hours in one of the many small valleys, which abounded in the terrain through which they were travelling.

The horse archers had strict orders that they must keep up with the army by travelling only during the hours of darkness, guided, much to his annoyance, by Abdulla, who seemed to be a very irritable and unhappy man whenever he was forced to be separated from Oscar.

Aelnoth knew that the enemy's scouts or spies would soon learn that the army had marched, and would attempt to shadow them.

He hoped that they would surmise that the only horsemen the army possessed would be the two thousand lancers, for he had learned from the old Generals that two thousand lancers had been the exact amount of cavalry who accompanied the Emperors last three armies.

The army followed the coastline along the inland sea, making their way through fertile lowlands, which abounded with crops and livestock, whilst the low hills to their east were dotted with large flocks of sheep and goats.

The farmers and herders of livestock plagued the warriors each evening, as they sought out those few warriors who were rich enough to afford the outrageous prices, which they demanded for their products of milk, cheese, butter, and meat from slaughtered beasts.

However, the majority of the warriors were unable to afford the fresh food, and were forced to stand in line each evening, and to join their fellow warriors as they waited for their daily ration of dried meat, porridge and small leather bottles of diluted wine.

They passed through the townships, of Zonguldak and Bafra, where the residents stood at their doorways and watched in silence and in awe as the massive army passed by.

Two weeks later, the army camped around the beautiful town of Samsun, which nestled in a picturesque bay on the Black sea, and it was here that the commanders decided that they should remain in camp for a few days, in order to rest both men and animals, and to enjoy the abundance of farm produce and fish, which seemed to abound in the area.

Commanders, warriors and animals bathed in the warm sea and refreshed themselves, with the exception of the large number of scouts who had been sent out in all directions, so that there would be no surprise attack by the Seljuk's, who had ventured into this area on more than one occasion.

Ten days later the army passed through the town of Fatsa, which sat a mile or so inland from the sea, at the foot of a range of mountains, which Aelnoth was informed, were known locally as. 'The Mountains of the Moon.'

The terrain had altered from the green pastures of Samsun, into a countryside that had been burned brown and dried out by a sun, causing the sun to have seemingly grown into a ball of fire, and it's searing heat appeared to be so intense, causing Aelnoth some difficulty to understand how anything could be so hot without actually burning, for it had turned almost every living thing, including the few humans, who they met, into dry and withered beings.

Water holes began to dry up, and rivers, which had obviously once been raging torrents, (for Aelnoth could see the remains of debris, which had been swept down in the recent floods, high in the trees and shrubs along the river banks) had become mere trickles of their former glory.

A week later one of the scouts galloped into the camp and screeched to a halt in a cloud of dust before the small leather tent, which served as Aelnoth's quarters.

'My Lord,' said the breathless scout.

'I saw a troop of enemy scouts on that hill there,' as he pointed to a small hill that was perhaps a mile to the east.

'They showered me with arrows but I managed to escape.'

'How many?' asked Aelnoth?

'Perhaps ten my Lord.'

'Thank you! You may resume your patrol.' Said Aelnoth, as he turned to one of the four Generals who had joined him.

The man was the General who commanded the lancers.

'General.' Said Aelnoth, 'I want you to order your Lancers to form a line on both sides of our army and drive the enemy scouting parties before us.'

'I do not want any of their scouts to penetrate your line and discover our horse archers, who are, as you know, some five miles to our rear.'

'Is that clear?' he snapped.

'It is my Lord,' said the white whiskered General, who was about to turn in order to carry out his orders, when Aelnoth added.

'Make sure that your Lancers take their shields with them.'

'We all know how deadly our enemy can be with those bows of theirs, do we not?'

'Yes my Lord.' Answered the General in a sourly tone, for he was one of the many older veterans who resented being led by a Northman, no matter that he was reputed to be 'The White Wizard,'

To this General and probably to many other Officers of the old guard, Aelnoth was little more than an untried young man, who was supposed to be lethal with those two silly, straight swords of his.

Towards sunset, Aelnoth received word that the line of lancers had seen no less than three separate squads of the enemy, and had succeeded in driving all three eastwards, and away from the army.

Aelnoth ordered the sentries to be doubled to two hundred men to guard their night camp, and ordered the lancers to camp in a long line adjacent to the main body of his army, in order to deter any of the enemies horsemen from penetrating their line and locating his six thousand horse archers, who in turn, had been alerted to the possible danger of being discovered, and had been ordered to light the minimum of the smallest of fires possible when they to cooked their evening meal.

He met with his Generals that evening in order to discuss the discovery of the Seljuk scouts.

'Who amongst you knows this area?' he asked.

Only one of them answered his question and said. 'I was with General Omar Aitschar when he fought the Seljuk's forty years ago.'

'Of course I was nought but a boy then, but I have a good memory for places, and we covered much the same ground that this army has taken thus far.'

'Did you do battle with them? Asked Aelnoth.

'Yes, my Lord. We did.' Answered the old General.

'And did you win?'

'We did my Lord,' answered the General with pride.

'Where did the battle take place?'

'About a hundred miles or so further east.'

'In Armenia,' my Lord, 'close to the sea of 'Sevan,' which is near the furthest borders of Armenia, but of course in those days, Armenia was within the Empire of Constantinople, whereas today, it is a country that has almost entirely been conquered by the Seljuk Turks.'

'When you say, 'almost entirely.' What do you mean?'

'My Lord,' answered the man as he ran his fingers lovingly through his long white fluffy beard.

'I believe that there are still a number of regions in Armenia where the Christians still hold out in their mountain fortresses, and have so far resisted the inroads of the Seljuk's.'

'Would it be possible to reach these Christians?'

'Well, I do know where one or two of these enclaves are, but it would be very risky to pass through the Turkish areas in order to reach them.'

'If I gave you a squad of chosen men, could you reach one or two of them?'

'I am an old man my Lord, and the way would be too strenuous for my old bones.' he said, as he put on the wining voice of a frail old man, which was in stark contrast to the gruff voice, which he had been using a few brief moments ago.

Whilst Aelnoth had learned to value this particular old Generals knowledge of the terrain over the last few weeks, he was slightly put out that the General had more or less refused to journey into the mountains in order to contact the fortresses and groups of Christians, who he had mentioned'

However, he was not too concerned and asked. 'Could you draw a map, which some of my younger warriors could follow to reach the Christians?'

'Of course my Lord.'

'Do so, and whilst you are drawing your map. I shall have my scribe write parchments to these Christians, asking for their help in defeating the Seljuk's.'

'I shall expect your map by daylight on the morrow.'

'So soon, My Lord. I am not sure that I can do it so quickly.' He said in his old man's voice.

'No excuses. Do it' said Aelnoth harshly.

Aelnoth stooped over the large map that had been given him by one of the Emperor's advisors who had been born in Armenia, and had travelled to visit his family though the mountains a number of times during the past thirty years.

'We are approximately here.' He said, as he stabbed his finger at an area of the map that showed the army was in a cluster of small mountains.

'How far are we from that lake?' he asked.

One of the other old Generals joined him.

'That will be the 'Sea of Van,' and I would say that it is about fifty or so miles from where we are now.' Answered the man.

'It is a beautiful area,' he added. 'I lived at Van for eight years.'

'What kind of terrain would we have to pass through to reach it?'

'Much the same as we have here my Lord.' Answered the General.

'A jumble of small hills and pleasant valleys until we reach the Kackar Mountains.'

'Is it possible for an army of this size to get over these mountains?'

'Not over them my Lord, for their heads are in the clouds, but I can guide you through the passes between the mountains.'

'Plenty of water?' he asked.

'Oh yes my Lord.' There should be plenty of water, especially at this time of year.

'And what is the countryside like? Once we reach this 'Sea of Van?'

'Again, My Lord. For a few miles the land is much the same as it is here, but after we reach the district of Van, there are more mountains and a large flood-plain around the sea, which floods after the rains have drained off the eastern mountains.'

'What time of year is that?'

'It is difficult to say my Lord, but it could be around the time that we reach Van, if my Lord, that is your intention?'

'It is indeed. We leave for the 'Sea of Van' on the morrow.'

It took them three weeks to reach the town of 'Karakose,' which was the single town of any note in the area.

Karakose was tiny compared with the more crowded towns and sophisticated cities which they had passed through, and the smell of goats hung like a grey veil over the entire valley.

After they had left the stench of goats behind them, they made an arduous journey through a tangle of mountains, hills and valleys that left Aelnoth in awe by the vastness of the country.

Three days later, after tramping through the town of Patnos, they made a fortified camp outside a small village that was called 'Ercis.'

'Ercis,' said Aelnoth to Magnus, as he heard the name of the town.

'Tis as close as dammit is to swearing, to the name of my own sire. 'Edric Sylvaticus.'

'Many folk may accuse me of leading our army here, but that certainly is not the case, for I have never heard of the place until a few moments ago.'

'Perhaps you are the White Wizard after all,' said Magnus, as he clapped Aelnoth on the shoulder and gave him a wry smile.

'I think not.' Said Aelnoth.

'I am still nought other than an exiled Englishman, who is just as homesick as you are, and I am merely trying to make the best of the options that life has thrown at me.'

'How are the fortifications going?' he asked.

'Reasonably well,' answered Magnus.

'Most of the trees have been felled and a ditch has been dug around the entire perimeter of the camp, and about one third of the stakes are in place.'

'They should be finished within a couple of days, and then all we have to do is to build platforms along the top, which will probably take another week.'

'Can't you assign more men?'

'Not really.' Answered Magnus.

'We have so many men already on the job that they are already falling over each other.'

Aelnoth nodded solemnly as he looked towards the crowds of men who made up the construction teams, causing him to cast his mind back, and liken the hill to the swarms of wood-ants, which he used to see when he disturbed their nests in the forests around Wentnor.

'How far are the scouts going on their patrols?

'At least twenty miles.' Said Magnus.

'Do you know if our horse archers have been discovered?'

'No. At least I don't think so.'

'So many questions.' Growled Magnus.

'We have covered these points every day since we arrived here, and NO, before you ask. We have not yet sighted the enemy.'

'What about the men we sent out to contact the Christians in Armenia.'

'No news my young friend,' answered Magnus, who saw something happening along one side of the palisade which concerned him, and strode manfully away in order to rectify it.

Aelnoth left the noisy crowded camp, and rode a few miles to the east, where he had assigned a squad of two hundred men to clear the crest of a low hill, which overlooked, and dominated a large flat area of grassland, bordering the sea of Van.

He did not lead his small escort up the slope to the hill, but rode around the 'Sea' for a second time, musing to himself that whilst the 'Sea of Van,' was indeed large, in his own mind, it did not seem to be large enough to hold the title of 'Sea,' and in England it would have been called a large lake.

Nonetheless, he did concede, that it would be very, very large lake.

After the best part of a day spent riding around the 'Sea,' though marshlands and bogs, which sucked the strength out of the horses legs, and reed beds, which were so high that they towered over the heads of the mounted men, they finally found themselves at the bottom of the hill where Aelnoth's men still toiled, felling trees and clearing the undergrowth, as well as levelling off the top of the hill, and building a mound of logs and earth into, what he hoped would be such a strong fortification, that would, he hoped, make it practically invulnerable from anything, other than a long and costly siege.

After they had camped at Van for more than three weeks, a weary messenger slithered his lathered pony to a halt in front of Aelnoth. My Lord,' panted the breathless rider.

'We have sighted the enemy.'

'They are coming from the east, and will be upon us in less than two days.'

'Did you count their numbers?' asked one of the old Generals.

'No, my Lord,' answered the scout.

'Their scouts chased me off, but they are many thousands, for the dust from their army blotted out the sun.'

CHAPTER 22

As daylight broke the following morning, Magnus, Oscar, Abdulla and Aelnoth stood on the hill and stared into the distance, in order to have their first sighting of their enemy, but even though the day dawned bright and clear, there was no sign of the Seljuk Turks, or the cloud of dust, which the scout had reported.

After a brief discussion, the three other leaders left Aelnoth, in order to ensure that their individual sectors of the army were in their assigned places, and the officers and lower ranking warriors all understood what was expected of them, once the battle had commenced.

The two hundred men who laboured on the hill were urged to put the few finishing touches to their work.

Hallandor and his three thousand bowmen made their way through the one and only entrance that had been left open, before it was sealed, thus enclosing them, plus two hundred ordinary archers and two hundred spearmen who manned the defences, should their wooden citadel be attacked by the Seljuk's.

Aelnoth stood on a raised platform with his small group of his signallers, as they overlooked the flood plain, and watched as their army assembled around the lower slopes of the hill.

During the last few days' hundreds of men had been sent into the reed beds in order to cut the reeds, which had been cut and woven into hurdles.

Two hurdles, seven feet high and seven feet long had been tied together, with a twelve-inch layer of the leaves from the reeds, crammed tightly between the two hurdles.

The hurdles were now lying flat on the ground in front of the assembled warriors, as they waited for their enemy to appear.

The morning was well advanced when suddenly a single horseman appeared from a small dip in the landscape, some half a mile away.

He sat on his stationary mount and surveyed the prepared positions of the Aelnoth's army.

'Ah,' said Aelnoth quietly. 'He is just a scout.'

He could not have been more mistaken, for no sooner had the mumbled words left his mouth, than a torrent of horsemen rose from behind the 'scout' and thundered across the flood plain towards his men.

The torrent continued and became a flood of horsemen, who had silently and secretly advanced during the night and the early hours of the morning, into a position that would allow them to catch their enemies unaware.

'Order the barriers raised.' Shouted Aelnoth to his signallers, who immediately raised their yellow flags, and the pre-arranged signal was immediately obeyed as the hurdles were raised, erecting an instant wall in front of the foot soldiers.

Most of the unit commanders saw the signal, and began to pull on the ropes in order to haul the hurdles off the ground, thus creating an instant wall, which should have prevented the anticipated barrage of arrows and spears from slaughtering their men, but a single commander lagged behind his peers, and was slightly late in raising his hurdles.

His lethargy was immediately exploited by the horsemen, who sent clouds of arrows into and through the gap, decimating the warriors who were struggling with the ropes, as they attempted to haul their barriers into position.

From his position on the hill Aelnoth could see the danger, and knew that it only would be a matter of seconds before the enemy horsemen followed their arrows, and poured through the gap on their agile ponies.

The nearest groups of Seljuk's began to urge their ponies into the gap, decimating the nearest warriors of Aelnoth's army, with arrows, swords and spears as they cut through the ranks of panicking warriors, and out into an open space between the two sectors of the army.

The General in charge of the front sector managed to rally his men, who formed up into a ragged shieldwall, which bristled with spears, whilst the second sector stood firm and presented a second wall of resistance, causing the enemy horsemen to circle in the open space, as more and more horsemen poured through the gap to congest the milling horsemen even further.

It was an opportunity that the three hundred Greek slingers could not ignore, and they ran out through the shieldwall, and commenced to bombard the horsemen with clouds of slingshot, striking both horses and riders alike, causing many to panic, as riders tried to control their horses, which had been struck by slingshot, whilst many of the riders themselves fell to the deadly swathes of slingshot, which pounded into their heads and bodies.

Archers from within the Aelnoth's army joined the slingers, and sent clouds of arrows over their own ranks and into the milling jumble of the Seljuk horsemen.

Like the tide ebbing amongst the rocks, the surviving horsemen surged back through the gap, leaving at least half of their number dead or wounded, in a space that had become a killing zone.

'Bowmen.' He shouted to 'Hallandor the Scythian,' whose bowmen were lying on their backs in readiness to shoot.

'Get ready.' Shouted Hallandor, and his archers immediately placed their feet on the body of their bows, and notched one of their six foot long arrows to the string, and hauled back the string with both of their arms.

Hallandor looked up at Aelnoth, and the moment that Aelnoth dropped his arm, Hallandor screamed 'Loose,' at the top of his voice, and with a sound that was akin to a gale screeching through a gap in a cavern, three thousand, six foot long arrows were launched into the sky.

Aelnoth watched the dark cloud sail lazily up and over the ranks of his own men, to fall upon the Seljuk's army like a hailstorm, but it was a hailstorm that contained not hail, but long deadly bolts of death, which penetrated mail, man and beast, sending hundreds to the ground, and causing such panic amongst the surviving horsemen and foot soldiers, that they gazed up at the heavens in wonder and fear, not knowing where these long bolts of death were coming from.

Their wonder and fear was accelerated when a second cloud of arrows fell out of the sky onto them, and when Aelnoth gave the order for the rest of his archers to join in, the five thousand ordinary archers inflicted even greater slaughter, as their smaller arrows joined with those of the longbowmen, to create clouds so black that they blackened the sky and blotted out the late morning sun.

Above the noise from the two armies, Aelnoth heard the sound of a horn, and noticed that the Seljuk horsemen immediately broke off from the battle, and streamed away, disappearing into the slight gully, out of which they had emerged a short time before.

The jubilant warriors of his army pushed their hurdles to the ground and seethed over them, to loot their fallen enemy, who they knew, not only carried their wealth with them, but also adorned their weapons, horses and saddles with gold and silverware.

Aelnoth sent men out to collect any arrows that had not been damaged, in order to re-use them.

He personally led a troop of fifty men to bring back both the bows and the quivers full of arrows, which were lying in profusion around the bodies of their slain enemies.

The army remained on alert for the remainder of the day, and were only allowed to retire to the foot of the hill, as the sun began to set behind the distant mountains.

After assuring himself that the warriors had been given food and drink, and had been either allotted guard duty or had been given permission to retire for the night.

Aelnoth met with Oscar, Magnus, Abdulla and the rest of the Generals in order to discuss the day's battle, as well as the strategy for the battle, which would probably take place on the morrow.

'What will they do next?' he asked.

'They will bring hurdles of their own,' suggested one of the Generals, 'and then they will be safe from our arrows and slingshot.' He added.

'They cannot carry hurdles on horses.' Said another.

'They may not come on horses.'

'They are horse warriors.'

'Not all of them.' Said an old General sarcastically.

'They always ride into battle.' Said the original General adamantly.

'They may try to burn our hurdles.' said Magnus.

'And then we would be open to their arrows.'

'Yes, they could try that.' Said Aelnoth, as he ran his fingers through his sparse beard.

'We will counter that by soaking the barriers with water from the lake before dawn.' He suggested.

'See that it is done.' Ordered Aelnoth.

The General nodded and placed his fist on his chest in acknowledgment.

'I think you should let Abdulla and myself go out at midnight, and see if we can discover their plans,' said Oscar.

'That would be very dangerous.' Said Aelnoth, 'and I would be reluctant to lose you.'

'The battle today was dangerous. Tomorrow's battle will be even more so.' Countered Oscar.

'The simple fact that our being out here, in this Godforsaken land in the first place, is bloody dangerous.'

'It's all bloody dangerous, but it might be a little less dangerous if we can find out what they intend to do.' Said Oscar.

'Take half a dozen men with you then.' Said Aelnoth.

'No. That would make it more difficult for Abdulla and myself to melt into the darkness.'

'I know man who good in dark.' Said Abdulla.

'He thief.'

'I don't want a bloody thief out there with me,' said Oscar.

'Trying to dodge a hundred thousand bloody Seljuk's is bad enough without having a bloody thief to worry about.' He snarled angrily.

'Not thief no more.' Said Abdulla.

'Good friend. I trust.'

'Good with knife.' He added as he put his index finger to his throat and croaked as he ran his finger across his throat.

*   *   *

After the three men had eaten, they walked around the foot of the hill until they were at the rear of the area, where the previous days battle had taken place, and after having a quiet word with the sentries, they entered the sparse woodland and became part of the shadows.

It took them over an hour before they turned towards the east, where they suspected their enemy had made their overnight camp.

They flitted like ghosts from one tree to another. From one bush to another, and from one shadow to another for a long time before they eventually noticed a lightening of the dark sky, which was caused from the glow of many fires in a valley about half a mile ahead of them.

Yet again, they did not go directly towards the valley, but walked in a semi-circle until they were at the rear of the huge encampment, which covered the whole of the valley floor.

The three men crouched down as they watched the enemy sentries patrol their given areas, and were about to make their way towards them, when Oscar heard a loud thump, and then he felt a slight quiver of the ground under his feet.

'Someone has just felled a tree.' He whispered.

'I hear too.' Whispered Abdulla.

'It came from over there,' said Manga the thief.

Who pointed towards the dim outline of a hill that was perhaps a half a mile to the west?

'Let's go.' Whispered Oscar as he rose and disappeared into the shadows.

The clouds began to float away to the west, leaving the landscape bathed in the glow from the moon, which made it more difficult for the three men to move unseen through the eerie landscape.

Nonetheless, they crawled slowly from bush to bush towards the distant hill, frequently pausing to scan the way ahead, as they probed their way forward.

'Stop,' whispered Oscar as he dropped to the ground and prevented his two colleagues from passing him.

'I can see sentries up there.' He said as he pointed to a ridge.

Another and much louder crash echoed out of the woodland as another tree crashed to the ground.

'Well, we definitely know that they are felling trees but we don't know their purpose.' Whispered Oscar.

'They could be building a fortress and preparing for a siege.' He added.

'More likely to be towers to attack us with.' Manga the thief whispered.

'I go look.' Said Abdulla quietly.

'I'll go too,' said Oscar.

'Me too,' said Manga the thief. 'I shall go too.'

Oscar shrugged his shoulders in frustration.

'Why not.' He hissed.

'The more the merrier.'

All three wriggled through the sparse tufts of grass towards the ridge, and as they got closer they were able to see a complete line of sentries, who were standing at intervals of four or five feet apart, in a large circle around the whole of the valley and it's still distant hill.

'It's no good.' Whispered Oscar. 'We had best go back.'

'I can get through,' said Manga the thief, and refused to stop as he slithered past Oscar and Abdulla, and although Oscar grabbed the cuff of his jerkin, he shook it free and wriggled forward.

Oscar and Abdulla had no alternative other than to allow him to go, and although they could see the slight gap in the long line of sentries, they could see no sign of Manga.

The two Albino's quietly retraced their steps until they were some one hundred yards away, where they crouched under a small bush and gazed across the moonlit landscape to the place where they had last seen Manga.

'I can see him.' Whispered Oscar.

'Where?'

'Well, I can't actually see him, but I did see a tuft of grass move by that sentry who is leaning on that tree over there.' He said, as he pointed towards a lone windswept tree that sat on the crest of a ridge.

'I see.' Mumbled Abdulla, who was about to say something else, when they both heard a loud shout, and saw the sentry by the tree snatch up his spear and stab downwards twice.

The sentry shouted to his fellows, who ran over to him and joined him, as they stared down at the thing that was on the ground a few feet away.

'I think that is the end of our friend Manga the thief.' said Oscar.

Abdulla nodded sadly and said. 'We go,' and they both turned to retrace their steps towards their own encampment.

They arrived a little while before dawn to find the sentries alert, and a camp, which resembled a wasp's nest that had just been disturbed, with men and horses moving in every possible direction, and everyone, be it man or beast trying to make as little noise as possible.

When they managed to push their way through the throng of men and horses, they found Aelnoth speaking to three of his Generals as he gnawed on a cold leg of mutton.

'Ah, here you are.' Exclaimed Aelnoth with glee, as he moved away from the three Generals and walked quickly towards them.

'You had us worried.'

'Thought we had lost you.' He added.

'We thought we had lost us.' Said Oscar with a wry grin.

'What did you find out?' Asked Aelnoth, ignoring Oscar's casual remark.

'What did we find out, you ask?' Replied Oscar.

'Not a lot, although a man might say, almost nothing, and yet, quite a lot.'

'You are talking in riddles.' Said a rather annoyed Aelnoth, for his mind was reeling with the trials and tribulations of commanding such a vast army, which brought with it, an equally vast array of problems.

'Did you or did you not find out any thing of use?' he snapped.

'Well, we found their camp, and from what we saw, I would say that they probably outnumber us by three, or even four to one.'

'They are also chopping down a hell of a lot of trees, but we could not get close enough to find out what they are going to do with them.'

'Will they attack us again today?' asked Aelnoth.

'Don't really know,' said Oscar, 'but they certainly have enough men to attack with, and still build whatever they are building in that valley of theirs.'

No attack came that morning, or in the afternoon, and by evening the men were weary from standing and sitting in their formations, in readiness for a battle that had not materialised.

Aelnoth recalled them to their evening quarters, as darkness fell over the silent plain, which stretched towards the marshlands, and the placid waters of the sea of Van.

The huge camp settled down for the night, with the warriors congratulating themselves, believing that as they had repelled the famous horse archers of the Seljuk Turks once, then they could do it again, with some of the loudest braggarts of the army claiming that they had given their enemy such a bloody nose, that they had turned tail and had ran home to their mothers.

It was a rude awakening, when an hour before dawn, the sounds of battle rang out from the heights above their encampment, causing the Generals to rush about in alarm as they stared up the hill behind them, where an obvious battle was taking place.

Aelnoth rushed out of his small tent with his two swords held in readiness for battle.

'What is happening?' he demanded from his startled guard.

'I am not sure my Lord.' Answered the obviously confused guard.

'Its, its. The noise is coming from the heights.' He stuttered as he looked up the hill.

'How the hell did they get up there?' screamed Aelnoth.

'We had guards right around the hill.' He shouted to anyone who was close enough to hear.

'Slingers.' He shouted. 'Get the slingers and spearmen to me. NOW.' He shouted at the top of his voice, and his guards ran towards the area where the slingers and spearmen were billeted.

Within the space of a few minutes an assortment of slingers, archers and spearmen had gathered around him.

'Follow me.' He roared, as he half walked and half ran up the lower slopes of the hill, on which the core part of his strategy depended.

A few days ago the steep slope had been thickly forested, but Aelnoth had ordered his men to clear the forest, and haul all the sizable logs up onto the top of the hill, in order to construct a fortress that would be not only a strongpoint, but would also be a last retreat, if the battle went badly for his forces.

He could see the turbans of his enemies above him, as they fought with the defenders in their attempt to take the fortress, before Aelnoth and his men could reach them.

They immediately came under attack from their enemies, who rained arrows, spears, and rocks down on them.

They weathered the storm and continued upwards, under the protection of their shields, and although Aelnoth could see that he was losing men, he also glanced down the hill, where he was pleased to see that hordes of his own men were following him upwards.

They eventually came close enough for the slingers to send their heavy projectiles upwards and into the attackers, which had an immediate effect, as the Seljuk's were also being assailed from the defenders who were on the palisade of the fort.

Many of the Seljuk's turned their attention to the slingers, spearmen and bowmen, who were slowly clawing their way up the hill towards them.

The leader of the Seljuk must have realised that he had lost his battle to take the fort, and in a futile act of desperation, he ordered his men to follow him, as he hurled himself down the hill and into Aelnoth's warriors.

It took the Seljuk's perhaps half a minute to cover the distance between them and Aelnoth's men, but to Aelnoth that half a minute turned into a nightmare, for as he prepared himself to receive the attack from above, the frantic sounding of horns and drums from below, caused him to look down the hill towards his army, where to his dismay he could see the vast array of the Seljuk Turkish army surging towards his own formations, accompanied by no less than two siege towers, as well as a large number of battering rams.

Aelnoth had no time to study the army of the Seljuk's, as the men who had been attacking his hilltop fortress slithered and ran down the hillside, crashing into him and his men.

A turbaned warrior hurled himself at Aelnoth, slashing at him as he crashed into him, but Aelnoth caught the sword-cut on his raised shield, and heaved the man over his shoulders and down the hillside, where he was cut down by one of his spearmen, who stabbed the man twice before the grinning spearman continued his upward journey.

Many of the Seljuk warriors simply embedded themselves onto the spears, which Aelnoth's men held aloft as the Seljuk's hurried downwards to their death, and if they were not slain by the front rows of Aelnoth's men, then his second and third row of warriors slew them, as fewer and fewer of them reached the men on the lower slopes.

Aelnoth clambered upwards until he reached the ramparts of his hilltop fortress, and climbed up the rope, which had been thrown down to him.

He ran to the platform where his signallers were stationed and gazed down at the battle that was about to take place on the flood plain below the hill.

He screwed his eyes up and held his hand over his eyes in order to assess the situation, but the last rays of the sun sent its beams directly through the black clouds and into his eyes, preventing him from seeing the overall scene.

The signallers stepped back in alarm, as the rays flickered upon Aelnoth for a long minute before they suddenly disappeared.

Their disappearance was followed by a crash of thunder so loud that it deafened the men.

The awe struck warriors watched in amazement and fear, as a single bolt of lightening flashed out of the black clouds, striking the tower on which Aelnoth was standing, sending its flame sizzling around its outer structure, leaving it blackened and smoking.

Aelnoth appeared to be oblivious to the lightening and shouted to one of his cowering signallers.

'Signal the army to retreat to the lower levels of the hill.'

The signaller had just enough time to obey, before the very heavens opened up, and a deluge of rain fell on them that was so severe that it almost drove them into the ground.

Aelnoth held his fathers old shield over his head, not merely to shelter from the rain, but also to enable him to watch his army as they retreated the two hundred paces towards the bottom of the hill.

During the final days of their march to Van, Aelnoth and his Generals had watched the ominous black rain clouds that had appeared to follow them over the mountains.

They had been confident in their belief that the coming storm would by-pass them, and would continue on it's westerly course, but for some unknown reason, the weather system had altered, and had sent the inky black clouds to it's present position, which was directly above the two opposing armies.

The heavy black clouds proceeded to empty themselves.

Despite the rain, and the storm of arrows, which fell upon them from both the normal archers and the longbowmen of Hallandor the Scythian, the Seljuk Turks continued their advance, and followed Aelnoth's men towards the hill, hauling their tall towers and battering rams through the soggy ground.

As the two sides closed with each other, more and more arrows flew from both sides, causing death and destruction, but despite their dead and dying, the enemy warriors marched over their dead, and continued to advance until they reached a point where the ground began to rise, some one hundred yards from their foes.

Whilst the archers of Aelnoth's army were competent archers, the Seljuk's, whose years of warfare had made them some of the most formidable warriors in the east, out-shot them.

The Seljuk's loosed two arrows for every arrow shot by Aelnoth's men, and whilst the Aelnoth's archers merely shot their arrows in the general direction of their enemies, the aim of their opponents bordered on miraculous, with perhaps eight out of ten of their arrows finding its mark, sending swathes of warriors to their deaths, and causing great gaps to appear in their wavering shieldwall.

The Seljuk's warriors surged forward, forcing Aelnoth's men backwards step by step.

Aelnoth ordered his reserves into the line and they stepped forward the few paces, which separated them from the front line warriors, filling the gaps and bolstering their wavering line, steadying it against the ferocious slaughter, which continued unabated, sending scores of men the ground, screaming in agony as they fell, either dead or wounded.

Both sides were intent on the business of killing and not being killed.

Spears, slingshot and arrows still flew through the air, forcing many men to shelter behind their shields.

Very few men noticed that the trickle of a river, which the Seljuk army had crossed a few short minutes before had suddenly been converted into a raging torrent by the numerous rivers and streams, which had cascaded down the hereto dry mountain slopes, to join the already swollen river, which now roared like a banshee out of the mountains.

Within seconds, the river surged over its banks, sending huge waves, carrying boulders and uprooted trees with it, in an eight feet high torrent, which swept into the rear echelons of the Seljuk army.

Perhaps half of the Seljuk's were horsemen, who upon seeing the disaster that was about to overtake them, savagely spurred their mounts in an effort to outrun the surging flood, but the deluge overtook hundreds of them, sweeping them off their panicking horses into the muddy waters, where they sank like stones in the turbulent torrent.

The Seljuk foot soldiers were swept away like chaff in the wind, so that within a short space of time, the area that had contained their vast army was replaced by a surging tide of brown muddy water, which contained floundering men and horses as they strived to keep their heads above the foaming brown water.

All that could be seen of the assault towers were floating logs, which were bedecked with Seljuk survivors, who Clung on to them for dear life.

Many of the heavily armoured Seljuk foot soldiers tried to evade the torrent, and were forced to close with the Aelnoth's warriors, who eagerly cut them down.

Aelnoth's men screamed and shouted with glee as they slaughtered their panicking enemies.

The ranks of the Aelnoth's army who were on the lowest part of the hill, were forced to retreat a few paces higher up the hill, in order to avoid being engulfed by the surging waters, but even as they retreated, they joined in with the rest of their fellow warriors in cheering and clashing their weapons upon their shields at the joy of such a victory.

The sun suddenly appeared through a hole in the black clouds, and a bright spear of brilliant light shone on Aelnoth.

His army cheered even louder, turning as one man to raise their weapons in homage towards Aelnoth, who in turn, held his own sword and shield aloft, acknowledging their acclamation.

One of the younger Generals climbed the few steps to join Aelnoth on the platform.

'My Lord,' he said almost reverently.

'We have won a great victory but some of the Seljuk's horsemen escaped.'

'They outran the flood.' He added, with a grim smile.

'Yes. I know.' Answered Aelnoth.

'I have already sent a messenger to our horsemen, and ordered a pursuit.'

'We cannot afford to let them escape' He added, 'or we may have to fight the same men again, in another place and another time'.

Oscar, Magnus and Abdulla climbed through the newly opened doorway in the fortress and joined him.

They did not slap him on his back, or clasp his shoulder in friendship, as had been the normal thing that had been done in the past, when they had joined up after a dangerous battle or assignment; they merely stood in a circle around him with silly grins on their faces.

'Well?' he said.

No one answered.

'What?' he asked.

'What's wrong?'

'Nothing is wrong old friend.' Said Magnus.

'We are all a bit shocked. That's all,' he added.

'Shocked!'

'Why shocked? We won didn't we?'

'Yes we did win, but you must admit. It was a bit spooky?' said Oscar.

'Nothing spooky about it,' said Aelnoth.

'We had a storm. The sun shone.' That's it.'

'What about the lightening?' asked Oscar?

'And the flood?' Echoed Magnus.

'Well you are the one who reads the runes and looks into the future. So you tell me?' snapped Aelnoth, as he stared towards Oscar.

The three friends relaxed a little and stepped forward to shake the hand of their friend 'The White Wizard.' Aelnoth two swords.

Aelnoth beckoned one of the Generals over to him and ordered. 'Give the order for the men to stand down, and allow them to glean what treasures they are able from the fallen.'

'They have earned their booty today.'

'Make sure they are fed and are given clean water.' He added.

CHAPTER 23

The three Englishmen and the Nubian watched with pride as the long procession of horsemen emerged out of the valley and onto the still flooded plain, splashing through the water, which was rapidly subsiding, and was now perhaps no more than ten or twelve inches deep.

The Lancers who accompanied the six thousand horse archers rode down the far side of the soggy valley, causing the ground to tremble beneath the feet of the cheering army, as they began their pursuit of the remains of the shattered Seljuk army.

The horsemen raised their weapons above their heads in response to the cheers of their fellow warriors, as they galloped past the army, eager to make contact with their enemies, after spending such a long time hidden and idle, whilst their colleagues had taken the brunt of their enemy's fury.

As Aelnoth watched the receding horsemen spread out into their individual units of one hundred men, he remarked. 'I have given them orders not to take prisoners, and to by-pass any strongholds, which they cannot immediately take, and to ride to the very borders of Armenia.'

'We can send men to take the strongholds once our horsemen report back to us, and thus take back the whole of Armenia for the Emperor.'

'Who are THEY?' asked Magnus as he pointed to a large column of men approaching from the east.

'Where?'

All four men stared at the column of men, which consisted of perhaps four or five hundred men, who were a mixture of foot soldiers and horsemen.

'Turks?' asked Abdulla glumly.

'I don't think so.' Said Aelnoth.

'The banners look like Christian banners.'

'You are right.' Said Magnus excitedly.

'Some of them bear the Holy Cross.'

'It's probably the men from the Christian enclaves. Come to help us.' He added.

'Bit late.' Growled Abdulla.

'Nonetheless,' said Aelnoth.

'Let us make our way to the bottom of the hill and greet them.'

'We may yet have need of their arms, and their knowledge of the country.'

They had a little time to wait at the bottom of the hill as the slow moving column of Christians made their way around the perimeter of the soggy flood plain, which allowed Aelnoth a little time to survey the area where the Seljuk army had been swept away.

The plain was splattered with bodies of men who had been looted by the men of his army.

The Christian column halted before Aelnoth, and their ranks opened in order to allow a small group of noblemen to approach him.

The leader of the group was an elderly man of average height, who wore a white shirt, which had a large red cross-embroidered on it.

He had a thick leather belt around his waist, plus an additional leather belt strapped around his left shoulder, which held a huge, two handed battle-sword, whose ornately carved silver hilt protruded over his shoulder.

'I am named 'Mikkis of Ganja,' he said as he struck his broad chest with his right hand, 'and this is my good friend 'Hinius of Kapan,' and this man here,' as he pointed to the huge figure of a giant who was on his left, 'is, Sarka the bold, who is the King of the kingdom of Barda.'

'We are the last Lords of the Christian Kingdoms in the whole of Armenia.'

Aelnoth and his friends bowed their heads in formal greeting and shook the hands of the newcomers.

'You are most welcome.' Said Aelnoth, 'although I must admit that I am a stranger to this part of the world, and have no idea where your kingdoms are.'

'Oh, I would not have expected you to,' said Mikkis with a smile, but we have heard of you, for you are the long awaited White Wizard, are you not?'

Before Aelnoth could answer the man continued.

'I am the lord of the Kingdom of Ganja, which is a small city, lying some fifty miles over the mountains of Goygol, and my friends here have cities that lie far to the north of Goygol.'

Yet again Mikkis prevented Aelnoth from speaking, and Aelnoth surmised, quite correctly, as it was later proven, that he was a man who liked to hear the sound of his own voice and did not thank any man who upstaged him.

'It seems that we are a little late for the battle.' He boomed in a loud jovial voice.

'Did you leave any for us?' as he slapped his friend huge Sarka on his shoulder and laughed aloud.

'Oh I think that we left a fair few for you,' said Aelnoth, realising that he had just uttered the word 'Fair,' which was a word used by the country folk around his home village of Wentnor, and he mused to himself, that it was a phrase, which he had encountered no where else on his wide travels.

He visibly shook his head in order to dispel the verdant green valleys of England, which had been invading his brain of late, and he said to the small gathering of leaders. 'I would say that although we destroyed the main body of the Seljuk's. I think that perhaps a quarter of their army escaped, and they could be somewhere out there regrouping in readiness to strike again.'

'Did you slay Arslan?' asked Mikkis.

'Who's Arslan?'

Mikkis looked stunned as he realised that the young leader of the Emperor's vast army did not even know the name of his enemy.

'Only the leader of the Seljuk Turks,' said Mikkis, as a look of distain crossed his face.

'I was led to believe that this Seljuk army was led either by Arslan himself, or by a man called 'Mjahan,' he said.

'Oh, Mjahan is the right hand man of Arslan, and although he is a sadistic shit, he is not half the man that Arslan is.'

'I am not a man to fear death or defeat.' Said Aelnoth, 'but the name of Arslan has just sent shivers down my spine, as if, as we say in England.'

'It is as if someone had just walked over my grave.'

'We have a similar saying in Armenia.' Said Mikkis, with a sympathetic smile.

It was as if Mikkis had not spoken, for Aelnoth continued, and said. 'I fear that this man Arslan will be ill for the world of Christ.'

The group was silent for a long time and gazed down upon the sodden flood plain.

*   *   *

The Christians were allocated a reasonably dry area of the hillside where they could make camp, and after they had settled down, Aelnoth asked the three Christian leaders to join him and his generals for an evening meal, but they were forced to wait for over an hour before his workmen finished erecting a large leather tent, which would be his new headquarters.

After a meal of roast mutton and an assortment of vegetables and fruit, washed down by red wine, Aelnoth stood at the head of the table and held his hand up for silence.

'My friends.' He said as he formally nodded to the Generals and the leaders from the Christian enclaves.

'With the help of God, we have just won a great victory over the Seljuk Turks.

'You mean 'Thor,' said Magnus loudly, causing most of the assembled lords, who were Christians to glare at him, causing Aelnoth to note that the right hands of several of leaders flew to the hilts of their curved swords.

Aelnoth held his hand aloft.

'Silence.' He said loudly, 'whether it was Christ or Thor matters not to me.'

'The thing that is important is that we defeated them, and with a little luck, our victory should secure Armenia for Christ and the Emperor, and set the Seljuk's back for many years to come.'

'Friends,' he said loudly as he raised his glass aloft.

'To our Victory.'

The entire assembly rose to their feet and raised their glasses. 'Victory,' they roared and emptied their glasses, with a number of them following Magnus in his age-old heathen custom of hurling their glasses onto the floor.

Some time later Aelnoth met with the Christian Armenians.

'Mikkis.' He said.

'I would like you and your friends to return to your Kingdoms, and extend your domains into the areas that have hereto been ruled by the Seljuk's.'

'In most cases I would prefer that you allow the inhabitants to remain, providing that they accept you as their overlord, thus continuing to maintain a stable population and economy.

I would also like you and allow the people to follow either Christ or any other religion they choose.'

'However, if they do not agree to serve you, then you have my leave to evict them and send them into exile, or if they still refuse, then you must oust them in a way that is best suited to yourselves and to the teachings of Christ.'

'Is that understood?'

'It is my Lord,' answered Mikkis who placed his right hand on his heart and bowed his head, as is the way when a lesser lord of the east acknowledges his masters wishes.

Late afternoon on the following day, Aelnoth and Magnus escorted the Christian leaders on their way, passing through the still soggy plain, where the bodies of the slain Seljuk's lay in swathes.

As they gazed westwards to the sea of Van, they could see even more bodies along the shoreline where the receding waters had deposited them.

Vultures rose in clouds as they were disturbed from their feasting, and foxes and hyenas reluctantly slunk off, as the small army of men approached.

'My God.' Swore Magnus, as he pointed towards the centre of a large tree, which had been uprooted by the flood and lay on its side.

A mans corpse was lodged high in its branches, but it was not the body that both Aelnoth and Magnus stared at.

It was the three wolves, who had scaled the lower branches of the tree.

The wolves snarled and ripped their last bites off the corpse before they leapt to the ground with chunks of flesh still in their reddened jaws.

The largest of the trio carried a human hand in its jaws.

The beast dropped the hand and snarled defiantly at the approaching horsemen, showing its teeth and gums, in a kind of a smile that Aelnoth had seen on certain men and women, who, when they had smiled, had also bared their teeth and their gums in a similar way.

The wolf quickly snatched up the hand, and loped off almost casually after its kin.

Both Aelnoth and Magnus did not speak, but they both knew that they had just witnessed part of the prophecy, which Oscar had seen during one of his 'predictions,' back in England.

After silently riding alongside Aelnoth for a considerable time, Magnus said quietly.

'During the battle, we were also four men standing on a hill.'

'Oh I know we were, but that's just a coincidence. Could have been anyone, anywhere,' he answered as nonchantly as he was able, although he knew, even before he uttered the words, that there would be no way that he would be able to convince the superstitious Magnus that it had not been foreseen, and had not been pre-ordained.

After escorting the Christian leaders for a further ten miles, Aelnoth, Magnus and their small escort took a different rout back to the sea Van, passing through dry but pleasant, sparsely populated countryside, full of wild game.

Three days later the army broke camp, with each division of ten thousand men marching along pre-arranged routs, which took them through the main areas of the populated areas of Armenia.

After learning the lesson, which had been so cruelly taught in England by the all-conquering Normans?

Aelnoth gave orders that garrisons were to remain in the major towns, and in strategic crossroads and hilltops, where his Generals were to impose their will upon the populations of those towns, and to force those populations to construct solid castles in order to pre-empt any possible uprisings.

After besieging and taking two of the main towns, which delayed the main body of his army for more than nine months, they marched onwards in a wide semi-circle, in order to make their way back to the shores of the Black sea, where they followed its scenic coastline back towards Constantinople.

Even after Aelnoth had left nearly one third of his men on garrison duty in Armenia, the army was still too large to be allowed into the city, and Aelnoth was forced to have each unit of one hundred men draw lots, thus allowing the fortunate fifty men out of each hundred to join him and his fellow leaders, in their triumphant entry into the city of Constantinople.

People thronged the walls and the rooftops, and the streets were so full of cheering citizens that as the army marched four men abreast, the outside ranks of the warriors virtually brushed shoulders with the adoring populace.

Fifty Drummers led the parade, followed by fifty Pipers, who in turn, were followed by One thousand men and five hundred horsemen, who were followed by a further fifty Drummers, fifty Pipers. One thousand men and five hundred horsemen, and so on, until the last division of men passed through the cheering crowds, to join their comrades, who had assembled in their silent divisions in the huge square that stood before the white palace of the Emperor.

Aelnoth had been persuaded to ride a white stallion, and as the drummers and pipers halted before the palace steps, he dismounted and accompanied by Magnus, Oscar, Abdulla and six of his senior Generals, he led them up the one hundred marble steps towards the

Emperor, who sat solemn and immovable on his marble throne on the wide platform at the top.

The Varangian guards halted them as soon as they had reached the shining marble platform, whereupon the Emperor had appeared suddenly to come to life, for he had been sitting upon his marble throne with his head bowed as if asleep for the entire time that it had taken the regiments to march into the square and assemble.

He sprang to his feet and walked quickly towards Aelnoth.

He placed his left arm around Aelnoth's shoulder, whilst he raised his right hand in the air to quell the noise from the huge mass of his citizens who thronged the square below.

'Citizens.' He said in a loud voice.

'I welcome our hero.'

'The White Wizard.'

'And I join you in your joy at his victory and his safe return.'

The crowd roared their approval, forcing him to wait for some considerable time before he could continue.

'He has won back our lands in Armenia, which have been safely returned to us, and are now reunited into the Kingdom of Christ.'

Again they roared and clapped, causing the resident pigeons to rise into the sky in several huge flocks.

'He has performed a miracle, and has called upon our lord God Jesus Christ to fall upon the heathens and sweep them from this earth.'

'It was Thor the Thunderer.' Snarled Magnus, and although the Emperor heard him, he chose to ignore the remark, and merely gave him a glowering look.

'As a reward for returning Armenia to us, I am promoting our beloved White Wizard to the position of the Senior General of our beloved Varangian Guard, and I will bestow upon him a palace and riches beyond his wildest dreams.'

Again, the crowd roared their approval, and were accompanied by the drums and pipes of the army, whose warriors, who had, up to that point been standing to attention in the hot sun, but now they gave way to their urges, and joined in with the crowd, crashing their weapons onto the metal edges of their shields and adding their voices to the clamour, causing the streets and alleyways of the city to echo with their cheering.

The Emperor turned and beckoned his servants to join him, and as soon as the bearer of the Royal Parasol had shaded the head of his Emperor, and the bearer of the Royal Fan had commenced his work, the Emperor turned to Aelnoth.

'I have been too long in this hot sun.' He said.

'Follow me,' and walked swiftly towards the Palace, where he and his retinue disappeared through the darkened doorway.

*   *   *

A group of eight Varangians had been assigned to show Aelnoth to his new 'Palace,' which was situated on a small hillock overlooking the Sea of Marmora, and as they walked through the huge gate, which appeared to be the sole entrance through the white wall that surrounded the Palace, Aelnoth became overawed by the beauty, not only of the building itself, but also by the well kept gardens, which were awash with flowering shrubs, shady trees and babbling water fountains.

He was even more impressed when he entered into his new living quarters, which had been furnished with such luxurious furniture, carpets, statues, busts and tapestries, which caused his mind to fly back to his Fathers cold Hall at Wentnor, with its open windows, bare walls and reed-strewn floors.

He suddenly stopped walking and stood, shaking his head in amazement at the total opulence of his new abode.

The smiling Varangians who had been assigned to him, left in order to return to their duties and to take up their positions by the entrance.

He walked over the spotlessly clean courtyard, which was dotted with huge pots, out of which sweet smelling flowering shrubs emerged, and he sat on a stone bench, close to a gurgling fountain, from which water gushed through the mouth of a stone lion, and fell bubbling into a sparklingly clear pool, which contained three very large golden fish, of a variety that was unknown to him.

He raised his face to the sun, wallowing in his new riches, but was suddenly brought back to reality, when he heard the sound of a door somewhere deep inside the house, being closed rather loudly.

He could not have been more surprised when the Emperor himself walked regally through the door, accompanied by his usual guard of ten Varangians and a small crowd of palace officials.

He rose to greet the Emperor, who clasped his hand in friendship, and bade him to sit on the stone bench beside him.

'I hope you are pleased with this humble abode, which I have given you?' he asked, and was about to say more, when the small assembly parted to allow the small figure of Agio 'the Witch' to approach the Emperor.

Agio came hobbling along with the help of her golden staff and her huge mute slave 'Abbi,' whose massive hand was placed on her elbow, as he helped her to hobble along. Shuffle plonk, Shuffle plonk, was the only sound to be heard in the wide courtyard.

They were followed by the slight figure of the slave girl 'Nike' who wore a gown, which Clung to her figure, making her look more like a princess than a slave.

Agio halted suddenly before the Emperor, and was nearly bowled over by the gigantic figure of Abbi, who had been looking at something to the left of him, and had failed to notice that his mistress had stopped.

The dumb slave could not speak his apologies, but his face gaped in a look of horror as his hand shot out and saved his mistress from falling to the ground.

'Careful you idiot.' She spat as she looked up at her slave who towered over her.

'Or I shall have you whipped to within an inch of your life for your impudence, and send to the slave market.' She hissed.

Abbi stepped back in alarm as his huge hand flew to his empty mouth in horror.

But it was all an act. Or at least, he hoped it was an act, for he had been threatened with such punishment a number of times in the past, and nought had come of it.

The Emperor gave a weak smile, and wished that the old witch would flog the dumb giant, for he had no particular liking or sympathy for the man, who had once, (accidentally,) or so it had seemed, slain one of his favourite courtier's in a 'friendly' joust, after one of the Emperor's infamous dinner parties.

Aelnoth broke the silence as he turned towards the Emperor.

'The Gift is wonderful your Majesty, and the view over the sea is unsurpassed by anything that I have ever seen.'

'I really don't know how I can ever repay you for such bounty.'

'You have already repaid me White Wizard.' Said the Emperor.

'For you have restored Armenia to us, and the cost of this small house will be repaid to me a thousand times over, once my Armenian taxes begin to flood into to my treasury.'

'I have brought you more gifts.' He added with a beaming smile.

He clapped his hands, and said in a loud voice. 'Bring the slaves.' And two Guards pushed their way through the crowd, as they escorted three slaves towards Aelnoth and the Emperor.

The Guards moved to one side to reveal two female and one male slave.

'For you.' Said the Emperor.

'My thanks your highness.' Stammered the shocked Aelnoth, for he had been brought up in a society of slaves, and was familiar with the ownership of slaves;

indeed, he had yet to meet a tribe or a nation who did not own slaves.

He bowed his head to the Emperor and thanked him for his generous gift.

The three slaves who stood before him were unlike most of the slaves in the city.

The male was a young man in his early twenties.

He was tall and slim, and had the aura and bearing of a nobleman.

The Emperor invaded his thoughts and said. 'The slave master who owned them, assured us that the females and the male, are chaste and pure, and as such he demanded an outrageous price for them, but if you find that this is not the case, then please inform me and I shall replace them, and have the slave masters head on a spike for misleading me.'

The eldest of the females was a little younger than the male, whilst the other seemed to be around the age of fourteen or fifteen.

All three were obviously from Northern Europe, for they were pale skinned and fair-haired, and whilst the young man had the bearing of a warrior.

The elder of the two girls was undeniably beautiful, but had the arrogant look of nobility about her, and gazed boldly into his face.

The young man stepped two paces forward and bowed his head slightly, as he held forward a casket and presented it to Aelnoth.

'It is merely a box full of trinkets, which I no longer have use for.' Said the Emperor with a gesture of nonchalance.

'It will pay for the cost of running this palace and feed your new slaves for a year or two.'

He added as he turned to leave, but as he was about to exit through the door, he turned again towards Aelnoth, and with a smile on his face he said. 'Agio, my sage tells me that you yearn for your homeland and may leave us soon.'

'I do not wish it. And bid you stay with us for a while longer.'

Aelnoth bowed his head in acknowledgment and said.
'As you wish, your Majesty, but one day my destiny will force me to leave Constantinople.'

'Let it not be soon.' He ordered.

Aelnoth opened the lid of the heavy casket to reveal that it was filled to the brim with all manner of precious stones, some of which Aelnoth recognised, but there were many others, of such different hues which were strange, and unknown to him.

The Emperor turned on his heel and without a word of farewell; he walked through the door, followed by his guards and his retinue, leaving Aelnoth and his three new slaves in the sunlit courtyard.

Agio was the last of the Emperor's retinue to leave the room, but as she was about to leave, she turned towards Aelnoth and said, as if it was an afterthought.

'I know that you were fond of my slave 'Nike,' when you were part of my household, and I have wearied of her, and have recently purchased two younger maidens to replace her.'

'She is yours, if you wish it.'

'And if you do not wish it, then you may send her out onto the streets to fend for herself, or sell her to a brothel, for I understand that a Madam would pay you a small fortune for a pretty little virgin like her.'

She clapped her hands twice, and a few moments later the door opened to allow the exotic looking Nike to enter.

An even more beautiful girl entered the room behind her.

Aelnoth looked at her and then looked away, surmising that Agio had brought yet another slave for him, but then he suddenly stood still and shook his head, for he had suddenly realised that he recognised the face.

He turned to look at the fair-haired maiden again, and slowly his brain told him that it was Ingrid, for although he had occasionally thought about her, during his three year campaign in Armenia, his thoughts had been about a skinny, pimply child, and yet the maiden who had just entered the room, and who now strode confidently towards him with the sun behind her, shining through her fair hair and the thin garments which she wore, outlining her voluptuous figure, portrayed the very essence of a young and a very beautiful, self assured and expensively dressed young lady.

She stopped before him and held her hand out to him, as she gazed up into his eyes, with eyes that were neither green nor blue, but an exotic mixture of both colours.

'Well met Aelnoth,' she said in a cultured voice in the language of Greece.

In a mood that hovered between shock and awe, he took her hand and lowered his reddening face to kiss it, too stunned to speak, and it was only after he had raised his head again that he managed to utter the words.

'Ingrid; By the Gods! How you have changed.'

'Indeed,' came the answer.

'So have you, my Lord, or should I address you as, The White Wizard.'

'Neither! Aelnoth will suffice, he said quietly.'

'May I congratulate you on your victory over the Turks?'

'You are the most famous warrior in the whole of Constantinople.' She added demurely.

'I always knew it would be so.'

'Did you indeed?' he said as he took her hand and began to lead her towards one of the stone benches, which had been placed under the shade of a large palm tree.

Agio hobbled away smiling to herself, for the success of the youngster who she was now proud to call her protégé, had re-asserted her standing with the court and especially with the Emperor.

Without another word Agio turned and left the shocked Aelnoth in the courtyard with Ingrid, Nike and his three new slaves.

Aelnoth called the three new slaves over to him.

'How are you named? He asked.

After a moments silence, the young man said in an accent that Aelnoth found it hard to understand.

'I am called Roger and I am from Suffolk.'

'How is it that you have a Norman name, and yet you come from Suffolk?' asked Aelnoth.

'My Father was one of King Williams men who fought at Hastings, and as a reward for his service, the King gave him the holding of Felixstowe, which is in the shire of Suffolk, and one evening when was I walking along the dunes near my home, I was captured by Barbary Pirates.

'I See.' Said Aelnoth who then turned his gaze towards the two girls.

'And you?' he asked.

The younger girl lowered her head further onto her chest and said nothing, but the elder of the two, thrust out her chin and stared boldly at her new owner.

'I am called Margaret, and I was taken into slavery by these Norman swine, so I have no love for him,' as she nodded towards Roger.

'Her name is Morag, and she was my serving maid.' She added, with a heavy hint of arrogance.

Aelnoth ignored her manner and nodded towards the door.

'Follow Nike and Ingrid.' He said.

'They will show you to your quarters and inform you of your duties.'

Nike and Ingrid made their way through the passageways, which led to the servants quarters, and once Ingrid felt that she had reached a wide open area, where the servants could relax in the sun, and was a place where she thought that she could not be overheard, she halted, in order to have a quiet word with his Lordships new slaves, for although all of the guards were Varangians, she knew that they had been chosen by the devious Agio, who, she suspected, had bribed one or more of them to report anything out of the ordinary to her.

'Those are your living quarters.' Said Nike, as he nodded towards a number of doorways that led off the small courtyard, 'but I would speak with you before you enter them.'

'That end door leads to the largest room, which will be Ingrid's.'

'Go and prepare it.' She ordered Morag.

The girl made a slight courtesy and made her way across the courtyard towards the door.

'Now, you two.' Said Nike. 'I shall be putting not only my very life in your hands but also the life of my Master when I tell you what I am about to reveal.'

She looked into the eyes of both Margaret and Roger, whose eyes suddenly lit up for they knew only too well that this was not the way that an overseer of slaves spoke to the property of their master, especially to new slaves, who had only just entered their new quarters.

Aelnoth walked across the courtyard to join them.

'There is no need for you to tell them.' Said Aelnoth.

'I will tell them myself.'

'You may think that because I am a lord in this city, he said to the two new slaves, 'and because I speak the Greek tongue that I am a Greek.'

'But it may, or perhaps it may not shock you to learn that I am an Englishman from the green pastures of Mercia.'

Both Margaret and Roger looked up in amazement and Margaret's hand flew to her mouth in astonishment.

'I too have been exiled from England by the Normans, as were my friends who you will, no doubt, meet soon, and as long as I am here in Constantinople, I shall serve the Emperor to the best of my ability, and I shall remain loyal to him and to his empire.

'But, I yearn for the cold rain and the green pastures of my homeland, and one day I do intend to return.'

He paused for a moment in order to allow his new slaves to absorb the news, which had just revealed to them, and watched their shocked faces, for this was obviously not the sort of slavery that they had anticipated.

'To all intents and purposes, you must appear to everyone, that you are nought to me other than just a couple of slaves, doing what slaves do, and providing you do just that, then I shall treat you with kindness and with understanding, and when the time comes for me to leave, then I shall take you back to our homeland, not as slaves but as freemen.'

'However, if any of you should betray me, then you will either be slain or assigned to the slave block to be sold.'

'Is that clear?'

The slaves chorused and nodded that they understood.

'No one. Not your handmaiden, Morag. Nor any of the Guards must learn of our plan.'

'Do you understand?'

They nodded at such an unexpected turn of events, and then their nods turned to smiles, which became beaming smiles, cracking their hereto serious faces, but as Aelnoth looked at the face of Margaret, his own face became pallid as he stared open mouthed at her, for as she laughed, the lips of her mouth rose high over her teeth and over her gums, causing him to see, not a beautiful woman who was laughing, but the snarling face of a wolf, who had just dropped the human hand, which moments before, had been firmly clutched in its blood red, slavering jaws.

A shiver shot through his body.

He suddenly realised that he had probably made a grave error in revealing his plans to her, before he had taken time to assess his new slaves in more detail, but then he became more rational, and decided that although his vision of her, and his recollections of the wolf warned him of her potential treachery, he realised that she had no idea of his suspicions, and as such, he may be able to use this knowledge to his own advantage.

'My sister, the Lady Ingrid will be staying with us in her own quarters, and I expect both of you to treat her with politeness and respect.' He said.

'If you do not, then you will find yourselves on the slave block.' He warned.

'You and Morag must keep all our living quarters clean, and I shall expect you to oversee Morag, and to help me in any way possible to entertain guests.' He said.

'Roger,' he said as he turned to the young man.

'I shall expect you to join me in the main courtyard each morning, and train with me and my Guards in the arts of swordplay and axe work, and when I am satisfied that you are up to the high standards that make a good Varangian Guard, I shall expect you, not to become one of them, but to join with my household Guards in protecting myself and this household.'

'Is that clear?'

'It is my Lord. Crystal clear, and may I thank you for the way that you are treating the three of us.'

Aelnoth cleared his throat. 'Hrrr.'

'Don't thank me too soon, for if you do not perform as I expect you to, or if you betray me in any manner whatsoever, you will find yourself in the ranks of the army, in some outlandish garrison in Lydia.'

'Lydia. Is that a person or a place, my Lord?' asked the bemused youth.

'It is a country,' answered Aelnoth with a grimace, 'and a dangerous place for our people, for it is a country where we lose more men than any other, in our border outposts.'

'Come,' said Aelnoth.

'I have things to do, and I suggest that you get settled into your new quarters before nightfall

CHAPTER 24

During the following weeks, months and years, the household appeared to be running smoothly, with the house itself being kept spotlessly clean by the two girls, and whilst the food that they prepared, did not have the spicy taste that he had become accustomed to, but other than that, it was wholesome and filling.

Aelnoth spent the first two hours of each morning in mock combat with Roger and a number of the Varangian Guards, in order to keep himself and his Guards, fit and skilled enough to take up arms at a moments notice.

On every occasion that he met with the young Emperor, he was given a gift.

Oftimes it was no more than a simple silken scarf or a small intricately woven tapestry, but on many occasions it was a priceless gold ring or a silver bowl, or perhaps a golden coin, which contained the head of Roman etched upon it.

Aelnoth added these trinkets to the growing riches that he was amassing from his many other enterprises, and although he did not advertise the fact, he soon became one of the richest men in the city.

As he was the Major General of the Varangian guards, he spent each afternoon in a room, provided for him by the Emperor in the Palace, or in drilling and weapon training one of the many sections of the Varangian Guards.

The Soothsayer Agio now treated him in a very different way.

Instead of lecturing to him as if he was an errant schoolboy, she now hung onto every his word, and oft times he caught her gazing up at him in awe, rather than staring angrily at him, as had been the case before he had led the army out of Constantinople to defeat the Seljuk Turks.

Despite his youth, the gnarled and battle hardened Varangians appeared to have accepted him as their commander.

Indeed many of them held him in such high esteem, causing him to be aware that many of them would willingly give their lives to protect him.

On the occasions that Magnus visited him. He often accompanied Aelnoth riding around the perimeter of the city walls.

Magnus spoke sparingly of the opulence and riches of his new life in Constantinople, for he was very homesick, and would have made his way home to England many months ago, had it not been for his loyalty to Aelnoth.

Oscar and Abdulla had become very popular with the Emperor and his court, who showered the two Albinos' with gifts of jewels and golden trinkets, but despite the companionship and love he had for his two friends, Aelnoth felt that they were drifting apart.

Aelnoth could hardly believe that five years had passed since his victory over the Seljuk Turks at the battle of Ercis.

All appeared to be quiet with the vast Empire of Constantinople with the exception of the usual border raids for cattle, loot and women.

His duties within the city took up so much of his time, causing him to spend more and more of the sparse periods of leisure with Magnus and Roger the Norman, who he now counted as one of his closest friends.

During the first few months and years, the Emperor had been a regular visitor to his home and had repeatedly invited Aelnoth to the Palace, in order to seek his advice on matters of court and of the army, but these visits slowly became fewer and fewer as the Emperor appeared to spend more time in the company of his few select friends.

Oscar and Abdulla had become rich members and affluent members of court, and spent much of their time either at court, or at their new villa overlooking the 'Hellespont', which they informed him had originally been named 'Sea of the Helle.' (Greeks)

On the odd occasion when Aelnoth found time to visit his friends, he reluctantly agreed with them, that they had found their own type of Heaven.

As the three of them sat under a palm tree, shaded from the blazing sun and sipping at their cool drinks. They gazed across the straits at the myriad of shipping, which plied to and fro across the azure blue sea.

His two friends rarely spoke of England and seemed to be totally absorbed and happy with their new life.

Both Oscar and Abdulla proudly escorted him around their large estate, causing him to marvel at the host of slaves and servants, who tended their villa and their numerous fields of olives and vines.

'Why on earth do you want to return to England?' asked Oscar.

'I really cannot understand why you would yearn to tramp about in the snow and slush, and freeze your balls off with every winter, which would seem to be longer and more miserable than the last one.

'I made a vow.' Answered Aelnoth.

'I swore that I would avenge the death of my brother and take back my Hall and my lands, which have been in my family for generations.'

'What about the Normans?'

'They will not willingly give back what they have owned for these long years?'

'Oh I shall cross that bridge when I come to it.' He said glumly.

'What about you?' He asked.

'What would you do if you came back with me?' he asked.

'I'd buy an Inn or a Brothel or some thing like that. Said Oscar.

'But, my friend, I'm afraid I shall not be going with you.'

'Why on earth should I leave all this?' He waved his hand to his front as if who whole of the Hellespont was his.

'I would be a fool to leave this, just to end up on the spear-point of some flea ridden Norman who took a dislike to me.'

'No. My old friend; I shall remain here with my good friend Abdulla and allow all these servants and slaves to continue to pamper me, for as long as the good Lord sees fit.'

'Aelnoth nodded glumly and said no more on the subject, for he could see the wisdom in his friends reasoning.

His mood became morose as he journeyed back to the city, as his mind dwelt on the words, which Oscar had uttered, and although he was forced to agree that he would probably freeze his balls off in the winter, he began to cheer up a little as he thought of the warm spring days, and the shrill sound of the larks as they sang and hovered above the flower speckled meadows, where happy men and women sang their ancient songs as they harvested the sweet smelling hay.

He could almost smell the hay, and hear the loud, curdling song of the curlew, as it flew over the marshlands, wheeling up and down as it attempted to lure intruders away from its nest.

He envisaged meeting again with good honest English folk who spoke the good English language, and not the difficult languages of the Greeks and their associate nations.

He smiled to himself, as he pretty well knew that when, at last, he finally met with an English peasant, then one of the first conversations he would have with that peasant, be it a man or a woman, it would be about the weather.

His mood lightened and he was still smiling as he rode through the gates and into the city, ignoring the guards as they stared at this famous nobleman who rode past them with a stupid smile on his face.

It was a balmy spring evening when Aelnoth, Magnus and Ingrid sat under a shady shumac tree, sipping red wine and nibbling on roast chicken and chunks of freshly baked bread.

'It is evenings like this that make my belly ache for England.' Said Magnus with a sigh.

'Me too,' answered Aelnoth.

'The beech and the oak will be out now, and the spring showers will turn the meadows into a rainbow of wild-flowers.'

'Ah, I long for the smell of the wet woodland,' said Magnus and he raised his head and loudly inhaled the dry, lifeless air of the courtyard.

'Pah,' he swore. 'Tis time we left this hot, arid land, and set our feet on the green fields of England again.'

He emptied his silver tankard and hurled the empty vessel across the courtyard, where it clanged along the flagstones, and crashed to a halt at the base of a large terracotta pot.

'Funny you should say that.' Said Aelnoth with a smile.

'I have long thought the same, and as we are alone at the moment, I think it is time to share my plans with you.'

Magnus sat bolt upright and then leaned closer to his friend.

'What plans?' he said quietly.

Ingrid stood and carried her own wicker chair, which she placed in-between the two men.

'Yes! What plans?' she asked excitedly.

Aelnoth also leaned towards Magnus, and said. 'Of course you know that during the past few years I have been owner of two merchant ships, and both of my captains have been honest and trustworthy men, who have been totally loyal to me.'

'They have both made trips to Crete, Cyprus and the other islands to sell their wares, and have returned here laden with food and goods for the city, and the profits from their endeavour have helped to make me a very rich man.'

'But what you probably do not know,' he said quietly, 'is that a few days ago, as a reward for his loyalty. I sold my ship, the Porpoise to the Captain at a price that gave him no option other than to snatch my hand off, and I have hidden the proceeds of the sale, along with the coin and gifts, which I have received from the Emperor, and from the merchants who have sought my favours over the years.'

He paused for a moment, as the amazed Magnus and silent Ingrid digested the news.

'As you already know, I have always vowed to return to England and avenge the slayers of my family and to reclaim my inheritance, and now I have the wealth and the means to do so.'

'It is my fervent wish that both of you.'

'You Magnus, who are the oldest and most loyal of my friends, and of course you, my dear Ingrid, will join me in my quest.'

'Willingly and with all my heart.' Exclaimed his friend as he clasped Aelnoth's right hand and placed his left hand on Aelnoth's shoulder.

Ingrid literally jumped off her chair, and plonked herself on Aelnoth's lap where she showered his face with kisses.

'Oh, my dearest Aelnoth. How wonderful.'

'When do we leave?' She said in a loud and excited voice.

'Shh my Love.' Said Aelnoth as he held his index finger to his lips, and gazed around the courtyard to assure himself that no one had heard her.

He prised her arms from around his neck and rose to his feet, carrying her back to her chair, where he gently replaced her onto her original seat.

'Don't get so excited my little wildcat.' He said.

'It won't be for a little while.'

'Just act normal for the next couple of days, and I will give you the full details when the time comes.'

'My remaining ship,' added Aelnoth. 'The Dolphin,' is due to sail on the ebb tide in two days time, and I think the captain could find room for a few extra passengers.'

'Are you serious?' asked Magnus whose tanned face broke into one of his very rare smiles.

Ingrid could hardly contain her excitement, and rose from her chair, causing Aelnoth to hold his hand out to her in an attempt to calm her down.

'Quiet.' He hissed quietly.

'I have told you about this in complete confidence, and it is vital that only we three know about it at this moment in time.'

'Besides.' He added. 'I do not trust all of our house servants, for both your good selves and myself are well aware that both the Emperor and that old witch 'Agio' have armies of spies throughout the city, and certainly have more than one in this very household.

'I am very serious, for like you. I too yearn to return to England. Normans or no Normans.'

'Gather your valuables, and take only what you can pack into one bag, and meet me here tomorrow evening, so that we can make our way to the docks, and we can board the Dolphin during the night.'

'We should be able to sail with the tide, which will be about an hour before dawn.'

'I shall be taking my three servants, as well as Nike'' He added.

'Is there anyone who you want to take?'

'No, not really.' Said Magnus.

'Of course, you do know that I have four ladies here, and have fathered three children, but I am not close to any of them and they would not be made welcome by our people, if I were to take them home.'

'What about Oscar and Abdulla?' asked Magnus.

'I have already spoken to them, and they have decided to remain here.'

'They both have a good life here and have little to gain, and probably a lot to lose if they were to return to England.'

'No.' said Magnus.' If they were to come with us, they would certainly be ostracised, and may well meet an early death in England.'

Aelnoth did not speak of his plans to any of his servants (slaves) until late the following evening, just as they were about to go about their usual duties of bolting the doors, and closing the shutters for the night.

He beckoned them to him and said. 'Come with me Roger,' and began to walk towards Roger's quarters.

'And you three ladies.' He said, as he ushered Margaret, Nike and Morag before him.

Once they reached Rogers sleeping quarters, he said. 'Gather up anything that is dear to you and follow me.'

Roger stood for a moment before he moved to a small chest that lay alongside his bed.

'I have little of value.' He said, 'only this jewelled dagger.'

'Why my Lord?' He asked in a nervous voice.

'Where are we going?'

'Have I displeased you?'

'Are you selling me?' he asked in a voice that had begun to shake with emotion.

'No, my friend,' answered Aelnoth. 'Nothing like that.'

'But.' He added.

'You and these three ladies here will accompany me on my voyage home to England.'

Gasps and exclamations of joy came from the three girls, and Roger rose to his feet with the dagger in his hand, causing Aelnoth a moment of doubt, which was speedily dispelled, as Roger thrust the dagger into his own belt and threw his arms about Aelnoth's shoulders, and as he hugged him.

'I had begun to fear that I should never see England again, and would spend the rest of my days as a slave in this hot hellhole of a country.' He said emotionally.

Aelnoth escorted each of the girls to their rooms, where they were allowed to collect just one bagful of their belongings, before he ushered them to the rear of the Villa.

'Some of my Varangians have agreed to leave with us.' He told them.

'They will escort us to the docks, and will accompany us on our voyage.'

He made his way to the doorway and said. 'I urge you all to remain silent, no matter what happens once we leave the protection of this Villa.'

'Not a word or a squeak out of any of you! IS THAT CLEAR?' He said menacingly, as his left hand fell upon the hilt of his Saex, as if to emphasise his point.

The three girls and Roger nodded and muttered. 'Yes my Lord,' and stooped to pick up their bags in their readiness to follow him.

'Put your bags down, for it will be some time before we leave.

'I have things to attend to.'

'Stay here.'

'Roger, I want you to stay here, and do not let anyone in or out of this room until I return.' He added, as he left the room.

He walked quickly to the rear gate, where the Guards silently greeted him.

'Has the cart arrived?' he asked.

'Not yet my Lord, but I think I can hear it approaching.' Replied the Guard.

He peered into the darkness and saw the outline of the cart, which approached, almost silently on its four lagged wheels.

'Let it in.' he ordered, and the Guards opened the two gates to enable the cart and its stinking contents to pass through.

As quietly as they could, the Guards and the driver performed the grisly task of unloading the bodies, which they had scavenged from Constantinople's midden, where the bodies of the paupers and criminals were deposited.

The bodies were carried into the Villa, where they stripped them of their stinking rags, and the men struggled to dress the male corpses in the clothes of the Varangians, whilst Aelnoth manhandled one of the three male bodies, and dressed the body in his own old robes, carefully inserting some of his own rings onto its rotting fingers, and placed his own expensive silver chain of office around its neck.

It was more difficult to turn the other corpse into something that resembled the tall figure of Magnus, but after decapitating it, and placing the ornate Helmet, which Magnus favoured above all others, onto the detached head; Aelnoth hoped that the burned corpse would pass off, as being that of Magnus.

Two English axes and a number of knives and swords were strewn around the room.

The four female corpses were dressed and adorned with some of the belongings, which had belonged to Ingrid, Nike, Margaret and Morag.

The men then doused the bodies and the furnishings of several rooms of the Villa with oil, which had been purchased for that particular purpose, and set it alight, before they ran back to the gate, where they found his small party, ready and waiting.

After closing the gates, they made their way through the darkness towards the docks.

The sky behind them illuminated the darkness as the fire took hold, and the flames leapt into the sky.

The road upon which they travelled was pitch black, with no sign of the moon.

As the cart was quietly negotiated its way around a narrow corners, no one noticed the slight form of Margaret, as she grinned to herself with the smile of the wolf, and slipped off the rear of the cart, disappearing quickly into a darkened doorway, where she waited for a few moments before she ran as fast as she could towards the Emperor's palace.

An hour later the weary horse, carrying the girls and the assortment of sacks and baggage made its way quietly along the quay to the ship.

It was only when they began to unload the girls and the baggage from the cart that Aelnoth realised that Margaret was missing.

'Where's Margaret?' asked Aelnoth.

Nike or Morag, who had been snuggling together under a blanket, shook their heads in disbelief, for they had not noticed until that very moment that she had disappeared.

'Ah well,' said Aelnoth quietly.

'She's gone, and gone of her own free will by the looks of it, and if I am not mistaken, she will be at the palace gates demanding an audience with the Emperor.'

'I had long suspected her to be a hornet in our nest.' He added.

'We had best be on our way or we shall have the night Guards upon us.'

'Is everything set?' Aelnoth asked the Captain.

'It is my Lord, as soon as you and your party board.' He answered

As he quietly ushered the ladies, Roger and the Varangians aboard, he approached the Captain.

'Are all the weapons and trade goods that I ordered aboard?' He asked.

'They are my Lord, and the crew are all slaves who I have purchased, and are all from the north of Europe.'

'They were all either seamen or warriors before they became slaves, just as you ordered, and once we are under way, I am sure that they will work their hearts out, for I have already told them that you will allow them to sling their chains into the ocean, and will be set free, providing they help us to reach England.'

'How many?'

'Forty two my Lord, enough to man the oars and handle the ship.'

'When can we sail?'

'Right away my Lord. The tide has just turned and is on the ebb.'

'Let's be on our way then.' Ordered Aelnoth, as gazed at the men in the ship who were all looking at him and the Captain in anticipation, keen to leave this city whose empire had enslaved them.

'Let go fore. Let go aft.' He said quietly, and men dashed to do his bidding and quickly untied the thick ropes that held the ship to the quay.

'Out oars.' He said in a quiet voice, and as several of the oars clunked against the quay.

'Quiet you idiots.' Snarled the Captain.

'Do you want to leave this city in one piece, or do you want the Harbour guards to hear you, and raise the alarm?'

'Now row.' He hissed. 'Quietly,' and the oarsmen dipped their oars into the still waters of the dock and heaved, propelling the heavily laden ship forward towards the mouth of the harbour.

It had cost Aelnoth a small fortune in silver to bribe the port guards who were in charge of the chain, which prevented ships from entering or leaving the port during the hours of darkness.

Aelnoth breathed a sigh of relief as the Dolphin glided serenely a few feet over the huge chain, which was visible in the moonlight, as it glowed in the crystal clear waters of the harbour.

The ship was over a mile away from the city when dawn broke over the seven hills, on which the city of Constantinople had been built, throwing its red shadow over its still sleeping inhabitants.

Aelnoth gazed back towards the city that had bestowed such riches on him.

'Well. That is the last time that we shall see Constantinople.' He said quietly.

'Let us hope so.' Answered Magnus, as they stood by the Captain, who had just adjusted the steering in order to avoid a small cairn of jagged rocks, which had appeared to the east of the channel that the ship was passing through.

'Cease rowing.' Shouted the Captain and the tired oarsmen brought their oars up and out of the water and rested on their oars.

'Ship oars.' He ordered and the oarsmen heaved their heavy oars in and shipped them alongside the sides of the ship.

'Up sail.' He bellowed causing a number of men to heave on the ropes and pull the heavy sail up the mast until it reached the top.

Aelnoth and Magnus stood beside the Captain, who was guiding the helmsman in the vital job of manoeuvring the ship through the myriad of channels, rocks and small islands, which dotted the dark blue sea.

Aelnoth noticed that the Captain periodically turned to gaze back into the distance from whence they had come.

'What are you looking for?' he asked.

'Pursuit.' Was the blunt answer.

'And do you see any?'

'No, my Lord. Not yet.' He said, as he held his hand up in order to shade his eyes from the morning sun, which now blazed over the eastern horizon.

'It would seem that our ruse has succeeded.' Said Aelnoth.

'Let us hope so my Lord.' Said the Captain in a noncommittal voice.

'For should the Emperor discover that we have tricked him, and left his city without his permission, he could send a hundred warships to hunt us down, and if we are caught, his wrath will be awful to behold.'

Aelnoth joined Magnus, who, as a result of their conversation with the Captain, had also turned to stare into the distance behind the ship.

'What is that?' Said Aelnoth, who pointed towards a dot, which had appeared on the horizon.

The Captain immediately joined the trio and stared at the dot.

'I can see nought.' He said.

'I can.' Said Magnus.

'Where?'

'Over yonder, just to the left of those two small islands.'

'Well I can see the islands but I cannot see ought else.'

'Your eyes are younger than mine,' added the Captain.

'Keep your eyes concentrated on the spot, and if they look like ships, then for Christ sake tell me.' as he returned to the rudder, in order to help the helmsman guide the ship past a clump of rocks that protruded out of the shallow sea.

By mid-day the ship was clearly visible, and was accompanied by two other vessels, which were trailing her by a good sea mile.

'All three are Galleys out of Constantinople.' Growled the Captain, who was becoming more and more agitated.

'Can we out-run them?' asked Aelnoth.

'No chance.' Was the muffled answer.

'They have three tiers of rowers, and the leading ship will be upon us before nightfall.'

'So we have no chance?' said Aelnoth glumly, as he looked at the equally glum face of the Captain and Magnus.

'Well, I didn't exactly say that.' Said the Captain, as he touched his nose with his index finger and gave a wry smile.

'I know these waters like the back of my hand, and if we can make it to those islands before dark, then we may, just may be able to lose them.'

'There is a maze of islands down there,' he added, 'and if we can reach them in time, then we might be able to get away.'

'Is there any way that we can make this ship go faster?' asked Aelnoth.

'Not really,' answered the Captain.

'We cannot make any more sail and the rowers are tiring.'

'Come Magnus,' said Aelnoth.

'Gather up all the seamen and the Varangians, and we will relieve those men who are tiring and get our hands blistered,' and he walked a few feet towards one of the rowers who was struggling to hold his stroke with his fellow oarsmen.

Aelnoth helped the man to his feet, and sat in his place and began to row.

Magnus gathered all the other men who were not rowing, and pulled out a number of the tired rowers, replacing them with fresh men, before he plonked himself down on the bench behind Aelnoth and commenced to heave on the heavy wooden oar.

Despite the fact that Aelnoth and Magnus were now quite at home on the sea and were familiar with oarsmen, they had never actually rowed, and once they had sat on the bench and began to row, they did not find it as easy as they had expected.

The rowing itself was not the problem, for in the past they had handled small boats as well as the occasional skiff.

The problem was keeping their own stroke in time with experienced oarsmen, and they found that as they attempted this seemingly easy task, they either dug their oars in too deep, which put their own stroke behind their peers, or they went too high in the water, and skimmed the top, thus crashing into the man who rowed to their rear.

However, after a few initial mistakes and a lot of cursing, they began to get it right, and assisted in sending the ship skimming over the calm water towards the still distant islands.

The Captain stayed at the helm, whilst his helmsman periodically walked the length of the ship with a large jar containing watered down wine, which he ladled out to the oarsmen as they strained at the oars.

All of the crew were aware that if the ship did not reach the tangle of small islands, which lay ahead of them before they were overtaken by the Galley's, then their one and only hope of freedom would be well and truly doomed.

With their backs to the prow, the rowers could not see how far the Islands were.

All they could see was the back of the man in front of them and as they glanced over his shoulder, they could also see the enlarged figure of the leading Galley, which seemed to be less than half a mile to their rear.

'Pull Lads,' gasped Aelnoth Loudly.

'Pull for all you are worth or you will never see your homelands again.' He shouted, causing the oarsmen to dig their oars a little deeper in the sea, and pull until their arms felt that they were being pulled out of their sockets.

The pace of the ship seemed to pick up, and to Aelnoth it felt that they were skimming over the calm sea like the schools of dolphins that had oft times raced alongside the ship, in happier times.

He glanced over his shoulder and with relief he saw that they had almost reached a small cairn of large rocks that bordered the nearest Island.

'Pull men. Pull!' He urged.

'Just a little further and we shall out-run them.'

As he pushed himself to force his own tired muscles to continue to obey him.

The Captain ordered the Sail down, causing two of the weary men to shuffle forward and lower the sail.

'Port oars in.' he shouted, and the rowers who were on the port side of the ship ceased rowing and hauled their oars aboard.

'Aft, row two strokes only.' He ordered and the men on the aft side of the ship obeyed, and held their oars out of the water.

'Oars in.' he ordered. The men obeyed, and gazed in wonder as the ship glided serenely through a small passageway between two small islands, which were just wide enough to allow the ship to pass through, scraping the one side as it did so.

The ship's momentum took it over a sandbank with less than a foot to spare, but just as they thought that they were clear, the ship suddenly lurched to a stop.

'You men there.' Shouted the Captain.

'Jump out and lighten the ship, and try to lift her off this sandbank whilst the rest of you pull on your oars for all you are worth.'

After a lot of heaving, the ship slid sluggishly off the hidden sand bank, causing the men who were still in the water to scramble forward and grasp onto the oars, in order to enable them to be hauled aboard.

The Captain gave the crew no time to celebrate his seamanship, and ordered. 'Oars out.'

'Now row for all you are worth.'

'We are not clear yet.' He shouted as the weary men dipped the heavy oars into the water and groaned as they strained on the oars again.

As Aelnoth glanced again over his shoulder, he could see that the nearest Galley had stopped short of the rocks, and could see the sea foaming, as the Galley's rowers were furiously attempting to cease the onward rush of the ship, in order to prevent its impetus from sending it crashing onto the rocks.

'Why are we still rowing?' shouted the angry Aelnoth, for the Captain was his man, and was thus subservient to him.

'We are clear and the Galley cannot reach us.' He gasped.

'I know these waters my Lord,' said the Captain in a controlled voice, 'and I know full well that the other two Galleys are already on their way around this cluster of Islands, and if we are lucky, we may be able to cross the open water, which lies ahead of us, before those Galleys reach us, and then, with a bit more luck, we can disappear into the darkness and be free of them.'

The ship passed through the channel into the open water, which the Captain had predicted, whereupon he ordered the sail to be raised, and with the help of the sail and an additional hour of backbreaking rowing, they crossed the wide stretch of open water and vanished behind another larger island into the growing darkness, as the sun began to drop below the horizon.

'There are no islands for a while,' said the Captain, 'but we need to be well out of sight from the Galley's by daybreak, so it means that the men will need to row throughout the night.'

'They are already exhausted.' Said Aelnoth.

'Surely you cannot expect them to row through the night?'

'I know that I am your man,' said the Captain in a surly voice, 'but whilst we are on board the Dolphin. I am the master, and if you want to stay alive and reach your homeland, then you need to allow me to do what I do best, and that is to handle this ship.'

'Besides,' he added. 'I know full well that the men are tired, but I intend to leave the sail up and arrange the crew, including your good selves, into three sections, who will take it in turns to row.'

'One third of the crew will row, while the other two sections sleep.'

'I shall, of course, remain at the helm throughout the night.' He added.

After a long and tiring night, there was little sign of the sun, merely a thin light, which shone through a heavy sea mist.

The sail lay limp against the mast, allowing the ship to move very slowly through the eerie and silent sea, as the exhausted oarsmen propelled it ever slower.

'Cease rowing.' Said the Captain just loud enough for the men in the front rows to hear.

'Ship oars and have a rest.' He ordered.

'As quietly as you can.' He added.

'Noise will carry for miles in this fog.'

'I'm going to get an hour of shut-eye,' he said.

'Wake me if you hear anything,' and he made his way wearily towards his own sleeping bag.

Aelnoth felt that he had been up for half of the night, and almost tripped over a sleeping man, as he made his way to the helmsman who had taken over the tiller.

'Do you think we have lost the Galleys?' he asked.

'No way of telling my Lord.'

'They could be over yonder just out of sight, or they could be fifty miles away.'

'If we hear any voices or the clumping of oars then we will know they have found us.'

By mid-morning the sun had burned away the mist, revealing an immense and empty sea, with no signs whatsoever of either land, or of the Emperors Galleys.

The ship was urged slowly along by a gentle breeze, allowing everyone, except the helmsman and the lookouts, to catch up with some much needed sleep.

After a few hours, some of the men began to wake and stretch their aching limbs.

One man began to sing softly to himself.

Other men joined in.

The small band of Englishmen started to sing a very old folk song of the green fields of England, of the damp woodlands and of the song of the larks, which sang, as they hovered over the fragrant meadows.

The four Norwegians sang a mournful song of their Fjords and of ice covered waterfalls.

The two Icelander's appeared to sing of mountains belching fire and brimstone, although no one else could understand much of what they sang, for their words were intermingled with sobs and sighs, as tears streamed down their blonde beards and onto their sweat stained shirts.

Roger the Norman was the only one who did not sing.

He sat alone as he listened to the conglomeration of noise, which the crew and passengers made, unable to distinguish one song from another.

Nonetheless, he too was dreaming of home.

He was thinking of the beautiful town of Felixstowe, and the clear streams, as they gurgled over stones and tiny waterfalls, as they made their way to the coast.

At this moment in time he was not aboard an old trading vessel, accompanied with a crew of reevers who would willingly kill him if they were given leave to.

He was a mere boy again, paddling barefoot down the stream below his fathers new hall, in the old Saxon land of the south folk, attempting to catch the wily brown trout who lingered beneath the overhanging banks in their attempt to elude Roger, the famous catcher of trout.

He had been too young to remember his earlier childhood, before his Father had left the warm climes of southern Normandy, in order to join Duke William on his conquest of England, although many of the happy stories, which his Father had told him of his warm southern home, were still vivid in his mind.

He had literally hated his two years as a slave in the smelly city of Constantinople, but did, nonetheless recall the warm sunny days and the balmy nights, which he had spent in the city, as his confused mind attempted, without success, to compare them with the freezing cold winter days and nights that he had spent in Suffolk.

As the ship sailed serenely over the deep blue sea, Aelnoth made it his duty to speak to every member on board, in order to assure them that they were now free men, and once they reached the shores of England, they would all be allowed to go their own separate ways.

Much to his astonishment, most of the Englishmen, which included two of the Varangian Guards, were reluctant to return to England.

'What will we find there? Asked Edward of Braintree.

'More bloody Normans, ruling over us like Gods.'

'My parents were evicted from their farm' Edward added.

'They died of starvation whilst I was with Hereward in the Fens.'

'Both of my sisters were taken by the Normans.'

'Bastards!' he spat into the sea, and glared at Roger, who was the sole Norman amongst the crew.

The two Icelanders, Ingar and Ivar, told Aelnoth of their plans to make their way across England to the town of Bristol, where they planed to purchase a skiff, and sail along the coast of Ireland, and wait in the City of Dublin until they could join one of Bjorn's trading vessels, in order to sail home to Iceland.

'Bjorn could be dead.' Said Aelnoth quietly.

'I was with him when we were defeated at Exmoor, and I have heard nought of him since the storm scattered his fleet. Or at least, what was left of his fleet.'

'So?' said Ingar surly. 'If he's dead, then he's dead.'

'Someone else will have taken over his leadership, and we will join him.'

CHAPTER 25

'The wind is getting up,' said the Captain to Aelnoth.

'If you agree, my Lord.' He added. 'I will steer to the west and haul the Dolphin out onto the beach for a day or two.'

'She is slowing and shipping a lot of water, and I suspect that she was damaged on that damned sandbank, and is in need of a little attention before we pass through the straights of Gibraltar.'

Aelnoth nodded his consent, for although he considered himself to be a seasoned sailor, he was well aware that compared to the Captain, with his many years at sea, he was still a novice regarding the ways of the sea and ships.

The breeze turned into a howling gale, tossing the Dolphin about like a cork and sending cascades of water into the ship.

'Bale for all you are worth or she will sink,' shouted the Captain, and even the three women snatched up helmets and helped the men, in their attempt to empty the ship of some of its water.

The Captain steered the Dolphin sluggishly towards the shore, but as he did so, one massive wave swept over the ship and carried Morag overboard.

Her head reappeared just once, about fifty feet away from the ship before it disappeared, never to be seen again.

It had all happened in a moment, shocking the men, several of whom were on the point of diving into the swirling waves in an attempt to save her, but they were thrown about by the motion of the ship, which appeared to have a mind of its own, as a number of huge waves almost swamped her, and drove the waterlogged ship away from the spot where Morag had been seen, forcing the ship to float sluggishly away in the opposite direction.

Nike broke down in tears as she leant over the side of the ship, screaming at the top of her voice as she held her arms aloft, as if pleading for Morag to reappear, and leap into her open arms.

She fell onto her knees with the water lapping around her waist, and clasped her hands together as she turned her face up into the rain and stared up into the clouds.

'Dear Lord,' she prayed. 'Please do not take her from us.'

'She is young and is dear to us.'

'Please Lord God in Heaven, don't let her drown. Send her back to me. I beg you to save her,' she sobbed.

The driving rain lashed her face, merging with her tears, which ran in torrents down her face, but the storm continued with its ferocity, forcing her to grasp the side of the flooded ship, in order to prevent herself from plunging face first into the water.

The heart of Magnus went out to Nike, but he could do no more than slosh his way through the flooded ship to grasp her by her shoulders and hold her close to him.

He knew that Morag was gone, and yet as he held Nike close and felt her sobbing against his chest.

His mind was saying to him that her prayers were in vain, and thought to himself that this moment in time had been destined long ago, but as he held her close to him, another strange thought entered his mind, telling him that of all living creatures that dwelt upon the earth, as far as he knew, only mankind prayed.

Ingrid merely looked solemnly at Aelnoth, and continued bailing out the water, wiping a strand of her wet hair out of her eyes before she looked away.

Darkness was falling as the Captain struggled to steer the waterlogged Dolphin to a halt as the surging foam propelled her up onto a sandy beach.

'Bale her out and help me haul her further up onto the beach.' Shouted the Captain and all of the crew and passengers continued to empty the water out of the hull before they jumped out into the surging waves, and hauled the Dolphin high above the high-water mark.

They eventually managed to light half a dozen small fires, which they huddled over in their attempt to dry their saturated clothing.

Most of them slept like the dead for much of the night, waking to a dry warm morning, and a sea, which was so calm that Aelnoth found it difficult to understand that this was the same sea, which had taken poor Morag and had almost drowned him and the rest of his shipmates.

After days of hesitation and indecision Magnus broached the subject of Nike to Aelnoth.

'Aelnoth,' he said, as he sat near the fire next to Aelnoth.

'When you and I met all those years ago in Broseley. I did consider taking the leadership from you, as you were nought but an untried youth.'

'I was older, and was, and still am, the nephew of King Harold, and I had fought at Stamford Bridge.'

'Therefore at the time, I did consider myself to be superior to you.'

'However,' he hesitated, and became unsure what to say next.

'During the past seven years, my decision to leave well alone, has proven to be the correct decision, for you are a born leader, and where you have led, I have willingly followed, whether it has been in peace or in war.'

He was aware that he was waffling, and was fearful of reaching the point. Not because he was afraid, but because he was simply fearful of the answer.

'I have loved Nike since the first day that I saw her, and have always known that she adores you and follows you about like a love sick calve, thus I have been afraid to approach you regarding her.'

'After all, she is your slave is she not?' He added.

'Why of course she is.' Answered Aelnoth.

'But although I like the girl, she has never been anything to me, other than a slave.

'However, as you are well aware, I have promised freedom to all who joined me on this voyage home, and that goes for Nike too, so she is free to choose whosoever she pleases.'

'So I suggest that instead of pouring your heart out to me like a love-sick calf, you go over to her and tell her just what you have told me.'

Magnus was so shocked at such a simple and straightforward solution, that he simply sat still with his mouth open, whilst Aelnoth turned and walked over to the Captain who was gazing up at the surrounding hills.

'I have seen no signs of human activity.' Said the Captain.

'I think that it should be safe to make camp here while we have a look at her Hull,' as he nodded towards the Dolphin, which had began to list over onto one side.

'I agree,' said Aelnoth, 'Nonetheless, I think it will be wise to post sentries,' and without further ado, he hailed the two Icelanders.

Ingar and Ivar approached him.

'I want you Ingar, to climb up that hill over there and keep watch until noon, when I will send a man up to relieve you.'

'Ivar. You go up that hill the other side of the beach and keep watch until I relieve you, and make sure that both of you stay awake.'

'If you should see anyone approaching who you think could be a danger to us, sound your horns. But if it looks like a shepherd or a fisherman or an odd man or two, then I would like one of you to run back to me here, and I can make arrangements to deal with the situation.'

'Is that clear?'

385

'Aye my Lord Aelnoth.' Said the pair in unison, as they turned and ambled off to collect what they needed for their watch.

Whilst the crew were eating their bowls of warm oats, which contained a mere taste of honey, the Captain mingled with the men, in order to discover if any of these former slaves and Varangian Guards had any knowledge of boat building.

Much to his surprise, at least a third of the men had been brought up in the coastal areas of England, Ireland or Scandinavia, and had spent much of their childhood and younger years, either fishing or helping their families construct or repair sea-going vessels.

Aelnoth, accompanied by two new sentries, relieved the two Icelanders.

'Have you seen or heard anything unusual?' he asked.

'Are there any towns or villages near?'

Both men confirmed that they 'appeared to be alone here.'

'Wherever here was.' Remarked Ivar with a hint of sarcasm in his voice.

'So neither of you have seen smoke rising out of the valleys and woods?' he asked.

'No my Lord.' Answered the men.

Satisfied that they appeared to have landed on an uninhabited, or at least, on a quiet sector of the coast, he walked down the hill and commenced to watch as the Captain and a dozen other men started their work on the Dolphin.

Aelnoth could not help noticing the envious looks that the crew gave him as they began to settle down for the night, when Ingrid rolled up her now dry sheepskin bedding by him and snuggled up alongside him.

As was his habit before settling down for the night, Aelnoth looked around the camp to ensure that the guards were awake, and patrolling their given sectors, but he was suddenly forced to cease his patrolling, and smiled to himself, as he saw the prone figure of Magnus open his own sheepskin blanket to allow the trim form of Nike to join him.

The following morning Aelnoth was roused from his slumbers by the sounds of men waking from their sleep with grunts and groans, as they stretched their stiff limbs and ambled to the outer limits of the camp to relieve themselves.

Aelnoth noted with satisfaction that the Captain had chosen an ideal place to beach the Dolphin, as she now lay on one side, with a large part of her keel showing.

The Captain was standing by the keel with his hands on his hips as he studied the ship.

Aelnoth joined him.

'Any problems?' he asked.

'No, my Lord,'

'Well, yes my Lord, there are a few, but nothing I can't handle, providing we can get the right kind of wood, and can remain hidden here for a few days.'

'Whilst you and your men are doing the repairs, I will send men out to hunt, in order to provide fresh meat.' Said Aelnoth.

'By the way, do you know where we are?' he asked.

'Of course, my Lord.'

'We are in Italy.' Said the Captain almost nonchantly, as if every man and his dog should know that he had beached the Dolphin in Italy.

'What part of Italy? Asked Aelnoth, for he had long been aware that the southern half of Italy was part of the greater Norman Empire.

'Pretty well on the most southerly tip.' Said the Captain.

'So this part could well belong to the damned Normans?' asked Aelnoth.

'Yes it could be, but in many parts of the south, they are still at war with the locals,

'Who are the locals?'

'Oh they are people who are supposed to owe allegiance to the Emperor in Constantinople, but there are also a lot of Lombard's in this area, and they can be pretty savage opponents.'

'Oh,' said Aelnoth, as he stroked his sparse beard and digested what he had just been told.

'How long will it take to get the ship repaired?'

'At least two or three days.' Said the Captain.

'In that case I shall have a word with the men,' said Aelnoth as he left the Captain and walked towards the area where the majority of the men lounged about playing dice, or merely sunning themselves in the morning sun.

'Gather around.' He shouted to the men who were furthest away, and waited for a few minutes whilst they made their way towards him.

'Men,' he said loudly.

'You all know that I have promised you your freedom, and I can assure you that I will abide to my promise.'

'However, whilst we are here or in fact whilst we are aboard the Dolphin, I will expect you to obey me without question, until such time as we reach England.'

'The good Captain here informs me that we shall remain here for at least another couple of days.'

'He also tells me that we are in the south of Italy, and it is an area where the Normans are still fighting with the local population.'

He paused a moment in order to allow the men to absorb the news.

'I think it would be wise to make preparations to repel any Normans or local tribesmen who may take it into their heads to raid us, for they will recognise the Dolphin as a trading ship belonging to the Emperor in Constantinople, and it would be a rich prize for them to capture.'

'I am also aware that some of you are rich men, who have a wealth of silver and gold, which you have accrued over your years in Constantinople, and, like myself, you would be reluctant to lose it to some greedy Norman, or a peasant with a sickle.'

Some of the men nodded in agreement, whilst many of the other men, who had been purchased off the slave block, gazed in awe at their shipmates, who they had previously assumed to be penniless ex-slaves or mere soldiers, and not the wealthy men that Lord Aelnoth had just revealed them to be.

Aelnoth continued. 'I want you Varangian Guards to organise the men into sections, and instruct them to construct a marching camp as if you were still in the Guards.'

'You know the sort of thing I mean,' he explained.

'The type of a marching camp that the Roman legions used to make, which is exactly the type of a daily task that the armies of Constantinople performed each evening.'

The Guards and himself were familiar with the procedure, but the word 'Marching camp' would be a completely unknown word for those of the crew who were ex-slaves.

'Dig the ditch to the standard depth of six feet,'

'Cut as much turf as you can find in order to construct a good barrier.'

'Cut logs and erect them in a circle around the camp, which we will make there.'

He pointed to a small mound, which was about fifty feet away from the beached ship.

'Unload the ship of all the personal effects and storage chests, and everything else that is not nailed down.'

'Carry them on the mound where they should be safe.'

'Then, when the tide turns we will be able to lean the ship over onto the beach and allow the Captain and his men to complete their repairs.'

'Right men,' he said loudly. 'I want the defences completed before dusk.'

The men shuffled and grumbled as the ex-Varangian guards began their task of organising the crew into a number of teams.

One team would dig the ditch, whilst three teams would search for turf and the appropriate trees, which they would fell, trim and haul back to the camp, whilst other teams of men would dig the post-holes in readiness for the sharpened stakes to be dropped into, and pounded into place.

Aelnoth urged the Captain and his men to redouble their efforts to replace the damaged timbers and scrape the barnacles off the hull.

He also placed three men on the small hills, which overlooked the bay as lookouts.

The camp was thus turned from a place of idleness, into a hive of activity.

Aelnoth spent some time in assisting the Varangian Guards to organise things, and once he was happy that all was going to plan, he took a hunting bow and a quiver of arrows, and walked quietly through the sparse scrubland, in the hope that he would be able to chance upon a wild boar, or a deer, in order give the men a taste of fresh meat for their evening meal.

Noon came and went without any sign of wild game, except for a small covey of quail that rose from below his feet, and disappeared over a small mound before he could raise his bow.

He made his way down a narrow valley towards what looked like a small stream, but when he reached it, he found it to be nothing more than the damp bed of a waterway, which had not seen flowing water for many months.

Deducting that there was probably water downstream; he followed the valley downhill, and did eventually find a dip in the streambed, where there was a small pool of clear water.

He laid his bow beside him as he knelt down, in order to scoop some water up, but froze before he reached the water, as a voice said. 'What have we here?'

Aelnoth slowly straightened his back and looked over his shoulder to see a young man standing some six feet away, holding an expensive looking sword in his right hand.

As Aelnoth slowly rose to his feet, his shocked mind was trying to tell him something, and he suddenly shook his head as he realised what it was.

'You are a Norman?' he gasped in astonishment.

'God's blood. He is quick?' Uttered a sarcastic voice, which came from his left, to reveal another and much older man, who held a large hound on a leash, whilst in his other hand he carried a sturdy spear.

'He is no Lombard my Lord.' Said the elder of the two.

'Apparently not,' said the youngster.

'But the question is. Who is he? And what is he doing hunting on my land?'

Aelnoth had a little trouble following the conversation, for although both of the men were speaking in Norman French, their accents appeared to be mingled with another language, which seemed to alter the pronunciation of many of their words.

'I am named Aelnoth,' he said boldly in Norman French, 'and I have spent some years in the Varangian Guard in Constantinople, and am returning home to England with a small party of men.

'Are you Norman or English?' asked the older of the two.

'I am English.'

The elder of the two cleared his throat and spat into the dust.

'No matter.' Said the young man.

'If he was a Varangian Guard, then he is a proven warrior, and as such, he is probably quite skilled with those two swords.' Nodding his head slightly towards Aelnoth's swords.

He turned and shouted 'Pierre. John. You may join us now,' and two men rose from hiding, and took the arrows from their bows, as they casually ambled down the slope towards Aelnoth and the two Normans.

'Come.' Said the young man as he turned and commenced to lead the way down the valley.

He slowed his pace a little until he walked alongside Aelnoth.

'I am Herman,' he said, 'and I am the legitimate son and Heir of Lord Robert, who is the Lord of this part of Italy, as well as being the Duke of Normandy.'

'Well met Lord Herman,' said Aelnoth.

'I am called Aelnoth, and I am the only son of an English Lord who held sway in the old Kingdom of Mercia before you Normans came.'

'Well met Lord Aelnoth.' Said Herman in a civil tone.

'Is your Sire still alive?'

'He disappeared.'

'Oh.'

'Where are the rest of your men?' he asked.

Aelnoth ignored the fact that this young man either knew or had surmised that there were 'other men,' and answered.

'At the moment they are on the beach, although how long they will wait for me is in the lap of the God's.'

'How many are there?'

'A full ships crew.' He answered, for he was not quite sure if he was to be a captive or a guest of this young Lord.

'Are they all Varangians?'

'Quite a few, but of course the Captain and his helmsman are mere seamen.' He answered carefully.

Herman turned his face towards Aelnoth and with a wry smile he said. 'You give nothing away my friend, and that is to the good, for it tells me that you are not a fool.'

'I know that you are unsure as to whether or not you will be welcomed in the Hall of my Father as a friend or as a prisoner, but that is for my Father to decide.'

'In the meantime, I will offer you my hand in friendship, and you will know that my offer is genuine, for you will, no doubt have noticed that I have allowed you to retain your weapons, and have not placed a guard upon you.'

He removed the suede glove from his right hand and held it towards Aelnoth.

Aelnoth did likewise and found Herman's grip to be strong and friendly.

The old hunter with the large hound led the way onto the plain, and relaxed a little, for he was pleased to be free from the valleys where his Lord preferred to hunt, and he felt much safer with the vista of the flat countryside that now lay before them.

He relaxed even more and smiled happily to himself as he envisaged his comely wife and the taste of the roast lamb, which she had promised him on his return.

He did not see or hear, and probably never felt the two arrows, which thudded into his chest, and propelled him backwards onto the very feet of Lord Herman.

Aelnoth's reaction was speedier than the rest of the party, and he dived towards Herman and pushed him to the ground, behind a large ant-hill, a mere heartbeat before a second shower of arrows zipped through the empty space where Aelnoth and Herman had been, and sped on to slay the remaining Normans.

Aelnoth peered around the ant-hill, and saw no less than ten men rise from behind tufts of tall grass.

The men discarded their bows and brandished a variety of weapons, and screaming their war cries, they ran towards the two survivors.

Aelnoth glanced down at Herman who was still lying down behind the ant-hill.

'Up. Herman. Up.' He repeated to the prone figure, who looked up into the face of his erstwhile prisoner as he leapt to his feet.

The speediest, thus probably the youngest of the attackers, and again, possibly the most inexperienced of them, reached Aelnoth first.

Aelnoth stepped forward two paces and caught the man unawares, plunging his sword into the mans belly and withdrawing it from the dying man whose speed drove him past Aelnoth into Herman, who fell in a tangle with the dying man.

Cursing loudly, Herman heaved the man's body off him and scrambled to his feet.

Aelnoth had no time to look at the dying man before two other attackers faced him and jostled one another in their eagerness to get at him, and it was that slight moment of hesitation, which gave Aelnoth the tiny advantage he needed, and he wielded his two swords, sending both of his assailant's to the ground with a flurry of hacks and parries that not only caused their faces to look shocked as they fell to the ground, but also caused a gasp of astonishment from Herman who had, as yet, not lifted his sword in anger.

Then the final seven attackers launched their attack and assailed the two defenders with such a flurry of blows that they were forced backwards, over the bodies of the slain men, forcing them to retreat up the track that they had recently covered.

One man began to attack Aelnoth on his left hand side, with the obvious intention of attacking him in his rear, but as the man reached the back of Aelnoth. Aelnoth swung the whole of his body around and sliced through the man's neck with a backward slash, and then resumed his confrontation with the rest of the assailants.

Herman managed to slice the right hand off one of his attackers, sending the wounded man backwards, thus allowing Aelnoth to slice through the man's neck as the wounded man gazed down in horror at his missing hand, which lay on the ground in front of him, and the dying man fell still clutching his handless arm.

Aelnoth suddenly felt serenity surge through his body, and he appeared to fall into a kind of a battle trance, which gave him the gift of knowing exactly where and when the next attack would come from, and using his skill of being ambidextrous, he knew that the time of retreating before these villains was over, and took the fight to them, swinging both of his swords like flails.

He cut down one man after another, until the sole survivor threw his sword to the ground and turned tail, and ran as fast as he could, leaving Aelnoth and Herman leaning on their swords as they gasped for breath.

'Oh Mon Dieu. Oh Mon Dieu.' (Oh My God) Uttered the astonished Norman Prince.

Herman dropped onto his knees and with his two hands on the hilt of his sword he raised his face to the heavens and whispered: 'Dieu et mon Droit. (God on my right).

He then rose and placed his hand on the shoulder of Aelnoth.

'The Lord God, Jesus Christ sent you to me, for there is no doubt that this day that you have saved my life.'

'My friend.' He continued as he stood a mere handsbreadth away from Aelnoth and gazed directly into his eyes, as if he was searching for something.

'My friend. My friend,' he repeated.

'No matter what my Father says when we meet him. I shall inform him that you are to be unharmed.'

'Nay. You are to be rewarded, and given the orders of a Knighthood.'

He was about to continue when the rumble of horsemen caused the ground to shake, as a large group of riders appeared and spurred their mounts towards them.

'More enemies?' queried Aelnoth as he stooped to retrieve his bow.

'No my friend,' said Herman as a wide grin spread across his young face.

'These are no Lombard's.'

'They are Normans,' and he walked forward to meet them.

Aelnoth lost sight of him as a swirling cloud of horsemen engulfed him, emerging a little later astride a grey stallion, which he rode slowly towards Aelnoth, accompanied by his horsemen.

The riders were an array of battle-hardened veterans, who carried dents and holes on their well-worn armour and shields.

Herman rode up to Aelnoth, whilst his horsemen formed a silent line some yards away and stared this stranger who, according to their leader, had slain no less than eight out of the nine men whose bodies lay strewn about the scene of the battle.

'Rupert,' he shouted. 'Your mount for my friend here.'

'You can jump up behind Gistard.' He added.

*   *   *

Aelnoth mounted the horse and was about to follow Lord Herman and his men when he suddenly reined his mount in.

'Hold.' He said loudly.

Prince Herman, who had already spurred his horse into a canter, pulled his own mount to a skidding halt, causing a number of his followers some confusion as they too attempted to halt their own eager mounts.

'What's wrong?' he shouted.

'Nothing is wrong my Lord,' shouted Aelnoth.

'But I am rather reluctant to follow you to meet your father, for if I do so, then my friends may well think that I am dead, and they will sail home to England without me.'

'Ah. Quite right. Quite right.' Said Herman, who then shouted to one of his men.

'John. I want you to ride to the bay and find the ship.'

'When you have done so, then you may inform the Captain and his men that their Lord and Master are accompanying me to my Father. Lord Robert of Normandy.'

Aelnoth held his hand up in order to prevent the messenger spurring his horse in order to carry out his Master's wishes.

'Not so my Lord,' he said.

'I think that my friends could think it a ruse, and may well not believe your man.'

'They might well think it a trap and will set sail all the speedier.'

' I shall have to return in person, and then, with your permission, I will order the Captain to sail around the bay, in order to meet with your goodself and your esteemed Father in his Capitol.'

'So be it my friend.' Said Herman with a wry smile.

'And myself and a dozen of my burly lads will accompany you, in order to protect you on your way to your ship, and then we will be on hand, should we meet any more unsavoury characters on the sea.'

Before Aelnoth could object, Herman added. 'I fancy a pleasant sea voyage home, rather than sitting upon this bony Destrier for another long hot day.'

He singled out a number of men, and followed by them, he urged his steed towards Aelnoth.

'Lead the way,' he said jovially, and spurred his horse, leaving Aelnoth sitting on his own horse, facing the wrong way.

Herman immediately sent two of his men ahead in order to ensure that they did not ride into any trouble, and rode alongside Aelnoth for most of the afternoon, chatting in a friendly way to the ever-cautions Aelnoth, who answered all of his questions, albeit in a way that he considered to be non-committal, for he did not really want to spend too much time in Italy, as it was getting rather late in the summer, and his previous disastrous experience of autumn gales at sea, had given him a genuine reason not to repeat the performance.

Aelnoth heard the horns sounding their warnings, long before they reached the beach, which gave him a feeling of satisfaction, as well as the knowledge that not only the ship and his men were still there, but also that the sentries had spotted his approach and had sounded the alarms.

They found the two scouts waiting for them at the beach.

The beach itself was deathly quiet, but Aelnoth could see a number of the crew on board the ship with bows in their hands, and shields and weapons nearby.

The completed 'Marching camp,' bristled with men and weapons, all anxious to see if the mounted men who had appeared on 'their' beach would turn out to be friends or enemies.

Aelnoth urged his mount forward and held his right hand in the air, for he recalled one of his father's sayings, for he had often said that, 'a friendly arrow can make you just as dead as an arrow from a foeman.'

'It is Lord Aelnoth,' came the shout from one of the men on the ship, and his statement was followed by a series of cheers, which were quickly taken up by the men who manned the 'Marching camp.'

But it was not until Aelnoth reached the ship, and had assured the men that it was not a ruse, and he was not a prisoner, that the men began to jump down from the ship to greet him.

A short time later the bulk of the men who were in the 'Marching camp,' opened up the sturdy gateway and began to stream out to greet him, loudly cheering their noisy welcome.

Magnus was the first man to meet him, and as Aelnoth dismounted, he clapped him on the shoulder and said. 'Some of the men were getting concerned about your safety and thought that you had been slain or taken captive, but of course I had no doubts that you were fine, for who in their right minds would tackle 'Aelnoth two swords.' 'The White Wizard?'

Herman had also dismounted and walked up to them.

'What's this about a White Wizard?' he asked.

'Tis nought but a joke.' Said Aelnoth.

'Not so,' intervened Magnus.

'This man here is the most famous and well loved man ever to live in Constantinople.'

'He called on our Lord Jesus Christ, who sent floods and thunderbolts to sweep away an army of two hundred thousand heathens.'

'Tush,' said Aelnoth. 'It was just a storm that happened to come at an opportune moment.'

'Rubbish,' snorted Magnus in a good-natured way. 'This man is a saint.'

'That's what he is.'

Herman made no comment. He merely glanced towards Aelnoth, but there was a look on his face, which Aelnoth had not previously seen, and it was a look that he could not make up his mind whether Herman's face portrayed confusion, or perhaps fear, or even a little awe, or perhaps, Aelnoth thought, it might be suspicion.

Herman noticed the confusion on the face of Aelnoth and said, as if to chase the suspicions from both himself and Aelnoth.

'So these are your crew of cutthroats eh?'

'I do not see many Varangians amongst them.'

'Oh we do have a few with us, but most of the men are freed slaves who are escorting me to England.'

'Freed slaves,' said Herman with a shake of his head. 'How novel.'

'Who are the women?' he asked, and then half whispered as they approached her.

'They are both very beautiful.' He added with a glint in his eye.

'This is Nike, who is the wife of my good friend Magnus,' said Aelnoth.'

Nike, who on her approach, had heard her master's remark, and rushed up to him, and flung her arms around Aelnoth's neck and kissing him on his cheek.

'Thank the good lord that you are safe, my Lord,' she gushed.

'Magnus and I were beginning to fear for your life.'

'Nike,' Said Herman. 'That is the name of a Greek Goddess, is it not?'

'It is indeed,' said Aelnoth, 'and I think that she was well named, don't you agree?'

'Yes, she is,' answered Herman reluctantly, and turned his face away from the pair as if he had accepted the fact that this was one plum that he could not sink his teeth into.

'And the other?' as he pointed to the approaching form of Ingrid.

'Ah,' said Aelnoth. 'This is my wife Ingrid.' And almost immediately regretted telling a lie, for although he realised that if he told this young Norman prince that she was his wife, as such, she should be safe from his clutches, and would not be treated as a slave or a peasant, to be preyed upon by a man of his rank. On the other side of the coin, as his Wife, and IF this young Prince actually fell for her beauty, it could raise all sorts of very difficult questions.

Aelnoth held the hands of both Ingrid and Nike as he approached the Captain and asked. 'Is the Dolphin repaired and ready to sail?'

Herman appeared to have been deterred from the maidens and accompanied Aelnoth to the ship.

'She is my Lord, and we await your order.'

'Good. Load the provisions and storage chests.'

'Already on board my Lord.'

'Even better,' said Aelnoth with a smile.

'The tide is in my Lord,' said the Captain. 'We are ready when you are.'

'Well done Captain.'

'Get the men aboard.'

As the men began to board the Dolphin, Herman organised his own men so that four of them would make their way home overland with the horses, whilst the remainder of his men would accompany him on board the Dolphin.

By mid-day they were half a mile off the coast, cruising along with the blessing of a stiff southerly wind.

They passed through the straits of Messina and gazed towards the coast of Sicily, where the mountain of Etna spewed plumes of black smoke high into the clear blue sky.

The Captain skilfully navigated his way through the maze of small islands and rocky outcrops, safely mooring the Dolphin in the small harbour of Scylla.

'That is the latest of my Fathers Fortress's.' Said Herman as he pointed to a gleaming white fortress, which was situated on a hilltop, overlooking the town.

'He builds them everywhere he goes.' He added almost nonchantly.

Aelnoth and the rest of the men had already seen the Fortress, and gazed in awe at the massive stone structure, which sat majestically astride the highest hill, dominating the area.

'Aelnoth said quietly to Magnus who was standing alongside him.

'Just like they did in England.'

'Aye. The bastards.' Whispered Magnus as, he nodded and returned his gaze to the citadel on the hilltop.

The bay and the shoreline were crowded with all manner of craft.

They were immediately met by a squad of ten guards, who strode angrily towards this impudent Captain who had docked his old trading ship at the pier without their permission.

They abruptly halted when they recognised the tall figure of Lord Herman, as he leapt nimbly onto the dock.

'My Lord.' Uttered the shocked leader, at the unexpected appearance of the son of Earl Robert, who had been the last person in the world who he had would have expected to be aboard an old trading ship.

He dropped to one knee, saying 'My apologies, my Lord. I did not see you.'

'No matter,' said the smiling Herman.

'I thought that I may just enjoy a cruise in this lovely ship with my good friend Aelnoth here.'

'Follow me my friends,' said Herman to Aelnoth and Magnus as he strode forward, followed by his own men at arms.

'Come,' said Aelnoth as he beckoned Nike and Ingrid to join them, and both of the girls walked demurely a pace behind him, as was the Norman custom.

Before he left, Aelnoth turned to the crew, saying. 'I shall leave you my good Captain and my valiant Varangians in charge, but non other than the Captain himself must leave the ship until I return.'

He called one of the senior Varangian guards over to him and said quietly. 'You and your fellow guards must guard the ship whilst I am gone, and make sure that no-one interferes with my crates.'

The Guard saluted and said in a grave voice. 'You can trust me my Lord.'

'No one will touch them, or anything else that is on the ship.'

Herman and his escort, including Aelnoth, Magnus and the two ladies, who were provided with mounts, and rode regally up the hill to the castle, passing through the open gateway and under the portcullis, which was guarded by four burly looking guards.

The courtyard was a hive of activity with male and female servants, dressed in their colourful livery, rushing hither and thither, whilst at least two thirds of the open spaces were taken up with men at arms, who were training with an assortment of weapons, including a clutch of archers who were shooting at round targets with the strangest type of cross-bow's that Aelnoth had ever seen.

Grooms rushed over to take the horses, allowing Aelnoth and his party to follow Herman through the throng, and up a wide flight of stone steps, leading to a large iron studded doorway, which was guarded by another pair of stern sentries.

The guards saluted as Herman sped past them into a wide hallway, and strode along a brightly lit passage way until he reached yet another large iron studded door, where he halted for a moment in order to thump on the door with the pummel of his knife, and without waiting for an answer, he opened the door and walked boldly in.

Aelnoth and Magnus, closely escorted by the demure figures of Nike and Ingrid followed the Prince of Normandy into the room.

The opulent furniture of the room and its decorations were so vivid that the astounded Magnus nearly bumped into the stationary figure of Herman, who had abruptly halted some ten or twelve feet from a huge polished table, around which a number of noblemen were bending, as they studied some papers and a large map.

Herman dropped to one knee and glanced behind, as if he was ordering the two Englishman to kneel, and although he did not say a word, they immediately took the hint and obeyed.

'My Lord,' he said boldly to a man who emerged from a small cluster of men, and who was the exact replica of Herman, albeit a man of middle years, whose fair hair was speckled with white, and whose girth was somewhat larger than that of his son.

'Herman,' the man roared with delight, as he literally threw the papers, which he had been holding, onto the table and strode forward to greet his son.

'Thank the good Lord you have returned safe and well.'

'On your feet boy,' he roared. 'On your feet.'

'Tell me.' He asked. 'Did you put the rebels to flight?'

'No, My Lord,' answered Herman, but then he hesitated a little, which was so unlike a man who had never known defeat, and who prided himself on his skill at arms, as well as his forthright manner.

'Well, yes, in a manner of speaking.' He added.
'Make your mind up boy,' stormed Robert.
'Either you did or you didn't.'
'Which is it to be?'
'We had a minor skirmish with them my lord, and put them to flight, but they split up into a number of warbands, so we were forced to give up the chase, as I was reluctant to split up my force and leave our men open to attack.'

'Oh,' said the Father glumly.

'Then we still have bands of rebels in the south, destroying my manors?' and he turned to rejoin the men who were still clustered around the table.

He paused and looked towards Aelnoth, Magnus, Ingrid and Nike who stood behind Herman.

'Who are they?' asked Lord Robert curtly,

But before Herman could answer he continued. 'They look like they are from Constantinople and if that is so, then they are not welcome at my court.'

'Not so father,' answered Herman boldly.

'They are English.' Conveniently ignoring Nike, as he knew that she was Greek.

'English.' Roared Duke Robert.

'ENGLISH!!' He bellowed again.

'What makes you think that I should welcome English serfs into my Hall?' he roared.

'Firstly my dear Father,' said Herman as sarcastically as he dared, without fear of either being disinherited or having his head hewn from his body. 'They are not serfs.'

'Both of them are the sons of Lords, and this young man,' as he turned and placed his hand on Aelnoth's shoulder. 'Slew eight Lombard's, whilst I, your son, who is a prince of this realm, and although perhaps I should not say so. I am also a warrior of some note, could only manage to better one man.'

'Father.' He said loudly, so that not only his Father could hear him, but in order that every Lord, Lady and servant in the hall could hear.

'Aelnoth slew eight men who had already killed my servants and men-at-arms, and who would undoubtedly have slain me.'

Earl Robert halted, and remained where he was for a several seconds, whilst every living thing in the Hall, including the four hounds, who lay before the fire, froze.

He turned to face his son, and on seeing the determined look on the face of his firstborn, he turned his gaze to the rather grubby young Englishman who stood some six or eight feet behind Herman.

'Eight men you say?' asked Lord Robert.

'Eight.' Confirmed his son.

'Were they drunk?'

'No. My Lord.'

'Perhaps they were inexperienced youngsters or men in their dotage?'

'Neither Father,' answered Herman.

'They were all hardened warriors who were in their prime.'

'I see.' Said Lord Robert in a quiet voice.

He proudly strode the few paces back to his son and stood close to him, saying in a quieter voice, in order that the two of them would be the only ones in the room who would be able to hear his words.

'What would you have me do for him?'

'Bestow a citadel or a province upon him?' He said sarcastically.

'Indeed, I have lords in this very room who have served me since before you were born, and who have performed deeds of valour, and they are still no more than lackeys to me, so why should I honour him?'

'Indeed, even if he did save your life, and I do have some trouble in believing that. He is still a bloody Englishman, and as such, he is no more than a serf belonging to a conquered people, so I do not feel inclined to furnish him with a Citadel or a Province.'

'I have given him my oath that you would honour him with a knighthood.' Said Herman loudly, in order that the whole congregation could hear.

Aelnoth could not hear the Duke's reply, for it was literally hissed into the ear of his son, but he could see, as those men who stood near could also see, that the face of the Duke of Normandy had altered from its normally colour, to a colour that resembled the breast of a Robin.

Duke Robert realised that he was in danger of being out-manoeuvred by his son, and forced himself to smile and relax his arms a little, un-clenching his fists and flexing his stiff fingers.

'Ah my son,' he said loudly.

'I see that the Grand Master has been out-played by the novice Chess student, and I note with great pleasure that my boy has at last, come of age.'

'If I am to agree with you, and make this young man one of my knights, then I have nought to lose and everything to gain, for in doing so, I shall please my own heir, who will have no reason to gainsay me, and I shall be gaining a Knight who is, by all accounts, a warrior who any man would be proud to call friend in a battle.'

'No time like the present.' Said his son loudly.

The Duke gazed at his son with eyes that glared with venom, whilst his face belied his true feelings and smiled something of a forced and a false smile.

'Kneel.' He growled.

Aelnoth was rather stunned at the sudden turn of events, and as Duke Robert walked the few paces towards him and drew his sword with a flurry of bravado.

Aelnoth hesitatingly went down onto his one knee, and watched apprehensively as the Duke speedily brought his sword down and touched him on first his left shoulder and then his right, saying loudly. 'Arise Sir Aelnoth.'

'You are now a Knight, and one of my men belonging to the Royal Duchy of Normandy.'

'You cannot just be a Knight.' He said sarcastically.

'You must be a Knight of somewhere.'

'Where are you from?' He growled.

'I came from a small village called 'Wentnor, My Lord.' Stuttered Aelnoth.

'Never heard of it.' Snorted the Duke.

'No matter.' He said nonchantly.

'Kneel again.' He snarled.

'This time, we shall do it properly.' And he drew his sword again and touched Aelnoth's left and right shoulder.' Quite a lot harder, or so thought the kneeling young man.

'Arise Sir Aelnoth of Wentnor.'

He replaced his sword into its scabbard with a loud clang.

'My scribe will give you the necessary scroll and a ring, which will verify your new status.' He said, as he abruptly turned his back on them and returned to his Barons at the table.

As Aelnoth rose to his feet to receive a few polite cheers and an isolated clap or two from the audience, and an odd man here and there shouting 'Bravo'.

Ingrid leapt forward, flinging her arms around his neck and smothering his face with kisses.

Herman smiled and congratulated him, and Magnus slapped him on his shoulder.

'Congratulations my friend,' he said.

'Your new title should give us free passage throughout the duchy of Normandy, should we need to pass that way.'

'And England.' added Aelnoth, who was still a little shocked, as the realisation of what had just taken place slowly entered his brain.

'England,' said Herman, who was standing beside Aelnoth, 'Now I am not too sure if my Father's charter will carry too much weight there, for he and my uncle Rufus have drifted apart, and each have their eyes on the others Kingdoms.'

'No matter,' said Aelnoth.

'Your Fathers charter must be a good thing to have, rather than a thing not to have.'

Herman shook his head and moved away muttering something about the weird way that Aelnoth spoke the Norman tongue.

Aelnoth, Magnus, Ingrid and Nike were ushered out of the Hall, and after a long walk through corridors, and through a number of ornately furnished rooms, they were escorted through a small door, which led into a wide courtyard, where a large and imposing house stood at the end of a stone walkway.

Their two escorts left them in the house where no less than six servants bowed before them, and quietly introduced themselves to the four awed newcomers.

There were more than enough bedrooms to accommodate them, and Aelnoth chose a large room, with panoramic views over the harbour.

After they had eaten their evening meal and they had enjoyed a glass or two of red wine, they parted and made their way to their individual sleeping quarters.

Aelnoth undressed before the open window and strode onto the stone balcony dressed in a thin wrap, which covered the lower half of his body.

He spent a long time studying the assortment of ships that lay at anchor.

He stretched his arms and made his way to the bed, and as he drew back the sheets he was shocked and yet delighted to see the beautiful face of Ingrid smiling up at him.

'What? Why?' he stammered, but was interrupted as she stretched her arms up at him and said. 'I just couldn't sleep in that big room all by myself, and I knew that you wouldn't mind if I just snuggled up with you.'

Without another word, he joined her, and although she did indeed snuggle up to him, the snuggling blossomed into much more, as they both knew that it would.

It was not the most restful night that Aelnoth had ever had, but it was certainly one of the most enjoyable, for although he had dallied with a number of ladies in Constantinople, he found that Ingrid possessed a passion that almost consumed both of them, and when daylight eventually came, he gazed lovingly at the beautiful face of this English beauty who lay beside him.

As he lay on his side and looked at her, he found it hard to believe that this beautiful maiden was the same scrawny child, who he had seen at her father's table in Pitchford, mourning the death of the young lord of that place, what seemed to be a lifetime ago?

He mused not only at the startlingly beautiful women, who she had blossomed into, but also at her bravery and determination that had caused her to follow him, and remain chaste and pure for him, over the past seven, or was it eight years?

'She is the girl that I shall marry.' He said aloud, and as he looked down again to her, he found, much to his surprise, that she had wakened and was looking up into his own eyes with tears oozing out of her own blue eyes.

'So, you will marry me, will you?' she said in a husky sleep-ridden voice that contained a hint of doubt in it, for she was unsure that he had intended her to hear what he had said.

'Indeed I will.'

'If you will have me.' He added.

'Of course I will, you silly man.'

'It has been my dream and my intention since first I saw you all those years ago in Pitchford.'

'And when do you. 'Lord Aelnoth.' 'The White Wizard, two swords' intend to marry this lowly peasant girl?' she asked with a hint of suspicion in her voice.

'As soon as we reach Mercia. And less of your sarcasm of this White Wizard, two swords business.'

'Do you remember my father's house in Pitchford?' she asked.

'Of course.'

'And do you remember seeing me at the table?'

'Well, to be honest, I remember seeing a small flock of children at the table, but I did not really recognise you when you followed me, and met me half way across England.

'I know.' She said.

'But what you probably don't know is that when I was sitting at the table, I did look up through the veil of my hair, and I saw you. But, if it makes any sense, I didn't see you as the hungry boy who had come into our house, seeking food and shelter.'

'What I saw was a proven warrior standing, triumphant on a hill, bathed in light.'

'Just as you were described to me after your victory over the Seljuk Turks, when you returned to Constantinople.'

'Really?'

'Really!'

'Now that is weird.'

'Indeed, and that is why I followed you.' She cooed as she gazed up into his eyes.

'Not because I was unbelievably handsome then?' he said with a smile.

'No.'

'Neither, I will warrant, was it because I was immensely strong?'

'No. In fact you were not immensely strong at that time.'

'It seems that we were destined to be together.' She said.

'It would seem so.' He agreed quietly.

He placed a gentle kiss on her cheek and rose from the bed, ready to take on the world.

Although life was pleasant at the villa, and they wanted for nothing, as their servants saw to their every need.

The two men, Nike and Ingrid spent many sunny afternoons exploring the town and the surrounding areas, spending many pleasant hours at a small Inn near the docks, sipping the local wines, as they watched the comings and goings of merchant and warships.

Aelnoth visited the Dolphin daily, and eventually relented, giving the Captain permission to allow one third of the crew to alternate, and spend one afternoon of each day in the town, providing they returned to the ship before nightfall,

Herman occasionally joined them and delighted in showing Aelnoth and his (wife) some of the more unusual parts of the growing city and its surrounding areas, especially the small castles, which were being constructed in all of the surrounding townships.

Aelnoth whispered to Magnus. 'Just like the bastards did in England. Hold the natives down. Don't give them the freedom or the opportunity to revolt.'

However, due to the fact that he was an honoured guest of Herman and his Father, he did not voice his opinions to them, and showered them with compliments (many of which were quite genuine) regarding their conquest and occupation of most of the southern parts of Italy.

Herman joined him one Sunday afternoon as Aelnoth was leaving the Docks, and as they walked together up the slope into the town, Aelnoth broached a subject that had long been on his mind.

'I have been buying up a few provisions of late, and will resume my voyage home as soon as possible.' He said.

'Yes. I know.' Answered Herman.

'My Father has spies everywhere, and he is aware that you are preparing to leave.'

'Does he object?'

'No. I don't think that he has any objection, although he did mention to me that he would prefer your good self and your men to be on his side, if we were to go to war.'

'But as every thing seems to be quiet at the moment, except for a few raids from a couple of small groups of Lombard rebels, he has no real need of you and your men, so I suggest that if you do intend to go, then now might be as good a time as any.'

'Thank you my friend.' Said Aelnoth.

'I shall inform the Captain to leave with the tide tomorrow afternoon.'

'I shall be at the dock and see you off.' Said Herman, 'and I shall forever be in your debt for saving my life.'

*   *   *

The Dolphin pulled away on the high tide without ceremony, and the only activities on the quayside were the usual layabouts and a gang of slaves who were unloading a recently arrived merchantman.

Aelnoth, Magnus and Ingrid gazed at the receding docks, and were shocked to see the reasonably quiet docks suddenly turned into a state of chaos, as a small band of horsemen spurred their steeds down the street, and onto the wooden dock, making the quay tremble as they galloped along the wooden planking, scattering the slaves in all directions as they sped towards the end of the quay.

The leading horseman was waving his hands in the air and shouting something, although he was too far away to be heard, and as he neared the end of the pier he reigned in his mount a few feet before the pier ended, but two of his escorts failed to do so, and crashed into him, sending themselves and their leader, who was still astride his horse, tumbling over into the foaming waves.

Three horses surfaced and immediately began to make their way to the shore but it was some time before the three human heads appeared, and as they did so, one of them waved his hand furiously in the air towards the Dolphin, and bellowed more unheard words.

'That looks like Herman.' Said Aelnoth.

'Indeed it does.' Answered Magnus with a smile. 'Indeed it does.

CHAPTER 26

'That is Sardinia over there.' Said the Captain.

'Why don't we spend the night there?' asked Aelnoth.

'That would be unwise. Too many Pirates.'

'Are there any other islands where we can spend the night?'

'No. At least there are non that are close enough.'

'The eastern shore is riddled with nests of pirates.' He added.

'We will have to drop the night anchor out here, and hope for the best.'

It was an unpleasant night, for as the night progressed, so did the wind, and with the wind came the waves, which became larger and larger, so that by the time that dawn had broken, the Dolphin had dragged her anchor to within quarter of a mile off the coast of Sardinia.

Fortunately the waves were too savage for any Pirates to launch their vessels, so the Dolphin was in no immediate danger from them, but the Captain was very concerned about the ship being forced further inshore, where a savage ridge of rocks protruded a hundred or so yards from the shore.

'Oars out.' He shouted, 'and as soon as you start to row, you men there. Haul in the anchor.'

With the anchor up and the men pulling on the oars, the Dolphin slowly edged away from the looming rocks and headed for the open sea.

By midday the men were exhausted, forcing the Captain to order them to cease rowing and rely solely upon the sail, as he slowly tacked the vessel away from the treacherous shoreline and out into the sea.

Sometime around the middle of the afternoon the clouds retreated to the east, allowing a weak sun to penetrate the gloom, and when the wind started to blow westwards, all the men breathed a sigh of relief as the Dolphin made its way majestically in a westward direction, up and down the long troughs.

The evening was dry and sunny as the Captain steered the ship into a secluded cove, where he beached the craft high on a shingle beach.

The weary men lit a number of fires from the driftwood, which abounded on the beach, and enjoyed their first hot meal for more than two days.

Aelnoth allotted sentry duties to six unhappy men whilst the remainder of the crew enjoyed a dry and restful night,

For the following six days they made their way westwards, sailing within sight of the coast, spending the nights in the secluded coves, which the Captain's unerring skill and knowledge of the coastline seemed to find at will.

Two days later the darkening storm clouds forced the Captain to steer the Dolphin into the small harbour of Gibraltar.

'It is one of the most dangerous ports on this coastline.' He said to Aelnoth, 'but we cannot possibly pass through the straits in this weather, and this is the only protected harbour for the next fifty miles.'

'What makes you say it is dangerous?' asked Aelnoth.

'It looks like a nice little place from here.'

'You will see what I mean once we have docked,' said the Captain.

'I have only been here once before, and then it was full of cutthroats and Pirates from both sides of the Mediterranean, and almost half of my crew were slaughtered or taken to the slave blocks.' He added grimly.

The Dolphin gently docked alongside the jetty, which contained three other vessels, which, by their look, all appeared to be from the eastern shores of the Mediterranean.

A small crowd of grubby men gathered along the quayside, and Aelnoth noticed that all of them were heavily armed with a wide variety of weapons.

He ordered his men to don their chain mail, so that they would be ready to meet any trouble that may arise.

Aelnoth jumped onto the wooden jetty and shouldered his way through the small crowd of men, who reluctantly moved out of his way, and walked unharmed out of the crush and along the walkway towards the small town.

Two men sat on an upturned boat at the end of the jetty, and as he approached them, the larger of the two rose to his feet and stood in the centre of the walkway, with his hands on his hips and his legs akimbo.

'Who are you to walk along my jetty without my permission?' he snarled in one of the worst Norman/French accents that Aelnoth had ever heard.

'And who are you to ask such a question?' Said Aelnoth quietly.

'I own the bloody thing?'

'Then may I walk on your precious pier?' said Aelnoth, in the most amiable tone that he could muster, for although he was not looking for trouble, he literally detested bullies and did not believe the man, when he had claimed that the pier belonged to him.

'You may not. Unless you give me the contents of one of those chests you have aboard your ship,'

'You must be jesting.'

'You will see who is jesting you silly young puppy,' said the large man, whose hands flew to the dagger and sword that nestled in his belt.

The second man rose to his feet, and as he walked over to join his friend, he too produced two weapons.

They both stood facing Aelnoth.

'Last chance you silly young fool.' Snarled the large man.

'A chest of silver or your life,' and as if they were joined at the hip, they both advanced the few paces towards Aelnoth, who stood facing them with his hands close to the two swords, which lay snugly in their fleece lined scabbards.

'What makes you think that I have anything of value in the chests? Asked Aelnoth, hoping to avoid a confrontation.

'It's a ship from Constantinople, aint it? And it is carrying men who were in the Varangian Guard by the looks of things, and they are always weighed down with the silver that they have hoarded over the years, so what else could be in those chests of yours?' He snarled as he advanced towards Aelnoth.

The two men could not believe what happened next, for in the space of two heartbeats, they had both been disarmed, and stood clutching their wounded right hands, whilst this harmless looking young man stood before them with each of his two swords prodding their necks.

'Permission to use your pier or your lives?' asked Aelnoth with a smile, as he thrust his swords a mere hairsbreadth into their necks.

'It. It is not really our pier,' stammered the smaller of the two, as he attempted to back away from the sharp blade that simply followed him backwards, pace for pace.

'We were but jesting.' He added.

'The pier is free for anyone to use, providing they are not Raiders or Pirates.'

'Go.' Said Aelnoth as he retracted his swords from their necks, leaving a trickle of blood, which seeped from the barely visible scratches that had been made on the necks of both of the men.

'But if you give me any further trouble, I shall set my men upon you, and they are all berserkers, and I can assure you that they will not be as friendly as I have been.'

The big man scowled.

He was furious that this young fledgling had humiliated him so easily, and struggled with himself not to open his mouth and anger this youngster any further.

Aelnoth strode past them and walked into the huddle of houses and shacks that called itself the town of Gibraltar.

He made his way along the main thoroughfare where Blacksmiths, Tanners and an assortment of shops plied their trade, and was eventually directed towards a man who sold the sort of provisions that he needed.

After a lot of hard bargaining, he managed to purchase enough drink and foodstuffs to see him and his shipmates through the straits of Gibraltar, and at least half of the way home, and although he gave the dealer a silver piece, in order to seal the deal, he refused to pay the full amount agreed for the goods, until they had been delivered to the Dolphin some time the following morning.

As darkness fell, he allotted half of the men to stay awake and guard the ship and its cargo for half of the night, whilst the other half of the crew slept until one hour past midnight, when they would be relieved their shipmates, who would stand guard until daylight.

Aelnoth remained awake until long after the exchange had been made, but weariness eventually overcame him, and he retired to his bed an hour or two before dawn.

A hand that gently slapped his face roused him, after what seemed to be minutes after he had settled down, causing him to open his eyes, to look up into the lovely face of Ingrid.

She put her index finger to her mouth in order to deter him from speaking and put her mouth close to his ear.

'Something knocked the hull beneath my bed.' She whispered.

He rose to his feet and crept along the deck, noting with satisfaction that all of the men who were guarding the Dolphin were awake.

As he past the men he whispered. 'Have you seen anything?'

'Each man answered 'No,' or shook their heads as they continued to gaze into the misty dawn that hinted to the prospects for another blazing hot day.

He reached the rear of the ship where the helmsman was curled up under a sheepskin, and as he was about to turn and return to his own berth, he was amazed to see two hands suddenly appear on the side of the ship.

He rushed the few paces forward and as he did, the dripping wet head of a man appeared between the two hands.

With an angry grunt he dashed forwards and almost without thinking, his sword had appeared in his right hand and was brought down onto the head, cleaving it in two, and leaving the sword embedded in the side of the ship.

Some of the men had seen his action and leapt to their feet, shouting in alarm in order to waken their sleeping shipmates.

For a few moments the deck of the ship was in a state of pandemonium, as men leapt to their feet and attempted to snatch up their weapons and shields, bumping into one another and tripping over the late risers, or some of the storage boxes, which were stacked along the sides of the Dolphin.

More faces appeared along the sides of the ship as more and more men attempted to climb aboard.

But more worrying to Aelnoth, was the large crowd of armed men, who he had just appeared at the end of the pier and were running along the pier towards the ship.

Aelnoth grabbed Ingrid and literally threw her down along the overlap of the ship and covered her with his father's old shield.

'Lie there, and don't move. I will keep an eye on you.'

He left her hidden, and ran along the centre of the ship, calling to a group of his men who were not engaged in repelling the raiders.

'With me men,' he shouted.

'Follow me onto the pier and we will tackle this lot.' And he jumped onto the pier and stood as he waited for a group of his men to join him.

As the attackers on the pier neared him, Aelnoth noted with a grim shrug that the man, who led the attackers, was none other than the large man who he had tangled with on the previous day.

If it is at all possible, men should not run into battle, for if they do, then they may well reach their enemies either tired or out of breath, and either, or both of these factors could well put them at a disadvantage when they eventually met with their foes.

These attackers were probably men used to bullying seamen out of their wages, and men who spent a lot of their time drinking in the taverns of this seedy little town, or else, merely sitting on the sea-front idling their time away, and waiting for their next victims to arrive.

They were not especially fit or battle hardened, as were Aelnoth and most of his men, and the attackers did arrive out of breath to do battle with Aelnoth and his ex-Varangian Guardsmen.

The leader plunged into the fight hacking to his right and to his left with a huge sword, and literally swatted one man to the ground with his small round metal shield.

Aelnoth saw the move and recognised the man who lay dazed on the ground as non other than Roger the Norman.

Aelnoth quickly stepped forward and prevented the attackers' sword from reaching the shaking head of Roger, with a blocking movement that jarred his arm and sent bolts of pain up through his shoulder and into his head.

'You again,' snarled the man as he raised his sword to attack Aelnoth.

Aelnoth took half a step backwards to allow the sword to slash through thin air a foot away from his neck, and then he counter-attacked with both of his swords, assailing the man with a whirlwind of strokes, which sliced and cut his large body, completing the task with a thrust that drove his long sword through the neck of his opponent, sending him writhing to the ground in his death throes.

As he helped the still dazed Roger to his feet, who shook his head and said. 'Yet again, you have saved my life.'

'I shall forever be in your debt,' as he shook his head again and plunged back into the fight.

Aelnoth and his men commenced to decimate the attackers, so that within the space of a hundred heartbeats, not one of the attackers remained standing, and all that was left of the large crowd of men who had raced down the pier, were half a dozen men who had turned tail, and were now running back along the pier, leaving their comrades either dead or wounded, as their life's-blood seeped through the wooden planks, to redden the shallow water below.

Aelnoth glanced back at the Dolphin and found most of the crew standing and watching the remaining attackers disappear into the town.

Aelnoth could see at least four of his men lying on the deck, whilst another eight or ten were sitting, and having their wounds attended to by their comrades.

After carrying the four slain men to a pebble beach, the crew erected a large pyre, which Aelnoth lit and sent their spirits to the afterworld, be it Valhalla or Heaven.

The ships provisions, which he had ordered had not arrived by noon, so Aelnoth took a squad of ten men with him, and marched along the pier and up into the town.

He was rather surprised to find the town, which, on his previous visit had been a solemn and practically empty place, was now seething with shops and stalls, which were selling all manner of goods to the crowds of men women and children, who thronged and jostled with one another in their eagerness to purchase goods from the heavily laden stalls.

Aelnoth stopped one of the men who almost bumped into him and asked 'How come there are so many people here today, when on the yesterday, the place was like a ghost town?'

'Ah well,' answered the man.

'Yesterday 'Osterig the cruel' ruled here, but he was slain by the men on the ship from Constantinople, and now we are free to walk the streets without being set upon by him and his men.'

'May his soul rot in hell'? He added, as he spat onto the dusty street.

Aelnoth and his men eventually found the trader with whom he had made a deal for provisioning the Dolphin, but his shop was so busy with customers that Aelnoth was forced to order his men to clear the place, in order to speak with the owner.

After a lot of pushing and grumbling, his men evicted the shoppers and Aelnoth approached the trader, who was furious that his potential customers had been forced to leave.

'What right do you have to evict my customers?' stormed the trader.

'The right of arms.' Snarled Aelnoth, as he drew his Saex from its scabbard.

'And the fact that you and I struck a deal on the yesterday and it is a deal that I expect you to keep.'

'Where are the provisions for my ship?' he growled menacingly.

'Sold my Lord,' squeaked the startled trader as the sharp Saex snipped one of the leather thongs, which held his grubby shirt together.

'The people are paying treble the price that you offered me.' He said feebly.

'Tough,' snarled Aelnoth, for he had no liking for traders such as he.

'I want my provisions, and I want them now.' He snarled.

'Close your shop and get your assistants to load what we agreed onto yonder cart and my men will escort it to the docks.'

'I cannot.' Wept the trader, wringing his hands in despair.

'It has already gone.' He said.

'Edward.' said Aelnoth. 'You take a couple of men and search the back rooms and see what this blaggard has hidden in his storerooms.'

Edward nodded towards to two of his colleagues who followed him through the back door.

They returned within seconds and Edward.

'Tis full of trade goods my Lord.' Said Edward.

'You,' snarled Aelnoth as he faced the trader.

'Go into your store room and have your assistants load my goods onto the cart.' He ordered with a flourish of his Saex.

'And if you tell me any more lies, then I shall slice your fingers off. One by one.'

He then emptied his purse onto the counter saying. 'That is the full amount we agreed on yesterday.'

'Take it and be grateful that I am a lenient man and don't take your head off and load that onto my cart with my goods.

The trader glumly scooped up the silver, and sullenly stood aside as he allowed his two assistants to help load the cart, with the trade goods, which had been agreed on the previous day.

Once the cart had been loaded with casks of fresh water, flagons of wine, barrels of flour and dried meat, Aelnoth, followed by his men began to make their way back to the ship, through the crowded streets.

At the final junction where three streets converged, they were forced to halt, due to the sheer number of citizens who pushed and shoved in their attempt to make their way through the junction.

One of the women recognised Aelnoth, and screamed at the top of her voice. 'It's him. It's the Englishman who slew Osterig.'

The people who heard the women, ceased their pushing and stared at Aelnoth and his men for a moment, but one middle-aged man stepped forward and put the small sackful of bread onto the cart.

'Please take this.' He said as he touched his forehead with his knuckle, as if in homage.

'That's for killing Osterig the cruel, and freeing us from his tyranny.'

Almost by magic. The crowds opened to make way for Aelnoth and his men, and as they passed through the people.

The grateful citizens piled food, beer and wine unto the already heavily laden cart, until it could hold no more.

Nonetheless, the people followed Aelnoth to the ship, and once the goods had been transferred to the Dolphin, they continued to throw all manner of foodstuffs to the men on the ship, who caught it and stowed it in the holds of the ship.

The Captain edged the Dolphin away from the docks, and steered her into the centre of the channel where the ebbing tide took hold of her, and she glided serenely through the straits and out into the ocean.

A favourable wind drove the ship across the Bay of Biscay and into the English Channel, where, after three days, the majestic white cliffs of Dover shone through the morning mist, heralding that they had reached their destination.

Aelnoth opened one of the six chests, which he had closely guarded during the voyage.

He dragged the chest along the deck and as he came alongside his men, he gave each and every one of them a leather bag.

Once he had reached the Captain and the helmsman he turned to face his men and said. 'Men, we have now reached England, and I now release you from any pledge or debt that you have with me.'

'You are all free men to go wherever you wish.'

'The men cheered and stamped their feet on the deck until the poor Captain begged them to cease, for he was afraid that their continued stamping would damage his precious ship.

'To the Captain I give the ship and two bags of silver, and to the Helmsman I give two bags for his skill and devotion in bringing us safely home.'

'The bags that I have just given you, each contain twenty silver pieces, to do with what you will, although I would caution you not to gamble away such a fortune, for if you lose the small fortune that is in each and every bag, it would bring to nought all that you have fought and bled for over the past years.' (Knowing full well that there were at least four of the crew who were addicted to the dice, and would probably end up either dead or destitute within the next few weeks)

He continued. 'With twenty silver pieces, you could easily purchase a small village, several good farms or even a stately Hall, so I urge you to use it wisely.'

'My thanks for your loyalty and companionship and I wish you all god-speed.'

'My wife Ingrid and myself will make our way to my home shire, which is in the wild lands, bordering Wales, where we hope to make our home.'

'Again I wish you God-speed.'

'Fare you well.'

The men cheered and began to make their way to the front of the ship where the Captain had driven the prow of the Dolphin onto the white pebbly beach

Although most of the crew disembarked in order to stretch their legs, a mere sixteen men and women intended to remain on shore, and these included Magnus and Roger the Norman, five men of the Varangian guard who were oath sworn to Aelnoth, the two Icelanders Ingar and Ivar, and of course Aelnoth himself, Ingrid and Nike.

One man, who had been one of the slaves who the Captain had purchased in Constantinople, who called himself 'Aelfgar of Kendal,' and who purported to be an Anglo Saxon from the north of England, and who declared that he had been taken in battle and sold into slavery over fifteen years ago, but on the several occasions when Aelnoth had spoken to him, Aelfgar had been vague about his origins, and his tongue was not that of the north, causing Aelnoth to suspect that he was a man hiding some deep and dark secret.

Nonetheless, Aelnoth was pleased to have Aelfgar join him, for he had proved to be a good man with the large ornately carved eastern scimitar, which was never far from his right hand.

CHAPTER 27

Aelnoth had been the first man to leap off the Dolphin, and landed on the shingle beach with both of his feet deeply embedded into the pebbles.

He walked a few paces up the beach and fell on his face, burying his face in the wet, rough shingle and stretched his hands.

He grasped two handfuls of pebbles, before he rose to his feet and shouted at the top of his voice.

'I am home. I am home.' He shouted joyfully.

'I have returned safely to Mother England. Just as I said I would.'

A number of the men followed Aelnoth's example and fell on their knees, delighted to be in England again.

Once their belongings had been carried above the high water mark, they waved, as they watched the Dolphin leave the beach, and make its way around the white cliffs, as it headed northwards to the Northlands, where the majority of the crew had been whelped.

'My lord, My Lord.' Said the excited voice of Ingar, who pointed towards the top of the cliffs, where he could see a number of horsemen, sitting upon their mounts and gazing down at them.

'So my hopes that we could land here unseen has come to nought,' said Aelnoth aloud.

'No matter,' said Roger the Norman.

'If they come down then I will talk to them.'

'It will be fine.' He assured them.

Aelnoth dismissed the horsemen out of his mind for a moment as he looked at the six chests and four bundles of belongings, which lay on the sand.

Everyone began to carry as much as they could off the beach, and were on the point of entering into a small valley between two sand dunes, when the ground began to shake as a cavalcade of twenty horsemen appeared a mere one hundred yards away, and thundered towards them.

Aelnoth and his men drew their weapons and waited behind their shields as the horsemen galloped towards them, sending clouds of sand and clods of mud in their wake.

The expected impact did not come as the horsemen skidded to a halt a few feet away from them.

The leader was a middle-aged man, with a large white moustache and long white hair, who was dressed in expensive clothes, and sat proudly astride a shiny black stallion, which screamed 'wealth and status.'

'I am John of Dover.' The man said loudly.'

'Who are you varlets, who land secretly on my beach on this bright sunny day, and not into my port of Dover?'

'I suspect that you think you can escape paying the tax, which all who enter my port must pay?'

Before Aelnoth or Roger could answer, the man continued. 'Seize them.' He spat, 'and we shall see what manner of goods they dare to land on my beach, before I allow you to hang them.'

Half a dozen of his men dismounted, whilst the rest of the horsemen remained on their mounts grinning.

The leader himself had finally noticed Ingrid and Nike who had tactfully remained behind two of Aelnoth's men.

'Ah. Women.' He leered, 'and beauties too.'

'I might not hang them.' He sneered. 'At least, not for a while.' He snarled gleefully.

Two of the Normans approached Aelnoth and were about to grab his arms when, to their horror, they found that each of their necks was suddenly pricked by a razor sharp sword.

'Oh we want to play tough, do we?' said the snarling leader, who dismounted and drew his own sword as he approached Aelnoth, whose two swords lingered at the necks of the two Normans, whilst his steel blue eyes watched their leader strut towards him.

'Sire.' Said Aelnoth. 'We are mere wayfarers who have strayed onto your beach, and are unaware that your town of Dover is nearby, so we will gladly pay our dues to you and be on our way. With your kind permission.' He added with a smile as he withdrew his two swords from the necks of the two men.

'No matter,' said the leader.

'You have trespassed upon my domain, and the penalty for that is death.'

'Seize them.' He hissed again.

Aelnoth took a step backwards and as he held his two swords aloft he said angrily.

'Enough of this niceness. I have given you the lives of your two men, and have eaten more humble pie that I can stomach.'

'My friend here and myself are lords in our own right, and my other friends here are men who have served the Emperor of Constantinople in his Varangian Guard for many years, and as such, we have slain more men that we can remember.'

'If you want a fight, then you shall have one, although I can assure you that neither your goodself, nor any of your men will be alive for more than a few minutes.'

'On the other hand, if you would care to read the parchment that I possess, which is signed by no other than Lord Robert, who is The Duke of Normandy, then I may, just may allow you to live, and return to Dover unharmed.

The man took a pace backwards in alarm, as his fuddled brain tried to assimilate what this stranger had just said, and IF what the man had said turned out to be true.

'Indeed,' he thought. 'Upon reflection, the man himself and the rest of his men did indeed have the look of proven warriors about them, and again, IF what he had just said about 'The Duke of Normandy' was also true, then the stranger had just given him an escape route, as well as a way of saving face in front of his own men, and possibly, a way of not dying here and now on this desolate beach, thus leaving behind all that he had gained since he had deserted his own kind and begun to serve King William.'

'I will see the document?' Said John in a tone of voice that shouted. 'Bravado.'

Aelnoth reached inside his shirt and brought out the parchment, which was wrapped in kidskin, in order to protect it from inclement weather and seawater.

John the friendly calmly took the parchment and studied it carefully.

Looking at the seal and the signature several times before he grunted and handed it back to Aelnoth.

John sheathed his sword and with a forced smile, which was little more than a grimace, he said. 'My apologies stranger.'

'I am merely patrolling the lands of my liege lord, Sir Phillip of Dover, and carrying out his orders.'

The leader of the horsemen looked around in alarm and became even more docile, saying, 'I am called John. 'John the friendly' by some, and I am Lord Phillip's of Dover's right hand man, so if you would be good enough to follow me, then I will introduce you to him, for I am certain that he will welcome men such as you into his Hall.'

Roger the Norman had not said a single word during the confrontation, and as the leader of the horsemen returned to his horse and began to mount, Roger turned to Aelnoth and said quietly. 'Beware my Lord, for although it is many a long year since I was in England. I still remember stories of the treacherous and dastardly deeds of an Englishman who had deserted his own kind and joined the Normans, and he was called 'John the Friendly.'

Aelnoth nodded and said quietly. 'Thank you my friend. I shall watch him like a hawk.'

'John,' he said loudly.

'Alas, I have urgent business in the west, and much as I would like to meet the Lord of Dover, I am afraid that I must decline your generous offer.'

John the Friendly reigned in his steed and looked back over his shoulder, rather shocked that this young stranger had the nerve to gainsay him, and although he was tempted to insist that the stranger and his men must follow him to Dover, he recalled just how easily this man had defeated two of his finest men, so he nodded and with a face as black as thunder, he turned and spurred his horse onwards, whilst his agile and evil brain said to him.

'They are few, and are afoot, and I shall be in Dover before nightfall, and by dawn I shall return with fifty men, and see what that young puppy is guarding so keenly in those chests of his.'

As the horsemen disappeared over the brim of the hill, Aelnoth turned to his men and within a few minutes they were trudging over the sand dunes, laden with their belongings.

They had travelled no more than a quarter of a mile before Ingar sank to his knees and fell forward, dropping the heavy chest, which he had been carrying on his shoulders.

'By Odin's balls, that thing is bloody heavy.'

The rest of the men halted, and heaved their own chests onto the ground, grunting with relief as they straightened their shoulders and stretched their aching backs.

Aelnoth, who had also been carrying one of the chests on his shoulders, grunted as he too heaved the chest onto the ground.

'We need pack horses, or a cart.' He said again in a weary voice.

'I noticed a farm near that copse over yonder,' said Magnus.

'They may have pack animals there.'

'You and Roger go and find out,' said Aelnoth, 'and make sure that you pay for the bloody things, and don't cause any trouble.'

'Here, take a couple of silver pieces,' he said as he plunged his hand into the leather purse. We don't want more bloody Normans chasing us.'

Magnus and Roger loped off and soon disappeared in the tangle of undergrowth, which infested the untilled fields.

The men sat down on the sandy soil, resting and waiting for the return of Magnus and Roger, and within the hour they leapt to their feet when they heard the thunder of horse's hooves drumming onto the sodden earth.

'Weapons ready,' shouted Aelnoth, and his well trained men drew their weapons and swung the shields, which they habitually carried on their backs, around to the front, in readiness to defend themselves.

Aelnoth breathed a sigh of relief as the dreaded troop of Normans turned out to be non other than Roger and Magnus, who each rode a packhorse and pulled two spare horses behind them.

'Did you have any trouble?' asked Aelnoth as the two men halted in front of him.

'Non at-all,' answered Roger.

'The farmer can buy a dozen nags like these for the two silver pieces that he charged us for these four.'

'Right, lets load them up and be on our way,' said Aelnoth, and the men leapt forward to carry out his orders, relieved that they would not have to carry the heavy chests, and all their other belongings throughout the length and breath of England.

They walked beside the packhorses all afternoon and well into the night, before Aelnoth called a halt, stopping in a small, dense wood, which nestled along a south-facing hillside, overlooking the well-trodden road, upon which they had been travelling.

The dawn chorus wakened the travellers with an overwhelmingly loud cacophony of sound, as each of the hundreds of thousands of birds shrilled their claim to their own particular patch of the woodlands, meadows and sky.

After a quick breakfast, they made their way down onto the roadway, and commenced to trudge doggedly along it, passing through farmyards, small hamlets and villages as they moved slowly and steadily in a westerly direction.

*   *   *

John the Friendly flung the reins at one of the grooms, and almost ran into the Hall, and despite the fact that he was an Englishman, he pushed his way through the Norman guards as he rushed into Lord Phillip's dining hall.

'My Lord.' He said loudly, as he dropped to one knee before his liege lord.

'Oh my God John, you made me jump. I nearly choked on this lump of pork.'

'What is it now?'

'Some bloody peasant who has stolen a lamb or a chicken?'

'Spit it out man, and for God's sake get up off your knees.'

'Strangers my Lord.' Said John boldly.

'They landed off seal point.'

'Sixteen of them including two girls.'

'And they were both strikingly beautiful.' He added with a leering smile, which sent a shiver down Philip's back, for he was well aware of John's sadistic way of dealing with prisoners, especially female prisoners.

'So! I have seen pretty girls before. Or are you blind,' he added as he pointed to two very attractive English serving maids, who hovered near the panelled walls of his elaborately decorated dining hall.

'No my Lord,' said John.

'You mis-understand. If I may be so bold as to point out.'

'It's not the girls my Lord. It's their chests.'

'So we have girls here with big chests. If that is what is getting you so excited.' Said his Lordship, laughing at his own jest.

'I have seen many wench's with big chests since I came to England.' He continued jovially.

'No my Lord,' said John as his face reddened, and his anger grew in his chest in his attempt to tell his stupid Norman overlord his vital news.

'These men. My Lord.'

'They have no less than twelve chests, which I am sure are all filled with silver or even gold.'

At the sound of Silver and Gold, Lord Phillip spat out the lump of pork gristle, which he had been chewing on, throughout this hereto-tedious, yet jovial conversation.

'Gold.' He hissed. 'Did you see the Gold?'

'Not exactly my Lord,' said John. 'But the chests were heavy.'

'It took two men to lift one of them.'

'Pah! Could be stones or Holy relics.' Spat Phillip.

'No my Lord,' contradicted the still fuming John, who was fighting within himself, in order to attempt to control his anger, at this mans stubborn reluctance to believe him.

'I swear they are full of silver or gold.' He said,

'Give me fifty men and I will bring them to you.' He added vehemently.

Lord Phillip ran his greasy fingers through his greying hair.

'I have nought to lose and everything to gain.' He said aloud.

'Who were they again?' he asked thoughtfully.

'Some travellers from Normandy.' Answered John.

'Normandy. How do you know that?' asked Lord Phillip.

'They showed me a parchment.'

'Parchment. What parchment?'

'Oh, just some parchment signed by Duke Robert. Or so he claimed.'

'And did you see this document?'

'I did my Lord. I studied it at length and although it looked to be genuine, I think it was a fake.'

'Why?'

'Well! Why would the Duke of Normandy give such a document to a lowly knight like that?'

'What!' Shouted Phillip at the top of his voice as he thumped his fist upon the table causing a goblet of wine to spill its contents over the table.

'And now you telling me that this man has a document signed by Lord Robert? Who is not only the brother to our own King Rufus, but is also 'The Duke of Normandy,' and is a man who owns half of bloody Italy?'

'And the man is now, no longer a mere wayfarer, but a Knight of the Realm.'

'Are you stark staring mad?

'If this man is assaulted on my land, what do you think would happen?'

'I will tell you what would happen.' He added before the alarmed John could answer.

'You would lose your head, but more importantly.

'If I was not executed along with you, then I would certainly lose Dover, and would be exiled, and The Duke of Normandy would have a long awaited reason to invade England, and kick his brother Rufus off the throne, in order to add England to his already huge bloody Empire.'

'God's blood man. I should hang you myself for putting me in such peril.'

Lord Philip walked over to the fireplace, scratching his sparse beard.

He turned, walking past John as if he were not in the room, and snatched up a goblet of red Burgundy, which he drained in one long gulp.

He strode the few additional paces and stood in front of John, with his face a mere inch or two from john's blanching face, and stared fiercely into his eyes.

'You have caused me this unasked for headache,' he snarled, 'and as I see the situation.'

'As it is you who caused the problem, then it should also be you who must solve it.'

'How many men were they?'

'I think there were either fourteen or so, my Lord.' Plus two women.' He added.

'Fourteen or sixteen. You are not even sure of their numbers you idiot,' He repeated.

'At first light on the morrow, you will ride out with half a dozen men, taking sixteen fully saddled horses with you.'

'No nags mind you.'

'Take good steeds, including your own black stallion, and catch up with this Knight.'

'Present him with the horses, as well as my kindest wishes, and give him a parchment, which I shall furnish you with, that will allow him and his men free access across the lands of Kent.'

'Yes my Lord.'

'Thank you my Lord.' Said John, as he bowed his head, acknowledging his liege lord's orders.

'Thank me not.' Said Phillip scornfully.

'For I shall deduct the cost of the horses from your salary, and if my calculations are correct, that will mean that you will labour in my service for the next six years without any pay whatsoever.'

John quickly nodded again and turned to walk away, as he attempted to prevent his liege Lord from seeing his reddened and furious face.

He left the room before his anger got the better of him, and forced him to do or say something silly, purposely closing the door quietly behind him to the voice of his Lordship, who bellowed.

'Scribe. Scribe.'

*   *   *

Ingar had been set the first watch of the night, and although he was not actually asleep, he certainly was dozing when the thunder of horsemen caused him to shake his head, in order to assure himself that he was not dreaming.

'Damn and Blast.' He shouted, as he realised that it was not a dream, but was if fact stark reality, as what looked like fifty horsemen thundered out of the darkness towards him.

'Alarm. Alarm.' He shouted, as he slung his shield off his back and brought it across his chest, and took up the required position, which had been knocked into his thick Icelandic head when he had first joined the Varangian Guards, and had been taught how to resist an attack from horsemen.

The small encampment was immediately thrown into turmoil at this unexpected pre-dawn attack, as men tumbled out of their blankets, and snatched up their weapons, with one half awake man stumbled into and over the fire, causing sparks and half burned logs to light up the darkened camp.

The horses were brought to a skidding halt a few yards short of the crouching figure of Ingar, who was about to hurl his spear at the leading rider, who sat proudly on a pitch black stallion, which was in the act of rearing up, with his iron shod hoofs flashing in the moonlight.

Aelnoth and the rest of the men were a little way behind Ingar, but due to the suddenness of the attack, they had not yet had time to form a shieldwall, or any other form of defence, and stood isolated and dotted about the camp.

Although Aelnoth was still a little shocked at being attacked at this time of morning, he was equally shocked at the suddenness in which the attack had been brought to a sudden halt.

He beckoned the rest of his men to join him, and they advanced in a shieldwall to join the solitary figure of Ingar, who still stood on his guard with his shield and spear held to the fore.

Aelnoth gazed up into the smiling face of John the Friendly, who made no attempt to dismount, but sat, straight backed on his black stallion as he gazed down at him.

Neither man spoke.

Aelnoth briefly glanced at the rest of John's men and thought it rather odd that only about half of the horses were mounted, noting, as was his life long habit that John the Friendly had twenty four men with him.

It was now John's turn to be nervous, for he knew that he had a mere two dozen men behind him, and he also knew that the men who now faced him numbered fourteen warriors plus two women.

He also knew that although his own men were experienced warriors, if things did turn ugly, they would be totally outclassed by these opponents who had served in Constantinople's famous Varangian Guard, and as such, each of them was likely to be a champion in his own right, and had probably slain more men than he'd had hot dinners.

'It is I.' He said in as bold a voice as he could muster.

'John! John the Friendly.' He added.

'John.' Aelnoth acknowledged with a slight nod of his head, whilst he still held his weapon in readiness before him.

'What brings you to my camp at this time of night?' he asked gruffly.

'Cheeky young swine.' John thought to himself.'

'I bring greetings from my liege Lord. Phillip of Dover.' Said John in his well-rehearsed and cheerful manner.

'He has ordered me to give you these horses as a gift, with a warrant that will allow you to pass freely through the lands of Kent.'

'Give?' he queried in a clearly suspicious tone, asked Aelnoth.

'Why would he do such a thing?'

'What does he want in exchange?'

'Naught my Lord. He wants nothing from you.'

'He merely wishes you 'Godspeed,' and merely asks that you will speak kindly of his generosity, when next you meet 'The Duke of Normandy,' or indeed, should you meet his brother, our own good King Rufus.'

'Step down and join me in a jug of ale and a bite of cold beef.' Said Aelnoth who was still suspicious at this much unexpected bout of generosity.

John dismounted, and as he did so, he ordered his men to tether the horses.

'Join me after you have seen to the horses.' He added.

Aelnoth accompanied John to the fire, where a large leg of beef had been left sizzling over the logs, in readiness for the morning.

Before he sat down, Aelnoth called Aelfgar over to him, and whispered to him.

'Scout around the camp and down the roadway which our friends came.'

'See if this traitorous Englishman has left any nasty surprises in his wake.'

Aelnoth sat at one side of the fire whilst John sat opposite him.

Their men sat in a semi-circle around their respective leaders.

Several leather bottles containing both beer and wine were passed from man to man, thus breaking the awkward silence, which existed between the two groups.

After each man was presented with a couple of slices of half- cooked beef and a large slice dry bread, Aelnoth said to John. 'I understand that despite your dress and your obvious loyalty to Lord Phillip, you are, in fact an Englishman?'

John nodded, saying somewhat guardedly.

'Indeed I am, but the Norman's have brought law and order to England, and that can be no bad thing.'

'Can it?'

'I thought that we had law and order before your Norman friends arrived.' answered Aelnoth as pleasantly as he was able, despite the fact that he was seething with rage at this traitorous worm of a man, who sat across the fire from him.

'Maybe so,' said John, who added sarcastically, 'but we always seemed to be fighting the Welsh, or the Scots, as well as amongst ourselves, did we not?'

'Every Kingdom that is rich and prosperous is envied by its neighbours.' said Aelnoth as he tried to close the subject, and not be forced to sink his Saex into the chest of a man who had just given him a small herd of valuable horses.

The next hour of so was spent pleasantly enough, with a lot of small-talk and a lot of ale, before the two bodies of men retreated to their sleeping areas, with both the Normans and Aelnoth's men posting sentries who patrolled their individual camps until the camp stirred, a couple of hours later, with the dawn.

Aelnoth had suspected that John planned an act of treachery, and spent a large part of what was left of the night, either lying in his sheepskin with his eyes open, or patrolling the perimeter of his camp, in order to satisfy himself that all was well, and that John and his Norman escort were asleep and not up to any mischief.

The two groups of men broke their fast around their individual fires before they packed their belongings onto their animals and went their separate ways, with John and his men retracing their steps towards Dover, whilst Aelnoth's group set off in the opposite direction.

CHAPTER 28

After a mere half a mile, John reined in his horse and waited for a few moments until all of his men had gathered around him.

'As you already know,' he said to his men. 'I have known most of you for many years, and have chosen you to join me on this errand, due, not only your ability as warriors, but also because I have watched you, and learned over the years that you, like myself, are not best pleased at remaining as common Men-at-arms for that jumped up toad, the so called Lord Phillip.'

'When we all joined the Norman cause in England, it was because we were promised that if we did so, then we would be given Manors and farms, and would be wealthy men.

He paused for a moment as he looked around at the nodding heads of his men, smiling his famous, well-rehearsed smile that had given him the name of 'John the Friendly.'

'And yet, here we are. Common Men-at-arms with nought to show for our loyal service, except for a coat of mail and a straw pallet to sleep on.'

'Where is the wealth we were promised?' he asked vehemently.

The men growled their agreement.

'I will tell you where it is.' Snarled John.

'Phillip has kept it all for himself. That's where it is.'

'Have you seen any of the silver that he collects from his tenants?'

'No,' said John slyly.

'Do you have any of the money, which comes from the ships that sail in and out of Dover each and every day?'

'No. None.' Growled the men.

'When I asked you to join me on this patrol, I promised you riches. Did I not?'

'Aye, Aye.' Said the men, for they were eager to reap the riches, which they had been promised.

'I will tell you where the riches are.'

'They are in those large wooden crates that those 'damned Englishmen' were hiding in their camp.'

The men looked at one another in amazement, for although they were keen to get their hands on the riches that had been promised by John, they all knew that John himself was a 'damned Englishman,' and the question which crossed the minds of one or two of them was, why was this particular 'damned Englishman' betraying his own people and using Normans to do his dirty work for him.

'Did you see them?' Asked John.

'I saw a pile of boxes.' Said one man

Other men grunted and nodded their heads, for they had also seen a pile of boxes, but had paid them no heed; expect to suppose that they contained the belongings of the men and women, who were in the act of taking them to their homes.

'Well,' said John. 'Those boxes are full of gold and silver, which those men have brought back from Constantinople, and that gold and silver will be ours if you do as I say.'

The men crowded around John as he issued his orders.

John knew the area well, for he had patrolled the lands of his Lordship on many occasions, and had often used this very road.

He knew all of its twists and its turns, as well as the hills, valleys, woodlands and marshes.

'Then you had best follow me, and we will all be rich men.' He snarled as he turned and mounted his steed.

He led his men away from the road, and over a small hill, which took them into the next valley, and followed the valley through woodlands and meadows for five miles, before he led them in a south westerly direction in order to cut across the original road.

They followed the road westward until they reached a small wooded valley, where he halted and assigned his men to take up positions on either side of the road.

'We must take them by surprise,' he snarled, 'whilst they are strung out in ones and two's.'

'Remain in hiding until I blow the horn.' He said, 'and when you hear the horn, mark your man and hurl your spears at him, and then charge down to finish off the survivors.

'Should be easy.' He said with the confidence he did not really feel, for he knew that even if half of his targets escaped the initial shower of spears, he and his men would still have a fight on their hands, but his calculating mind hoped that he would lose at least half of his own men, for if that did happen, then the riches would be shared out amongst surviving men, rather than the full compliment of twenty-four men who were with him at the present moment.

*   *   *

Aelnoth had been riding alongside Magnus, enjoying his company as they reminisced about their adventures in the east.

Both of the young men agreeing just how wonderful it was to be home, as they rode slowly through the meadows and occasional strips of farmland, enjoying the birdsong and hum of the warm English countryside.

Ingrid and Nike rode behind their men and as they too chatted, catching snippets of the men's conversation, sharing their men's happiness, causing both Nike and Ingrid to smile with pleasure at their men's joy at being back in England.

Although Nike was still a little unsure, and felt slightly daunted by this cloudy and verdantly green country, where the fates had brought her.

Aelnoth suddenly hauled on the reins, and brought his horse to an abrupt halt.

The suddenness of the halt caught Magnus by surprise, and he rode a further six or eight feet before he could bring his own horse to a halt.

He looked back towards his friend.

'What's wrong?' he called back to Aelnoth.

'Can't you hear?' said Aelnoth.

'Hear! Hear what? I can't hear a thing,'

'That's just it. I can't hear anything either, and not a few yards back, the world was full of birdsong and the sounds of the countryside.'

'Something is wrong' he added.

Magnus turned his horse around to face the line of horsemen and shouted to them.

'Men. Shields to the fore and ride in two's along this valley.'

'You four men. Protect the ladies.'

'Aelnoth senses that something is wrong, so be on your guard.'

The men urged their mounts closer and held their shields outwards, as they snatched their helmets from their saddles and quickly put them onto their heads.

As soon as he could see that his men were ready, Aelnoth turned his horse around again and led his men along the road, into a pleasant, bush speckled valley.

They were half way through the valley when the sound of a hunting horn blew loud and clear.

Before the sound of the horn had ceased, they were subject to a shower of heavy war-spears, which rained down upon them from both sides of the valley.

Some spears fell short and two over-shot their intended victim's heads, whilst the majority were well aimed and thudded into the shields of Aelnoth's men.

One struck Aelnoth's own shield with such force that it penetrated the shield, leaving the leaf shaped point of the spear two inches from his chest.

He threw his now useless shield to the ground as he quickly glanced at his men; he was alarmed to see two of them writhing on the ground with spears protruding out of their bodies.

He drew both of his swords and ran towards the nearest wounded man who he instantly recognised as Aelfgar of Kendal, but as he knelt by Aelfgar, he saw his spirit leave him and fly to the afterworld.

Despite the fact that he knew that men were charging down the slope towards him, he pushed his way through the pack horses to the other side of the line, where the second man lay groaning, and dragged Ivor the Icelander into a sitting position.

He covered the wounded man with a shield, before he turned to rally his men.

'Slay the pack animals.' He shouted, 'and form a shieldwall around them.'

'Get into the middle.' He yelled at the two women, who immediately edged their way past the men into the centre of the shieldwall.

Within seconds the pack animals were slain, and as soon as they had fallen, he joined his men in the pitifully small shieldwall.

The attackers paused for a moment when they reached the valley floor, and as if an order had been given; then they began to walk boldly towards the shieldwall from both ends of the valley.

Being slightly outnumbered did not concern Aelnoth too much, for in the past he had been outnumbered by greater numbers, but as the twelve opponents approached him from the east, he did notice that they were a little farther from him than the other twelve men who approached them from the west.

He stepped out of the shieldwall, (which was THE THING NOT TO DO,) and an order, which he had attempted to drill into the thick heads of the numerous recruits who he had attempted to train over the past years.

He literally loped towards the west.

The very fact that this stupid man had left the protection of his shieldwall, and who was now running towards them, made the Normans halt for a brief moment and glance at one another in awe, but they were all experienced warriors, and as one of them grinned from ear to ear, his glee infected his friends, who smiled and shouted with joy as they, in turn, raced towards the man.

Once the first man had began to run, his fellow warriors immediately joined him, as each man vied with his friends in their eagerness to kill this particular idiot, before they went on to slay the few men in the pitifully small shieldwall.

Their laughter and sniggers ceased as the man suddenly leapt to one side and sliced the head off their friend Maurice.

The man did not stop there, but immediately attacked the next man with both of his swords raining blows down on the helmet and shield of the unfortunate man who eventually succumbed to a sword-cut, which sliced away half of his chin, sending him reeling backwards onto the mossy floor.

The remaining men attacked Aelnoth with a vengeance, but due to the narrowness of the valley, only two could reach him at any one time.

Aelnoth dropped down onto his knees and sliced through one of the legs of one warrior.

Aelnoth immediately sprang up again and attacked a second man, forcing him backwards into the small crowd of his friends, causing them to retreat in confusion.

Aelnoth glance backwards towards his friends in the shieldwall, where he could see that two of his men were on the ground lying in pools of blood, whilst the rest of his men were being pressed hard by their attackers.

He raced back to them, sliding his Saex into the neck of one of the attackers whilst his long sword sliced into the thigh of another man, sending both men to the ground.

The suddenness of his attack threw the Normans into confusion, and their confusion was speedily accelerated as Magnus and his friends, who screamed their shouts of triumph, and rushed forward to attack them, sending two of the remaining attackers to the ground,

The survivors fled back up the slope, nursing their bruised and battered bodies as they did so.

They met John the Friendly, who had sensibly remained at the top of the hill, from where he had witnessed the fight.

'Four.' He screamed.

'You only managed to kill four of them.'

'Christ alive. What were you playing at?'

'That madman with the two swords would have killed us all if we hadn't run,' gasped one of the survivors, who was clutching at cut on his shoulder, which was oozing blood.

'We were forced to leave our wounded men down there.' Growled another bruised and battered veteran.

'Never seen anything like it.' He added mournfully.

John ignored their moans and excuses and resumed the persona of his smiling countenance.

'Still, we thinned them down a bit.' He said cheerfully.

'They bloody well thinned us down a bit too.' Snarled one man, who then added.

'I for one ain't going up against them again.' And turned away from John, and began walking towards his tethered horse.

'Stop.' Shouted John, but the man continued to walk away.

John could see his cunning plan slipping away from him, for if this man deserted him, and then he felt sure that others would follow, so he lifted his spear and hurled it into the back of the man, sending him sprawling and twitching under the legs of his horse.

'He broke his word.' Snarled John.

'No man can break his word and get away with it.'

'You all agreed to follow me to get our hands on those treasure chests, and that is what we will do.'

'It is not over.' He snarled.

'Mount up.' He ordered and the remaining men reluctantly untied their horses and mounted.

*   *   *

Aelnoth surveyed the scene and walked over to the dead and wounded, carefully inspecting the enemy wounded, but in order to assure himself that it was safe to examine their wounds, he collected their fallen weapons and threw them out of their reach

He did not need to be so careful, for each of the men who he had wounded, were either dead or in the last moments of their lives.

Aelfgar, Ivor and two of the Varangian Guards had been slain.

All of his remaining men, with the exception of himself had suffered minor cuts and bruises.

'Short but savage.' Remarked Magnus.

'Indeed,' answered Aelnoth glumly.

'The sods were good fighters.' He added.

'Mmm. Bloody Normans.' Said Magnus angrily.

'Build a pyre.' Ordered Aelnoth. 'We will burn them.'

Two hours later, Aelnoth led them away from the scene of conflict, leaving a thin plume of smoke rising from the burned out pyre.

They had managed to catch four of their attackers horses, and after some reluctance, the once proud Norman steeds were loaded with the belongings from the slain pack animals, as well as the captured armour and weapons, which had belonged to their riders.

Their journey took them through the towns of Beckenham and Maidstone, reaching the noisy and smelly capitol of London by early evening of the third day.

After a tiresome search, they eventually found a small open space at Southwark where they made their camp.

Each man took a turn on sentry duty throughout the night, patrolling their small encampment, which was soon hemmed in by other travellers, who arrived during the evening and throughout the night, unrolling their bedding and making their fires to within a few feet of Aelnoth and his men.

After two weeks in London, Aelnoth and Ingrid led the way through the north gate, followed by Magnus and Nike who rode alongside each other, followed by the remaining ex- Varangian guards and a solemn Ingar, who was still mourning the death of his Icelandic friend.

After seeking permission from Aelnoth, Roger the Norman had left, and commenced his journey to his own home on the east coast.

All the men now wore the latest in Norman chain mail and the sturdiest and most modern helmets that Aelnoth had been able to purchase, plus modern and un-damaged shields, which had been adorned with green and red chevrons, which matched the pendant that one of the Varangians held aloft.

To all except the very observant, his small band of fellow travellers looked like any other wealthy band of Normans, escorting their ladies in a modern four-wheeled carriage, as they traversed the old Roman road, which led to the northwest of England.

CHAPTER 29

John the friendly and the single member of his band who had not deserted him, had been sitting near the window in a hovel, which the folk in those parts called a tavern, for the best part of eight days, as they watched the travellers who made their way southwards towards London, or northwards towards the midlands and to the north-western parts of the country.

After another weary day of watching and consuming more drinks that he cared to remember, he was suddenly shocked into action, when he glanced, almost casually at the rear horseman of a small party of Normans, who were literally in the process of passing the tavern.

Aelnoth had been ill at ease, since he had roused himself from his slumbers at dawn and felt that they were being followed.

His eyes searched the faces of the travellers who followed him along the road, and he watched each and every man who rode past him with suspicion, ready to spring into action should the need arise.

If Aelnoth had not turned in his saddle for the twentieth time that day, in order to scan the road behind him, and satisfy himself that they were not being chased or followed. John the Friendly would not have even bothered to search for an English face beneath what was, quite obviously Norman garb, as his eyes fell, almost nonchantly upon the face of Aelnoth.

'Jesus Christ,' he exclaimed, as he leapt to his feet, knocking the small table over, and spilling the dregs of their drinks over his fellow conspirator, Edwain of Everex.

'What the Hell?' growled Edwain as he attempted to brush off the dregs of his already filthy breeches?

'It's them.' Hissed John.

'Quick. Get the horses.'

Within a few minutes they had saddled their horses and had ridden around the corner of the Tavern, where they became entangled with another party of Normans who were heading in the opposite direction, towards London.

After the initial confusion, they untangled themselves from the Normans and urged their steeds up the road in pursuit of Aelnoth and his party.

'I can see their banner.' Said John loudly, in order for Edwain to hear over the hustle and bustle, which their fellow travellers were making.

'So can I.' Said Edwain. 'Green and red.'

'Drop back a bit.' Ordered John.

'All we need to do is to follow that flag and we can pick them off one by one until we get the treasure.'

They eased their horses to a slow walk, allowing a number of riders and a couple of carts to overtake them, and continued to follow the banner, until the light faded into darkness.

The travellers on the road became fewer and fewer, until the only people on the road were Aelnoth and his party, and John the friendly and Edwain of Evreux.

Following the Norman custom, the Green and Red banner had been embedded in the ground and fluttered boldly as John and Edwain rode past Aelnoth's small camp.

As they rode past, they gazed nonchantly in the opposite direction to ensure that no one from the camp saw their faces, until they disappeared again into the darkness.

John guided his mount off the muddy roadway into what looked like a small wooded area, where both men dismounted, un-saddled their horses, and after lighting a small fire, over which they roasted two partridges, which they had purchased from the tavern.

They devoured the birds, covered themselves with their sheepskin horse-blankets and lay down to await the arrival of the dawn.

The noise from early risers woke them, causing John to curse, for allowing himself to sleep past dawn, fully aware that his quarry could well be part of the small clusters of people who were already up and hurrying in both directions along the road to their own personal destinations.

Edwain gazed over the top of his horse as he struggled to pull the girth tight, and exclaimed in disbelief.

'That's them now. Look.' He said loudly.

'There's that bloody Green and Red Banner.'

John, who had been stooping to pick up his sheepskin, jumped up and cursed loudly.

'Blast and Damnation.' He spat.

'That's another day lost. We can't take the bastards in the daylight.'

'I was hoping to sink one of these little beauties in one of 'em.' Snarled the bloodthirsty Edwain, as he tapped the bundle of iron-headed crossbow bolts, which hung on his belt in a brown leather quiver.

'We will just have to follow them until we are right out in the countryside, where there are no people.' Said John, as he spat into the dying embers of yesterday evenings fire.

The day was clear and bright, and the old Roman road was as straight as old Roman roads are reputed to be.

They followed the banner, which fluttered in the warm morning air some half a mile ahead of them.

When the banner stopped at mid-day. They stopped.

When the banner began to move, then so did they, always keeping a healthy distance between themselves and their prey.

However, as they moved farther away from London, the travellers became fewer and fewer, until by the end of the second day, there were so few travellers on the road that John the Friendly felt that it would soon become obvious to their intended victims that they were being followed, and could themselves be the victims of an ambush.

He cursed long and loud.

'God's teeth,' he shouted aloud.

'How in the name of Hell are we going to thin the buggers out and get our hands on that gold?' he fumed.

'Ride through the sods as soon as they have settled down for the night.' Suggested Edwain, 'and kill a couple or three of them on the way.'

'That way, we will be in front of them again and there will be two or three of the swine less to deal with on the morrow.' He added.

John smiled at Edwain's suggestion and grunted in agreement.

As soon as they saw the banner cease its forward movement, they pulled over to the side of the road and ate a mouthful of dried mutton, which they swilled down with a couple of mouthfuls of tepid beer from their leather flasks, whilst they checked their crossbows and readied themselves for action.

As they neared the banner, they primed the bolts into their crossbows and spurred their horses out of the darkness, thundering off the road and into their victim's camp.

Aelnoth and his friends were in the act of finishing their evening meal when their peace was shattered by two horsemen who galloped out of the darkness, and into their camp, causing men to jump to their feet and snatch up their weapons, but almost before they had drawn their weapons, the horsemen had careered through the small camp, leaving its occupants in disarray.

'Is anyone hurt?' shouted Aelnoth.

A few 'nay's' followed by a groan, answered his question.

He walked towards the groan and in the darkness and stumbled over something soft.

His fears were justified as he knelt and felt the body of a man who was lying on his face.

He heaved the body onto its back to reveal the face and the lifeless eyes of one of the Varangian guards who had served with him for five years in Constantinople.

It took Aelnoth some time to find what had slain the man, and it wasn't until he ran his hands over the man's chest that his hands felt the leather fletching of a crossbow bolt.

'Blast,' he snarled. 'All this way, just to die here in the darkness.'

A shout shook Aelnoth back to reality, 'Aelnoth,' the voice shouted and he rose and walked to the other side of the fire, where he could see Magnus crouching by the inert form of Ingar the Icelander.

'He's dead,' said Magnus, as he held his own left shoulder, where a crossbow bolt protruded through his chain mail shirt.

'How bad is it?' asked Aelnoth.

'Oh it's not too bad. Only went in an inch or two.'

'Could have been worse.' He added. 'If I hadn't been wearing my mail shirt.'

'Pull the sodding thing out.' He ordered.

Aelnoth placed his one hand on the chest of Magnus, and he gripped the metal bolt with his other hand and gave a sudden pull, ripping the offending shaft from the shoulder muscles of his friend.

Magnus made no sound other than a grunt as he clasped his throbbing shoulder with his other hand and sank slowly onto the ground.

Holding her hand to her mouth in horror, Nike had watched as Aelnoth had withdrawn the bolt, but as Magnus fell to the floor, she rushed to his side and held his head in her lap, cooing like a broody hen as she watched in awe as Magnus's eyes suddenly opened and stared up at her.

Aelnoth looked down towards the wounded man, satisfied that the iron will and toughness of his friend would pull him through.

He then gazed towards the body of Ingar, who lay just out of the meagre light of their nearly dead fire.

He could see the shaft of a spear, which still stuck in the Icelanders body, and his logical mind tussled with something for a moment, before he solved his newly found problem.

'Two horsemen,' he mumbled.

'For the few seconds that they were in our camp, they released two crossbow bolts, and still managed to hurl a spear and hit three of us?'

His mind was working as if he was talking to, and questioning himself, and he uttered the answer that his mind had found.

'Normans,' he said aloud.

'Normans learn how to ride by steering their steeds with their legs and knees, so that they can keep both of their hands free in battle.'

'That's how they managed to handle a crossbow AND hurl a spear at almost the same time.'

He turned towards Nike who was still attending to Magnus's wound. 'How is he?'

'Why don't you ask him yourself,' snarled Magnus, as he looked up into the darkened face of Aelnoth.

'Well. How is it then?' asked Aelnoth.

'Hurts like buggery.' Growled Magnus, as Nike finished tying a knot in the piece of linen, which she had wrapped around the wound.

'He will be fine.' She said quietly as she wiped the blood from her hands, and threw the damp cloth into the fire.

'But he will need to rest for a few days, or the wound could go bad.' She added.

'Well, we are in no great hurry, so I suppose we can stay at the next place we get to.'

'My friend,' said Aelnoth.

'You and I have followed the path of the sword together for the past nine years, and yet, here we are, perhaps no more than a few miles from the very spot where you collected a crossbow bolt all those years ago, and now you have attracted another lump of iron.'

'Do you have an urge to gather these things?' He asked with a forced grin on his tired face.

Magnus merely grimaced as another spasm of pain shot through his body.

'It is at times like this when I miss our old friends Oscar and Abdulla.'

'If they had been with us this night, then we would have not been caught napping like a couple of untried recruits.'

'True. True.' Said Aelnoth. 'I too miss them.'

He said, forcing the two men to put the thoughts of their two Albino friends out of their minds.

'In the meantime we had better bury our dead.'

Aelnoth helped his two remaining men to scoop out shallow graves for the slain men, and after they had been laid to rest, they covered their bodies with their saddle blankets and covered them with dark English soil.

Rugalf, who was one and only survivor of the Varangian Guards turned to Olaf, who had become his best friend, and who was also the sole survivor of the released slaves, who the old Captain of the Dolphin had purchased to man the ship.

'Just you and me now.' He whispered.

'And the two Lords,' said his friend in an equally quiet voice.

'We will both be rich men when we get home.'

'IF we get home.' Whispered Olaf grimly.

Aelnoth said a few words over the graves and returned to the campsite.

'Do you realize that we are being hunted?' he asked Magnus.

'Surely not?' Was the reply.

'I had thought that the attackers were just a couple of Norman braggart's out for a thrill.' He added.

'Not so, my friend.' Said Aelnoth.

'Just think about it.'

'Since we left the ship, we have been travelling through what is supposed to be a peaceful land, and yet we have been attacked on two occasions, and have lost a large proportion of our men.'

'No my friend,' he said.

'Someone has got wind of our wealth and is making a damned fine attempt at taking it from us.'

'Mmmm, I suppose you could be right, said Magnus, as he rubbed his aching shoulder with his good arm.

'They are certainly thinning us out a bit. There are only six of us left, and that includes me with a useless arm and young Nike and Ingrid, which makes our situation somewhat precarious. Don't you think?'

'Indeed,' answered Aelnoth thoughtfully, 'and there is little we can do about it until it gets light, so I suggest that you try to get a little sleep while I keep watch.'

He rose to his feet and commenced to walk out into the darkness in order to allow his eyes to become accustomed to the darkness.

As soon as they had eaten a hasty breakfast, they followed the attackers' tracks through the sparse woodland and onto the road, where the raiders tracks disappeared on the compacted earth of the roadway.

Aelnoth led them off the road and down a farm track, towards an isolated farmhouse, where the startled farmer and his wife gazed in alarm at the small party of savage men and two ladies, who invaded their cobbled yard.

It was obvious to Aelnoth that intruders had visited the old farmer before, as both he and his wife fell down onto their knees and bowed their heads in unison.

'My Lord,' said the old man in a voice that quavered with fear.

Aelnoth stepped slowly off his horse and said in a friendly manner.

'There is no need for that my good man. Despite the attire, we are Englishmen, just like yourself, and we mean you no harm.'

The man looked up and slowly and painfully rose to his feet as he continued to look directly towards Aelnoth.

'English?' Said the man in a bold voice.

'You do not look English.'

'Well I can assure you that I am, although one or two of my friends here are not.'

'What can I do for you my lord?' Said the still suspicious farmer.

'I have a wounded man here, and we need a place to stay whilst he heals.'

'I will pay you for your trouble.' He added, as he dismounted and walked towards the couple, placing two silver pennies in the farmer's shaky hand.

The man's weathered face softened as he looked down at the two coins saying. 'My thanks my Lord.

Unfortunately I only have one room to offer you, but the rest of you are more than welcome to the barn.'

'It's dry and warm, and the cattle and our one and only pig are out at this time of year.'

'That will do fine.'

'Help me get Magnus into the house,' said Aelnoth, and his men half carried the wounded man across the cobbled yard and through the front door.

The old couple followed them into the house and stood holding hands by the small fire, which glistened in the fireplace.

'My son Finn sleeps here,' nodding towards a wooden chest, which was covered by a straw mattress and a spotlessly clean sheepskin.

'He'll be back soon.'

Aelnoth said nothing as he helped one of his men to lay Magnus down upon the chest, and gazed at his wet face, realising that he was obviously suffering from some sort of fever.

'He has a fever,' said the woman, echoing his own thoughts, as she released the hand of her husband and walked over to another small chest, where she fumbled about for a few brief seconds, before she rose and carried three small earthenware bottles and a wooden bowl over the Magnus

She knelt down by him and commenced to wipe his damp forehead with a clean cloth, before she raised his head and urged him to drink some of the contents from one of the bottles.

'There,' she said with a satisfied smile.

'He should sleep for a while, and with a little help from his God, the fever should abate.'

It suddenly struck Aelnoth that despite the grubby and sparse surroundings of the two roomed farmhouse, the woman's speech and her rather refined manner did not seem to him to be the way of a lowly farmer's wife.

'How long have you lived here?' He asked.

'Just over five years,' answered the man.

'Where were you before then?'

The couple exchanged looks of alarm and shuffled their feet, as if each of the two expected the other to answer.

'We lived at the manor at Hartshill,' said the man.

'Were you servants there?'

'Good lord No!' said the woman indignantly, and then she brought her hand up to her mouth, as if she was attempting to stop herself from adding to the words that her pride had forced her to blurt out.

'I am called Athelston,' said the man in an attempt to prevent his wife from saying anything further.

Aelnoth was about to say that he had suspected that the couple had been of the English nobility, when the door suddenly flew open, and a huge man bowed his head to allow himself access into the room.

The man who seemed to be around the age of his mid twenties, raised his head to its normal level and surveyed the strangers who were standing in the room speaking with his parents.

A rather silly grin crossed his face and he said. 'Ma, Who? Who is here?'

'It's all right Finn,' said his mother as she crossed the room to place one of her hands upon one of his massive arms.

'They are friends.'

'They won't hurt you, never you mind,' she cooed as she gazed up lovingly into her gigantic son's face.'

'They are going to stay with us for a while.'

'Until the sick man is well enough to travel.'

'Go into your fathers' room and I will bring your supper in for you.'

'Off you go now.'

The man gave his mother the kind of a look that a trained puppy might give its master, and pushed his way through the standing men and stooped to enter the room, which served as a sleeping room for the family.

'That was Finn, our son,' said the father.

'He was wounded at the Battle of Hastings.

'Some blasted Norman staved in his helmet with an iron mace.'

'He is lucky to be alive. Isn't he Aethelflaed?'

'He certainly is my dear. He certainly is!'

'Aethelflaed. Now that is a noble name,' said Aelnoth with a smile.

'Indeed it is,' answered Athelston with a face that shone with pride.

'She was so named after 'Aethelflaed.' 'The lady of the Mercian's.'

'I have heard of her,' said Aelnoth.

'She was a great lady.'

'A warrior woman who led men, and won many battles.'

'She helped her brother to recapture Mercia from the Danes. Did she not?'

'She was the daughter of Alfred the Great.' Said Aethelflaed.

'She was a wonderful woman.' Said Aelnoth

'Finn was one of King Harold's housecarls.' Said Athelston, as if he was trying to steer Aelnoth away from the couple's noble heritage.

'He was a skilled warrior.' She added.

'When he was young, he practiced every day with my own weapons until he was good enough to join up with the Kings guards. He was as strong as an ox.'

'He still is.' Said his wife.

'Aye. I know he is, but much of the time he seems to live in a strange little world of his own.'

'I don't know what will happen to him when we are dead and gone.'

'Oh he will be fine.' Said Aethelflaed.'

'He's getting a little better with every day that passes.'

'We will retire to our room and leave you here for the night.' Said Athelston.

'Make yourselves as comfortable as possible and we will see you in the morning.'

And as he turned to exit through the door he said, 'there are a couple of extra rugs in yonder chest,' as he nodded to a large carved oak chest that stood near to the door.

Aelnoth was wakened at least three times during the night when Aethelflaed crept into the room to attend to Magnus, but other than that, he and Ingrid slept peacefully in each other's arms.

It took two weeks before Magnus had recovered sufficiently to allow him to stand and walk a few paces, and during that time both Aelnoth and his small band of travellers had become firm friends with their hosts and their son.

Finn managed the small farm, doing the work of two men, mostly in silence but on the odd occasion, Aelnoth had heard him either talking to himself, or singing loudly at his work, or as he walked behind their single milking cow, as he brought her in for milking.

At dawn one morning, as Aethelflaed was sitting on her three legged milking stool, squeezing the final drop of milk out of her cow, a rough hand closed over her mouth, causing her scream to be muffled, whilst her assailants other hand drew his razor sharp knife across her throat, sending her to the floor in a pool of blood that mixed with the milk from her overturned bucket.

With a sadistic smile Edwain of Evreux patted the already dead woman on her head.

'There, there old lady,' 'No more milking for you,' he muttered, as he stepped past her body and made his way into the shadows in the corner of the barn.

Minutes later, her husband entered the barn, and upon seeing the body of his beloved wife lying on the floor in a pool of her blood, he ran over to her and dropped on his knees, holding her head in his hands, unable to comprehend what had happened, as his fuddled brain refused to believe that his wife was dead.

Moments later, as he cooed and sobbed, Edwain's knife entered his back and plunged into his heart, sending him into an embrace of death with the lady who had been his wife for the past forty seven years.

Finn had been expecting his mother to return some time ago with her usual bucket of fresh warm milk, which she always poured over the large bowl that was waiting on the table before him, full of crushed oats and nuts, which she usually laced with honey.

As the men and women who had been staying with his family for the last few weeks were out feeding and watering their horses, Finn was alone in the house, sitting, rather forlorn at the table as he waited for his mother.

Tired of waiting, he eventually rose and ambled over to the barn to see what was keeping her.

As he pushed the already open door and entered the barn, the shock of seeing both his mother and his father lying in the straw, in a pool of blood brought his huge frame to an immediate halt, and he stood and literally stared unbelieving at their bodies.

As he stood there, his muddled mind heard a slight sound, which came from behind him, and he slowly turned to see the figures of Edwain of Evreux and John the friendly creeping up on him. Edwain held a bloodstained knife in his right hand whilst John carried a sword, which was pointed towards Finn's chest.

Something in Finn's mind seemed to tell him that he was back in the shieldwall at Hastings, and these two Normans had just slain two of his fellow warriors.

The noise of the battle deafened him, as men screamed in defiance and agony as they killed or were being killed.

His head spun as he realised that the only weapon that he had managed to retain during the fight was his eating knife, which was always kept in its usual place in a sheath on his belt.

He snatched the small knife out of its sheath just as Edwain stepped forward and plunged his knife into Finn's chest.

It seemed to Edwain that his knife thrust had not happened, for his massive opponent merely stepped forward as if he had been bitten by a gnat, and grabbed Edwain's head with both of his huge hands and with a feral growl, he literally twisted his head so that before his spirit left him, Edwain's last glimpse of life was the astounded face, and the open mouth of John the friendly.

John quickly recovered his wits and brought his sword down with all of his strength, slicing through Finn's shoulder and sending him backwards.

Finn shook his head like a large dog that had just emerged from a river, and looked to his left where he could see his bloodied arm hanging loosely.

He rushed forward and crashed into john, who was in the process of bringing his sword down again in order to finish the job, but was thwarted as the huge form of Finn crashed into him, under the sword, sending both men crashing to the floor with Finn landing on top of the smaller form of John, rendering his sword useless.

John was in the process of trying to reach his poniard, as Finn grabbed his throat with his one and only good hand, and with a grip of iron, he squeezed his opponent's throat.

John managed to grasp the poniard, which he plunged time after time into Finn's side, but was finally forced to cease his attack as blackness overtook him, and he died with his hand still firmly grasping the hilt of his poniard, as the already dead Finn's hand failed to loosen its grip from around his throat.

Half an hour later Nike led one of the horses into the barn to find the five bodies laying haphazardly on the floor of the barn, causing her to scream in horror.

Her piercing screams brought Aelnoth and Magnus running to her side with their weapons at the ready, only to find that the time for weapons had passed, as they stared at the dead bodies of their hosts and his son, whose huge body lay upon the corpse of the man who they instantly recognised to be 'John the Friendly.'

The two men moved from corpse to corpse, with a false hope that perhaps one of them may yet still be alive.

'All dead.' Said Aelnoth, stating the obvious.

'I think we have found the two who swept through our camp that night.'

'I think so,' answered Magnus.

'It looks like Finn sorted those two buggers out.' He added.

'God, he must have been strong.'

'Well, he has done us a good turn, although it was a costly win.'

'I suggest that we drag these two swine out of the barn and throw them onto the midden for the eaters of carrion.' Said Aelnoth.

'And then we should load up and leave this place, but not before we have arranged for the bodies of Finn and his parents to be placed alongside each other, and we can set the place alight and send their souls to heaven.'

'Or Valhalla,' said Magnus.

Who added thoughtfully, 'for I really do think that Finn was a warrior of old, and his soul will thank us for giving him a proper send off.'

Aelnoth and Magnus helped their two remaining men to load the treasure chests and the rest of their belongings onto the horses, and mounted their own horses in order to join the two ladies who were waiting for them near the far end of the stackyard.

Rugalf had asked Aelnoth if he could light the fire, and after a nod from Aelnoth, he stepped forwards a couple of paces and tossed his lighted torch into the barn.

He mounted his own horse and joined the rest of the party, where they all paused for a few minutes, and turned to watch the flames consume the dry hay, sending black plumes of smoke into the clear morning air.

'Time to go.' Said Aelnoth and led his horse away, tugging on the rope that had been tethered to one of the packhorses.

The two other men pulled their own packhorses behind them and began to make their way westwards.

'Another few miles and we will be in Mercia,' said Aelnoth.

'And then we will be home.'

CHAPTER 30

They travelled along dilapidated and overgrown roads, pausing each evening to camp on the outskirts of towns and villages, in order to avoid the newly installed Norman lords, who ruled from their freshly constructed keeps, which varied from a mound that was topped by wooden stakes and surrounded by a dry moat, to the more elaborate stone towers, which were almost always built on top of a mound or a hill and were often surrounded by deep moats, fed from nearby streams or freshly dug canals.

On the few occasions that they were visited by the rulers of these towns and villages, the Normans readily accepted Aelnoth and Magnus's word that they were travellers on their way to their own keeps on the Welsh boarder.

Only on one occasion were they asked for proof by one obnoxious individual, who, from his accent, they could tell had been, and not that long ago, a mere man-at-arms, who, for some unknown reason, had been given the sizable village of Toddington, over which he ruled with a sadistically iron fist.

As the man studied the parchment, which Duke Robert had given to Aelnoth, it became obvious that he could not read, and only agreed to their passage through his domain, when Magnus had pointed out to him the seal and coat of arms of Duke Robert of Normandy.

It was with soothing words and a false smile that Aelnoth declined his surly invitation to sup with him that evening, for he had seen the lecherous look, which the man had been giving both Ingrid and Nike, and suspected that once the six of them had entered his keep, then there would be a good chance of them losing not only their silver, but also their ladies and their lives.

It took them nearly two weeks to travel through Lutterworth, Tamworth and Lichfield, before the countryside became more familiar to them.

Magnus started to recognise hamlets and features on the landscape, which they had passed through, when they had rescued Oscar, and had made their way towards Kent and Wessex, in their quest to locate the Godwinson treasure.

As they neared the township of Broseley, Aelnoth brought his own horse alongside Magnus.

'If you have any secret plans to avenge the ill treatment, which you received whilst you were a captive here,' he asked. 'Then I think now might be a good time to tell me.'

'After coming this far and being so close to home.' Answered Magnus thoughtfully. 'I would rather not get embroiled in yet another fight with my former captor.'

'I have thought long and hard about wreaking vengeance on De-Bracy,' he added, 'but since it was me who killed his only son, I think that he will have suffered enough for the pain and hardship that he caused me all those years ago.'

They rode around the village, quietly passing the three cottages, which made up the hamlet of 'Willey' towards the more substantial township of 'Much Wenlock,' which had been one of Aelnoth's fathers manors, but had, alas, also been lost to the Norman's these long years past.

They walked their horses down the steep track which led them down the line of hills that the local's had named 'White-rock Edge,' and made their way to Pitchford, where Ingrid was hoping to meet with her parents and siblings.

It was early evening when they halted their horses in front of the cottage.

'It is so quiet,' remarked Ingrid quietly.

'That's because the place is empty.' Said Aelnoth.

'Just look around you, and you will see that the leaves and debris from winter are still up against the door and around the corners of the cottage, where the March winds have blown them, and here we are in mid-summer, so no one has been in the house for a long time.'

'We may as well stay here for the night, and we can look for your kinfolk in the morning.' Said Aelnoth, as he alighted from his horse.

Once inside, it became quite obvious from the state of the cottage that it had been deserted for several years, but once the fire had been lit, the roaring fire appeared to drive the musty smell away, and give the two-roomed cottage a more homely feeling.

After rekindling the dying embers of the previous night, and a hasty breakfast of stale bread and cold meat, they packed their belongings onto their horses and rode into the village.

Ingrid was shocked, and could not help gasping in astonishment when she saw the small village in which she had spent her childhood.

'There are so many people.' She exclaimed, 'and those three cottages were not there, and that one over there is new.'

'And just look at that.' She said as she pointed to the large stone tower, which had been erected on a high mound.'

'Even that mound wasn't there when I left.'

Aelnoth, who was riding alongside her, reigned in his own mount and looked up at the new Norman keep, and although he could understand her astonishment, he was not really impressed, for he thought that it was quite a diminutive building, after the enormous, multi turreted stone castles and buildings, which he had seen, and even destroyed, in Armenia.

'Mmm,' he muttered as he urged his horse forward.

'Let's see who's at home.'

'Careful,' warned Magnus, who was a few feet behind him.

'It obviously belongs to the new Norman Lord of Pitchford, and you and I know just how bloody tricky and devious these bastards can be.'

Aelnoth merely nodded in agreement, and continued to urge his mount up the ramp, which led to a large iron studded oak door.

On reaching the door, he hammered on the door with the butt of his Saex.

A few minutes passed before a small aperture was flung open and the wary eyes of a man stared up at Aelnoth.

'Yes.' Said a gruff voice.

'I am here to see the lord of this keep.'

'And who be you?'

'I am a Norman knight and if you know what's good for you, you had better inform his lordship that I am here, or your head may not stay on your shoulders for much longer.'

'Oh, came the shocked reply, 'but his lordship has not yet finished breaking his fast.'

'I will open the gate and let you in, but please stay in the courtyard whilst I run and tell him of your arrival.'

Aelnoth nodded his head and made the appropriate grunt.

The gate swung open, allowing Aelnoth and his retinue to clatter into the cobbled forecourt. Aelnoth's hand immediately fell on his sword as Ingrid screamed at the top of her voice, and she literally rolled off her horse, landing lightly on her feet, as she half turned and stared at the white haired old man, who was in the process of closing the gate, and who she and the rest of the group had ridden past without giving a second glance.

'Father,' she screamed, and raced towards him, throwing her arms around the startled man's neck.

The old man grabbed her in a bear hug, and as he lifted her off her feet he swung her around twice before he almost tenderly placed her back on her feet, gazing into her eyes, as a look of pure joy crossed his weather-beaten and heavily lined face.

Tears streamed down his cheeks as he held her at arms length.

'Ingrid, my darling Ingrid,' he sobbed.

'Your mother and I thought we had lost you years ago, when you ran away after some stray boy who lodged with us for a night.'

'And just look at you.' He continued as he gazed lovingly at her.

'All grown up and as beautiful as I always knew you would be.'

'And those clothes. I still can't believe that it is you.'

'Your mother is going to faint when she sees you.'

'Elfreida,' Elfreida,' he shouted, and almost immediately an old lady who Ingrid barely recognised as her mother, appeared in a doorway a few yards away, wiping the dough off her hands and her face with a white cloth.

'What is it now? She said with a tinge of annoyance in her voice, for she was in the process of taking her second tray of baking out of the oven, and was not at all pleased to be called away without having the chance of taking the piping hot small cakes off her baking tray.

'What is it?' she repeated.

'Come here my love,' said Leofric loudly.

'Come and see who has just entered our courtyard.'

'Another waif and stray begging for a bite to eat I'll warrant.' Grumbled Elfreida to herself, in a voice that still showed a little annoyance, but her tone also included a little pride at the knowledge that her husband still loved her, and needed her advice, even in petty situations such as this.

Her mutterings suddenly ceased as she came within ten feet of the strangers, and her eyes registered on the face of the beautiful young woman, who was dressed in Norman attire, and not just ordinary Norman clothing, but the type of clothing that only a lady of breeding and wealth would be able to afford, and wear.

'It cannot be.' She exclaimed, as her hands flew up to her face in alarm.

'It cannot be.' She repeated, for her mind was in turmoil, and was telling her that the child, who she had long thought to be dead, had suddenly come back into her life, and not as the scrawny fifteen year old child who had disappeared many years ago, but had returned as a beautiful and well dressed young lady.

Her head spun and she fainted in a heap onto the cobbled courtyard.

The mists slowly cleared from her eyes and as she looked up, causing her to slowly realise that she was lying on the table in her own kitchen.

She turned her head and saw the faces of her husband Leofric, and the lovely face of Ingrid, who were both looking down at her, whilst the kitchen. Her Kitchen was crowded with figures and faces, which were unknown to her.

'Come my dear,' said her husband as he placed his arm around her shoulders and helped her to sit up, and slowly cajoled her, as he helped her to ease herself off the table and onto her feet.

She struggled free of his grip, and hugged Ingrid so hard that Ingrid was forced to prise herself away from her mothers arms in order to regain her breath, which had almost been squeezed out of her.

'Mother,' said Ingrid, as she took her mother by the hand and led her a little way away from her friends.

'This man here is the boy called Aelnoth, who I followed when I left you.'

She paused for a moment to her startled mother to turn and look, with apprehension at Aelnoth, before she continued.

'He is now a wealthy knight, who was knighted by 'Duke Robert of Normandy himself, and he and I are betrothed to be married.'

'The other man there,' as she pointed to Magnus.

'Is no other than the nephew of King Harold Godwinson, and is a loyal friend of my Aelnoth, and he is betrothed to the dark haired girl, who is my very best friend, named Nike.'

Both parents looked at one another in shock, hardly being able to comprehend that not only had their long lost daughter returned to them, but she was now telling them that, low born as she was, she was engaged to be married to a wealthy Norman knight.

'But you said his name was Aelnoth,' said the father, 'and if my wits do not deceive me, the name Aelnoth is an English name and yet you are telling me that he is a Norman knight.'

'Are you speaking the truth daughter? Or are you trying to lie to your old mother and father?'

'Even as a child you always were a bit of a strange one.' He added.

'No, Father dear.' She answered demurely.

'Let me assure you that Aelnoth is as English as you and me, but he really is a knight, and was knighted by the earl.'

'Has he deflowered you?'

'No father. I am still chaste.' She lied, haughtily.

'We are soon to be wed, and then, and only then will we be united as man and wife.'

'Aelnoth,' she said in a louder voice.

'Come over here and allow me to introduce you properly to my parents, and please bring your parchment to prove to them that you really are who I say you are.'

Aelnoth obliged, and after the formal introduction, he produced the parchment and pointed out his name and Lord Roberts's seal to Ingrid's parents, for neither had accomplished the art of reading.

'Tell me,' said Aelnoth in a pleasant yet inquiring voice.

'Are you the Lord of this manor?'

Both Leofric and Elfreida glanced at one another, and after a short pause Leofric smiled and said. 'No. Well not really,' he said cagily, and then he added. 'You see after the old lord of Pitchford died in a hunting accident, his son Henri took over the estate, and my wife Elfreida did all the cooking for the old Lord.'

'She knew Henri quite well, and then Elfrieda asked our daughter Harriet to help her in the kitchens.'

'One day young Henri walked down into the kitchens and saw her, and he was smitten by her comeliness, and married her a few weeks later.'

'We jumped at the chance when Henri and Harriet asked us to move into the Hall, and we have lived here for nigh on five years.'

'We also have two grandchildren here in the Hall with us.' She said with pride.

'Oh your mother and I don't actually live in the Hall.' He explained.

'We live over there in that annex.' As he pointed to a door at the far end of the wall, which surrounded the Manor house.

'Come with me.' He said. 'I will show you.'

'Don't you think we should introduce Aelnoth to Lord Henri first?' Said his wife, as she shook her head as if she was correcting a naughty child.

'Oh yes, of course my dear.' Said her husband rather shamefacedly.

'I am forgetting my manners.'

'I will take them over right away.'

'Come with me my Lord.'

'Er, should I call you my Lord?' he asked.

'Aelnoth will do,' was the answer.

'Especially so, if I am to become your son-in-law.'

Aelnoth followed Leofric through the front door and along a short passageway, where Leofric paused for a moment before a large oak door, which he banged upon, and without waiting for an answer; he opened the door and walked boldly in.

Ingrid, who had followed Aelnoth and her father into the building, and who was close behind Aelnoth, nearly deafened him as she screamed 'Harriet' in a most un-ladylike manner, and rushed past both of the men, to cross the room and hug her sister, who had been seated at a large table with the man, who was obviously her husband, and the new Lord of Pitchford.

Lord Henri was a small, fair-haired man with a short beard and a moustache, which rose up at the corners, giving his already pleasant face an even happier countenance.

Unlike the severe hairstyle, which most Normans continued to favour, he had allowed his hair to grow in the style of the English.

As Aelnoth shook his hand, he felt an immediate fondness for the man, and it was as if Henri's generous nature flowed through his hand and surged up Aelnoth's arm and into his heart.

As he released Henri's hand and sat down upon the chair that was offered to him, he experienced a feeling that was unknown to him, during the many years since he had been evicted from his home.

During his travels in the east, he had met numerous people, and had shaken more hands than he cared to remember, but on most, if not all of those occasions, the people who had shaken his hand had wanted something from him, and on times their treacherous hand-shakes had sent shivers down his spine.

The warmth of Henri's hand still tingled, and as he looked across the table at the young man who was soon to be his brother in law, and he saw from the warmth of the smile on his face, that Henri also knew that he too, had found a new friend.

Food and drink was brought in by Ingrid's other sisters, causing squeals of joy, and excited laughter, followed by a lot of embracing and floods of tears.

As all of the siblings sat at the table with Lord Henri and the newcomers, with the exception of the two ex-Varangian guards, who seemed to have been embarrassed by this noisy family re-union, and had tactfully withdrawn to the kitchen, where they were provided with warm beer and hot food by the two remaining serving wenches.

The following morning, they were disturbed at the breakfast table by the ten year old son of Leofric and Elfreida, who burst through the door like a winter storm, causing the diners, especially the newcomers to pause from their repast and leap to their feet in alarm, forcing them to cease eating their breakfast of freshly made bread, bacon, eggs and sausages.

Leofric, who merely looked up from his plate, and shook his head in annoyance, calming down the startled Aelnoth and Magnus.

'Good God boy,' shouted Leofric.

'How many times have I told you to walk quietly into the house, NOT to rush in like an invading army?'

'You are lucky that one of Henri's guests has not run you through with a sword.'

'Come Aidan.' He beckoned the boy over to him. 'Meet our noble guests.'

'This is Lord Aelnoth of Wentnor, and this man here, as he indicated to Magnus.

'He is Lord Magnus, who is the nephew of the late King Harold Godwinson.'

Aidan bowed his head slightly and shook hands with Aelnoth and Magnus.

'These ladies are Nike, and of course you do recognise your sister Ingrid. Do you not?' he asked sharply.

'Er, well no. I didn't recognise her.' He said boldly.

'For I was only three years old when she left, and I certainly don't remember her as looking like this.'

'Nonetheless. It is Ingrid and she is betrothed to Lord Aelnoth.'

'Which brings me to a thing that I should have mentioned sooner?' Said Aelnoth.

'I have promised Ingrid that I would marry her when we reached home, and although we have not quite reached my own home, I think it would be appropriate for us to marry here in Pitchford, rather than wait until I have reclaimed my inheritance at Wentnor.'

'Would that be in order?' he asked, putting the question to Ingrid, her father and to Lord Henri.

The immediate answer came from all three of them, plus a jumble of words and happy laughter from pretty well everyone in the room, causing Aelnoth to ask.

'Is that a yes?'

'Of course it is, silly,' said Ingrid as she leapt to her feet and flung her arms around his neck, and plastered his neck with kisses.

Magnus intervened, saying loudly. 'I think we should make it a double wedding.' 'Don't you Nike?'

More shouts of approval filled the hall as Nike and Magnus joined the other couple, who were still wrapped up in each other's arms.

*   *   *

The tiny church was so packed with villagers and well wishers, that many people were forced to stand outside, where they showered the four newly-weds with rose petals, as they emerged from the doorway.

The wedding feast was laid out on long trestle tables, which had been erected in the courtyard in front of the

Hall, where the guests enjoyed all the food and drink that they could consume.

Despite his joy, Aelnoth could not fail to notice that the few Normans who had been invited, formed a tight group, and did not mingle with the much larger group of English guests, and continually stared with open hostility at the commoners who they obviously thought of as inferior beings.

Aelnoth was extremely proud of being an Englishman, and felt that now that he had been bestowed a knighthood by Duke Robert of Normandy, he had equal rights with these petty lords, who, he knew had been little more than common soldiers a few short years ago,

He forced himself to stride over to them, speaking to them in a friendly manner.

In the first instance, he addressed the group in the language of Constantinople, noting with smug pleasure that not one of the group could understand him.

With a smile he spoke in Norman French, asking 'May I extend my greetings to you and thank you for attending my wedding.'

They grunted and nodded cordially.

'Is the food to your liking?' He asked.

Most of the men answered with an amiable, 'Oi,' whilst one man said 'Si' and two others said 'Ja,' telling Aelnoth that perhaps a narrow majority of these new lords of the villages of England were actually Normans, whilst many of these so called 'Normans' hailed, not merely from Normandy, but from many of the other nations of Europe as well.

'The food is good,' said one of the younger men, in broken English.

'I am Sir Reynauld of Mont Saint Michel, and have been in your country for the past seven years. I love it here, although I do miss the long summer days of my homeland.'

Aelnoth was tempted to say that if he missed his homeland so much, then there was nothing to stop him from returning to it, but he refrained, and smiled sweetly as he made small talk with the man.

After mingling with both his Norman and English guests for a while, he made his way back to his bride, who was chatting with a small group of giggling women.

Ingrid was radiantly happy, and greeted him with a peck on his cheek before she introduced him to the ladies.

'This is the Lady Beatrice of Condover,' she said indicating a fair-haired young lady who demurely lowered her eyes and curtseyed.

'It is good to meet you Lord Aelnoth,' she said politely.

'And this is my sister the Lady Gillian, who is the wife of Sir Steven,' as she pointed to a gaggle of young ladies and a slim young man, who were speaking with Henri.

Ingrid, Aelnoth and Lady Gillian walked over to the group, where Henri greeted them with enthusiasm saying.

'Ah here you are Aelnoth, and you too my lovely sister in law.'

'Allow me to introduce you to these ladies here, who are the Lady Eve Maria of Betton, Lady Michelle of Acton, Lady Emma of Hughley, and Lady Gillian, who you have already met.

'This is Gillian's husband,' he said affably, as he touched the shoulder of the young slender man as if to urge him forward.

'This young man here is not only my cousin, but he is also a very good friend of mine.'

'Aelnoth may I introduce you to my cousin, Lord Steven of Streeton.'

The ladies curtseyed and Steven shook hands with Aelnoth.

'Well met Aelnoth,' he said with a smile.

'I have heard many good things about you, for these ladies seem to be unable to talk about anything other than you, and your adventures in the east.'

The mention of 'Streeton' had sent alarm bells ringing in his ears, as his mind raced with the possibilities, both good and bad, of this chance meeting with the new Norman lord of Streeton.

When he had left his home many years ago, Streeton had been the nearest, and in fact the only town of note that had been close to Wentnor, and as such, during the past few years, this new owner of Streeton would most probably have had regular contact with his Norman neighbours in nearby Wentnor.

Therefore, he surmised, there would be a distinct possibility that this young Norman, to whom he had just been introduced, could have close ties with the Normans who had slain his brother, and usurped his hereditary Hall.

Steven queried him about his heritage, and did not seem unperturbed when Aelnoth told him that he was pure English, and despite being a Knight, he had no Norman blood in his veins.

'Not to worry my friend,' he said jovially, 'for nearly all of us have an English wife, so within a few short generations all of our children will be English.'

The young man chatted happily away, causing Aelnoth, much against his will, to fall under the happy spell of the geniality of the man, causing Aelnoth to laugh for the first time since he had entered the room,

He was introduced to yet another bevy of ladies, to whom he smiled and muttered a few words, before he made his excuses and nudged Ingrid away, whispering to her.

'Come. Let us join Magnus and Nike.'

'I think we have more in common with them, rather than these chattering sparrows.'

The four newly weds enjoyed a couple of additional drinks before they left the hall and made their way to their bedchambers.

Despite the fact that it was his wedding night, the passion of his new bride surpassed his expectation, for although he had not been celibate during his time in the east, the ladies with whom he had dallied, had been the type of ladies who followed armies and men with money.

Many had been young and attractive, but all seemed to have possessed the same dull and uncaring attitude towards men, and had given him blessed relief, but sparse pleasure.

Aelnoth and Ingrid had been lovers for some considerable time, but despite their previous encounters, the love and tenderness, which she gave him on this, their first night as man and wife, surpassed all of their previous nights of lovemaking.

Fully sated and extremely weary, he lay beside her, gazing at her beautiful face, which shone in the flickering candlelight as she slept, and yet sleep evaded him as his thoughts sped towards the days which lay ahead.

The breakfast table was laden with all manner of food and drink, when the four newlyweds joined Henri and Harriet, who were already seated and had begun to eat.

Steven and Gillian entered the room and joined them at the table, sitting on the bench opposite Aelnoth and Ingrid.

'How long have you been the lord of Streeton?' asked Aelnoth, as he plunged his eating knife into a large pork sausage?

'Seven years now,' came the answer as he chewed on a large slice of crispy bacon.

'We love the place, although we do seem to get more than our fair share of rain.'

'It's the hills that attract the rain.' Said Aelnoth amiably.

'Indeed! We do seem to have a climate all of our own.'

'On a number of occasions I have travelled just a couple of miles down the valley, away from rainy Streeton, only to find that the sun is blazing away at my friend Simons hall.'

'Where does Simon live?' Asked Aelnoth.

'Longnor.'

'Ah yes, I remember Longnor. Thane Edward lived there when I left.'

'I know the name,' said Steven as he speared another slice of bacon, and brought it up to his mouth as he continued to nibble on it and speak at the same time.

'I have heard that he was a good man.'

'What happened to him?' asked Aelnoth.

'Don't really know,' said Steven casually as he swallowed the last of the bacon.

Aelnoth thought that he had continued the small talk for long enough, and was determined to cut out this banal chit-chat, so he broached the subject which he had wanted to talk about since the man had walked into the room.

'Who holds Wentnor now?' he asked as casually as he could.

'Oh. The Le-Mare's are at Wentnor.'

'Are the Le-Mare's the people, (he carefully avoiding mentioning the word 'Normans') who took it from my family?' he asked politely, forcing himself to smile as he asked this vitally important question, for if these were the people who took Wentnor, then they were also the people who had slain his brother and had stolen his ancestral home.

Steven ceased chewing and his mouth fell open, as he gaped towards Aelnoth, for he had, at last, begun to realise the real reasons for Aelnoth's questions.

'I, I, I didn't like Simon Le-Mare very much.' He stuttered.

'What do you mean?' 'Didn't?'

'Is he dead?'

'Indeed he is. These long years past.'

'His wife Marianne holds the place now.'

'Well, she and her man Hugo hold it.'

'There was much suspicion about Simon's death,' he continued.

'He was an excellent horseman.'

'He had been riding long before he could walk, and yet there he was, in an open meadow. Lying on the ground with his head caved in, and a bloody great, blood covered rock beside him.'

'And within a couple of weeks, Hugo the Breton turned up, and he has been running the place ever since.'

'He is a big brute of a man. I wouldn't like to tackle him.'

'Him and Marianne are a sadistic couple, and run the place with a rod of iron.'

'Nobody likes them.' He added as he wiped his greasy plate clean with his last crust of bread, which he then stuffed into his mouth.

'I will join you when you return to Streeton.' Aelnoth said ominously.

'Of course. Of course.' Said Steven, nodding his already balding head, for although he had initially liked this new son-in-law of his cousin, he was beginning to see another side of him, and he realised that this victor of battles in the east, who still appeared to be nought but a boy, could possibly turn out be, either a very good friend, or a very dangerous enemy.

Steven rose from the table and walked out of the room as if in a daze, for he realised that he had been manoeuvred into a somewhat difficult situation.

He considered that both Aelnoth and Marianne Le-Mare to be equally dangerous, but he felt that he needed a little time to think which of them would be the most likely to prevail.

He walked slowly over the courtyard and out of the gate, mumbling to himself, as his active mind tried to consider which of the two would be the more dangerous.

'Aelnoth or Marianne and Hugo?' He mumbled aloud.

Marianne and Hugo were Normans, and were well established in a fortified village.

They also have at least a dozen or more warriors in their pay.'

'I must choose.' He mumbled aloud.

'Aelnoth, on the other hand is still English, despite holding the title of Knight.'

'That factor alone did not make him a Norman,' he mused, 'and both the late King William and his successor Rufus had decreed that Normans must hold all the towns and villages of England.'

'Aelnoth has a mere three men with him, but those three looked tough enough to take on double their number, and he also had the element of surprise on his side.'

'Surely the title of Knight, dubbed by the Duke of Normandy, who was the King's brother, must count for something,' he reasoned.

'Aelnoth.' He muttered aloud.

'Besides,' he added. 'His wife and mine are sisters, so he is family.'

'I shall foster a friendship with Aelnoth, whilst at the same time; I shall go out of my way NOT to make enemies of Marianne and her sadistic henchman.'

Steven felt pleased with his decision, and stopped in mid-stride, turned and retraced his steps, entering the dining hall where Henri and his guests were still finishing their meal.

He walked up to Aelnoth and placed his hand on his shoulder.

'Well my friends, when you have finished stuffing your faces.' He said jovially.

'I suggest we say our farewells to my cousin and get ready to ride, for the day has half gone and we have many miles to cover before we reach Streeton.'

Half an hour later they waved farewell to Henri and the rest of Ingrid's family, riding through the gateway, to be greeted by a bright sunny day, which was full of birdsong and the sounds of the countryside.

They rode through the hamlet of Frodesley to reach the old Roman road, which led them through woodland, interspaced with dappled meadows and glades, before they reached the villages of Longnor and Lea-upon-the-bottom-wood, where the mountain of Caradoc rose on their left, and the massive rounded hills of the Longmynd stretched away to their right.

It was mid-afternoon before they reached their destination of Raynard's keep.

His small castle had been built upon the old Saxon fortress, which, long before the Angles and the Saxons had conquered what was then the Island of Britain, had been one of the famous British fortresses, destroyed by the Romans in their conquest of Britain seven or eight hundred years ago.

CHAPTER 31

Riding two abreast, they rode up the steep incline to the fortress, where scores of men laboured; dismantling the stakes, which still circled at least half of the wooden palisade, whilst masons and their labourers were busily building a sturdy stone wall that would eventually encompass the complete fortress.

'Are all of the masons Norman?' asked Aelnoth as they rode through the half completed gateway.

'Good lord No.' answered Steven.

'There are only two Normans.'

'The rest are from Brittany and Aquitaine. Oh. And there are eight Englishmen learning the craft.' He added with a smug smile.

The manor house itself was much the same as Aelnoth remembered it from the many times he and his father had had visited it, what seemed to be a lifetime ago, with the exception of genuine glass windows, which had replaced the old English shutters.

They dismounted and handed the reins of their mounts to a gaggle of youths, who led the horses away to a new stable block.

Aelnoth helped Magnus and his two stalwart Varangians to unload their personal belongings and the chests off the pack animals, and carried the heavy chests into the Hall.

As soon as Steven had accompanied Aelnoth and his party to their quarters, he left them to settle down, and made his way hurriedly towards his own rooms, beckoning his servant Alfred to accompany him.

'Close the door.' He ordered, and Alfred carefully closed the heavy oak door behind him.

'Alfred,' he said to the young man. 'You have been with me for nearly seven years, and during those seven years you have been more than a servant to me.'

'Indeed, I look upon you as a dear friend.' He said in a friendly manner.

'I want you to carry out an important task for me.' He said with a smile.

'I want you to saddle your horse and ride out of the gates.'

'Ride slowly,' he said, 'so that no one will suspect that you are out on a mission for me, and then ride up 'Ashes valley,' onto the top of the Longmynd.'

'Ride across the hill and turn westward when you reach the old wooden hunters hut.

'Take the track-way leading to the Coates farm.'

'When you reach the farmhouse, you will need to take the lane that leads westward, and that will take you directly to the village of Wentnor.'

'When you have reached the village. I want you to hand this note to Marianne Le-Mare.'

'Not to Hugo, or to anyone else.' He stressed, wagging his finger in order to emphasise the point.

'Just the Lady Marianne.'

'Is that clear?'

'Yes my Lord.' Answered the youth, for although Lord Steven had called him 'a Friend,' it was a term that he had only used on two previous occasions, and on both of those occasions, he had ordered Alfred to risk his life and limb to perform a dirty or dangerous task.

On the face of it. This seemed to be an easy enough errand, despite recent news that a small band of brigands had recently been seen up in the hills.

'Upon reflection,' said Steven, interrupting Alfred's thoughts.

'I think that it might be unwise for me to put my thoughts in writing.'

'Evidence and all that.' He added, with a wry smile.

'I think it best that you learn the message, and repeat it to the lady Marianne when you meet her.'

'Say to her.'

'The young lord of Wentnor. Aelnoth Edricson has returned from the east, and will try to claim Wentnor for himself.'

'That is all. No more and no less.'

'Do you understand?'

'Yes my Lord.'

'Good. Repeat it.'

'Aelnoth Edricson has returned from the east, and will claim Wentnor back for himself.' Said Alfred.

'Good. Well good enough.' Said Steven with a smile as he patted the young man on his shoulder.

'Just for good measure. Repeat it again.'

Alfred repeated it again. 'Young Lord Aelnoth Edricson has returned from the east and will reclaim Wentnor for himself.'

'I suppose that will have to do.'

'Right, off you go.'

'Tell no one of your mission.' He added.

'Don't rush. Walk casually and saddle your horse.'

'Take your time and don't rush around and arouse suspicion.'

Alfred obeyed, and ambled slowly out of the house and over to the stables, speaking casually to an acquaintance here and there.

He saddled the horse and rode slowly across the courtyard and out of the gate.

Ashes valley was abloom with a carpet of bluebells, giving Alfred the impression that he was drifting through a sea of blue.

The ash trees, which covered the slopes were alive with birdsong, as nesting birds vied to make their voices heard above their numerous competitors, each competing with its neighbour in order to defend its own particular piece of territory.

He followed the babbling brook up-stream, until he reached the waterfall, where he was forced to dismount and lead his horse up a narrow track that had been made over the generations by deer, and travellers such as himself.

The narrow track led him up the damp hillside; by-passing mossy area's, which declared themselves to be deep bogs, and seemed to him to have been purposely covered by the devil himself with a thin layer of moss, in order to trap unwary travellers.

It was only after he had led his horse through half a mile of high heather that he was able to remount, and follow the track to the brow of the hill, where he met the main track, which had been used by riders and drovers for hundreds of years.

He urged his horse westwards along a track that led away from the hunters hut, halting and dismounting to allow both himself and his horse to drink from a clear spring, which bubbled up from the earth.

He rode past an empty shepherds hut, which looked as if it had been uninhabited for a long time, and rode down a farm track until he reached the Coates farm, where he was greeted by no less than four dogs, who barked loudly and snapped at the heels of his horse, causing the frightened animal to snort and prance about in alarm.

A shrill whistle caused the dogs to cease their barking, and sit quietly in a semi-circle around Alfred and his still nervous horse.

'Who are you?' said a man who had appeared from the rear of the farmhouse.

'I am Alfred of Streeton.'

'English then?'

'Indeed, and proud of it.'

'It's all right Alden,' shouted the man loudly.

'He's English. Don't shoot him.'

A young beardless youth appeared from behind a large holly tree, taking the arrow from his bow and replacing it into his quiver, as he walked towards Alfred.

'Right young man. You can step down now and join us in a jug of cider.'

'If you had been a Norman, then my son there would have offered you something a little sharper than rough cider.' He said, chuckling loudly at his own morbid joke.

'Or was it a joke?' thought Alfred as he began to alight from the saddle.

As if he had read Alfred's own thoughts, the man added. 'Those stupid Norman sods down in the valley, think that the Normans who disappear when they are travelling these hills and forests merely lose their way, and get eaten by wolves, but we know different. Don't we Alden?' as he nodded towards his son.

The youth merely nodded and gave his father a smirk.

Alfred spent an hour at the farm, drinking three horn tankards full of rough cider, before he staggered unsteadily towards his waiting horse, which he mounted with the help of a friendly shove from the farmer, and rode down the track towards Wentnor.

He urged his horse down the steep sided valley, where he dismounted and plunged his head into a large pool of crystal clear water, which gushed down the rocky valley.

After a short pause to allow his head to clear, he remounted, and rode up the other side of the valley, where he was eventually forced to walk his horse along a very narrow track, which circled the stone-walls of Wentnor.

The two guards' on the walkways above his head followed him and glowered down at him, sending shivers down his spine.

His apprehension was intensified when he reached the one and only gate, where two more guards confronted him, who seemed to be equally as hostile as their colleagues on the walkway.

'What do you want?' demanded one of the guards.

'I am Alfred of Streeton, and I am on an errand for Lord Steven of Streeton to see Lady Marianne?' said Alfred boldly.

'We shall see about that.' Said the guard.

'You hold this Saxon swine here while I go and see if her ladyship will see him,' as he handed over the horse's reins to the other guard, and walked casually through the gate and into the fortress.

'What do you want to see her ladyship for?' snarled the second guard, as they waited for the first man to return.

Alfred did not answer the man. He merely turned his back and left the guard holding the reins of his horse, as he casually gazed down the valley, as if he was enjoying the sunshine, and not at all nervous about meeting this lady, who was renowned throughout the district as being something of a sadistic bitch.

Eventually the first guard returned, and took the reins off the other man and walked back through the gate.

'Follow me.' He said, causing Alfred to hurry, as he was still some distance away.

Once they had entered the Manor house, the guard literally pushed Alfred through the door, where he was confronted by a stern faced lady, who sat on an ornately carved oak chair at the end of a highly polished oak table.

A giant of a man stood by the chair, towering over her, and to Alfred, he appeared to be so large that his head almost touched the ceiling.

'Well?' Said the lady haughtily.

'What is so important that you drag me away from my studies?'

'Lord Steven of Streeton sent me my lady.'

'And?'

'He ordered me to inform you that the young Lord who used to live here, has returned from the east, and will want to take Wentnor from you.'

'Christ alive.' She swore. 'I have oft times thought about him.'

'He was the little brat who bested four of our men.'

'William of Rouen never recovered from that bash on the head that the little bastard gave him.

Alfred, forgetting his loyalty, could not help himself from saying. 'He is not a LITTLE bastard any longer my lady.'

'Oh! How so?'

He realised that he should not have opened his mouth, and found himself compelled to answers her question.

'He is a man full grown, my lady, and it is rumoured that he is a warrior of renown, who was the victor over a huge foreign army, when he was a General for the Emperor of Constantinople.'

'Pa!' she spat.

'The bastard is still a bloody Saxon, and has no standing here, and I have Hugo and a dozen other men here who will tear the Saxon turd apart, if he stupid enough to show his face here.'

482

Again, Alfred opened his mouth, and put his foot in it.

'Not so my lady.' He said before he could stop himself. 'He is a Knight of the realm, who was Knighted by the King's own brother. The Duke of Normandy and he has some of the famous Varangian guards with him.'

'Varangian Guards. I have heard of them.' She spat.

'How many?'

'Three my Lady.'

'Three,' she snarled. 'We will still outnumber them five to one.'

'How is this pig of a Saxon called?'

'I. I. I fear that I cannot tell you my lady.'

'Why in the name of all that is holy can you not?'

'Doesn't the bastard have a name'?

'No my Lady. I mean, yes My Lady.'

'He does have a name but I am feared to tell you.'

'For Christ's sake why not?'

'I will not kill you for telling me his name.'

'Now. Again. What is the name of this pig?'

'And if you do not tell me, then I shall let Hugo loose upon you, and I can assure you that you will assuredly tell him after he has broken both your arms and your legs.'

It was now Alfred's turn to turn white, as he glanced upwards towards the towering figure of Hugo.

'He is called, Sir Aelnoth of Wentnor.' Alfred said quietly.

A froth of spittle appeared on the face of Lady Marianne, and her face reddened so much, that Alfred thought that she was in the midst of a fit, but somehow she took control of her rage, and snatched a goblet of wine off the table, emptied its contents down her throat and hurled the expensive glass across the room, where it shattered on the stone fireplace.

Her entire body continued to shake for several minutes before she calmed down, and clenching her fists she screamed. 'Sir bloody Aelnoth of Wentnor.'

'I will show the bastard who is, and who is not the lord of Wentnor.'

'Nonetheless,' she said in as calm a manner, as her rage would allow.

'The fact that this Saxon swine has Varangians with him does change the situation somewhat.'

'I have heard of them and know that they are warriors to be wary of.'

'I will need to give this a little more thought.' She snarled.

'Hugo. Show our friend here to the kitchens, and order the maids to give him food and drink, whilst I give this impudent upstart some serious consideration.'

'Come.' Growled the giant as he strode past Alfred and led him through a passageway and into the kitchen.

Alfred only dared to glance up into the pock marked face of the giant on one single occasion, where he was met with a glare that sent shivers throughout his entire body, causing him to walk behind the man like a motherless lamb.

'Feed him.' Ordered Hugo, before he turned and left the kitchen, causing the two kitchen maids to exchange glances and expressions, that were somewhere between a grimace and a smile.

As soon as Hugo had left the room the two girls fawned over Alfred, placing a steaming hot bowl of porridge and a tankard of small beer before him, plying him with questions about the 'outside world,' for it seemed that their mistress forbade any of the villagers to leave the village.

He merely had time to consume the porridge before the enormous figure of Hugo appeared in the doorway.

'Come.' He ordered, causing Alfred to jump to his feet and follow Hugo.

Once again he found himself in the hall, standing before Lady Marianne.

'Your name?'

'It was remiss of me not to ask your name.'

'Alfred of Streeton my lady.' He answered.

'Well. Alfred of Streeton.'

'Pray thank your master, the good Lord Steven for the news of this upstart, which he has been kind enough to relay onto me, and tell him that I have ordered you to take my ladies maid here, who I shall give to him as gift from me for his kindness.' as she nodded towards a fair haired girl, who seemed to be aged about fourteen or fifteen.'

'Say to your master that the maiden is named 'Mildred' is an honest and hardworking girl, whom I have found to be completely honest and trustworthy, and should your master wish it. I think that she would make an excellent ladies maid for his wife, the lovely Lady Gillian.'

'My man 'Bois.' She nodded regally towards a swarthy middle aged man, who stood to her left, 'will accompany you as far as the waterfall in Cardingmill valley, where he will camp and wait for either yourself or Mildred to meet him, and inform him if and when this man Aelnoth and his ruffians, intend to ride and attack us here at Wentnor.'

'Is that clear.' She asked with an evil smile, which sent a shiver down his already sweating back.

'Yes my Lady, very clear.' Said Alfred, for he was happy that his ordeal seemed to be coming to an end, and could hardly wait to be on his horse and riding away from this fearsome woman and her even fiercer gigantic bodyguard.

With Mildred riding behind him, Alfred followed Bois through the gates and down the hill towards Prolley moor, where they followed the one and only cart track that circled the boggy land, until they reached the slopes of the Longmynd, where they were forced to dismount and lead their mounts up the steep hillside until they reached the top.

After crossing six or seven miles of heathland, he left Bois at the top of the waterfall, where the man dismounted, and immediately began to unwrap his leather tent, with the intention of making himself as comfortable as possible, for what the three of them realised may be a long and tedious wait.

Once he had reached the fortress of Streeton, Alfred led Mildred into the hall and presented her to Lord Steven and Lady Gillian.

Both seemed to be delighted with Mildred, but Steven was silently furious, as he had not told his wife of Alfred's errand, and had intended to keep the mission a secret.

Whilst the Lady Gillian also gave the impression of being delighted with Mildred, she was actually very annoyed, as she realised that her husband had placed her in a difficult position by sending Alfred to Wentnor, with the intention, (she guessed) of warning Lady Marianne of the intentions of her new brother-in-law.

She also realised that as sweet as her new ladies maid Mildred seemed to be, she was quite obviously a spy, who would inform Marianne Le-Mare of any developments.'

As Aelnoth was now married to her sister, her husband's action meant that Lady Gillian's loyalty was being torn between her sister and her husband.

Mildred quickly settled in and became very friendly with the Lady Gillian, helping her with her clothes, and expertly braiding her ladyship's hair into the new Norman style, causing the villagers to gape in awe, as she rode her pure white pony through the township.

The people of Streeton knew that Mildred had been the ladies maid of the dreaded lady Marianne of Wentnor, and tended to treat her as a leper, ignoring her whenever she was in the township.

Lord Steven had been most unhappy in the way that Alfred had let him down, when he had told Lady Gillian about his errand, and had sent him out of the house to join the labourers, who were still working on the walls.

Aelnoth and Ingrid, Magnus and Nike and the two ex-Varangian guards seemed to be happy enough enjoying Raynard's hospitality.

Aelnoth and Magnus had taken to riding each morning, exploring not only the township of Streeton, but also ranging far and wide over the countryside, venturing on one single occasion to the brow of the Longmynd, where they sat on their horses, partially hidden by a gnarled hawthorn tree, and gazed down at Prolley moor and the village of Wentnor, which sat on a hill in the distance.

'How does it look to you?' asked Magnus.

'Much the same as when I left, except that the stone walls which my father began to build, seem to have been completed.' Answered Aelnoth.

Magnus was beginning to become frustrated with the lack of action that appeared to have taken hold of his friend, and broached the subject during the ride back to Streeton.

'Aelnoth.' He said as he rode alongside his friend.

'We both know the real reason that you have brought us to Streeton, and we know that you want to take back your ancestral home, but why in the name of heaven have you not already done so? For in truth, this waiting and riding casually through the countryside is beginning to annoy me.'

'I have lost count of the number of people who you have questioned about Wentnor and the Lady Marianne, and yet you still eat, drink and make merry as if you don't have a care in the world.'

Aelnoth rode along for a while without answering, and when he finally did answer, his answer shocked Magnus.

'My friend,' he said.

'Do you realise that we have been out riding each morning for the past three weeks, and yet today is the first day that I have chosen this route, and have seen my old home.'

'I have little doubt that the sentries on the walls of Wentnor have also seen us.'

'I wanted to look upon Wentnor once again, before I begin my plan to kick out that old witch who killed my brother.'

'Tomorrow morning I shall inform Ingrid of my intention to storm Wentnor and I shall make sure that her maid Mildred can hear.'

'She will, no doubt inform Alfred, who in turn will tell Lady Marianne.'

'I am not quite sure just how she will be informed, but I do assure you that the Lady Marianne will hear the news within half a day.'

'Her pride will not allow her wait behind her walls for us, where our attack will be witnessed by every living soul in the village.'

'I think that she will take her men up onto the Longmynd, and try to ambush us where there will be no one to witness our deaths, and with her superior numbers, she will feel certain that she will be able to destroy us.'

'Bearing in mind that Marianne is a Norman, whose husband was given Wentnor by King William for services rendered unto William, during The Battle of Hastings.'

'Therefore, much as I would like to. It would be folly to kill the bitch,' for it would undoubtedly bring the wrath of every Norman in the district down upon my head, which would undoubtedly prevent me from living peacefully in my Hall.'

'How then are you going to get hold of Wentnor without slaying Marianne?' Asked Magnus?'

'She has the reputation of a wildcat, and will not give up her holding without a fight.'

'Watch and wait my friend.'

'Watch and wait.'

CHAPTER 32

That evening, when Ingrid and Aelnoth were in their private room. Aelnoth said to her. 'Ingrid my love, after we have eaten this evening, I would like you to instruct the kitchen maidens to pack enough food and a couple of flagons of good ale for Magnus, our two stalwart Varangians and myself, and leave it near the door for us to pick up first thing in the morning.'

'We shall be away for a few days.'

'In the meantime I shall order the grooms to have our horses ready by dawn, as well as a couple of pack horses for our weapons and supplies.'

'Where are you going this time?' Asked Ingrid.

'Nowhere dangerous I hope?'

Aelnoth did not answer, merely gave her a light kiss on her cheek and left the room.

Mildred had been silent during the conversation, and seemed to be her usual pleasant self, as she continued to braid Ingrid's long fair hair, in readiness for Ingrid to look as beautiful and well groomed as normal.

* * *

Lady Marianne was wakened an ungodly hour before by dawn by her new ladies maid, who had crept fearfully into her dark bedchamber, holding the candle, which flickered in the darkness, and tip-toed up to her ladyships bed, nervously placing the candle onto the chest by the side of the bed.

'My Lady,' she whispered, but there was no response from her mistress.

'My lady,' she said in a louder voice.

The Lady Marianne continued to snore quietly, as she lay on her back with her mouth wide open.

The maid took her life in her hands and reached out to gently shake the shoulder of her mistress. 'My lady,' she said boldly.

'There is a messenger to see you.'

'Wha.' 'What is it you stupid girl?' She snarled, as she blinked her eyes in an attempt to rouse herself from the beautiful dream, which she had been having.

'What in the name of Hell is going on?' she demanded.

'You had better have a good reason for wakening me at this hour my girl or I shall let Hugo have you, and look for another girl to take your place.'

'Fetch me my shawl and be quick about it.' She snarled.

'Now. What is it?' she snarled.

'Bois has returned my lady, and he says it is urgent,' she stammered.

'Give me that shawl girl and prepare some food for myself and all of my men.' She snarled as she snatched the shawl off her cowering maid, and flung it around her shoulders.

Lady Marianne stalked out of her bedchamber like an avenging demon, and was about to give her maid another tirade of abuse, when she saw both Hugo and Bois waiting near the fire, which had been re-kindled into life, throwing an eerie light into the great hall.

'Bois.' She growled, as she approached the men.

'I take it something has happened?'

'Yes my lady,' he replied quietly, for he too had been roused from his sheepskin blanket where he had lain snug under his small leather tent, and had been rudely shaken awake by that grubby youth Alfred, who he had clouted around his ears for his trouble.

'The Knight called Aelnoth has given orders that food, horses and weapons are to be made ready for him to ride at first light this morning.'

'Christ's bones.' She swore.

'It will be first light in about an hours time, so we had better shift our feathers if we are going to trap him up on the 'mynd.'

'Hugo, Rouse the men.'

'Have them fully armed and mounted, and ready to ride within the half hour.'

'Jump to it.' She snapped.

Hugo spun around so fast that he nearly knocked Bois over in the process.

Marianne led a party of twenty-six fully armed men out of the gates as the first rays of the morning lightened up the eastern sky, cantering down the track-way at a pace that was perhaps a little too reckless.

Within half an hour they had dismounted and had led their horses up the steep incline until they reached the more or less level expanse of heather and stunted shrubs, which covered a large portion of the Longmynd.

She halted her men in a hollow. 'You four men follow me.' She ordered.

'I want the rest of you to remain here until I return.' She called over her shoulder as she spurred her mount, leaving the four men who she had chosen to follow her, in a shower of peaty earth before they could recover their wits and spur their own mounts in order to follow her.

She halted her sweating mount on the brow of a hill, where it was able for a person to see for at least two miles both to her left and to her right.

'You two ride that way.' She pointed to her right.

'And when you reach the brow of that hill. I want you to stop, and I want you,' as she pointed to the second man. 'To ride right up to the furthest hill which you can see in the distance, and remain there until you see either myself or our friend here to tell you otherwise.'

'Is that clear.'

Both men nodded and said, 'Yes, My lady.

'When you have reached the brow of the hill. I want you to remain hidden, and watch the tracks and trails that come from Streeton, and the second that you see someone coming, you must ride back to me, making sure that you ride below the ridge so that these English swine's cannot see you.'

'Do you understand?'

Again both of the men nodded.

'Off you go then and keep your eyes peeled, and if this English upstart should pass you without you warning me, then I will get Boise here to hold you down whilst Hugo cuts your balls off.'

Both men nodded glumly, mounted their horses and rode off to do the bidding of their sadistic mistress.

'Did you hear what I said?' she snapped to the other two men who had been standing nearby.

They both nodded.

'Good! Then I want you two to ride that way,' as she pointed to the left, 'and take your positions on those two hills over there, and make sure that you are both well hidden.'

'Do you understand?' she hissed ominously.

Both men nodded glumly, for perhaps they were a little unhappy to be used as simple look-outs, which was a task that she could have assigned to any ten year old boy on a pony, instead of allowing both of them, who were, after all, very experienced warriors, to remain with the bulk of their party and enjoy some of the cut and thrust of the battle they had been hoping for.

Within the hour, the man on the hill, which was furthest hill to the left, leapt onto his horse and spurred it back towards Marianne.

He skidded to a halt alongside her.

'They are coming my lady.' He shouted.

'How many?'

'Only four my lady.'

'Good! It must be them for I have been told that they would only be four in number.'

She rose in her saddle and waved at her other scouts who were high on the hills to her left and beckoned them to join her.

Pleased to see that they were both alert, she urged her horse backwards and began to lead her four men back towards the hollow, where her main body of her men were waiting.

'Mount but stay hidden.' She ordered as she rode down the slight dip in the land that concealed her men.

'How many my lady?' asked one of her bolder men.

'Four.'

'Only four.' He exclaimed with a wide grin.

'Cocky young fool.' Snorted Lady Marianne with a wide smile.

'We will chew 'em to pieces and blow out the bubbles,' said another.

'Six to one,' said a gnarled veteran.

'This is going to be a massacre.'

'Try not to kill the leader.' Said Lady Marianne.

'I want to see the little bugger squirm before I rip his eyes out.'

'What does he look like?' asked Bois.

'I don't really know.' She answered, 'But I think he may be the youngest.'

492

'Let us hope that they are not all wearing helmets.' Said Bois. 'Or we may not be able to tell 'em apart.'

'Are they getting near?' Lady Marianne asked the man who had been placed on the rim of the hollow, and peered through the bracken.

'Still a couple of hundred yards away my Lady.' Answered the man.

'Another couple of minutes then.' She said. 'And then we can have our fun.'

*   *   *

Aelnoth reined his horse to a stop and held his hand in the air.

'They are here.' He said grimly.

'I can't see anyone.' Said Rugalf quietly to Olaf, as he halted his own horse alongside his fellow ex-Varangian.

'Me neither,' said his friend. 'But none of us can see what Aelnoth sees. You know him.'

'Indeed I do.'

He was about to say more but was interrupted by Aelnoth, who shouted. 'Dismount and grab the spears.'

The four men dismounted and walked almost casually to the packhorse, where each man grabbed four spears and walked to the front of the horses.

'Shields at the ready.' Ordered Aelnoth to cause his three friends to fall into the well rehearsed drill of forming a small shield wall of four shields.

'Ready spears.' Said Aelnoth quietly, and all four of the men placed three spears against their shields whilst they held a fourth spear in their right hands in readiness to launch as soon as the order was given.

'Still can't see anyone.' Said Rugalf.

'You will in a minute.' Muttered Aelnoth, who was standing next to him.

In less than a minute, a jostling crowd of horsemen erupted from a small valley no more than a hundred yards away, fighting with each other, and yelling at the top of their voices, as they savagely spurred their horses out of the small hollow and towards their four waiting opponents.

'Wait.' Growled Aelnoth.

'Wait until I say throw.'

'Mark your man.'

'Steady. Steady. Throw.' He shouted, and all four men hurled their spears at the oncoming riders.

Three riders were hurled backwards off their mounts, whilst a very unfortunate fourth man fell, clutching two spears that were embedded in his chest.

'Ready.' Shouted Aelnoth.'

'Throw and a second volley of spears were hurled into the horsemen, sending another four men to the ground.

'In your own good time.' He shouted, as he looked at the crowd of milling horses and horsemen who were now no more than fifty feet away from him.

'Thank you very much my Lord,' shouted Olaf, and with a wide grin, which spread across his bearded face, he snatched up his third spear and hurled it unerringly into the chest of a horseman, who had only just managed to steer his horse out of the tangle of horses and horsemen, who still screamed and cursed as they tried to urge their horses forward.

The third spears of both Aelnoth and Magnus found their targets, sending two more men to the ground, but the third spear of Rugalf missed its target and sped away into the heather.

Lady Marianne, Bois and Hugo had been wise enough to allow lesser men to be in the fore of the fight, and stared in horror at the carnage, which the spears of these four men had caused.

'I'll sort 'em out.' Snarled Bois as he spurred his horse towards the still tangled mass of Marianne's men.

'Pull yourselves together,' he screamed as he struck man after man with the flat of his sword, causing several riders to ease their mounts out of the knot, and ride to one side of their fellow horsemen.

'Follow me.' He shouted as he struck the rump of his own horse with the flat of his sword and spurred the steed forward.

The fourth spears of both Aelnoth and Rugalf hurled him off his horse, sending him backwards into the three or four men who had untangled themselves, and had been in the process of following him.

'I'm enjoying this.' Shouted Magnus at the top of his voice.

'And we haven't even got to grips with the buggers yet.' He added gleefully.

'Look at those cowards.' Shouted Aelnoth, as he pointed his sword towards a number of horsemen who were in the process of spurring their horses away from this unexpected bloodbath in which they had found themselves.

'Not many left,' said Magnus.

'Six.' Said Aelnoth. 'And a woman.'

'That'll be 'er Ladyship.' Said Rugalf.

'Time to walk forward.' Said Aelnoth grimly.

'Let's go.' And the four of them locked their shields and walked purposefully towards the remaining horsemen.

Lady Marianne's remaining horsemen had eventually managed to untangle themselves, but were savagely shoved aside by the enormous figure of Hugo, who pushed his way to the front.

'This could be interesting.' Mumbled Aelnoth.

'By Odin's sacred balls. He IS a big sod.' Said Magnus.

'The bigger they come, the harder they fall.' Muttered Aelnoth as he strode forward to meet the man.

'How did I know you were going to say that?' said Magnus.

'Nonetheless,' he added.

'He is a bloody giant of a man, and he looks seriously dangerous.'

'I know. I know.' Mumbled Aelnoth as he tossed his shield to one side and drew his Saex and his long-sword.

Despite the noise made by the remaining Normans, and the high pitched screaming which emitted from the normally cool and collected Lady Marianne, the serene sensation of battle calm flooded into the mind of

Aelnoth, as he gripped his long battle sword in his right hand and his short Saex in his left hand, and walked forward to meet his gigantic opponent.

Both combatants reached a wide grassy area, where wild deer, or perhaps sheep had grazed the grass, thus preventing the invading heather to take hold, and the moment that Hugo reached the grass, he charged forward like an enraged bull, swinging the seven feet long Pick-axe, (which was a sturdy staff, with a sharpened steel bolt and a steel axe that had been forged by a blacksmith, and mounted upon the end of the thick wooden staff)

Aelnoth moved to one side as the pick-axe thudded into the ground a mere six inches away from his feet.

As Hugo wrenched his weapon out of the wet earth, Aelnoth stepped forward and slashed with his sword, making a long cut down his opponent's upper arm.

The giant grunted and paused, with his weapon held to one side, and glared at Aelnoth with bloodshot eyes, which looked more like the eyes of a beast than those of a human.

The Pick-axe was brought around with such speed that Aelnoth was forced to lean so far backwards that he nearly fell on his back, as the razor sharp weapon sliced though the air a mere inch away from his throat.

He countered the move with his sword and slashed at the staff, sending a six-inch sliver of wood sailing through the air.

For Aelnoth, there was no sound in the world except for the animal grunts of his opponent.

Nor did the earth contain another single being, other than the one who was confronting him at this moment in time.

His inner calmness seemed to merge with the obvious adrenaline, or perhaps it was called 'Battle madness,' which careered through his veins, allowing him to anticipate the Giant's every move, and giving him the split second needed to either avoid or counter the blows.

Hugo slashed and swiped, poked and prodded with his huge weapon, only to be totally frustrated by this youth, who countered or avoided his every move, and the more frustrated he became, the more wild and desperate were his attacks, for never once in his life had he been beaten, and his former opponents had always succumbed to his strength and prowess in no more than the first few brief moments of battle.

Aelnoth avoided most of his opponent's strikes, but on several occasions he was forced to block the two headed weapon.

The massive force of the strikes sent spasms of pain down his arm and into his shoulder, forcing him to retreat in order to regain some semblance of normality, before the next blow fell upon him.

Hugo could see that the power of his blows had damaged his rival, but he was furious that this strip of a boy was beginning to get the upper hand by allowing him to use up his power on blows, which hit either thin air, or were blocked, causing his brain to tell him that if he did not alter his tactics, then his strength would be sapped away, and he would lose this fight.

He paused for a second, and dropped his heavy weapon to the ground, whilst in the same instant he snatched his poniard from his belt, and charged forward, with the intention of shoulder butting his nimble opponent, only to find that his huge shoulder hit no more than an empty pocket of air, where his rival had been a split second before.

As the startled giant tried to turn towards his elusive opponent, he did not see and tripped over a small tussock of grass, falling face forward onto the ground.

Aelnoth dashed up to his fallen opponent and as he placed one foot on the giant's back, he pricked his neck with the point of his sword.

'Up you bastard.' He snarled, 'and no tricks or I will strike your ugly head off your shoulders.'

Other than a twitch from his right hand, there was no reaction from the fallen giant.

Aelnoth took half a pace backward and kicked the prone figure.

To no avail.

He motioned to Magnus. 'Come Magnus.' He said.

'You too Olaf.' Keep your weapons ready while Rugalf and I will turn this ugly sod over.'

His three friends joined him, and with the help of Rugalf, they hauled the supposedly unconscious man over onto his back.

'Christ alive,' swore Magnus.

'Would you just look at that'? He added as he gazed open mouth at the slim poniard that was imbedded up to its hilt in the giant's chest.

'The bastard fell on his own knife.' Said Rugalf, stating the obvious.

'Straight through his own heart.' He added with a grunt.

'Well. That's that.' Said Aelnoth.

'Now, what about that lot,' he added as he turned his head and looked towards the Lady Marianne and her remaining men.

He led his three companions towards Marianne and her group, but before they reached them, Marianne's men dropped their weapons to the ground in unison, and knelt with bowed heads in surrender.

'We yield to your arms Sir Knight.' Said one of the men in a subservient tone.

The Lady Marianne, however, stood firm with her chin high and her face full of pride and hatred, and snarled in a most un-ladylike voice. 'I yield to no man.'

Aelnoth walked up to her, and firmly, yet gently, took the slim sword from her right hand and threw it into the heather.

'You will not be needing this now.' He said calmly.

'So, you are the brat who my husband allowed to escape, are you?'

'It would seem so. Would it not?' He answered with a grim smile.

'And if I recall the incident. Your husband did NOT allow me to escape.'

'Had it not been for my unruly horse I would have stayed and fought.' He added proudly.

'And died like your brother.'

'Who you killed like a wounded bear.' He accused.

'He was a bear that had to be killed, or he could well have disinherited my husband of his legal right.'

'Your husband had no legal right.'

'He had the King's writ in his purse.'

'Enough of this banter.' Snapped the frustrated Aelnoth.

'Your men are either slain or have surrendered, and thus you have been beaten.'

He raised his sword to strike, but his arm seemed to resist his attempt to bring the sword down.

'She is a woman.' His brain told him.

'And yet, it was she who plunged a spear into my own brother's back, and killed him.' His other mind told him.

'You are a Christian and should not kill in cold blood. Especially a woman.'

'She deserves to die.' It said.

'And yet I have sent many men to their deaths, so I have sinned.

'Probably much more than her.' His mind told him.

'I still own Wentnor.' She retorted haughtily, with a snort, causing his sword arm to rise again.

His arm wavered and then strengthened again as he prepared to strike, but something prevented it, yet again, from swooping down and taking off her vile head.

His arm shook and brought the sword down slowly until it reached the ground.

'I too own Wentnor,' said Aelnoth.

'So I have heard, but your ownership was granted by a foreign Lord who has no right here in England.'

'He is the King of England's brother.'

'But I will exchange no more banter with you, other than to say that I have overcome your followers, and you are my prisoner.'

'I am now the owner of Wentnor, and as such, I now have the option of killing you here and now, or perhaps taking you back to Wentnor with me, and throwing you in a deep dungeon, where you can rot away without anyone being any the wiser.'

'What about them?' indicating her men who now stood in a small group, close enough to hear every word that was being said.

'They are witnesses.' She said haughtily.

'Oh they can join you, either in death or in the dungeon. I care not which.'

Marianne's shoulders sagged and her face softened just a little, as single tear oozed from both of her eyes.

'I never liked Wentnor much,' she said.

'It is a cold and windy place, and I do so yearn to return to Trouville, and to feel the warmth of the Mediterranean sun on my shoulders again, but alas, this measly village has not given me the riches that I had hoped for.'

'Indeed, it has given me little more than heartache and pain.'

'Ah.' She sighed.

'Trouville. I do so wish I could return, and flaunt my wealth in front of that bitch of a sister of mine.'

'I understand that you have brought back much treasure from the east.' She said with the most pleasant smile that she could muster, under the present circumstances.

Aelnoth was usually a person with an active and inquiring mind, but for some reason he had, so far, failed to grasp the logic of her statement, probably due to the fact that he had, a few brief minutes ago, been in a life and death struggle with a huge and aggressive opponent.

Her insinuations and hints suddenly dawned on him.

'Ah. I see your point.' He said.

'I cannot, for the life of me see what you mean.' She said demurely.

'What would you say if I were to offer to purchase Wentnor from you, for the price of one thousand silver coins?'

'Pa,' she spat.

'I would say that you are taking me for a fool, and I may be many things, but I am not a fool.'

There was a long silence, for one of the things that he had learnt during his stay in Constantinople, was the skill of bartering, and he knew full well, the reward of silence.

He turned his back on her and walked a few paces towards Magnus saying. 'Tie the prisoner's hands and load their weapons onto our packhorse.'

'I might, just might accept two thousand silver coins for my holding,' came the unusually quiet voice of Marianne, 'providing of course, that they are freshly minted and are not clipped or worn with use.'

Aelnoth did not answer her and said to Magnus.

'Oh, before you tie their hands, order them to strip the dead of any weapons and valuables.'

'Then have them dump the bodies in that hollow over there, and cover the bodies with some heather to deter the eaters of carrion.'

'Then you can tie their hands and we will have them join their friends in the ditch.'

As the prisoners sullenly began their task, he turned to face Marianne and said. 'It is a shame that we can not reach an agreement my lady, for it does present me with something of a problem, and it will be such a pity to add such a pretty body as your own to that pile of slain men. Will it not?'

The face of Marianne blanched and she shook her raven hair at the annoyance and frustration that this young upstart was causing her.

'I will sign the deeds of Wentnor over to you for the sum of one thousand and five hundred silver pieces. Not a penny less.' She emphasised as she shook her head yet again and stamped her foot, like a child, in annoyance.

'It would be cheaper to kill you.' Said Aelnoth.

'If you were to kill me, then you would have no document of ownership.'

'My friend Olaf is skilled in the art of forcing people to do what they do not wish to do, and he does so enjoy his work.'

Olaf was an experienced warrior, whose sole art was with his Danish battle-axe, but he was a man who slew only when it was absolutely necessary, and much preferred to spend his time in front of a roaring log fire with a tankard of ale in his hands and a pretty wench on his knee, but in this instance, he decided to go along with Lord Aelnoth's ploy and snarled savagely, as he ran his thumb along the edge of his razor sharp axe.

'Do we have a deal?' she asked quietly.

'We have a deal,' answered Aelnoth.

The prisoners, including the Lady Marianne were escorted across the bleak hill to the township of Streeton, where a deed of sale was drawn up.

It was signed by both Aelnoth and Lady Marianne, and witnessed by no less than five Norman lords, and sealed with their own individual seals, which, by habit and with Pride, had been forged upon the rings that each and every Norman lord worth their salt kept upon the middle finger of their right hand.

The Lady Marianne left the following day, escorted by her remaining warriors who guarded the packhorse and their mistress, as if their very lives depended upon it.

For indeed, their very lives did depend upon the safe arrival of Lady Marianne and the silver, which the packhorse carried towards her original home on the sunny shores of the Mediterranean sea, where she had vowed to pay each of her men twenty silver coins apiece, as well as a parcel of land upon which they could retire and enjoy a life of luxury as free-men.

'It never fails to mystify me that men will believe what they want to believe.' Said Aelnoth to Ingrid, as he watched the last of Lady Marianne's escort disappear in the distance.

'No, it will be nothing short of a miracle if she reaches her home alive,' said Ingrid.

'It will also be nothing short of a second miracle if those men ever receive a single piece of silver from the old hag.' Said Aelnoth.

Aelnoth gave one hundred silver coins to Olaf and to Rugalf, and after thanking them profusely for their loyalty and service; he watched them with sadness, as they too, mounted their horses and rode away.

Magnus had decided to take Nike to Ireland in order to find out whether his father had survived the battle of Exmoor.

'If he lives, then that would be good, and I will share my riches with him, but if he is dead, then I shall inherit his title, and will settle down in Ireland, as far away as I can from these damned Normans, and breed a litter of fine sons with my Greek Goddess.'

As he placed his arm around the shoulders of Nike, and gave her a kiss on her cheek.

Magnus and Nike left for Ireland the following morning, leaving a huge gap in the heart of Aelnoth, who had known Magnus for most of his adult life, and despite the fact that Magnus had been the elder of the two, he had always seemed to be like the younger brother that Aelnoth had never had.

The villagers of Wentnor welcomed Aelnoth and Ingrid home with cheers, and tears of joy, as the pair rode through the gate and into the tiny township.

The three serving maidens and two young men, who had cared for the household during the days of Lady Marianne, lined up in front of the manor house to welcome their new lord and his lady home.

The fireplace, which his father had built, lay bright and undamaged, and he was delighted to see that his father's carved chair was still placed at the head of the huge oak table that his father had personally constructed out of an old oak tree, which had been swept to the earth in a winter's gale, many long years ago.

Ingrid ordered her new serving maidens to burn the mattress, which had belonged to Lady Marianne, and gave them all of Marianne's personal effects.

Aelnoth ordered a feast to be laid out upon the courtyard in front of his Manor house, paying each and every one of his people with silver coin, which came from the one and only remaining chest, out of the original hoard, which he had brought home from the east.

The villagers watched in silence as Aelnoth rode his horse to the front of his manor house and stretched upwards in order to secure his father's old shield onto the post that still stood empty in front of the house.

'Our rightful lord has returned,' shouted one of the men causing the rest of the people to cheer loudly and clap their hands in joy.

That evening, after drinking perhaps a little too much ale and after eating just perhaps one too many mouthful's of delicious food, the new Lord and Lady of Wentnor lay on their new duck down mattress, and snuggled under two brand new woollen blankets.

'We are home my love.' He whispered.

'Indeed we are.' Whispered Ingrid, as she raised her hand and brushed a wisp of hair that had fallen over his eyes.

'Happy?' He asked.

'Very.'

'Now, after all of our travels and our adventures, we have finally come home, and home is where I intend to stay.'

'Me too.'

'Perhaps now is the time to start thinking about children.' He ventured.

'Funny you should say that.' She said demurely as she turned over to face him.

THE END

FACTS

A Saex is a short sword, after which the Saxon people were named

IE= Saxons (People of the sword)

It is something akin to a Roman Gladius.

A Poniard is a slender Norman/French dagger.

After the Battle of Hastings. The mother of King Harold Godwinson is said to have offered William the Conqueror. 'My son's weight in gold if you will bestow unto me his body.'

What happened to the gold?

The Normans defeated an army of English, Irish and Viking warriors on, or near to Exmoor. (Historians cannot agree exactly where the battle took place.)

Le-Tamaris is in the gulf of Morbihan, on the coast of the Mediterranean Sea.

Robert, who was the eldest son of 'William the Conqueror, The Duke of Normandy conquered a large part southern Italy, and was the brother of King William Rufus of England.

Previous names for present-day Istanbul have been Byzantium and Constantinople, but the city was also known as. 'Micklegard,' by the peoples of Northern Europe.

The Emperors of Constantinople employed only Norsemen and English warriors in the famous Varangian guard.

The 'Sea of Van' and the township of 'Ercis' are situated in present day Turkey.

Printed in Great Britain
by Amazon